GLOBALISATION AND THE ROMAN WORLD

World history, connectivity and material culture

This book explores a new perspective for understanding the Roman world, using connectivity as a major point of departure. Globalisation is apparent in increased flows of objects, people and ideas, and in the creation of translocal consciousness in everyday life. Based on these criteria, there is a case for globalisation in the ancient Roman world. Essential for anyone interested in Romanisation, this volume provides the first sustained critical exploration of globalisation theories in Roman archaeology and history. It is written by an international group of scholars who address a broad range of subjects, including Roman imperialism, economics, consumption, urbanism, migration, visual culture and heritage. The contributors explore the implications of understanding material culture in an interconnected Roman world, highlighting several novel directions for future research.

Martin Pitts is Senior Lecturer in the Department of Classics and Ancient History at the University of Exeter. Specialising in the quantitative analysis of consumption patterns, his research addresses the origins of mass consumption and the role of artefacts in large-scale historical processes and how such processes impacted on local cultural practices. Although his focus is on the northwestern Roman Empire, he has also published on consumption in the seventeenth, eighteenth and twentieth centuries. He is co-author, with Dominic Perring, of *Alien Cities: Consumption and the Origins of Urbanism in Roman Britain*. He has published articles in the *American Journal of Archaeology*, the *European Journal of Archaeology*, the *Journal of Anthropological Archaeology*, *Britannia* and the *Journal of World-Systems Research*.

Miguel John Versluys is Associate Professor of Classical and Mediterranean Archaeology at the University of Leiden. In 2010, he obtained a VIDI grant from the Netherlands Organisation for Scientific Research to build his own research group, Cultural Innovation in a Globalising Society: Egypt in the Roman World. In 2011, he was a guest professor at Université de Toulouse II – Le Mirail. In 2013, he received the Zenobia Essay Prize. His main research interest is cultural interaction in the Hellenistic and Roman Mediterranean. He has published many articles in international journals and is the author of several books, including *Egyptian Gods in the Hellenistic and Roman Mediterranean: Image and Reality Between Local and Global* (2012).

GLOBALISATION AND THE ROMAN WORLD

*World history, connectivity and
material culture*

Martin Pitts
University of Exeter

Miguel John Versluys
University of Leiden

CAMBRIDGE
UNIVERSITY PRESS

CAMBRIDGE
UNIVERSITY PRESS

32 Avenue of the Americas, New York NY 10013-2473, USA

Cambridge University Press is part of the University of Cambridge.

It furthers the University's mission by disseminating knowledge in the pursuit of education, learning and research at the highest international levels of excellence.

www.cambridge.org
Information on this title: www.cambridge.org/9781107619005

© Cambridge University Press 2015

First published 2015
First paperback edition 2016

A catalogue record for this publication is available from the British Library

ISBN 978-1-107-04374-9 Hardback
ISBN 978-1-107-61900-5 Paperback

CONTENTS

v

– Contents –

CONTRIBUTOR BIOGRAPHIES

Dr Tamar Hodos
Department of Archaeology and Anthropology, University of Bristol
Material Culture and Social Identities in the Ancient World (with Shelley Hales; Cambridge, 2010)

Professor Richard Hingley
Department of Archaeology, Durham University
Globalizing Roman Culture: Unity, diversity and empire (Routledge, 2005)

Dr Elena Isayev
Department of Classics and Ancient History, University of Exeter
Ancient Italy: Regions without boundaries (with Guy Bradley and Corinna Riva, University of Exeter Press, 2007)

Professor Ray Laurence
Classical & Archaeological Studies, University of Kent
The City in the Roman West c. 250 BC–c. AD 250 (with Simon Esmonde Cleary and Gareth Sears; Cambridge, 2010)

Professor Neville Morley
Department of Classics & Ancient History, University of Bristol
Antiquity and Modernity (Blackwell, 2008)

Professor Jan Nederveen Pieterse
University of California, Santa Barbara
Globalization and Culture: Global mélange (Rowman and Littlefield, 2009)

Dr Martin Pitts
Department of Classics and Ancient History, University of Exeter
Alien Cities: Consumption and the origins of urbanism in Roman Britain (with Dominic Perring; Spoilheap Monograph 7, 2013)

Dr Michael Sommer
Institut für Geschichte, Carl von Ossietzky Universität
*Roms orientalische Steppengrenze. Palmyra – Edessa – Dura Europos –
Hatra* (Franz Steiner Verlag, 2005)

Dr Francesco Trifilò
Classical & Archaeological Studies, University of Kent
Understanding Age in the Western Roman Empire: An epigraphic study
(with Ray Laurence; in preparation)

Dr Miguel John Versluys
Faculty of Archaeology, Leiden University
Isis on the Nile: Egyptian gods in Hellenistic and Roman Egypt (with
Laurent Bricault; Brill, 2010)

Dr Robert Witcher
Department of Archaeology, Durham University
'Life of an Ancient Monument: Hadrian's wall in history' (*Antiquity* 86
(2012) 760–71, with R. Hingley and C. Nesbitt)

Acknowledgements

This volume benefitted from a long genesis, with the idea arising following conversations between the editors and other contributors at the Theoretical Archaeology Conferences (TRAC) held in Amsterdam (2008) and Oxford (2010). The main impetus was a two-day workshop held at the Devon and Exeter Institution in April 2011, for which we are indebted to the financial assistance provided by the Department of Classics and Ancient History and the College of Humanities at the University of Exeter.

Martin Pitts would like to thank Professor Stephen Mitchell for advice and practical assistance with the organisation of the Exeter workshop, as well as his intellectual input at the event. He also thanks Classics and Ancient History students at Exeter who trialled an early draft of this book in 2013. Their varied reactions provoked some unexpected new perspectives and helped improve the overall clarity of the volume.

Miguel John Versluys would like to thank the Netherlands Organisation for Scientific Research (NWO) for granting him a VIDI project entitled 'Cultural innovation in a globalising society: Egypt in the Roman world', of which this book is a result; as well as Frederick G. Naerebout for the many fierce debates on 'globalisation' and the Roman world, and Thomas Späth for his kind invitation to the Center for Global Studies in Bern.

Both editors would like to thank the contributors to this book for their various forms of criticism and their intellectual engagement. For the editing process we are especially indebted to Tamar Hodos and two anonymous reviewers, as well as to Beatrice Rehl and her editorial team at Cambridge University Press. We thank Antonio Montesanti for contributing several illustrations, notably Fig. 1, and Marike van Aerde for her assistance with the editing and indexing of the volume.

Exeter & Leiden, November 2013

PART I

INTRODUCTION

1

GLOBALISATION AND THE ROMAN WORLD: PERSPECTIVES AND OPPORTUNITIES

Martin Pitts and Miguel John Versluys

> We should push the globalization analogy harder, applying to the ancient
> Mediterranean the same tough questions that scholars ask about
> connectedness in our own time.
>
> (Morris 2005, 33)

INTRODUCTION

Through a collection of essays, this book explores the value of globalisation theory to foster better understandings of the Roman world and its material culture. Why is such an exploration worthwhile? We believe globalisation theory has the potential to add significantly to several crucial debates in Roman archaeology and history. In taking this stance we are not alone: after a jolting start, the concept of globalisation has appeared with increasing frequency in publications addressing very different aspects of the Roman world.[1] However, using a term because it is currently fashionable will not suffice. Why *should* this concept be used, and what can it *add* that current conceptual and methodological apparatus lack? To answer these questions we must critically examine the current state of globalisation theory to determine if it is fit for purpose. Indeed, many Roman archaeologists and historians evoking the concept have arguably done so suggestively, without detailed attention to the theoretical debate that constitutes globalisation studies, or for the consequences that 'globalising the Roman world' implies for our understanding of antiquity.[2] This evocative approach, centred on what may be described as a buzzword, has been severely criticised by other scholars, and sometimes justifiably so.[3]

3

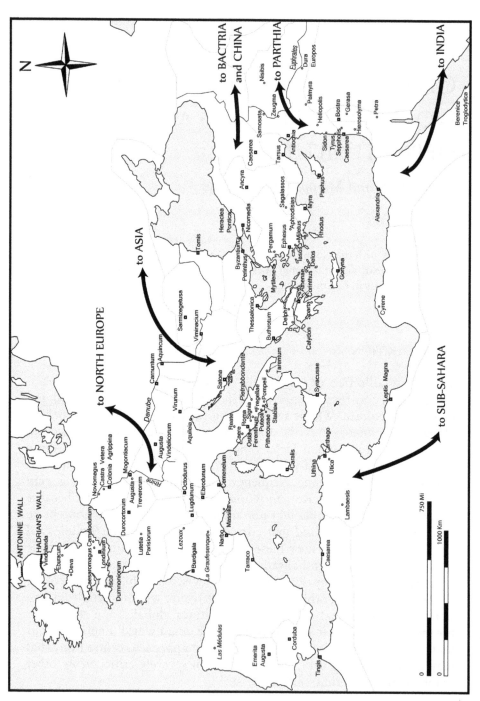

Figure 1: The Roman world in the second century AD, with additional places named in the text relating to other periods. Drawn by Antonio Montesanti.

4

It is crucial, therefore, to resolve whether we *can* use globalisation theory to understand the Roman world, and to determine if there is enough value in the theory to use it in an applied fashion. To address these questions we discuss the various definitions of globalisation, the principal themes in globalisation research and how the concept has been applied to other historical periods, as well as to the Roman world. Although we invariably identify potential problems and dangers, our answer is confidently positive. Not only is it methodologically sound to use globalisation theory in the study of Roman history and archaeology, but there are also many compelling reasons why it should be used and added to our theoretical toolbox.

FROM CULTURES TO CONNECTIVITY: BEYOND ROMAN AND NATIVE

> There is no going back to the fantasy that once upon a time there were settled, coherent and perfectly integrated national or ethnic communities. (Greenblatt 2009, 2)[4]

In recent decades, Roman history and archaeology have been tremendously successful in deconstructing several of their fundamental premises. The development of the Romanisation debate testifies to this, as does the fact that Romanisation is presently one of the central research themes in both disciplines.[5] From this deconstruction no new dominant paradigm has arisen. In some respects this is healthy and timely, demonstrating increased self-reflexivity in Roman archaeology as it moves away from the theoretical archaeologists' caricature as an atheoretical sub-discipline dependent on ancient texts.[6] However, in other respects, the conceptual vacuum created by the discredited concept of Romanisation is discomforting.

This state of affairs was clearly illustrated by many essays and discussions at the (Theoretical) Roman Archaeology Conferences held in Oxford in March 2010 (RAC IX/TRAC XX) and in Frankfurt in March 2012 (RAC X/TRAC XXII). In most cases, Romanisation was referred to as the main social, political and cultural process driving continuities and changes in material culture. However, few scholars were willing to use the word, instead preferring phrases such as 'Romanisation-between-inverted-commas' or 'what we used to call Romanisation'. This situation undoubtedly stems from the impact of predominantly Anglo scholarship, which regards the paradigm of Romanisation as 'defective' and 'intellectually lazy'.[7] However, if there are good reasons to abandon Romanisation instead of reformulating it, Romanists should be able to come up with alternatives. This has been tried in the past, especially by scholars working within post-colonial studies, but none of their proposals, such as 'creolisation', have found wide acceptance.[8] Building on these approaches, a similar buzzword, 'identity', has gained popularity in recent years, yet the use of identity as an analytical paradigm has all too often reverted to using the old terminology of Romanisation.[9] And this brings us to the present discomforting situation. Many scholars working in the field are aware of the pitfalls of Romanisation as used in the traditional sense (as acculturation),[10] and most try to understand the Roman world from a perspective that goes 'beyond Roman and Native'.[11] So far this has mainly resulted, however, in more ill-defined terminology. The most common formulations surmise that the Roman world was diverse and multicultural, due to its immense connectivity. While there is nothing wrong with this standpoint, it should be a point of departure rather than a conclusion in itself. The emptiness of much commonly used terminology in archaeological and historical studies becomes especially clear when the processes and mechanisms underlying such phenomena must be articulated. For example, it is common to encounter terms such as 'inter-culturality', 'crossroads of cultures', 'hybridity', 'confluence' or, popular in the French tradition, 'transferts-culturels' or 'métissage' – most of the time without an adequate explanation of what these concepts exactly mean or imply, especially for the interpretation of material culture.

In summary, the Romanisation debate has come to an unsatisfactory impasse. Most scholars are aware that they should not think in terms of the binary opposites of 'Roman' and 'Native', most crucially regarding the interpretation of material culture, but since no dominant alternative has arisen, and fruitful debates on the alternatives seem to have stopped, Romanisation remains the default framework for interpretation (even if it is less explicit). Scholars seeking alternatives to Romanisation seem to take two directions. On the one hand there are those favouring the post-colonial view, developing approaches that tend to focus on illuminating indigenous trajectories of change and identities. Although this remains useful, the subtle irony is that post-colonial perspectives often maintain the Roman–Native dichotomy (bad, imperialist Romans versus good, authentic Natives), and moreover, in privileging narratives of colonialism and imperialism in fact *strengthen* the dichotomy.[12] On the other hand there are those exploring notions of 'connectivity', but not always addressing its implications, as we have described above. The popular designation 'hybrid' is a case in point: what in the Roman world was *not*, in one way or another, a 'hybrid'? One might well ask. The explanatory value of the term as a label therefore seems extremely limited.[13]

WRITING 'ROMAN' HISTORY

Until not so very long ago almost all history was *national* history, an approach that has been usefully characterised as methodological nationalism.[14] It is within this intellectual framework that Area Studies first developed and flourished.[15] Methodological nationalism was born in the nineteenth and twentieth centuries and is directly connected to the emergence of the nation-state. As such it replaced the cosmopolitan, universalistic approach that characterised much of the eighteenth century.[16] Methodological nationalism had an immense impact on historical disciplines, which are now widely using globalisation concepts to develop new ways of thinking. However, it is arguable that the impact of methodological nationalism on archaeology is even greater owing to the very establishment of the discipline in the nineteenth and twentieth centuries. From its inception, archaeology had a distinctly local perspective and was effectively engaged in the practice of 'doing area studies' through the collection and description of material culture. This perspective has only changed slowly, and has bequeathed the continued dominance of ethnic labels and interpretations of material culture.[17] The fact that we still use the framework of *provincial* Roman archaeologies – as if Britain, France, Spain, Syria, Egypt, etc. would be useful historical categories to understand Roman material culture – is another case in point. Archaeologists, to paraphrase Appadurai, are good in mistaking particular configurations of apparent stabilities in material culture for permanent associations between space, territory and cultural organisation.[18] It is in this sense that much current conceptual apparatus, rooted in nation-state-thinking and Area Studies, is insufficient.

Within Roman archaeology and history, we argue there is an urgent need to transcend post-colonial approaches and a general concern with identity, and to engage more seriously with concepts of connectivity.[19] Writing 'Roman' history should move beyond methodological nationalism, especially where it concerns the understanding of material culture. We believe that globalisation theory is eminently suited to do this. While notions of hybridity and cultural mixing still form an essential part of this approach, the important questions remain: how and why? Globalisation offers a series of paradigms that might provide answers. These paradigms are especially relevant because, as we outline below, one of the main strengths of globalisation theories is that they concern 'a world of disjunctive flows [which] produce problems *that manifest themselves in intensely local forms but have contexts that are anything but local*' (our emphasis).[20] Through an emphasis on understanding differences in the context of larger

processes, globalisation theories have the potential to help Roman archaeologists and historians transcend oft-criticised dichotomies such as Roman–
Native, core–periphery and Italy–provinces, dichotomies that nonetheless
feature prominently in the structure of current understandings of the Roman
world.

BEFORE GLOBALISATION: WORLD SYSTEMS THEORY
AND ITS APPLICATIONS

Before concepts of globalisation gained currency, there was world systems
theory. World systems (or world-systems) theory derives from Immanuel
Wallerstein's *The Modern World System*, a neo-Marxist analysis of the
origins of modern capitalism.[21] A world system unites very large populations, spread over wide distances, through either political means (world
empires) or economic ties alone (world economies). World systems theory
is relevant to the discussion of globalisation for several reasons. Although
they are in fact strictly separate concepts, world systems analysis and globalisation have become increasingly intertwined. World systems analysis might
be best characterised as a specific methodology for studying globalisation as
a historical phenomenon, but focusing on the themes of macro-economics
and political integration alone.[22] World systems theory began as a means
of addressing the unique historical circumstances of modernity, but like
theories of globalisation, its application quickly acquired greater time-
depth. While Wallerstein acknowledged the existence of pre-modern
world systems, he regarded the present capitalist era as special because it
constituted the first world economy stable in the long term (i.e. 500 years)
that did not disintegrate or become converted into a world empire.[23]

For those wishing to make a direct link between globalisation and
capitalism, Wallerstein's date for the first world economy is often taken as
the benchmark for the origins of globalisation: AD 1500. This view was
challenged by Andre Gunder Frank and Barry Gills in the early 1990s for its
Eurocentric stance, and failure to consider broader system connections
before AD 1500. In their edited volume *The World System: Five hundred
years or five thousand?*, Frank and Gills argued that the present (single)
world-system was 5000 rather than 500 years old, largely on the basis of the
existence of long-distance trade relations.[24] Wallerstein's rebuttal to this
critique reveals the main points of difference between the two camps.[25]
Rather than being Eurocentric, Wallerstein claimed his position merely
exoticised Europe, highlighting the unique historical scenario that led
to the development of capitalism.[26] Wallerstein's position stressed a

substantial break, rather than continuity or a shift in the character of a pre-existing world system. Wallerstein pointed out that the long-distance trade connections cited by Frank and Gills were not underpinned by a single division of labour with integrated production processes. Furthermore, he stressed that such trade was in luxury goods between largely separate systems, and did not involve the exchange of bulk goods and necessities as would be expected within an integrated system. While not denying the existence of long-term interconnectedness, Wallerstein's argument for multiple waxing and waning world-systems before AD 1500 rather than a single world system (note missing hyphen) is compelling. Frank and Gills' insistence on a single 5000-year-old world system driven principally by capital accumulation is not sustainable from current evidence, especially given the prevailing view that the predominant mode of exchange in pre-modern tributary empires (or empire-systems) was socially embedded rather than based on 'free' market or profit-driven principles.[27] Crucially, neither position rules out the possibility of pre-modern globalisation.

Following Wallerstein, the principles of world systems theory have been attractive to archaeologists and historians working on pre-modern periods and realising the fundamental importance of connectivity.[28] Significant works applying the logic of world systems analysis to the Roman world include Keith Hopkins' *Conquerors and Slaves*,[29] and Barry Cunliffe's *Greeks, Romans and Barbarians*.[30] Building on the fundamental world systems structural opposition between core and periphery, such studies illustrate how asymmetrical flows of raw materials, goods and manpower from outer provinces to Rome were able to sustain urban populations and the military machinery of empire. Under the late Republic, the system was thought to be underpinned by territorial expansion borne of continuous successful warfare. When the empire acquired more stable boundaries, the essential inequality of the former system was maintained through the imposition of taxes, which guaranteed equivalent flows of resource from the provinces to the centre. Taxes collected in rich provinces such as Spain, northern Africa and Egypt were spent on provisioning frontier armies and other essential state infrastructure. This in turn was thought to encourage inter-regional trade as the core provinces sought to recoup their losses to pay further taxes. In newly acquired territories lacking monetised economies, taxes could be levied in kind in the form of surplus agricultural produce, which could in turn be converted into money through sale in urban markets. Thus, the impetus for the origins of urbanism in areas lacking cities before Roman conquest was seen as state driven and top-down, in order to guarantee the effective exploitation of new territories.[31]

Although effective in explaining how the Roman economy may have been integrated through politically determined means (i.e. taxation) as opposed to market forces,[32] the application of world systems models to the Roman world has not been without controversy. In the first place, the model as articulated by Hopkins makes several assumptions that have yet to be historically proven. For example, the degree of mutual *dependency* between Rome and the western provinces/periphery is unclear, both for the inward supply of raw materials and slaves to the 'core' on the one hand and the outward flow of luxury goods to the 'periphery' on the other.[33] Likewise, the extent to which taxes encouraged economic integration has been cast into doubt.[34] A second major criticism of the approach is that it privileges economic and political forces at the expense of the cultural and social.[35] World systems models implicitly assume cultural homogenisation over time (if culture is addressed at all), promoting a macro-scale view that is too unwieldy to explain regional and localised variations in material culture. Moreover, the models strengthen centre–periphery thinking that research on identity and memory sets out to undermine. It is for that very reason, from the mid-1990s onwards, when identity and memory developed into key concepts, that world systems models fell out of fashion. This is in some ways unjust as, despite their weaknesses, the models addressed the grand narrative of history head on, directly harnessing the potential of archaeological evidence as well as written sources, and developing ways of thinking beyond 'methodological nationalism' (see above). Building on world system approaches, the significant challenge is to address the universality of structure and practice in the Roman world, while simultaneously explaining the dialogues and divergences that defined local experience.

WHAT IS GLOBALISATION?

From the early 1990s, the use of the word 'globalisation' grew exponentially, from academic obscurity to mass-media ubiquity. In popular discourse it is a buzzword invoked to account for a variety of phenomena: global economic recessions, the relocation of Western manufacturing facilities to 'developing' countries, the erosion of local heritage in the face of capitalist consumer culture, and the future consequences of unchecked global warming. Globalisation is often linked to transnational corporate capitalism in the public imagination, aka the 'globalisation project',[36] which has led to a range of 'counter-globalising' political movements, ranging from international terrorism to anti-poverty protests and ethical consumerism.[37] In short, globalisation is seen by many as inevitable, unstable and uncontrollable; an ever-looming spectre of large-scale change in the contemporary world. While this viewpoint can be found in a burgeoning array of academic literature, there is also far greater diversity and debate surrounding how globalisation is defined, when it began, the nature of its effects and whether these are 'good' or 'bad'.[38]

In the most simple of terms, globalisation can be described as processes by which localities and people become increasingly interconnected and interdependent. Common denominators in most definitions are increasing connectivity and de-territorialisation. Variations and divergences have arisen as the concept has been reinterpreted within different academic traditions, typically depending on what is being 'globalised'. This in turn has ramifications for determining when and where globalising processes began. For example, in the field of economics, some regard globalisation as a matter of market integration leading to a single global economy, as demonstrated, for example, by the occurrence of global commodity price convergence in the early nineteenth century.[39] However, other economists have contested the methodology underlying this view, arguing for the key date to be pushed back to AD 1571 with the establishment of a trade link between Asia and America at Manila.[40] As discussed above, others have argued that a single global economy existed as early as 5000 years ago,[41] following some of the principles of Wallerstein's world systems theory,[42] and taking even less stringent economic criteria and focusing purely on long-distance exchange. Similar discrepancies are also evident in 'softer' approaches to globalisation within the humanities and social sciences. At a basic level, the classic 1990s' socio-cultural definitions of globalisation share the same core characteristic of increasing connectivity, sometimes stressing the idea of greater global consciousness through the compression of time and space.[43] Here are some examples:

1. 'the intensification of worldwide social relations which link distant localities in such a way that local happenings are shaped by events occurring miles away and vice-versa' (Giddens 1990, 64).
2. 'the rapidly developing and ever-densening network of interconnections and interdependences that characterize modern social life' (Tomlinson 1999, 2).
3. 'the compression of the world and the intensification of consciousness of the world as a whole' (Robertson 1992, 8).
4. 'a social process in which the constraints of geography on economic, political, social and cultural arrangements recede, in which people become increasingly aware that they are receding and in which people act accordingly' (Waters 2001, 5).
5. 'a world of disjunctive flows [which] produce problems that manifest themselves in intensely local forms but have contexts that are anything but local' (Appadurai 2001, 6).

Despite the quoted definitions exhibiting significant overlap, this coherence breaks down on closer analysis. On the one hand, theorists such as Giddens and Tomlinson (definitions 1 and 2, respectively, above) regard globalisation as a fundamentally new phenomenon, a unique condition of modernity facilitated by twentieth-century technological developments, most notably intercontinental jet travel and instantaneous mass-media electronic communication.[44] In contrast, while their primary interests also lay in the period of modernity, other leading figures such as Robertson, Waters and Appadurai (definitions 3 to 5, respectively, above) appear to concede that the processes, actions and social forces now understood as globalisation had precursors in the past and have been under way for several centuries, if not millennia.[45] Building on these views, Nederveen Pieterse was one of the first to suggest that globalisation should be understood from a *deep* historical perspective, criticising the 'globalisation as modernity' approach for its Eurocentrism, which he argues to describe a phenomenon of westernisation rather than true globalisation.[46] Similarly, Andre Gunder Frank dismissed the link between globalisation and modernity, presenting a powerful thesis for the leading role of Asia rather than the West in long-term global economic history.[47] Shami even proposed the metaphor 'prehistories of globalisation' to underline the need for a historical understanding of the process, which is necessary to reinforce a break with modernity theory.[48]

In considering the conflicting claims for globalisation's origins, it should be borne in mind that the theorists driving such debates rarely have sufficient grounding in history (let alone archaeology) to make measured assessments of pre-modern developments. Nowhere is this more striking than in Castells' concluding remarks to the edited volume *Connectivity in Antiquity*,[49] a volume that explores the application of theories of networks and globalisation in various archaeological studies.[50] Castells freely admits, in contradiction of his earlier work, that networks are not just a critical component of the modern 'Information Age': 'globalization is not new: under different forms, it appears to have happened not only in the 19th century of the common era, but thousands of years ago'.[51] A similar shift can be seen in the writings of Roland Robertson and David Inglis, who turned their attention to the existence of a global consciousness or 'animus' that characterised Greco-Roman thought, in which Rome is conceived as a truly 'global city' by modern standards.[52] These examples demonstrate the fragile presentism of many of the seminal globalisation texts of the 1990s, but perhaps more critically emphasise the current need for historians and archaeologists to engage with and contribute to the changing intellectual agenda on the subject. This call is in part answered by Jennings, who harnesses the idea of plural *globalisations* to characterise the origins of urbanism in Uruk, Mississippian and Wari civilisations.[53] Using as his earliest example the Uruk civilisation, a context which had long before been described in terms of being the first world system,[54] Jennings makes the case for the existence of all the defining characteristics of modern globalisation, including time–space compression.[55] Although applied with the usual caveats and disclaimers to distinguish ancient from modern, the work of Jennings demonstrates how the debate over the origins of globalisation has turned upside down. What were once seen as the distinct characteristics of later twentieth-century globalisation are increasingly being used to define the very start of urban civilisation.[56]

If the chronology of globalisation is contentious (see also further below), so too is its geography. Concerns over both the time and space of globalisation ultimately depend on whether the concept is regarded as option A – a process that can only begin once the bare bones of a single integrated worldwide economy have been established, or option B – a process simply involving the accretion of human networks. If the former, it follows that a fully globalised modernity is something rather different from the more geographically restricted 'archaic' or 'proto-globalisation' that preceded it.[57] If the latter, it is feasible to suggest that the phenomenon does not have to be truly global to exist at all, as Robbie Robertson suggested: 'the origins of globalization lie in the interconnections that have slowly enveloped humans since the earliest times'.[58] Both standpoints are not without their flaws. Whereas option B takes a holistic view of global human development, it encourages an evolutionary perspective, which, at worst, implies a seamless and fluid lineage from antiquity to modernity, glossing over the substantial qualitative and quantitative differences between the two eras. Likewise, although option A recognises the distinctiveness of contemporary globalisation, its myopic focus on modernity is at odds with the fact that many of the effects of globalisation are not exclusive to the last 250 years. Either way, as Nederveen Pieterse points out,[59] it is clear that a deep historical perspective is vital to the proper characterisation of conditions of connectivity in different epochs.

THEMES IN GLOBALISATION RESEARCH: CONVERGENCE, UNEVENNESS AND GLOCALISATION

> It [Globalisation] is marked by a new role for the imagination in social life.
> (Appadurai 2001, 14)

Compared with world systems approaches focusing on economic networks and exchange mechanisms, the 1990s studies of globalisation instead tended to explore the effects of increased connectivity. Although these effects are multifarious, a general consensus is that globalisation is an uneven process, reconfiguring social relations and political institutions, and fostering cultural diversity and social inequality. In the study of modern globalisation, the rise and declining importance of the nation-state has been a major theme for analysis, although in a longer-term perspective there is no reason to assume the existence of the nation-state as a pre-requisite of globalisation.[60] On the theme of unevenness and socio-economic inequality, Bauman, among many others, highlights the central paradox of globalisation to simultaneously create unity and division, suggesting that the collective process creates social fault lines according to social and spatial mobility. Some regard being local in a globalised world to be a sign of social deprivation and degradation, whereas elites are seen as being defined by their extraterritoriality and isolation from local communities.[61] This viewpoint is consistent with, for instance, epidemiological literature underlining the serious health consequences of deepening inequality in contemporary world societies, despite the increased availability of more advanced health care.[62] However, neither increased interconnection nor escalating inequality are new historical phenomena; both have simply become more apparent in the recent era of 'accelerated globalisation'.[63]

The impact of globalisation on culture represents an important focus for globalisation literature. Although the popular image of the faceless corporate machine of global capitalism destroying local distinctiveness has received much attention (so-called McDonaldisation or Coca-colonisation),[64] such processes of convergence and homogenisation are also acknowledged to occur hand in hand with increased heterogeneity.[65] This viewpoint is encapsulated in the term 'glocalisation', deriving from the Japanese *dochakuka*, loosely translating as 'global localization'.[66] The concept of glocalisation helps to emphasise how the homogenising elements of global culture (from institutions and commodities to social practices and ideas) are differentially incorporated into local cultures, which are in turn altered in the process. This is effectively summarised as follows:

> The globalisation of culture is not the same as homogenisation, but globalisation involves the use of a variety of instruments of homogenisation that are absorbed into local political and cultural economies, only to be repatriated as heterogeneous dialogues.[67]

To properly account for the cultural effects of globalisation, Nederveen Pieterse's theory of *global mélange* through 'hybridisation' provides a useful starting point.[68] While accepting that all cultures are in essence hybrid entities with permeable boundaries, global mélange is created through the mixture of phenomena that are regarded as being categorically different in a given historical moment.[69] The notion of hybridity is relational and context dependent, highlighting the fluidity of cultural boundaries.[70] A key element of this approach is the role of power and the relative status of individual elements in the mixing process.[71] Elites by definition have greater choice in the construction/expression of their identities than non-elites, who have more limited resources for cultural consumption and often lack empowerment to make equivalent choices, especially in colonial contexts. At the same time, as Appadurai, amongst others, has argued, minorities and the disempowered matter very much within globalisation, often serving as 'the flash point for a series of uncertainties that mediate between everyday life and its fast-shifting global backdrop'; a process in which they certainly have and can acquire agency.[72]

The study of globalisation, therefore, can be about many things.[73] What might be called 'globalisation theory' is less a unified theory or grand narrative than a set of theoretical paradigms in dialogue with each other. However, we propose that the theoretical toolbox associated with the study of globalisation and (material) culture offers the most potential for bringing new perspectives to the understanding of the Roman world and its archaeology. The friction of space is often overcome through the exchange of symbols, and material culture therefore plays an important role in time–space compression.[74] However, before pursuing these thoughts any further, we must first look in more depth at the question of whether globalisation *can* be applied to historical periods and, if so, what the criteria are for a civilisation to be 'eligible' for study via globalisation theory. So far it has become clear that the study of the Roman world can conceptually benefit from something like globalisation theory, and that although most globalisation studies are tied up with the modern world, there is a large group of scholars working on globalisation and culture that is convinced that globalisation can only be understood as a deep historical process. Nevertheless, those scholars work predominantly on modernity, and ask for historical insights from their own twenty-first-century perspectives. To answer questions relating to practical issues and methodology, we should also examine the extent to which parallel 'bottom-up' applications of globalisation theory in other pre-modern periods and civilisations have been successful.

GLOBALISATION AND WORLD HISTORY

A fine introduction to the historiography of the concept of globalisation within the historical disciplines is provided by A. G. Hopkins, who presents a rather personal story of his attempts to get globalisation established within the discipline of history.[75] This was difficult, but in the end successful: the present state of affairs in that field he describes as a truly 'global turn' (in combination with a 'material turn') – rightly characterising this development as a 're-turn' of these concepts.[76] In his edited volume *Globalization in World History* (2002), Hopkins made a forceful plea for globalisation as an agenda for historical research.[77] As a tentative taxonomy he distinguishes between (1) archaic globalisation (applicable to historical periods before industrialisation and the emergence of the nation-state); (2) proto-globalisation (roughly the period of AD 1600–1800); (3) modern globalisation (from AD 1800 onwards and characterised by industrialisation and the emergence of the nation-state; and (4) post-colonial globalisation (the beginning of new types of supra-territorial organisations), seeing these four not as stadia but as a series of overlapping and interacting sequences.[78] Archaic globalisation is not dealt with at length; instead the book focuses on the period after AD 1600.[79] Apparently it was still too early in 2002 for the combination of globalisation and world history to acquire real time-depth, although Hopkins is certainly aware of the importance of this perspective. Perhaps as a result of this awareness, he does not only focus on the economy (for many scholars an instant reflex when being confronted with globalisation: wrongly so, we think) and the role of the state, but also on the importance of cultural expressions.[80] His definition thus places emphasis on quantitative significance and qualitative changes alike: globalisation is about the emergence of something new.[81] Although this 'pushing back' of globalisation met with criticism, with hindsight it can be said that it has opened Pandora's Box.[82] Global history has become something of a new orthodoxy. Indeed, in a recent article on globalisation and the Roman empire, Hitchner feels confident to bluntly state that 'this fundamentally ahistoric stance [of earlier research] has now been successfully challenged by A.G. Hopkins and others'.[83]

It is clear that historians are increasingly embracing the concept of globalisation under the headings of 'global history' and 'world history'.[84] Their motivation is often practical: they hope that globalisation will provide new perspectives.[85] In doing so, they are not uncritical.[86] At the same time no 'eligibility check-list' has been developed for the analysis of historical contexts through globalisation theory. Here we encounter the approaches that have already been described above: option A sees globalisation as applicable to the present-day world alone, while option B sees globalisation as inherent to the development of human society since earliest times. In other words, historians and archaeologists can do either (almost) nothing with it or everything.[87] Here we cannot strictly solve this debate; but we can be more specific, and offer a third alternative.

If globalisation theory already *is* applicable to historical periods, for many scholars it is clear that we can speak about it in some way or another from around AD 1600. But what is this premise based on? Hopkins describes the era of AD 1600–1800 as follows: 'the chief characteristic of the period was the developing symbiosis between emerging state systems and growing cosmopolitanism'.[88] When, in the same book, Bayly describes 'proto-globalisation' in-depth, he sees the re-orientation of consumption as one of its main characteristics. According to Bayly, classes of consumers were created with a common goal of acquiring goods to signal position and status, which on an international level led to a net growth in production and retail.[89] This process has been very aptly characterised by Witcher for the Hellenistic and Roman periods as the universalisation of the particular, which goes hand in hand with a particularisation of the universal.[90] Moreover, the characterisation Hopkins provides of the period 1600–1800 is generally considered one of the main features of the Hellenistic period as well.[91] Both characterisations share several traits considered typical of 'earlier forms of globalisation': increased connectivity, the existence of a common market, the domestic impact of market integration, the idea of belonging to one world, a stress on the local as a part of global developments, the universalisation of the particular in combination with a particularisation of the universal, relatively dramatic time–space compressions and cosmopolitism. If we can study the world from around AD 1600 onwards through these themes, then we can certainly study the Roman (and Hellenistic) world from very similar perspectives. In structural terms, with regard to the topics that interest us as indicators of globalisation, the Roman world fits this framework very well.[92] Through this approach option A is bypassed, while the evolutionary perspective (and very general nature) of option B is evaded, leading us to option C.

We take globalisation, therefore, as a relative concept: connectivity has always been present to some degree but is, in certain historical periods, characterised by such dramatic punctuations that we can describe these as global (option C). Jennings shares a similar point of view and discusses 'multiple globalisations' – his most important point being, as we stress, that there is no long-term historical trend leading to modernity.[93] Globalisation is neither a single universal epoch for world history, nor is it a constant evolutionary condition for humankind. For Jennings, an instance of globalisation should involve both 'a significant leap in interregional interaction' and 'social changes that are associated with the creation of a global culture'.[94] The Roman era was such a period. A concern with culture ties in with another argument for seeing the Roman world as 'globalised', as opposed to simply being a historical period with increased connectivity:

the domain of perception. Did Romans perceive their world as global and act accordingly? This question is addressed in the next section, which also provides an overview of reactions of Romanists to globalisation and globalisation studies so far.

GLOBALISING THE ROMAN WORLD?

> Now in earlier times the world's history had consisted, so to speak, of a series of unrelated episodes, the origins and results of each being as widely separated as their localities, but from this point onwards [after the Second Punic war] history becomes an organic whole: the affairs of Italy and Africa are connected with those of Asia and of Greece, and all events bear a relationship and contribute to a single end. (Polybius, Histories 1.3)

Often quoted in the context of the question posed above is this passage from Polybius's 'world history', conceived between 160 and 120 BC.[95] The idea behind this text is strikingly similar to what, for instance, the Enlightenment scholar Johann Gottfried von Herder wrote about the eighteenth century in his treatise *Auch eine Philosophie der Geschichte zur Bildung der Menschheit* in 1774: 'When has the entire earth ever been so closely joined together, by so few threads'; strengthening the case for structural similarities between the Roman world and 'earlier punctuations of globalisation' after the Middle Ages. Moreover, the area seen as ruled or influenced by Rome was considered to be the *orbis terrarum*. Using a globalisation perspective to study a society that defined its territory as *imperium sine fine* and *oikumene* thus certainly makes sense from their perspective. This global network, moreover, shared a common cultural framework, which put notions of *paideia* and *humanitas* central.[96] The Roman perception of India – as being at the edge of the world – is a case in point here. Although India was not 'Roman' in a political sense and the Romans were not aware of its extent and geography in detail, it was very much part of their 'world' in a mental sense.[97] Around AD 150, this global perspective characterising the Roman empire is described by the rhetor Ailios Aristeides (XXVI. 101–102) as follows: 'And now indeed there is no need to write a description of the world, nor to enumerate the laws of each people, but you have become universal geographers for all by opening up the gates of the *oikumene* and by organising the whole *oikumene* like a single household.'[98] In the Roman period itself, therefore, there clearly was an idea of living in a novel punctuation of connectivity: they perceived their world as quintessentially globalised.

To date there have been several attempts by Roman archaeologists and historians to introduce globalisation and its conceptual apparatus to the study of the Roman empire. As seen above, the seductiveness of a global model to explain change across the wide expanse of territories controlled and influenced by Rome is not new, as is well-illustrated by the application of core-periphery models and world systems theory.[99] In the majority of cases in which globalisation is directly evoked, the concept is used as an alternative to traditional accounts of cultural change based on Romanisation.[100] As a paradigm for understanding the Roman world, Romanisation came to be seen to be problematic because it over-privileges the role of Roman metropolitan culture in associated narratives of change, which are typically linear (from Rome to the provinces), and neglect the non-elite and aspects of change in other spheres such as class and gender.[101] In contrast, approaches to Roman globalisation have often focused on its potential to offer a new perspective in which cultural change is viewed as being multidirectional, simultaneously fostering unity and difference in the genesis of 'provincial' societies *and* the 'centre'.[102]

In addition to cultural dynamics, globalisation has also found application in providing new perspectives on the extent of economic integration in the Roman empire.[103] However, the biggest impact of globalisation studies has arguably been indirect. As Mattingly demonstrates, the last decade or so has seen a shift in scholarship on Roman archaeology away from using the term Romanisation in favour of approaches to identity.[104] Such concern with identity did not occur in a vacuum. Rather, it is itself a sign of the times, a unifying theme in historical and social science research from the 1990s that arguably developed in response to the rapid pace of contemporary globalisation and its effects on society.[105] In a similar fashion, recent approaches to ancient Mediterranean history have effectively adopted some of the conceptual apparatus of globalisation with the recent popularity of new paradigms highlighting the role of networks and connectivity to explain changes in the region. Horden and Purcell's *The Corrupting Sea* is a key work in this respect, although they do not evoke (or comment on) the concept of globalisation, and have rightly been criticised for their rather ahistorical approach towards Mediterranean connectivity.[106]

Given the direct and indirect influence of globalisation concepts in the fields of Roman archaeology and history, it might appear that the application of globalisation theory to the Roman empire is uncontroversial and widely accepted. This is not the case. The extant literature on Roman globalisation consists of a handful of journal articles and chapters, many of which are admittedly explorative in nature.[107] There is one monograph on the subject by Hingley, containing a valuable discussion of Romanisation and identity in the context of approaches to globalisation, but which, perhaps illustrative for the debate so far, does not really deal with globalisation.[108] It is clear in his later work and in his contribution to this volume that Hingley's objective is not so much to use globalisation as a theory to explain the Roman empire, but rather to use the analogy as a basis to challenge ideas about the modern world.[109] Indeed, casting globalisation as an alternative to Romanisation is highly unusual in the context of the use of the term in other historical periods, illustrating the parochial concerns of many Romanists, and a failure to recognise the broader utility of the concept.

And here we encounter something of a paradox. Whereas there has been an undoubted paradigm shift towards identity, connectivity and networks in our understanding of the Roman world, the very concept that is widely discussed and debated in the social and historical sciences to understand all this – globalisation – is largely evaded.[110] On the one hand there are scholars suggestively putting forward globalisation; but perhaps not really exploring the concept and its implications (see above). On the other hand there are the silent majority, apparently perceiving globalisation as a distinctly modern phenomenon that has nothing to do with the Roman world.[111]

Exceptions to the latter category – and by no means silent – are the review articles of Naerebout and Greene which stress the fragility of approaches to Roman globalisation.[112] Both Greene and Naerebout are dismissive of the term on the literal grounds that the Roman empire was not global, whereas the latter presents a detailed criticism of the early formulations of Hingley and Witcher. Naerebout stresses that the concept will only outlive its 'current fashionableness' if it offers helpful tools in the study of the ancient world, but he sees no potential there. In his opinion globalisation should not be used outside the context of modern society, believing that the concept cannot be rescued as an analytical or heuristic tool (option A, see above).[113] Hingley's globalisation is rejected on the grounds that it offers nothing new, as Naerebout argues that the idea that there was diversity underlying unity in the Roman empire is long established. Similarly, although praising aspects of Witcher's approach, he criticises it for a lack of clarity over whether or not globalisation is a specific condition of modernity. Despite Naerebout's deliberately provocative stance, he raises several pertinent points that must be addressed if the application of globalisation in Roman archaeology is to become something more than a passing fad.

THE CONCEPTUAL CHALLENGE

There is a clear conceptual challenge to be faced in applying the concept of globalisation to the Roman world. This volume takes up the challenge.

This is necessary, as the evocative use of globalisation as a description of what goes on in the Roman world is quickly becoming popular (see Witcher, this volume). Often, those evocations are precisely what Greene and Naerebout (and Morley, this volume) warn about: a new buzz word uncritically applied by all longing for an alternative to (or just another name for) Romanisation, adding little to the debate and doing potential harm by mis-representing or steering discussion in an unhelpful direction. Although we sympathise with calls for restraint and proper theoretical reflection, we also believe that the arguments to not use globalisation have been countered in this chapter. We *can* use a concept developed to describe present day phenomena for the study of other periods – as many globalisation scholars presently believe, while some explicitly ask for such an exploration; the concept of globalisation *has* been used convincingly to describe other periods of history; globalisation *is not* exclusively tied up with modernity or capitalism and it *can* be fruitfully applied to the Roman world.[114] What remains then is the real challenge: the problematic nature of the concept of globalisation itself.[115]

The observation that scholars now stress fragmentation is as much contextual (and, probably, ideological) as was the focus on unity in large parts of the nineteenth and twentieth centuries: in this respect there is no escaping the circle (to borrow from Gadamer). Just like any other, this book is every inch a part of the intellectual climate in which it was conceived. As archaeologists and ancient historians studying globalisation we also duly follow developments within the social and historical sciences. Why would such a venture not be a failure from the start? We have two answers to such criticism. The first one is awareness – being aware of the conceptual challenge means evaluating the risks of using a particular concept. Having devoted attention to the problems of the concept for the study of the Roman world, we believe that that the same discussion exposes its great potential. We should use globalisation, therefore (and this our second answer), as an additional, alternative concept alone. Concepts like imperialism, Romanisation and creolisation are as contextual (and suggestive and misleading) as globalisation will inevitably turn out to be. But applying them has brought our understanding of the Roman world much further – as globalisation potentially promises to do. We consider this especially important at the current stage of the 'Romanisation' debate, where contemporary discussions of connectivity often return to (a reinvention of) nineteenth-century debates, like the one on imperialism. We think these developments are not the best way forward, as the much-maligned Roman-Native dichotomy is often reinforced by them. There is good reason, therefore, to make globalisation part of our conceptual challenge. It is possible that the concept can provide a better understanding of 'Romanisation' – but this is only part of what this book explores.

Perspectives and opportunities

> As scholars concerned with localities, circulation, and comparison, we need to make a decisive shift away from what we may call 'trait' geographies to what we could call 'process' geographies. (Appadurai 2001, 7)[116]

At the start of this chapter we asked ourselves if we *can* use globalisation theory to understand the Roman world and, subsequently, if there is enough value in its constituent theoretical approaches to use it in a more applied sense. Our answer is 'yes' in both respects. Let us summarise why we think globalisation theory should become important for the study of the Roman world:

1. There is a large and important group of globalisation scholars that do not accept that the relationship between globalisation and modernity is an exclusive one, and call for a deep historical understanding and contextualisation of the processes involved in the past. At the same time the focus within globalisation studies has shifted from topics that are not so relevant to the Roman world (the internet, for example) to subjects that are highly relevant to the Roman world (as connectivity, identity, inequality and cultural imagination).

2. Within historical research there has been a paradigm shift from Area Studies towards global history that has seen the fruitful application of globalisation theory in historical contexts which are, in terms of globalisation-characteristics, structurally very much like the Roman world.

3. Within Roman studies we are in the middle of a similar paradigm shift from 'Roman versus Native' towards connectivity, networks and identities. In several respects – directly and indirectly – this shift is intertwined with globalisation, both as a contemporary process and a subject for academic study. We therefore simply cannot afford to evade the debate. In other words: we *need* to push the globalisation analogy harder.

From this summary it becomes clear that (with some important exceptions) the two approaches that Romanists have so far taken towards globalisation theories are unsatisfactory. The first could be said to be impressionistic and even opportunistic, and the second is probably too reductionist: neither helps to push the globalisation analogy harder. The question of how to move forward from point 3 is perhaps most important. For some, using globalisation as a critical lens through which to view the current state of research on cultural and economic dynamics in the Roman period may suffice.[117] Alternatively, explicitly using globalisation theories to describe and explain aspects of the Roman world and its material culture may be preferable, provided the rewards are sufficient. Such rewards need not, however, be strictly confined to those with an interest in the Roman period. In writing this introduction we are mindful of the general tendency towards the writing of 'global history'. Although there is no reason why Roman archaeologists and historians cannot contribute to this endeavour, our review of globalisation literature suggests that their voices are not necessarily being heard, or understood. Engagement with globalisation and its theoretical apparatus certainly provides one potential means of breaking down the 'nationalistic' and disciplinary boundaries that have traditionally separated Romanists from other scholars.

Beck has argued that within the social sciences the concept of globalisation has gone through three phases: first was dismissal; second was a phase of conceptual clarification; and third, an epistemological turn.[118] We have the impression that Roman archaeology is at present somewhere between phases 1 and 2 in Beck's framework. It is hoped that this volume will make a vital contribution to the study of the Roman world by moving forward current debates and evaluating the potential for globalisation to bring a genuine future paradigm shift.

THE INDIVIDUAL CONTRIBUTIONS

> The historian's contribution to the study of globalization should therefore be to remind us that we may be living amid only the latest (but probably not the last) of globalization's diverse and disconnected pre-histories. (Armitage 2004, 173–4)

The book has a tripartite structure. The first part provides two introductions. The present chapter sets the intellectual agenda and outlines the main theoretical questions. Many of the points and issues outlined here are developed further by the individual authors, often with different emphases and outcomes. A second introduction is provided by Hingley, who takes up the discussion and criticism of his book *Globalising Roman culture*. In contrast to our introduction, which is primarily concerned with the application of the concept to the Roman world, Hingley stresses the dangers involved in attempting to separate knowledge of the classical past from the contemporary context in which ideas about the past are conceived. In particular, Hingley restates the need for post-colonial critique, and argues that in presenting the Roman past as 'globalised' or 'globalising', archaeologists and historians risk providing an alibi for global capitalism in the present. Taken together, the introductions cover the two substantial elements of current scholarship on the topic.

Part II consists of seven chapters presenting case studies with the aim of evaluating the usefulness of globalisation within thematic areas of study: Roman economic history (Morley), mass consumption and ceramics (Pitts), urbanism and connectivity (Laurence and Trifilò), demography and migration (Isayev), and visual material culture (Versluys). Additionally, Sommer examines connectivity in the Mediterranean in earlier periods and works from the Phoenicians to the Roman empire to examine how special (or not) was the connectivity of the Roman world in comparison to what happened before, and Witcher makes a connection to the present-day world (and a different discipline) by dealing with globalisation and heritage, linking with the theoretical and historiographic issues discussed by Hingley in Part I. The book, therefore, also aims to be an exploration in the sense of providing an overview of what can be done with globalisation (or not) in different subjects and sub-disciplines in Roman archaeology and history, as well as considering the heritage implications of presenting a globalised Roman world to the wider public. Each of the essays, therefore, comments on a set of specific questions: Does globalisation offer a valuable perspective for Roman studies? Does it offer anything new? How can it change the nature of current scholarship? What are the areas/themes that will benefit most from the application of the concept? And what new theoretical and methodological apparatus are required for the concept to be applied in a more practical sense? Several cross-cutting themes and debates emerge from the individual contributions in Part II, including the nature and extent of time–space compression; the creation and maintenance of global consciousness; the role of the Roman state and state institutions as drivers of globalisation; the question of understanding non-state networks; and decentring Rome in interpretations of visual and material culture. In their discussions the contributors share a cautious optimism. Despite the costs of introducing theoretical jargon with connotations of modernity, there is broad agreement that globalisation is 'good to think with' for a variety of reasons, including providing scope for better understandings of the differences between antiquity and modernity, promoting comparisons with globalising scenarios in other historical contexts, and addressing the complexity of the Roman world and its material culture in a more sophisticated manner than existing paradigms.

Part III provides perspectives from disciplinary standpoints outside the realm of Roman archaeology and history. As this book should be considered the first extensive exploration of the application of globalisation theory to the Roman world, such emphasis on discussion is crucial to examine the issue from different angles. Coming from outside the field of Roman studies, Jan Nederveen Pieterse places 'Roman globalisation' in a much longer-term perspective; anchoring it in the domain of Globalisation studies, and highlighting the wider relevance of the discussion beyond Roman specialists. Finally, Hodos, whose own research is on globalisation in the Mediterranean Iron Age, provides a general conclusion which binds the contributions together. The broader issues raised in Part III include the need to understand the form 'globalisation' takes in the Roman world as a product of particular historical circumstances as opposed to being a uniform agent of change spanning different periods of history; and the question of the contribution of Roman history and archaeology to the wider historical understanding of 'globalisation'.

This book is called 'Globalisation and the Roman world'; not 'Globalising the Roman world'. Its goal is not to arrive at the conclusion that we should replace Romanisation with globalisation (or not). Instead, our aim is to make a genuine theoretical exploration that might add new perspectives to the debate or possible avenues for further investigation. This book critically investigates *if* and *how* globalisation theory can help us to better understand the Roman world and its material culture. As such, it also aims to contribute to debates in 'global history'. Having taken in the warnings of Naerebout, Greene and others, our Introduction has focused on the 'if'; the individual chapters aim to answer the 'how'.

NOTES

1. Hingley (2005); van Nijf (2006); Sweetman (2007); Geraghty (2007); Hitchner (2008); Pitts (2008); Rüpke (2011). Recent publications not having the word 'globalisation' in their title but implicitly using the concept as a theoretical framework or alternative to 'Romanisation' are much more numerous, e.g. Revell (2009, 2).

2. cf. Hopkins (2010, 34) (on the discipline of history): 'At present, numerous books and articles display the word "globalization" in their titles, but only a small number show an acquaintance with the analytical literature.'

3. See in particular Naerebout (2006/7) and Greene (2008).

4. Greenblatt (2009, 4) also observes that: 'Literary and historical research has tended to ignore the extent to which, with very few exceptions, in matters of culture the local has always been irradiated, as it were, by the larger world.' We believe this to be true for much archaeological research.

5. The Romanisation debate has developed very differently within various national and intellectual traditions. For a balanced overview from an Anglo perspective, see Mattingly (2004); for the discussion within French academia on these issues see the contributions to the *Annales ESC* from 1978 and the

Annales HSS from 2004; the 118(1) volume from the *Mélanges de l'École française de Rome* from 2006 and volume 80 from the journal *Pallas. Revue d'études antiques* from 2009 dedicated to 'Rome et l'Occident'. For German and other continental perspectives, see the important volume by G. Schörner (2005). We cannot discuss the various approaches in detail here, but it is important to note that while the debate in and on (Roman) Britain has been most visible and guiding for the field as a whole, its conclusions and consensus have not generally passed into French, German or Italian traditions.

6. Johnson (1999, 182); Trigger (2006, 66–7).
7. e.g. Mattingly (2004, 2006).
8. Sweetman (2007, 66–7) and Roth (2007, 19) provide pertinent critique on the concept and its use.
9. Pitts (2007); Versluys (2008).
10. Cusick (1998). For a critique on acculturation as a theoretical paradigm to understand the Roman world, see Versluys (this volume).
11. Woolf (1997).
12. This approach seems to be characteristic of much current Anglo scholarship. Note that their plea 'to do away with Romanisation' is largely ignored in the German, French and Italian traditions. Malkin (2005a, 7) advocates the use of a Mediterranean paradigm for similar reasons of going beyond postcolonial theory.
13. See van Dommelen (2006a). It is debatable whether talking about 'hybridisation' or 'hybrid practices' provides enough explanatory value either.
14. cf. Wimmer & Glick Schiller (2002).
15. Appadurai (2001, 3) has characterised area studies within the United States as follows: 'the largest institutional epistemology through which the academy ... has apprehended much of the world in the last fifty years.'
16. Hopkins (2002b, 12); Thomas (2004, Ch. 5).
17. Approaches to identity are often based on ethnic interpretations of styles of material culture, cf. Versluys (2008, 2013, this volume).
18. Appadurai (2001, 8).
19. To name but a few important existing contributions on connectivity in antiquity, see Horden & Purcell (2000), Malkin (2005b) and Van Dommelen & Knapp (2010a). For further comments on this development, see below.
20. Appadurai (2001, 6). For this definition see further below.
21. Wallerstein (1974, 1980, 1989).
22. Two volumes illustrate this well. Denemark et al.'s (2000) collection *World System History* features eight of the same authors as Gills & Thompson's *Globalization and Global History* (2006). The former barely mentions the word globalisation, whereas the latter only sparsely refers to world systems. However, the same contributors in the 2006 volume have not noticeably changed their methodological standpoints, and seemingly use globalisation as a shorthand for integration within larger economic and empire systems.
23. Wallerstein (1974, 348).
24. Frank & Gills (1993).

25. Wallerstein (1993).
26. Wallerstein (1993, 292–5).
27. Bang's (2008) comparative study of trade and markets in the Roman and Mughal empires further strengthens the case for viewing the emergence of capitalism in early modern Europe as a qualitatively different phenomenon from the operation of markets within pre-modern tributary empires.
28. For applications outside or beyond the Roman empire see, for example, Schneider (1977); Kohl (1987a, 1987b); Sherratt (1993).
29. Hopkins (1978b). For further developed incarnations of the Hopkins model see K. Hopkins (1980, 1983, 2002).
30. Cunliffe (1988). Woolf (1990, 1993) provides detailed and nuanced consideration of the application of world systems thinking and related forms of grand narrative in the Roman world and beyond.
31. The link between urbanism and taxation is clearly articulated by Hingley (1982). See Laurence and Trifilò (this volume) for further discussion.
32. Current thinking does not deny the existence of markets in the Roman empire, but rather problematises the extent of their integration within a single unit of supply and demand (e.g. Saller 2002, 254).
33. Woolf (1993, 18).
34. Duncan Jones (1990, 30–47) provides a detailed critique of the economics of the Hopkins (1980) tax and trade model; cf. K. Hopkins (2002) for a rebuttal.
35. Although see Woolf (1990, 54–5) on the associated concept of world-symbols, and more recently Robertson & Inglis (2006) on Roman global consciousness.
36. e.g. Chase-Dunn (2005).
37. cf. the remarks by Appadurai (2001, 3): 'The academy (especially in the United States) has found in globalisation an object around which to conduct its special internal quarrels about such issues as representation, recognition, the "end" of history, the spectres of capital (and of comparison) and a host of others. These debates, which still set the standard of value for the global professoriate, nevertheless have an increasingly parochial quality.' Appadurai warns of 'an apartheid' between these debates and what he calls 'vernacular' (or 'grassroots') discourses about the global from 'below'. We comment on the 'conceptual challenge' that comes with using the concept of globalisation below.
38. For the historiography of globalisation theory, see also Nederveen Pieterse (this volume). Note that archaeologists and historians using globalisation often refer to older phases of the debate instead of current understandings.
39. O'Rourke & Williamson (2002); Nayyar (2006).
40. e.g. Flynn & Giráldez (2006).
41. Frank & Gills (2000). Denemark et al. (2000) and Gills & Thompson (2006) provide a range of sometimes conflicting views on the extent and development of long-term processes and structures in global history.
42. Wallerstein (1974).
43. The notion of globalisation as time–space compression was introduced by Harvey (1989).
44. Giddens (1990); Tomlinson (1999).

45. Robertson (1992); Waters (2001); Appadurai (1996, 2001).
46. Nederveen Pieterse (2004, 61). Jennings (2011, 1–18) radicalises this argument in discussing globalisation as 'Modernity's greatest theft'.
47. Frank (1998).
48. Shami (2001).
49. LaBianca & Scham (2006).
50. Castells (2006).
51. Castells (2006, 158).
52. Inglis & Robertson (2006); Robertson & Inglis (2006).
53. Jennings (2011).
54. e.g. Algaze (1993); Modelski (2000).
55. Contra Morley (this volume), who argues that the ancient world did not experience significant time–space compression. Jennings (2011, 123–5) suggests that ancient time–space compression was achieved through the introduction of the donkey in opening up new possibilities for inter-regional trade, in addition to the development of reliable road networks for the movement of goods through harsh landscapes. These arguments are paralleled by those of Laurence (1999) on the effects of the introduction of new breeds of draught animals (mules) and better road paving surfaces in the Roman period; see also Laurence & Trifilò (this volume).
56. Migration history shows an identical trend: where it first was focused almost exclusively on the nineteenth and twentieth centuries alone, it now goes back to an 'Out of Africa' perspective to study migration history in world history, see Lucassen, Lucassen & Manning (2010).
57. For the use and definition of these concepts see Hopkins (2002a) and Bayly (2002).
58. Robertson (2003, 3).
59. Nederveen Pieterse (2004, 26).
60. Cain & Hopkins (2001, 663) define modern globalisation in terms of the transformation of the state into the nation-state.
61. Bauman (1998, 2). See also Appadurai (2006), especially for the concept of 'grassroots globalisation'.
62. Wilkinson (2005); Wilkinson & Pickett (2010).
63. Nederveen Pieterse (2004, 23, 54). See also Morris (2005, 43) who underlines that in the ancient Mediterranean, globalisation is a process that created winners and losers.
64. See Horton (1998, 167–70).
65. Appadurai (1996); Nederveen Pieterse (2004).
66. Robertson (1992, 173–4); Clarke (2003, 191).
67. Appadurai (1996, 42).
68. Nederveen Pieterse (2004, 2009). For our reservations in using the term 'hybrid' for archaeological interpretations in particular, see the critique formulated below.
69. Nederveen Pieterse (2004, 72).
70. Ibid., 106. cf. Burke (2009) on notions of hybridity and related concepts.
71. Ibid., 108.

72. Appadurai (2006, 43) for the quote specifically. Relations between culture and power are thus more complicated than the routinely evoked dichotomy between elites and non-elites suggests; for this discussion cf. Gibson (2007).

73. An aspect not dealt with here, although certainly important, is the study of globalisation as fundamentally a philosophical subject, as forcefully argued and illustrated by the German philosopher P. Sloterdijk in his *Philosophische Theorie der Globalisierung* (2004). For Sloterdijk, globalisation is about the rationalisation of word structures, something he (rightly) sees beginning in antiquity.

74. Rightly Witcher (2000, 219) points out: 'It is not global material culture itself which serves to compress time and space and to bring us closer together, but the symbolic exchange which makes us aware of that fact.'

75. Hopkins (2010).

76. Appadurai (2001, 1) explains the initial reaction of historians as follows: 'Historians, ever worried about the problem of the new, realize that globalization may not be a member of the familiar archive of large-scale historical shifts.'

77. Hopkins (2002a, 2): 'The possibilities are as large as the concept itself.'

78. Ibid., 4–5.

79. Bayly (2002, 51). Bayly sees the main characteristics of archaic globalisation as (A) the notion of cosmic kingship, (B) universal religion and (C) humoral understandings of the body and the land.

80. Hopkins (2002b, 15). Note, however, that Waters (2001) maintained that time–space compression reaches its greatest extent in the cultural sphere.

81. Ibid., 16–17.

82. See Hopkins (2010, 25–6, 26): '"Is it new, is it true" asked one skeptic. "Do we really need this" intoned another.' Hopkins sees this radical change in approach as not having to do so much with his own book but with the *Zeitgeist*.

83. Hitchner (2008, 1).

84. cf. Stavrianos (1998) and Hopkins (2006). This trend is well illustrated by the volumes of the *Journal of Global History*.

85. Characteristically, Hopkins (2002b, 15) states: 'In short, globalization is a theme that promises to resurrect some old lines of historical inquiry, to open up new ones, and to stimulate revisions of established interpretations.' See also Witcher (2000, 214): 'I wish simply to suggest that globalisation offers both a vocabulary and a series of models with which to explore identities in Roman Italy.'

86. For instance, Harper (2002, 150) states: 'Here we run against the ever-present concern that the language of globalisation is for historians merely an opportunity to re-invent the wheel.' See also Pitts (2008, 505): 'globalisation remains a descriptive term rather than an explanatory concept in itself, and, like Romanisation, comes with much unhelpful baggage.'

87. Note, however, that increasingly within disciplines such as sociology there is a lot of interest in the historical development of global connections, see Wimmer & Glick Schiller (2002, 322).

88. Hopkins (2002b, 24).

89. Bayly (2002, 64–7).

90. Witcher (2000).

91. cf. Ma (2003).

92. See, for instance, the characteristics Rothschild (1998) provides concerning globalisation: a very rapid increase in (A) international trade, (B) international investment, (C) international communications and (D) international influence. All this very much holds true for the Roman world, as summarised by Hitchner (2008).

93. Jennings (2011, 9, with Fig. 1.2). It is for this reason that the term 'archaic globalisation' as used by Hopkins and others is not well coined. The same criticism applies to the term 'incipient globalisation' to characterise the early Middle Ages, as used by Harris (2007).

94. Jennings (2011, 13).

95. For this text (and its contextual understanding) see Isayev (this volume). It is interesting to note that to describe this globalised, Mediterranean perspective, Polybius sometimes has to switch to Roman concepts on both the applied level of language and the abstract level of ideas; cf. M. Dubuisson (1985, 172) on Polybius, calling the Mediterranean 'our sea'.

96. Pitts (2008, 494). In his conclusion, Witcher (2000) calls this system 'A universalisation of a particular model of elite social power, and a particularisation of that universal model for local requirements'.

97. Reger (2007); Parker (2008).

98. For this text (and its contextual understanding) see Sommer (this volume).

99. e.g. Hopkins (1978b, 1980); Cunliffe (1988); Woolf (1990).

100. As, for instance, within the now finished project, 'Reichsreligion und Provinzialreligion. Globalisierungs- und Regionalisierungsprozesse in der antiken Religionsgeschichte', in which globalization theories are used as a heuristic tool to understand ancient religion from a different perspective.

101. There is now a very large literature on the inadequacies of Romanisation, notably Hill (2001), Webster (2001), Mattingly (2004) and Pitts (2007).

102. Wells (1999, 192–3); Witcher (2000); Laurence (2001a); Hingley (2005); Sweetman (2007); Pitts (2008); Versluys (2013).

103. Geraghty (2007) outlines a complex quantitative model of globalisation to explain the development of the early imperial economy, whereas Morley (2007a, this volume) offers a more cautious account of the limits of ancient globalisation compared with contemporary economic processes of market integration.

104. Mattingly (2010). For examples of studies of identity in Roman archaeology see Laurence & Berry (1998); Mattingly (2004); Gardner (2007a); and Hales & Hodos (2010). Pitts (2007) provides some critique of this phenomenon.

105. Jenkins (2004, 8–14). Post-colonialism has played an important role here in preparing the intellectual terrain for pure studies of identity and the related notion of ethnicity, especially with scholars studying the Roman empire.

106. Horden & Purcell (2000). Malkin (2005a) and Morris (2005) have characterised their work as a paradigm shift in thinking about the ancient world. See also later

volumes, e.g. Malkin (2005b); Malkin, Contantakopoulou & Panagopoulou (2009); Van Dommelen & Knapp (2010a).

107. Of these, Hitchner (2008, 2) confidently asserts: 'it is the very fecundity and complexity of globalisation as a concept which makes it particularly fruitful as an explanatory mechanism to the Roman world.'

108. Hingley (2005). cf. the review by Prag (2006a) for why this is not really a book about globalisation and the Roman world and, in a similar vein, the postscript to Naerebout (2006/7). In this volume, Hingley responds to this discussion.

109. Hingley (2010).

110. In the index of Horden & Purcell (2000) it occurs only once, with a reference to p. 599. On that page we could not find the word. In Malkin (2005b) it is only the article by Morris that seriously points at globalisation as a way of understanding processes of Mediterranisation. Even a broader, theoretical book on archaeology and modernity (Thomas 2004) ignores the concept.

111. It is interesting to note that both groups are happy to use concepts that are tied up very much with globalisation – like hybridity – without further elaboration.

112. Naerebout (2006/7); Greene (2008). The observations and remarks on globalisation as an anachronistic concept for the Roman world in Dench (2005) also fall within this category.

113. Gardner (2013), reflecting on previous applications of globalisation to the Roman world, expresses similar reservations over whether globalisation offers analytical tools for examining the Roman period as a distinct entity. Nevertheless, his preferred alternative of 'institutional archaeology' can be seen to fall within the remit of globalisation, a theme which is productively explored by Laurence & Trifilò in this volume.

114. To briefly counter arguments 2–5 made in Naerebout's (2006/7) summary.

115. For a general introduction regarding the conceptual challenges facing archaeology, see Insoll (2007), with a useful Chapter 2 on globalisation. We find much to agree here, but not the caricature Insoll makes of post-modernism.

116. With 'trait geographies' Appadurai wants to indicate that area studies are always driven by ideas of cultural coherence, reasoning from some kind of 'trait list' of values, languages, material practices, etc.

117. See, if in a more general vein, Jennings (2011, 8): 'If the processes could be linked, archaeologists and other researchers who study the past would be able to mine the rich globalization literature to better understand the dynamics of these pivotal periods of widespread cultural change in world history.'

118. Beck (2004).

2

POST-COLONIAL AND GLOBAL ROME: THE GENEALOGY OF EMPIRE

Richard Hingley

> To think with ruins of empire is to emphasize less the artifacts of empire as
> dead matter or remnants of a defunct regime than to attend to their
> reappropriations and strategic and active positioning within the politics of the
> present.
>
> (Stoler 2008, 196)

INTRODUCTION

This chapter reflects upon how contemporary scholarship in Roman studies
relates to the politics of our world. Classical concepts of order, security and
civilisation are deeply embedded within political understandings of the
present. The Roman empire makes sense to us, in part, because our society
sees contemporary values and aims embodied in the evidence from the
classical past. This reflects the two-way relationship between classical times
and the present. Our comprehensions of order, logic and justice are bound up
with an inherited body of knowledge, much of which ultimately derives from
the classical societies of Greece and Rome. We transform and develop these
ideas, but we also build on them in the changing interpretations of the Roman
empire that are created within archaeology and ancient history. Whatever
academics may think about the strengths and weaknesses of globalisation
theory, many of the concepts on which it draws have become common
currency within the media and society in general. People in the Western
world draw upon these ideas just as directly as their ancestors drew upon
colonial concepts. This is why we cannot ignore globalisation when we
explore the culture of imperial Rome.[1]

My deliberately rather contentious book, *Globalizing Roman Culture*
(*GRC*),[2] contained an earlier version of this argument and this present
chapter reviews and updates the approach. In *GRC* I focused on the context

of some recent approaches that have been developed to address Roman identity and social change, commencing an exploration of the hermeneutical relationship of this field of knowledge to ideas about the present world-order. I aimed to extend the critical focus on Romanisation theory to address the recent works that had constructed what might be considered to represent broadly 'post-colonial' accounts of identity in the Roman empire. In particular, I explored the focus of some of the new approaches that have been developed to address the elite cultures of the Western empire ('becoming Roman').[3] I also addressed recent accounts of fragmented identities, exploring military, urban and rural ways of life, including detailed studies of the Lower Rhine Valley and northwestern Iberia.[4] The latter approaches are significant since they provide a rather more complex and less elite-focused view of the ways that Rome influenced people across the western part of its empire than the previous accounts of Romanisation and becoming Roman. My aim was to assess a variety of recent archaeological accounts, addressing the extent to which the Roman empire might be seen to have been fully connected. In the brief concluding section to my book, I returned to the issue of the ways that understandings of the Roman past reflect the concerns and interests of the present.[5]

In his review of my book, F. G. Naerebout observes that during an earlier conversation with him I had said that I intended the book to critique globalisation as a new paradigm for Roman archaeology, in much the same way that Romanisation had already been critiqued.[6] Naerebout argues that this aim is not clearly expressed in *GRC* and, although there *is* some emphasis,[7] I accept that I could have communicated this argument more clearly.[8] Building upon Naerebout's comment, Pitts and Versluys (Chapter 1, this volume) note that 'It is clear in his later work and in his contribution to this volume that Hingley's objective is not so much to use globalisation as a theory to explain the Roman empire, but rather to use the analogy as a basis to challenge ideas about the modern world'. I can see how Pitts and Versluys have come to argue this way. Since 2005, I have been drawing upon the critical accounts of contemporary 'Empire' to set imperial Rome in context.[9] The interrelationship of imperial Rome and Empire relates to the nature of the knowledge we develop of past and present, raising complex issues of interpretation that require detailed consideration. In addressing the globalisation of the Roman empire, I intend to critique both the contemporary world and our knowledge of the ancient world, since (as is often observed but also often ignored) our understanding of classical Rome can only exist in a contemporary context.

The argument in *GRC* was based on the hermeneutical relationship between past and present. Since the mid-1990s it has become fashionable to argue that the works of ancient historians and archaeologists during the early twentieth century adopted and modified colonial knowledge, creating and transforming political approaches that drew deeply upon Roman imperial models.[10] In this context, 'post-colonial' theory has been used to direct a critical focus on how ideas about the ancient past operated in the creation and perpetuation of forms of colonial knowledge.[11] The details of the critique of Romanisation outlined in Chapter 1 explain some of the background to this issue. My prime argument is that ideas about social change in the Roman empire have been transformed over recent decades to address the new political and economic context of the present while continuing effectively to recast the Roman past, at least in part, in the image of the present. This transformation occurs through the changing research agendas and theories of archaeologists and ancient historians. The use of classical Rome to contextualise contemporary imperialism in an early twentieth-century context has been replaced in many contemporary works by a focus on the global relevance of Rome.[12] This is the main reason that we cannot just dismiss globalisation as a viable model for the Roman empire, since past and present are too deeply interrelated to make this position viable. At the same time, images and messages derived from imperial Rome have maintained their relevance as the basis for political and military decision making. In Chapter 1, Pitts and Versluys emphasise that many ancient historians and archaeologists pick up the ideas inherent in globalisation theory while avoiding the use of the concept; my aim is to build on this observation by addressing why it is important that we are explicit about the transforming agendas we develop in Roman studies. The past is not dead, but continues to be brought to life through reference to the concerns and interests of the present. The Roman past has been globalised, whether we are happy to accept this or not.

The present chapter seeks to build on these arguments by addressing the changing intellectual tradition in Roman studies over the past decade. It seeks to express in clearer terms the argument that Naerebout failed to uncover in *GRC*, drawing on a number of other, more recent, accounts that supplement this approach, including two additional papers of my own.[13] The core argument is for the potential of articulating the idea of the genealogy of empire in order to provide a context for our interpretations of globalisation. This is a field of knowledge that explores the reception, memorialising, forgetting, rediscovery, contradiction, transformation and abandonment of the idea of empire from the classical past to the present. Although the term 'genealogy of empire' is used quite widely in the published literature,[14] the concept is yet to be developed in any detail and I shall return to this topic towards the end of this chapter.

THE HERMENEUTICAL RELATIONSHIP OF THE PAST AND PRESENT

Scholars who study the past usually construct a conceptual barrier between the present and the materials constituting the subject matter of their research, in order to create reliable knowledge. The act of delimitation on which this technique is based is elaborated through the creation of a linear sense of temporal order. This concept of sequence places the subject of our scholarship in a distant position, apparently entirely separated from the world in which we undertake our research and writing. This is achieved through a series of theoretical and methodological procedures that help to create a concrete concept of temporal distance. Archaeological methods for excavation, the creating of typologies and dating, together with the approaches adopted by classicists to textual analysis, seek to provide rigorous ways to create forms of understanding that can be defended as 'authentic'. As Pearson and Shanks have argued, 'What is found becomes authentic and valuable because it is set by choice in a new and separate environment with its own order, purpose and its own temporality – the time co-ordinates of the discipline of archaeology which give the object its date and context'.[15]

Distancing the past from the present might be seen to make it less relevant, but we also seek to bring this knowledge back to life by setting it in a contemporary context.[16] Laurent Olivier writes:

> Material things embed themselves in all subsequent presents; long after they have ceased to be of use or to exist, they continue to be. Thus, even though the Roman Empire collapsed for good in times which are completely over and done with, its material remains nonetheless continue to occupy our present, as they will continue to do so for those who come after us.[17]

This is a significant point, but it is not only the material relics of past societies that continue to haunt the present. All accounts of the Roman empire – its culture, religion, politics and economy – are based on assessments of the textual sources and the material remains that have been uncovered, but they also, inevitably, relate to the concerns and interests of the present. In addition to tangible remains, we inherit many intangible beliefs and concepts, ideas that are often held without a clear conception of where and when they originated.

It has been observed that the need to use theories about the present to interpret the evidence that we derive from the past arises, in part, from the fact that we have only fragments surviving. Many classical texts have been lost through time and the surviving fragments are constantly reinterpreted to draw out new meanings. Archaeological information is also highly fragmentary and requires interpretation before it can be drawn upon to provide information. Neville Morley has argued that the fragmentary nature of knowledge of imperial Rome means that modern analogies have often been used to fill the gaps in our information.[18] This is one of the factors that make it inevitable that interpretations of the classical world take on board current explanatory ideas, but we also have methods and theories to help distance the past from the present.

Kathryn Lafrenz Samuels has explored 'Value and Significance in Archaeology' and written about the idea of source criticism, arguing that the best reconstructions of the past are those that have managed to address the affect of contemporary influences and have worked back through the historical sources.[19] She also observes, however, that to argue that reconstructions of the past should be free of value judgements is to ignore the fact that archaeology is shaped by its practices and exists in a social context that is decidedly contemporary. Therefore, the insistence of a strict separation between past and present restricts the tools available for analysis.[20] Lafrenz Samuels promotes a form of understanding that leads to a 'dialogical conversation between past and present', an approach that 'blurs those barriers ... to show their interconnectedness, without disregarding their differences'.[21] I shall draw upon this approach to address the genealogy of our knowledge about the impact of classical Rome across its empire.

THE COLONIAL LEGACY OF ROMAN IMAGES

Images derived from classical Rome have a deep legacy that relates to the manner in which this ancient culture was (and is) drawn upon in the West. Since the Renaissance, people of power and influence have sought to create cultural capital through reference to imperial Rome. Rome has long formed an iconic image, drawn upon to inform and help redefine the present. This was the context of the European Renaissance, and images derived from classical Rome have continued since early modern times to operate in a complex variety of ways in many different areas of culture, politics, religion and economy. This is a vast topic and I cannot draw in any detail on the complex ways in which ideas derived from classical Rome have operated across Europe and beyond.[22] One important issue that has received detailed study concerns the intellectual process through which classical knowledge has been drawn upon in scholarly study in order to make this information relevant and apposite to cementing nationhood and creating imperial domination over others.[23] Although imperial Rome has often been received as a cultural paragon in the fields of politics, culture and architecture, many have reflected on it critically by drawing on ancient evidence for despotism, military force and enslavement.[24]

The role of Rome can change through time within a single society in order to address transforming political and cultural agendas. For example, a generally negative perception of imperial despotism typified the British attitude to imperial Rome for much of the nineteenth century, but a contrasting fixation on the efficacy of the creation of order and peace characterised the final decade of the nineteenth and the early twentieth centuries.[25] The inherent complexity of the cultural models offered by classical Rome explains its attraction to a broad range of societies from the fifteenth century to the present day. It provided (and provides) a contrasting set of concepts that often operate more effectively as a result of their inherent ambiguity.

The theory of Romanisation was effectively deconstructed in Britain during the period from the mid-1990s to the mid-first decade of the present century, based on the uncovering of the inherent imperial agendas, a process in which the particular interests of archaeologists and ancient historians drew upon the concerns of their own societies.[26] This critical approach drew upon the use of writings of 'post-colonial' authors, including Edward Said and Homi Bhabha.[27] A dominant element in this tradition represents the interrogation of the relationship between ideas about the imperial context of the twentieth century and the forms of knowledge created for Roman archaeology.[28]

Much of this research aimed to unmask and supplant the forms of imperial knowledge that used classical Rome to provide lessons, analogies, contrasts and morals for the colonial present. Relevant issues that became problematic during the late twentieth century included the idea that imperial contact encouraged a progressive transformation on the periphery of empire, from barbarity to civilisation. Post-colonial works focused on the implicit manner in which this idea of a Roman civilising mission fed on and supplemented the imperial agendas of certain Western nations during the first two-thirds of the twentieth century, in particular Great Britain.[29] Romanising was perceived as making indigenous people more progressive and modern, a process that would eventually lead, through the rediscovery of classical examples during the Renaissance, to the modern imperial context by which Western nations dominated indigenous peoples across much of the globe.[30] By the early 1990s, archaeologists were directing more serious attention toward the responses of native people to Roman control.[31] As Pitts and Versluys note in Chapter 1, however, there is something about the idea of Rome that continually resists unmasking.

CONTEMPORARY CONCERNS

Classical Rome, in its republican and imperial phases and also in its collapse, continues to hold immense cultural capital in our century, leading some to claim that Rome never died, but has been transformed into a global cultural phenomenon ('Empire') that has spread across today's world.[32] We only need to consider the widespread use of classical concepts in the military and political actions of Western nations since 2001, to reflect on the degree of continuity in the transforming systems that are used to regulate and order our world. Ideas about the bringing of civilisation, peace and order to barbarians and backward peoples at the margins, together with arguments about the 'just war' and the idea of securing the boundaries that define and defend the civilised, have been reinvented to form powerful political models, ideas that are used to justify political and military actions.[33] For some, Empire is alive and kicking and the extent to which classical Rome declined and fell is certainly open to sustained debate.[34]

Whatever perspective we take in the debate about the significance of globalisation theory to Roman studies, it is vital not to ignore the cultural and political power of imperial Rome today. Importantly, this image is also communicated, contested and contextualised through film and other forms of popular media.[35] The cultural currency of classical Rome provides part of the reason that over the past two decades, a number of archaeologists and ancient historians have aimed to unmask the roles played by our received versions of Roman imagery in the political and cultural actions of Western nations.[36] At the same time, scholarly approaches to the Roman past have been modified to articulate with the changing cultural and political contexts of Western thought.[37] To an extent, the battle that has been waged in Roman archaeology over the last decade and a half has been won. The linear concepts of progressive social change, together with the reified idea of Roman and native/barbarian identity on which these interpretations were based, have ceased to be popular.[38] Archaeologists and ancient historians today have more complex comprehensions of Roman identity and the flexible ways that contacts between Rome and the various indigenous peoples worked to establish and contest the growth of the network of power relations that formed the empire.[39] A number of influential accounts provide coherent ways of re-imaging classical Rome that appears particularly apposite in our global world.[40] Despite this, we need to continue the sustained analysis of the complex relationships that exist between, on the one hand, the forms of knowledge of the past that we seek to develop and, on the other, the politics, culture and economics of our contemporary age.

Roman imperial culture as global discourse

There is a lively debate amongst scholars about whether globalisation is an appropriate interpretational tool for the modern world and how ideas about the global world might operate today.[41] This debate has been explored in some detail in the introduction to this volume, but the particular issues in many studies include the breaking down of former geographies of oppositions between the core and periphery and the erosion of previous ideas about the centrality of the West.[42] Some works focus on the economic networking and connectivity of the modern world, while others concentrate more fully on cultural integration and fragmentation. These new research traditions and changing patterns of thought have created ideas of less dichotomous and more intricate patterns of inequality in recent interpretations of the Roman empire. These ideas have developed through theories that deal with the concept of 'becoming Roman' and various other attempts to explore the fragmented identities of soldiers, urban and rural dwellers.[43] As a result, the old ideas that constituted Romanisation theory – including those of the elite and non-elite, incorporation and resistance – have begun to break down, at least to a degree, in a global empire that is recreated through local engagement.[44] Thus pluralism, or heterogeneity, comes to be thought of as providing a binding force in the Roman empire, just as in the contemporary world. Cultural variation becomes a tool for the creation of a state of sustained imperial order.[45]

In pointing out these connections, I am not directly criticising the concepts of cultural pluralism and hybridity in either the modern or ancient world. Such approaches have formed a powerful and well-intentioned response to earlier ideas of the centrality and homogeneity of colonial and imperial power. They have served to help to undermine former colonial and post-colonial understandings of the ancient world, including the arguments inherent in ideas of progressive Romanisation and native resistance. Nevertheless, these pluralistic accounts appear to have effectively ceased to challenge the dominant ways in which the world is represented. In this context, I wonder whether the more inclusive accounts of peoples of various identities and statuses across the Roman empire generated during the past two decades effectively serve to exclude the critical perspectives that focus on the negative influence of global forces in the contemporary world.[46] Indeed, this would explain why Roman scholars are increasingly placing a greater emphasis on the observation that, in the Roman world, cultural difference was also used to establish opposites and to crush, marginalise and exterminate people.[47] In addition, as Robert Witcher has observed, we need to be suspicious of the reinvention of Rome as a model of inclusiveness since this has worrying and complex historical and contemporary resonances.[48]

GENEALOGY OF EMPIRE

One way to pursue the challenges laid out in this chapter is to consider genealogy as a way of addressing how empires have grown and been perpetuated by drawing on the example of a former imperial condition.[49] In an influential but contentious work on contemporary 'Empire', Hardt and Negri pursue a particular direct connection between the image of the Roman empire created by Polybius and the analogous structure they claim for the modern world.[50] To suggest that the Roman empire is in some way directly comparable to the modern state of 'Empire' is a rather naïve idea. It is more accurate to suppose that Hardt and Negri, and other scholars, have drawn upon Roman imperial models to provide a reflection, metaphor or analogy for contemporary global sovereignty.[51] Pitts and Versluys write of the 'fragile presentism' inherent in certain recent works that mirror contemporary global issues in evidence derived from the ancient world.[52] They emphasise the need for ancient historians and archaeologists to engage with and contribute to the changing intellectual agenda in globalisation theory. In this chapter I am echoing this suggestion, but also emphasise the complexity of this field of study. Rather than supposing that we can deal with this fragile presentism in works on contemporary globalisation merely through adding a classical/archaeological perspective, I propose that we add our own voices to this debate in order to show the interconnectedness of past and present without disregarding their differences.[53]

It is through detailed source criticism, including the analysis of comparability and difference, that knowledge of the past and the present is constructed, transformed and elaborated; our attempts to develop ideas of Roman globalisation in order to work with this approach. The popular field of reception studies in classics focuses attention on how some aspects of the past have been selected and 'appropriated' in order to create concepts of value, status and power in later cultures.[54] Reception study has considerable potential when it focuses attention on the representation of the modes of thought that lie behind our interpretations of classical Rome and on the messy business of the history of the transformation and contradiction of this knowledge through time.[55] Fragile presentism appears to be characteristic of an approach that links the present to the classical past without sufficient consideration of what happened in the centuries that separate classical Rome from contemporary Empire. It accepts the interconnectedness of present and past and allows no adequate form of analysis of alterity through source criticism.

To uncover the genealogy of thought about the global world, we need to keep a critical focus on the context of contemporary ideas about the Roman empire, an approach that explores the origin, source and transformation of these ideas. How have the ideas incorporated into our knowledge of empire been passed down through time? How have they been inherited and transformed? How have they been forgotten, rediscovered, adopted and contradicted? This approach focuses attention on the changing meanings of terms – including empire and globalisation – through detailed source criticism, aiming to address the affect of contemporary influences as a result of working back through the historical sources.[56]

The twin concepts of empire and imperialism inherited from the classical past have played a significant role in the creation of political power and the enforcement of order across the globe, in particular over the past two centuries. This tradition has built on a longer genealogy with roots in the classical past.[57] This does not mean that all forms of empire are particular reflections of a single grand conception, since meanings are constantly transformed and contradicted in different places and times; indeed, imperial Rome is not the only available ancient model for conceiving empire.[58] The centrality of Rome reflects its fundamental role as an origin myth for many Western empires since the end of classical times, and the reception and dismissal of imperial models in post-Roman times forms a fundamental part of the study of the genealogy of empire across the Western world. This means that cross-temporal studies of the concepts that lie behind imperialism are of fundamental importance in helping to define the ways that ideas have been inherited, forgotten, transformed and opposed. Recent accounts from a number of separate academic disciplines address how ideas of empire and imperialism have been constructed, transformed, contradicted and handed down in a variety of different periods.[59] Approaching the genealogy of empire requires a cross-disciplinary, cross-temporal perspective. Cross-cultural studies are also vitally important in helping to identify the links and discontinuities in the genealogy of empire.[60]

CONCLUSIONS

The inherently political nature of the ideas we derive from the evidence that exists for classical Rome and its empire is fundamental. My concern is that, in aiming to decolonise the subject of Roman imperial archaeology, we may write out aspects of the Roman imperial past that we feel to be in some way unpalatable or undermining. In addition, we have tended to create versions of the Roman empire that integrate more fully into the way we wish the contemporary world to be (whether these interpretations are created either in the form of positive or critical reflections). A post-colonial Roman empire often appears to be a place where all (or at least the vast majority) had some power to determine their own lives and live in active and creative ways. The hybrid or plural ideas of identity that have become common in much of the literature tell richer tales of (at least partial) emancipation from imperial force, but in some cases they also acknowledge the role of asymmetrical power relations in shaping particular forms of identity in which people were largely un-empowered and had limited choice or indeed knowledge to create/reshape their identities.[61] These accounts seek to replace previous colonial and post-colonial forms of knowledge that usually placed a far greater emphasis on the political and cultural dominance exercised by Rome over the peoples of its empire.

The creation of such approaches appears entirely justifiable as a response to the ideas of Romanisation that dominated Roman archaeology until the final decade of the twentieth century. Indeed, these new ideas in classical studies have formed part of a wider agenda to create a 'post-colonial' world, a society that is based on a fundamental challenge to the older binary forms of logic that characterised imperial and colonial discourses. The problem has become that the world has, in the meantime, moved on. It has transformed in a way that has helped to incorporate the idea of plurality into the common discourse of identity, the structure through which the culture and economy of the contemporary world is transformed and regenerated. Perhaps this argument about the context of study should cause some concern about the creation of ideas of plural pasts. My main concern, however, is that the idea of a critical reflection on the Roman empire continues to be subverted through an agenda that drives the conception of genealogical ancestry for the enabling power of contemporary connectivity.

Evidently, as the chapters in this volume clearly illustrate, a variety of different approaches to globalisation and the Roman empire are possible, including accounts that explore far more critical readings of the evidence for the past. Pitts and Versluys observe that 'the conceptual vacuum created by the discredited concept of Romanisation is somewhat discomforting'. In contrast, I would stress that it may be better that we do not seek to create too much consensus over such politically sensitive topics as empire and globalisation. Indeed, perhaps the highly contested nature of globalisation as a concept in itself helps to provide a reason to promote the adoption of globalisation theory in Roman studies.[62] Jean Baudrillard observed that 'the phenomenon of globalization is in itself random and chaotic, to the point where no one can control it'.[63] From this viewpoint, the proliferation of approaches that typify contemporary studies of imperial Rome is a sign of the intellectual strength of the subject; however, I must emphasise one final time that our approaches always need to engage with critical genealogies of thought in order to establish the ways that ruins of empire are re-appropriated within the politics of the present.[64]

ACKNOWLEDGEMENTS

I wish to thank Martin Pitts and Miguel John Versluys for inviting me to write this chapter. I have benefited from discussions of the topic of empire with David Mattingly, Phiroze Vasunia, Michael Shanks, Christina Unwin, Dimitris Grigoropoulos and Robert Witcher. I am also grateful to audiences at conferences in Berlin, Santiago de Compostela, Campinas (Brazil), Oxford (RAC), London (imperialism network) and Durham for comments on earlier versions of the arguments developed here. I am particularly grateful to the editors, to the two referees and to Christina Unwin for comments on an earlier version of this chapter.

NOTES

1. For recent definitions of the terms 'imperialism' and 'colonialism', see Mattingly (2011, 6–7) and Kiely (2010, 1–8). For 'globalisation', see Pitts & Versluys (Chapter 1, this volume).
2. Hingley (2005).
3. Woolf (1998); cf. Hingley (2005, 49–90). Laurence & Trifilò (this volume) point out that Martin Millett had already picked up the idea of a 'global' conception of the Roman empire in his earlier book, *The Romanization of Britain* (1990a), an issue that I did not address in *GRC*.
4. Hingley (2005, 91–116).
5. Ibid., 117–20.
6. Naerebout (2006/7, 167).
7. Hingley (2005, 117–20). These arguments build on earlier statements in the first chapter of the book.
8. Placing these observations in a short section in the conclusion may have detracted from the message I sought to convey, cf. Gardner (2007b, 390).
9. Including Balakrishnan (2003b), Meiksins Wood (2003), Passavant & Dean (2004), Boron (2005), Krishnaswamy & Hawley (2008). These works have developed in the context of the critique of Hardt & Negri's influential book *Empire* (2000). See the discussion in Hingley (2010, 54–64, 70–1) and Hingley (2011). This body of work forms one of a number of sub-disciplines that have

arisen in globalisation studies. For the broader context, see Nederveen Pieterse (this volume).

10. Mattingly (1997); Hingley (2000); Webster (2001).

11. In this context, the post-colonial writings that interest me are those that address the colonial context of past writings about imperial Rome. I am less concerned here with accounts that seek to use post-colonial writings to create a new understanding of the material culture of societies incorporated into the Roman empire. Pitts & Versluys (Chapter 1, this volume) argue that post-colonial writing often mirror Romanisation narratives by continuing to divide Romans from natives into two distinct groups, while inverting the focus of interest by placing a priority on native identity. By contrast, my interest in post-colonial theory has related more specifically to the interrogation of the colonial narratives incorporated in the works of ancient historians and archaeologists who address imperial Rome (cf. Hingley 2000).

12. Laurence & Trifilò (Chapter 5, this volume) and Witcher (Chapter 9, this volume) also consider this point.

13. Hingley (2010, 2011).

14. cf. Balakrishnan (2003a, xiii); Kelly (2009); Stoler (2010, 253); Hingley (2011).

15. Pearson & Shanks (2001, 115).

16. Hingley (2012, 9).

17. Olivier (2004, 206).

18. Morley (2010, 9–10).

19. Lafrenz Samuels (2008, 88).

20. Ibid., 89.

21. Such an approach has connotations for the debate summarised by Pitts & Versluys (Chapter 1, this volume) on when and where in the past the process of globalisation began. Another way of thinking about this issue is that the process of creating the past effectively writes the present into that knowledge. If we are going to ask where and when globalisation first came into existence, we also need to think about how we globalise the past through the questions we ask and the ways that we draw upon certain ideas and materials in order to create knowledge.

22. cf. Moatti (1993); Beard & Henderson (1995); Hingley (2001a).

23. cf. Marchand (1996); Mouritsen (1998); Hingley (2000, 2001b).

24. e.g. Shumate (2006).

25. Vance (1997).

26. Hingley (2005, 14–48).

27. cf. Hingley (1996, 2000); Webster (1996, 2001); Mattingly (1997, 2006).

28. Hingley (2013).

29. Ibid.

30. cf. Hingley (2005, 45–8); Mattingly (2006, xii; 2011).

31. Hingley (2005, 40–2).

32. cf. Hardt & Negri (2000); Willis (2007). Hardt & Negri's powerful but problematic writings on contemporary Empire draw upon classical Rome to define an idea of an ever-expanding global Empire that draws people into it through economic means. Some critical responses to Hardt & Negri are listed above in note 9.

33. Petras & Veltmyer (2001); Benton & Fear (2003, 268); Parchami (2009); Parsons (2010, 3).
34. Shumate (2006).
35. cf. Joshel et al. (2001). See Witcher's comments on Roman heritage (Chapter 9, this volume).
36. e.g. Hingley (2005); Morley (2010); Mattingly (2011, 3).
37. Hingley (2010, 54).
38. Hodos (2010a, 23–7).
39. cf. Woolf (1998); Hingley (2005, 47–8); Terrenato (2008); Morley (Chapter 3, this volume).
40. Hingley (2013).
41. For the particular sub-field of globalisation studies that has played a particular role in my research, see note 9. Pitts & Versluys (Chapter 1, this volume) and a number of other authors in this volume consider additional works that have addressed contemporary globalisation.
42. Pitts & Versluys (Chapter 1, this volume) write about the themes of increasing connectivity and deterritorialisation.
43. Hingley (2005).
44. Hingley (2005, 118); Hingley (2010, 61); cf. Balakrishnan (2003a, x).
45. This argument is considered in detail in Hingley (2005, 2010).
46. See Morley (Chapter 3, this volume) on how globalisation theory and Roman studies can tend to focus on elites and sideline violence and alternative responses to assimilation in the Roman empire.
47. Pitts (2008); Mattingly (2011, 22–6). See the discussion by Pitts (Chapter 4, this volume).
48. Witcher (Chapter 9, this volume).
49. The idea of genealogy developed here is derived ultimately from the writings of Foucault (1989); cf. Donnelly (1986); Barkan (1999), xxi.
50. Hardt & Negri (2000). For works that draw upon and develop such a conception, see Robertson & Inglis (2006, 36); Willis (2007). For the critical reception of Hardt & Negri's book, see references cited in above in note 9.
51. cf. Hardt & Negri (2000, 10–20, 163, 314–6); Robertson & Inglis (2006); Willis (2007, 330).
52. They quote papers by Castells and Robertson and Inglis, but do not mention Hardt & Negri.
53. Working with archaeological materials enables an engagement with the potential alterity of the past (see Pitts and Laurence & Trifilò, Chapters 4 and 5, this volume), but only if the issues of the present context of historical knowledge are addressed as part of the analysis.
54. Hardwick (2003, 3).
55. cf. Goldhill (2011, 15).
56. cf. Lafrenz Samuels (2008, 88).
57. Richardson (2008); Parchami (2009); Kiely (2010); Mattingly (2011, 5–6).
58. cf. Mutschler & Mittag (2008).
59. The following volumes illustrate the wide variety of current approaches to this broad topic in a number of disciplines: Shumate (2006); Münkler (2007);

Richardson (2008); Parchami (2009); Kiely (2010); Morley (2010); Mattingly (2011).

60. cf. Alcock et al. (2001); Munkler (2007).
61. Hodos (2010a, 26).
62. Pitts & Versluys (Chapter 1, this volume) write that 'globalisation theory' 'is less a unified theory or grand narrative than a set of theoretical paradigms in dialogue with each other'. I would add that some of the dialogue within accounts of our global world is often rather heated, reflecting opposing economic and political views. We need not seek a coordinated approach to globalisation and Roman culture when globalisation theory in itself is so fractured and contested, although debate and discussion is always to be encouraged.
63. Baudrillard (2003, 50).
64. Stoler (2008, 196).

PART II

CASE STUDIES

3

GLOBALISATION AND THE ROMAN ECONOMY

Neville Morley

In place of the old needs, satisfied by local production, new ones appear, which require for their satisfaction the products of the most distant lands and climates. In place of the old local and national self-sufficiency appears a universal traffic, a universal dependence of nations on one another.

(Marx & Engels 1964, 466)

For many nineteenth-century social and economic analysts, the phenomenon of global interconnectedness we now label 'globalisation' was seen as one of the defining features of modernity, clearly distinguishing it from all earlier forms of social life. This development, and the radical break with the past that it represented, was not solely a matter of the expansion of international trade and the increasing economic interdependence of different regions, but of the underlying processes that were creating this global traffic and transforming every aspect of social relations across the world. Even when these changes took different forms according to local conditions, they were clearly – at least to the eye of the discerning analyst – part of the same general process:

The ongoing revolutionising of production, the constant unsettling of all social conditions, the eternal uncertainty and agitation mark out the epoch of the bourgeoisie from all earlier ones. All firm, rusted-shut relations with their entourage of time-honoured ideas and opinions are dissolved, all new-formed ones become antiquated before they can ossify. Everything solid and permanent evaporates, everything holy is desecrated...[1]

Marx and Engels stand at the head of one tradition of interpretation in this field of enquiry, seeing globalisation primarily in economic terms as one of the products of the process of capitalist accumulation. There are plenty of alternatives. Under the general heading of 'globalisation', one set of theorists debates the workings of identity, hybridity and post-colonialism while another concentrates on the mobility of capital. For the most part, however, these different approaches share several basic premises with the Marxian interpretation that have significant implications for any attempt at applying the concept to the ancient world.[2] Firstly, they insist on the need for a theoretical and analytical approach, seeking to move beyond surface appearances to study underlying structures and processes; they caution against confusing phenomena and concepts, or reifying 'globalisation' on the basis of a miscellaneous assortment of symptoms. Secondly, they take the view that globalisation is primarily a product rather than an agent of change – it is the *explanandum* rather than the *explanans*, even if the products of that process do then have further consequences. The importance of the concept is not its explanatory power but the way in which it suggests that apparently disparate phenomena – the popularity of David Beckham in Japan and the 2008 economic crash, for example – are actually products of the same underlying process, and thus prompts consideration of the nature of that process.

Recent interest among Roman historians and archaeologists in employing the idea of 'globalisation' often seems to echo M. I. Rostovtzeff's century-old arguments about the high level of economic development of the ancient world.[3] The creation of a uniform worldwide civilisation and of similar social and economic conditions is going on before our eyes over the whole expanse of the civilised world. We ought therefore to keep in view that this condition in which we are living now is not new, and that the ancient world also lived, for a series of centuries, a life that was uniform in culture and politics, in social and economic conditions. The modern development, in this sense, differs from the ancient only in quantity and not in quality.[4]

This account clearly focuses entirely on symptoms rather than causes; the fact that the ancient development resembles, in Rostovtzeff's view, the modern development, understood in terms of the spread of a more or less homogeneous political and cultural system across a wider geographical area, is taken without question as proof that the process behind it must be identical. Recent studies offer a more nuanced view of the nature of cultural change in the Roman empire, emphasising local variation and two-way exchange (reflecting more nuanced views of cultural change in the modern world), but they make the same intellectual move. Effectively, this is to reify 'globalisation' (obviously Rostovtzeff did not use the term) as a transhistorical social phenomenon on the basis of a set of surface appearances that might, in different historical contexts, be the product of entirely different social and historical processes. Such an approach has the effect of erasing or obscuring differences between past and present, with all the ideological implications that entails; identifying modern phenomena as an echo, repetition or development of the classical past in this way goes hand in glove with the portrayal of that past as more or less modern.[5]

However, this critique of Rostovtzeff's assumptions is not the end of the debate, but rather the beginning. We can readily concede that in this instance he does have a case that merits consideration; the developments we see in the Roman period, above all from the material evidence that was so important to Rostovtzeff, do indeed seem in important respects to resemble the modern experience, both in the expansion of the variety of consumption at a local level, drawing on the products of a far wider geographical area than before, and in a tendency towards increasing homogeneity of consumptive practices at both regional and supra-regional levels. The question is, whether labelling this development 'globalisation' achieves anything beyond the rhetorical presentation of the Roman empire as analogous to the contemporary world.[6] It is worth emphasising, as Pitts and Versluys do in their survey of the history of the concept, that many theorists of globalisation have seen it as largely or entirely a modern phenomenon, something that distinguishes the present phase of human history from earlier ones. There is by no means consensus on this question, but the more that globalisation is defined in such a way that it can readily be identified in earlier periods – for example, by claiming that any long-distance trade links constitute globalisation – the greater the risk that it loses any content or analytical rigour.

There are two obvious analytical purposes for which we might make use of such a comparison between the Roman empire and the modern experience. Firstly, we can employ it as an ideal-typical description, distinguishing the process of change undergone by Rome from other kinds of process (most obviously in this context, 'Romanisation'[7]) and/or distinguishing this supposedly 'globalised' society from other, fragmented or less integrated, societies. In economic terms, this perhaps offers an alternative means of characterising the 'development' of the Roman empire and evaluating its progress in relative terms, emphasising the roles of connectivity and the mobility of capital rather than the usual themes of technological change and the spread of economic rationalism. Secondly, we can use it as a means of generating hypotheses: about the origins of this ancient development (on the principle that processes are replicated through history, and similar phenomena may have similar causes) and about its dynamics and consequences (on the principle that similar structures produce similar effects). The opposing case is, as always in ancient economic history, that the differences between modern and pre-modern economies are so fundamental that these apparent resemblances can only be superficial and/or tendentious; but that is precisely what we would seek to test through this approach, rather than rejecting any possibility of comparison a priori.

One obvious objection to this enterprise is the fact that the Roman empire was never remotely 'global', whatever the Romans themselves may have claimed or believed – and this is manifestly true even if we include in the analysis regions outside the political and military frontiers that were nevertheless economically part of its sphere.[8] Considering Rome from the perspective of global history – a different intellectual enterprise from the use of 'globalisation' as a concept – emphasises its relative marginality in relation to the ancient world as a whole. If 'globalisation' is a term that can only legitimately be applied to genuinely world-spanning developments, then clearly it is not applicable to the Roman empire per se; to put this another way, globalisation theory can be relevant and useful to Roman historians and archaeologists only if it has actually mistaken its own object of analysis, or at any rate adopted a rather misleading name.[9] In fact there are grounds for believing that this is the case: most globalisation theory focuses on exactly the same phenomena that had featured in the processes of economic, social and cultural integration within emerging nation states in earlier centuries, in what can be seen as the early stages of modernisation; and it is only a fetishisation of the nation-state, and hence surprise at or suspicion of any economic and social processes that transcend national borders, that makes modern globalisation appear as a unique phenomenon. There is an important analytical question as to whether the more recent shift in the scale and scope of activity from the regional to the truly global marks a genuine qualitative change from these earlier processes; but, whether or not all globalisation theorists would approve, there is no substantive problem with considering the application of their ideas to the study of change at a sub-global level, above all because this chapter is focused on the processes of globalisation far more than the nature of a world that has largely been globalised.[10]

A much greater difficulty with this project is discussed at length by Pitts and Versluys in Chapter 1: the fact that there is no generally agreed definition of globalisation, let alone a single theory of it. Just as 'modernity' as an all-embracing conception is so powerful that scarcely anyone doubts its existence, even as radically different theories of its nature are developed, so globalisation is taken for granted as a valid description of the current state of the world.[11] Further, there is wide disagreement about what, within the range of symptoms lumped together under the heading of globalisation, is most in need of explanation; economic, social and cultural approaches to the subject not only offer radically different analyses but constitute their object of analysis quite differently. The use of 'globalisation' as a basis for comparing the Roman empire with other societies and integrating it into a broader global history therefore requires the careful specification of what the concept is intended to mean, as well as consideration of the different ways in which the underlying processes generating these symptoms have been characterised. The relative incoherence and disparate nature of studies in this field do imply that we may be able legitimately and usefully to talk of 'Roman globalisation' in some senses but not others. This does, however, also open up the possibility – already seen in some recent discussions of the topic – of selecting a theory of globalisation that is compatible with current conceptions of the Roman empire, in order to be able to describe it as globalised and hence, implicitly, modern – not decentring Rome in the way that writers like Nederveen Pieterse have called for, but on the contrary ascribing to it a special status among pre-modern societies.

TIME AND SPACE

In this chapter I want to focus on two distinct but closely related phenomena, and the processes that lie behind them, that have been especially prominent in discussions of globalisation over the last two decades, each of which is particularly relevant to the economic aspects of the process.[12] The first of these is characterised by the geographer David Harvey as 'time–space compression'. To quote Harvey's definition:

> I mean to signal by that term processes that so revolutionise the objective qualities of space and time that we are forced to alter, sometimes in quite radical ways, how we represent the world to ourselves ... As space appears to shrink to a 'global village' of telecommunications and a 'spaceship earth' of economic and ecological interdependencies – to use just two familiar and everyday images – and as time horizons shorten to the point where the present is all there is, so we have to learn how to cope with an overwhelming sense of *compression* of our spatial and temporal worlds.[13]

In time–space compression, the world becomes effectively smaller, as time annihilates or reduces space, above all as a result of technological development: in the last two centuries, steam power succeeded sail and then jet aircraft succeeded sea travel; electronic communications now mean that individuals in different regions of the globe can communicate almost instantaneously and experience the same event simultaneously.[14] The average speed of long-distance travel thus rose from perhaps 10 mph before the nineteenth century to several hundred mph from the 1960s onwards. The world becomes ever more interconnected and integrated; this then results in an ongoing intensification of global social and economic relations and a rationalisation of the organisation of production. The potential thus exists for every region and every individual to become integrated into a single system (even if, obviously, the uneven global distribution of wealth and resources sets limits in practice on the degree and nature of that integration for different regions and individuals, and capital's ability to command space and time is always far greater than that of labour). Further, all social and economic processes become accelerated, as the time required to traverse space – to transport goods, to travel, to communicate ideas – shrinks ever more.

Recent discussions of the development of the Roman empire frequently, and correctly, emphasise its role in drawing together the disparate regions of the Mediterranean into larger systems (if not a single empire-wide system) and promoting the movement of goods, people and ideas between them; to use the term popularised in ancient history by *The Corrupting Sea*, its impact on connectivity. Horden and Purcell note the extent to which the expansion of the empire depended on the prior existence of reasonably high levels of connectivity, at least in the Mediterranean region – and that may suggest that we need to be wary of fetishising the role of Rome in bringing about change, rather than seeing the empire's expansion as a symptom as much as a cause of increased integration – but they do not deny that Roman imperialism then entrenched, altered and accelerated this process.[15] The main elements of this development were the imposition of a single, albeit fairly minimal, political structure, and hence the emergence of networks based on the movement of goods, people and information; the creation and diffusion of institutions like the law and coinage, that eased interactions between previously separate regions; the development of a improved transport infrastructure of roads, ports and canals; and the development of a more active and increasingly integrated system of trade and exchange, centred above all on the supply networks of the army and the city of Rome.[16] The archaeological record makes this unmistakably clear in the case of pottery and the goods that were moved in amphorae, which can reasonably be taken as proxies for a wider range of more perishable items: a far greater variety of goods from an ever larger number of places was distributed in far greater quantities over greater distances and an ever wider area.[17] Further, as Nicolet and others have argued, conceptions of space within Greco-Roman culture also changed as a result: a fragmented, mutually antagonistic world was reconceived, at least by members of the Roman elite and their Greek collaborators, as a harmonious whole centred on Rome.[18] These ancient accounts tend to focus on the effects of political and cultural rather than economic integration, but it is easy enough to expand the picture; see for example Aelius

Aristides' account of Rome, in which the whole world is presented as the city's agricultural hinterland:

> The city appears a kind of common emporium of the world. Cargoes from India and, if you will, even Arabia the Blessed, once can see in such numbers as to surmise that in those lands the trees will have been stripped bare and that the inhabitants of those lands, if they need anything, must come here and beg for a share of their own. Your farmlands are Egypt, Sicily and all of cultivated Africa.[19]

Of course the pattern of change was never uniform, either over time or space, but we would scarcely expect that. Equally it goes without saying that the primary driver of this process was the Roman state and its elite, supported by the local elites with whom the Romans collaborated, pursuing primarily self-interested political and military ends; with a few exceptions like the development of Ostia, the impact of their activities on trade and other economic development was entirely accidental – but none the less tangible for that. It is worth noting that one of the greatest potential attractions of globalisation theory for ancient historians, as opposed to other theories of economic development, may be that there is no suggestion that it is a directed process: 'globalisation' offers an account of historical change that is organised around complex impersonal processes, unintended consequences and unexpected feedback effects, which certainly offers a more nuanced perspective than the traditional narrative of top-down Romanisation.

So, it is clear that – relative at any rate to many other pre-industrial societies – the Roman empire experienced a significant degree of economic and social integration over a wide geographical area (though the depth of integration should not be exaggerated), as well as some form of economic growth (though the precise nature of that growth is a different argument).[20] The key question for the use of globalisation theory, however, is whether these changes amounted to time–space compression in any real sense or to any significant extent. Changes in transport and communications technology were fairly minimal; the construction of an infrastructure of roads, harbours, way-stations for the imperial post and the like certainly made some journeys easier, more predictable and marginally faster, but that is scarcely comparable to the sorts of step-changes seen over the last couple of centuries – it is difficult to imagine that journey times could have been reliably reduced even by a quarter, given the physical limits on the speed of sail and of draught animals, let alone by 80 or 90% as in the last two centuries. It is also relevant to note that the majority of infrastructural improvements under Rome were quite narrowly focused on certain specific routes, centred on the city of Rome and the military infrastructure of the empire, rather than being generalised; modern globalisation is of course also highly uneven, but not to such an extent. In a pre-industrial context, a reduction of 25% or even 10% in journey times could certainly be significant at an individual level; for example, it might make a substantial difference to a peasant farmer that he could travel to market and back in three hours rather than four, creating more time in the day either for marketing or for work on the land. This does not, however, amount to the sort of space–time compression that enables a substantial shift of human economic activity from a local to a regional context, let alone from the regional to the global.

Most of the impact of Roman imperialism on connectivity lay in the reduction of the costs involved in travel and transport; for example, the imposition of a higher level of security through the unification of the Mediterranean and actions (albeit patchy and of limited efficacy) against pirates and bandits; the provision of increased levels of information about different regions, travel routes, convenient ports and way-stations and the like; the development of legal structures to support the financing and insurance of trading ventures, the development of common means of measurement through coins and weights and measures, and so forth.[21] One might speculate that greater security and better information allowed some merchants to take more direct routes, thus cutting journey times to some extent, but that seems to be clutching at straws. There is no trace in Duncan-Jones's analysis of the length of time messages might take to reach distant corners of the empire of any significant improvements in the speed of travel or communication compared with any other pre-industrial society; and, given the nature of the changes that actually took place under Roman rule, there is no reason at all to expect any.[22]

Of course, reductions in the cost of travel, transport and communication, as well as increases in speed, have been a significant element in the process of modern globalisation – though this is something that has not been discussed extensively by many of its theorists, who often seem to treat it entirely as a product of technological change. As the example of Concorde versus subsonic air travel shows, it is not technology alone but affordable technology, appropriate to a specific economic context, that can bring about a step-change in average journey times and the effective size of the world. It is worth noting that the majority of Roman innovations in travel and transport were accessible to all at little or no additional direct cost, whereas to participate in the modern globalised economy requires substantial extra investment in communications equipment, technical skills and transport. I am not suggesting that the effect of all these improvements on the development of the Roman economy was negligible, nor that there was no significant increase in the volume of inter-regional economic activity – on the contrary – but simply that this does not amount, to any significant extent or in any real sense, to time–space compression.

Indeed, the opposite was the case: until well into the Principate, the Roman world was effectively growing rather than shrinking, albeit in fits and starts, as new regions were incorporated into its political, economic and social space. In cultural and conceptual terms, this might be seen as a kind of spatial compression, experienced as such by the inhabitants of newly incorporated areas as they came to think of themselves as part of a wider world.[23] In reality, however, the time and effort required to traverse 'the world' or communicate with its outer reaches was growing rather than shrinking.[24] A more appropriate historical comparison for the Roman experience than nineteenth- or twentieth-century globalisation might be the fifteenth to sixteenth centuries, when the world of the Europeans effectively expanded without any commensurate improvement in the technology of travel and communication; this has a range of consequences for those polities caught up in the attempt to master and control a much larger and less manageable space than had previously constituted their sphere of activity.[25] One of the consequences of this development was the creation of incentives for trying to increase the speed of travel in order to control and exploit distant regions more effectively, which eventually paid off in promoting technological change. Insofar as such incentives existed for the Roman empire – and they surely did, although the Roman state employed the alternative strategy of devolving significant power to local collaborators – they did not produce any substantial improvement.

Further, we see in the Roman empire few of the consequences of time–space compression that have been observed in the modern world, above all the rationalisation of production at the supra-regional level and the significant movement of capital between regions. As Greg Woolf has demonstrated in the case of Gaul, the inter-regional distribution of some goods actually decreased over time, as regional and then local production developed following an initial flux of imports – this can be seen in the diffusion of viticulture into regions which had previously imported Italian wine, and in the shift from imported *terra sigillata* in Gaul to local imitations – whereas the opposite tends to be the case in the modern development.[26] The analogy with certain modern global goods like Coca-Cola, now often produced at a regional level rather than exported from their country of origin, breaks down on the fact that those local producers are intimately connected to the mother company, whether as subsidiaries or franchises, whereas there is no trace of a Roman multi-national concern of this kind. The acquisition of lands across different provinces by members of the imperial elite affected the circulation of capital to some extent, with a surplus being creamed off by the centre rather than continuing to circulate at the regional level, but there is little sign of any rationalisation of production across these multiple holdings as has become common in the modern economy.

This is of course a chicken-and-egg situation. It may be attributed in part to the basic conditions of the ancient economy: the relative ubiquity of most of the key raw materials of production, the lack of any comparative technological advantage in their production and the limited development of wage labour, such that there was no great scope for reducing labour costs through the relocation of production.[27] Further, the objects of exchange were for the most part too generic, too easily imitated or substituted to sustain anything other than a short-term advantage for a particular region's products (e.g. Italian wine and olive oil initially dominating in the West and then being supplanted by Gallic, Spanish and African products). However, the persistence of decentred and small-scale production also reflects the very limited command of space and time of any of the dominant forces in Roman society; given the slowness of travel and transport, as well as their relatively high costs, it simply made more sense to organise things in this manner rather than on a large-scale inter-regional basis, and competing models of organisation – for example, inter-regional trading activities organised around locating family members or dependents in different ports and other strategic locations – were not institutionalised or sustained, as far as we can tell, beyond a few generations.[28] The Roman empire saw a significant increase in inter-regional economic activity, and a degree of integration between local and regional economies – but this development was constantly working against, and often impeded by, the constraints of time and space.

It is notable that even in the political sphere, where the state had the resources at least to attempt to overcome the established 'limits of the possible', including the friction of distance, the prevalent model for the organisation of space remained that of a myriad semi-autonomous communities, all in a direct relationship with the centre, rather than any more rationalised arrangement.[29] This does raise an interesting question for comparative study, given that all the European nations active overseas in the early modern period also had to devolve significant power to those on the ground in their colonies, and for the most part proved unable to maintain political control in the long term. How far should we contrast this experience with the Roman one – seeing the Romans, as Adam Smith did, as being happy to concede power to their colonies and to establish a relationship based on exchange and mutual advantage[30] – or compare the breaking away of Britain's American colonies with the increasing inability of Rome to maintain even limited political dominance over its more distant provinces from the third century AD onwards? If the Romans *were* much more content with a model of devolved rule, whether for cultural reasons or because that was how the empire developed, this would imply that the need to improve transport and communication technology was less pressing and less highly incentivised – and might thus help explain the absence of the time–space compression that is one marker of 'true' globalisation.

REFLEXIVITY, RELATIVISATION AND CULTURAL CHANGE

As Pitts and Versluys discuss in Chapter 1, there seems to be more mileage for Roman historians in the second major theme in globalisation theory: Robertson's emphasis on the growing consciousness of the world as a whole, an idea that is refined and developed in Anthony Giddens' arguments about the development of 'reflexivity' and the intensification of worldwide social relations:[31]

> With the advent of modernity, reflexivity takes on a different character. It is introduced into the very basis of system reproduction, such that thought and action are constantly refracted back upon one another ... The reflexivity of modern social life consists in the fact that social practices are constantly examined and reformed in the light of incoming information about those very practices, thus constitutively altering their character.[32]

The focus here is less on physical structures and processes – though clearly Giddens sees time–space compression as one of the primary forces involved in driving the changes he describes – than on social relationships, cultural practices and above all individual subjectivities. It is not just that individuals are increasingly integrated into wider social networks, and that local events are shaped by things happening many miles away and vice versa. It is the extent to which, in a globalised or globalising world, individuals increasingly view themselves in relation to a global rather than local context; they choose a social identity rather than simply accepting it as a given, and they do this in full awareness of and with reference to the whole range of possibilities that have now become available through the proliferation of knowledge of the world as a whole. Equally, their membership of different social groups becomes increasingly elective rather than a given, and many such groups are forced to redefine and reinvent themselves within this new context, or simply fade away as their traditional constituency declines or disappears. Globalisation makes such self-fashioning and self-examination possible, by making available both the information and the consumable goods required; but it also appears to make it unavoidable, so that an adherence to traditional forms and practices becomes a deliberate rejection of the alternatives, rather than simply a given.

There is a clear sense in many of the ancient sources, for example in geographical writings or the orations of Aristides, that the Roman empire came to be conceived as an increasingly unified whole which provided the context for any individual's or community's sense of its own identity.[33] Of course we need to be wary of taking this account completely at face value, rather than seeing it as, at least in part, a deliberate ideological project, a means for the Roman state of exerting political control by winning the assent of the provincials to their domination, and a means for certain Greek intellectuals of establishing a relatively privileged position for themselves within the new society. Equally, in contrast to the ideal of modern global consciousness, the imaginative construction of Rome as a single world ran in close parallel with an emphasis on the frontiers as marking a sharp divide between civilisation and barbarism, effectively an explicit rejection of the idea of globalisation in modern terms.[34] It is not clear how much that actually matters, if we ignore the modern emphasis on the literally global on the grounds that it represents a fetishisation of the nation-state; we are interested in the process whereby individuals are drawn into thinking of themselves in terms of a wider world and responding accordingly, rather than only cases where they think of themselves as being primarily inhabitants of that world rather than primarily members of nations or other, smaller communities or polities. However, it is important to keep in mind the specificity of Roman developments, the particular characteristics of Greco-Roman culture and *mentalité*, at the same time as developing parallels and comparisons with other phenomena.

The parallels between Giddens' ideas of reflexivity and relativisation and their consequences for individuals' material practices, and the processes of cultural change visible in the western provinces of the Roman empire, are still more striking. The arrival of Rome widened the range of possibilities for provincials (especially elites), offering new means of establishing and maintaining their status locally and the new possibility of gaining access to extra-regional power networks; in both cases, this involved identifying themselves through material practices with the ruling power. Such a change is never, globalisation theory suggests, a simple matter of abandoning one identity for another (or at any rate that is only one possibility), but rather of evaluating one set of possibilities in the light of other sets – which offers a reasonable interpretation of the sorts of 'hybrid' cultures we find in the western provinces, combining and negotiating elements of 'Roman' and 'Native' practices in ways that make something new of each of them (religious practices being probably the most striking example of hybridity and cultural negotiation).[35] Since these new identities are expressed, or at any rate manifested, primarily through changing patterns of consumption (including, crucially, the development of cities in previously less urbanised regions), this then has a significant impact on the nature and scale of demand for different goods. Changes in material practices driven by these processes of relativisation and reflexivity thus transformed the context of trade, exchange and distribution; at least to some extent and for a certain period of time in different regions, this also had knock-on effects on the location and organisation of the production of goods to meet these new forms of demand.[36] To this extent, then, we can talk of globalisation in the Roman empire in relation to economic change – even if, pedantically, this is more about the economic consequences of cultural globalisation, rather than economic globalisation in its own right – and explore its causes and consequences.

However, it has to be asked whether this tells us anything we did not already know: the consequences of changes in material practices in the provinces, especially in the West, for trade and economic development have already been recognised and discussed without any need for the term 'globalisation'. If the concept is to have any real utility for Roman economic history, it must be capable of helping us think differently about the nature and origins of these processes of cultural change in a way that alters our view of their likely consequences for the nature and scale of demand, the inter-action of local, regional and supra-regional economic systems and so forth. While Giddens' and Robertson's ideas do provide ancient historians with the useful concepts of relativisation and reflexivity, questions remain about how far this approach gets us beyond the issues that have already been identified with the 'nativist' approach to understanding cultural change under Rome, which has been proposed in recent years as an alternative to the top-down 'Romanisation' model.[37] Above all, there is a risk of concentrating solely on the activities and conceptions of the elite, because of their over-representation in the surviving evidence, and simply assuming that their experiences represent the experiences of the rest of society. In fact, while the incentives for the provincial elite to reconsider their identities and change their practices are clear, the same is not true for those who had no possibility of gaining access to super-regional power structures. The non-elite might be equally strongly affected by the forces of cultural globalisation, but in a quite different (and less positive) way.

It is notable that similar criticisms have been levelled at some modern globalisation theories, namely that they concentrate too much on groups with the power, resources, status and freedom to reinvent themselves without much fear of the consequences, rather than on the experience of the majority of the global population. This goes hand in hand with a tendency to neglect the possibility of resistance to globalisation except through overt, violent action, and the extent to which the benefits of the process are very unevenly distributed.[38] Whether the focus is on 'Native' elites fashioning new identities using the new repertoire of ideas, practices and objects of consumption made available through integration into the Roman empire, or on the modern international businessman, globalisation is often presented in positive terms as an exciting and liberating increase in possibilities, where the only constraint is access to the resources that allow full participation in this new world; that is not necessarily how it is experienced by everyone, even by those who can afford to join in if they wish. On the other hand – and this is true of both the Roman empire and modern globalisation – change is clearly not being imposed directly by an external force like the state.

The theoretical problem when it comes to the mass of the population is to explain how a more or less free choice to change one's material and cultural practices can nevertheless be experienced as compulsion. One interesting way forward here is offered by ideas from network theory, and in particular by those developed in David Grewal's *Network Power*. Networks are understood as shared forms of social coordination which may or may not be formally constituted and which require the acceptance of certain standards in order to be accepted into membership.[39] The modern compression of space and time enables, but does not provide, social coordination; that develops through the adoption, across a wide area, of particular standards that allow the emergence of inter-regional and global networks – some created deliberately for this purpose, others adopted for contingent reasons. The obvious example of such a network in the Roman empire is that of the Roman political-social elite, which offered the possibility of access to high levels of social, political and ideological power to those who were able to achieve membership; as has long been recognised, acceptance into membership of this elite involved a complex mixture of factors, including not only wealth and connections but also the acceptance and display of the correct forms of social behaviour, values, education, shared literary culture and the like.[40] In the case of most networks, including that of the Roman elite, the 'standards' for membership are never stable or clear-cut but constantly renegotiated, and acceptance into the network (at any rate for most people) is not necessarily a single one-off moment but a matter of having, time and again, to win recognition from fellow members as being 'one of us' by performing in a manner appropriate to that status.[41] Further, power is rarely evenly distributed across the network: some individuals, especially those firmly entrenched at the centre of power through their birth or achievements, held far greater influence in determining the acceptance of others, and equally could afford to be significantly 'unRoman' in some of their practices, effectively rejecting some of network's standards, without losing their membership. Greek elites, because of the importance of the Hellenic tradition for the 'hybrid' Roman elite culture, might need to make fewer adjustments to their behaviour in order to win acceptance than would be expected of 'barbarians'; arriviste Gallic notables might need to be far more Roman than the Romans, whether they liked this or not, in order to gain admission. The idea of networks and standards thus offers a way of re-describing the development of a Mediterranean-wide elite culture, and its role in regulating social and political relationships, in a way that engages with its complexity and diversity.

However, these ideas are much more powerful and interesting when applied to networks that cannot simply be described in more traditional terms as classes or status groups. We can think instead of ancient networks that were defined by their use of a particular standard: for example, the network of Latin speakers or the network of the users of Roman coinage or law. The decision of the individuals in such networks to adopt one of these standards was in principle entirely voluntary, a practical decision about the adoption of a useful tool or technique. In practice, however, it might be unavoidable if one wanted to do business or had to interact with Roman officials; the costs of being outside the network, of being unable to communicate or participate in normal exchange or social life, might be far too high to leave any other choice. The obvious parallel is with the dominance of English as the global means of communication; in many contexts, an insistence on using only one's native language becomes a decision to isolate oneself to a significant degree from the normal operations of society, to become as excluded as those who are unable to acquire the necessary language skills to participate. The dominance of certain standards may be largely or entirely unconnected to their intrinsic utility – the importance of English in the modern world is clearly a legacy of the past global power of the British empire and the United States – and the process of globalisation gives a clear advantage to standards that have already established some degree of extra-local reach.[42]

This offers a way of thinking about the persistence of Greek in the eastern half of the Roman empire despite the political dominance of a Latin-speaking polity; the inhabitants of that region already belonged to a powerful and well-established inter-regional language network, so the adoption of Latin offered an advantage at best only to those who had to interact directly with Roman officials, and in practice those Romans were more likely to learn Greek in order to participate in the network of the Hellenic cultural tradition. This implies, of course, that the eastern

Mediterranean was already fairly 'globalised' in cultural terms before the Romans arrived, with pre-existing inter-regional networks and standards, so had less incentive to adopt new ones except where these offered a clear advantage over existing practices. Clearly, the processes of cultural change in the ancient world cannot be understood solely with reference to the power of Roman imperialism, but need to engage with discussions of the spread of Hellenism in earlier centuries.

The consequences of adopting any such standard are not necessarily limited to the practical effects of acquiring a new skill or technique. The act of adoption of a standard does not require or imply any sort of identification with it, or with the wider values of the associated network, but that may happen in time, and not necessarily consciously. Membership of a network brings an individual into contact with new information, interpretations and practices, whether they like it or not: Giddens' account of reflexivity indicates that individuals in a globalised world have no option but to re-evaluate their identity in the light of the wider context, and involvement in a global network is one of the key ways in which this takes place. The user of Roman coinage, for example, motivated by its practical utility or compelled by the demands of the state or a landlord for payment in cash, was as a result exposed to imperial propaganda and the symbolic system of the ruling power, while the regular use of the Roman state's coinage entrenched its claims to legitimacy in the minds of its users. The use of Latin, meanwhile, spread through the western provinces for a whole range of reasons; it was not necessarily adopted in order to identify oneself as Roman, but the usual mode of acquisition, learning the language through the traditional literary canon, exposed the learner to the Roman cultural world and the ideology of imperialism.[43] Over time, many of these standards became ever more prevalent and dominant, and their adoption became less a matter of choice than an unavoidable necessity in order to participate in social life. This dominance was less because of their intrinsic superiority than because they had the backing of the dominant political and economic players; the benefits for peasant farmers in Gaul of the adoption of Roman coinage were marginal at best, but the benefits for merchants and the imperial system were enormous.

The economic significance of these processes lies in their role in the diffusion through the empire of institutions that lowered transaction costs and thus supported the expansion of trading activity. It was not simply a matter, as some accounts tend to suggest, of the Roman state creating such institutions (as always for its own purposes) to be adopted by a grateful population. Rather, the motives for their adoption and hence the dynamics of the process were more complex, and we might expect to find significant variations across both time and space, which in turn will have implications for the development of economic activity. It is again worth emphasising, as

Horden and Purcell do, that the Roman empire depended on pre-existing connectivity in order to expand its dominance, and that implies – especially for the eastern Mediterranean – the existence of at least some rudimentary networks and standards, some of which persisted and thrived under Roman rule. What Rome brought to the rest of its world were standards with ever wider global reach and, arguably, much richer ideological content; these standards helped to promote economic activity by lowering costs, but at the same time they were more likely to be adopted in regions that were already more closely involved in extra-regional trade – which in turn helped to promote processes of broader cultural change as their users absorbed something of the wider values of the network and made their own contributions to its development. The processes of the economic, the political and the cultural integration of the empire appear to be far more interdependent than is generally recognised.

'ANCIENT GLOBALISATION'

Grewal's account of networks and standards offers a way of thinking about changing patterns of social relations, identity and human behaviour that he happens to develop in the context of modern globalising society, rather than offering a theory of globalisation or assuming that it is an entirely new phenomenon.[44] That makes things easier for ancient historians insofar as it is not necessary for us to demonstrate that the development of the Roman empire was analogous in a strong sense to modern developments (rather than simply exhibiting some striking but perhaps superficial resemblances) in order to make use of these ideas in interpreting Roman history. On the other hand, it has to be noted that this does not actually require us to adopt the term 'globalisation'. Given the absence, in the Roman case, of the sort of time–space compression characteristic of modern developments, to say nothing of other fundamental differences between ancient and modern economic structures, we might conclude that the term does not offer any analytical advantages to outweigh the obvious problems of anachronism and the erasure of historical difference. Globalisation is of course 'good to think with', but I would see it primarily as a way of thinking through the differences between ancient and modern, highlighting how far these apparent resemblances actually stem from different causes and structures. Relativisation, reflexivity, networks and standards are the terms that may be more helpful in understanding Roman developments in themselves – as are the old favourites (albeit in need of greater precision and further analysis) 'integration' and 'interdependence'.

If globalisation has any utility as a concept for ancient economic historians, it lies in the way that it emphasises the complexity of developments: the
interdependence and mutual reinforcement of the processes of political,
social, economic and cultural change, and the significant variations in their
effects across both space and time. Many of the obvious alternatives for
characterising change in the Roman empire – imperialism, Romanisation,
development – seek to privilege certain processes as determinative of the
others, and they often have their own problems with anachronism and
submerged ideological content. Globalisation offers a framework for generating hypotheses about topics such as the relation between the diffusion
of Roman coinage and other cultural change, or the degree of correlation
between patterns of economic activity and patterns of language use –
admittedly in some cases hypotheses that it will be difficult to test adequately
with the available evidence. In the Roman empire as in the modern world,
we can see the far-reaching consequences of increased interaction between
and integration of different regions and cultural traditions, conditioned by
the uneven distribution of different sorts of power. If we could somehow
guarantee the absence of any suggestion that these processes were similar or
arose from similar causes to those observed in the contemporary world, then
'globalisation' is a reasonable label for what seems to be occurring in each
historical context. Perhaps a simple temporal marker will be sufficient to
emphasise differences as well as similarities. In modern globalisation, the
world changes as a result of becoming effectively smaller; in ancient globalisation, it changes as a result of becoming significantly larger.

Acknowledgements

I am very grateful to audiences at Cornell University, the Humboldt
University, the European Social Science History Conference at Ghent
University and the Roman Archaeology Conference at Oxford University,
as well as at the Exeter workshop, for their comments on earlier versions and
predecessors of this chapter. I have also benefited greatly from exchanges
around this subject with Colin Elliott, David Grewal and Martin Pitts.

Notes

1. Marx & Engels (1964, 465).
2. Pitts & Versluys (Chapter 1, this volume) offer a clear survey of key works
   in the history of globalisation theory. Good general introductions include

Rosenberg (2000), Waters (2001) and Held & McGrew (2008). On the nineteenth-century experience, Bayly (2004).

3. Generally on Rostovtzeff, see Wes (1990) and Shaw (1992).

4. Rostovtzeff (1926, 10).

5. See generally Morley (2004, 33–50) and (2009).

6. cf. Hingley (2005, 14–48; also this volume).

7. On 'Romanisation', see the various papers in Mattingly (1997), as well as Pitts & Versluys (Chapter 1, this volume).

8. cf. Whittaker (1994, 98–131) for a basic introduction to trade beyond the western frontiers, and Young (2001) on trade with India, both of which show Roman engagement with a wider world.

9. The alternative approach, not necessarily incompatible but a quite different intellectual project, is to shift the focus of attention from Rome to the wider world of which it was a part; cf. Nederveen Pieterse (Chapter 10, this volume).

10. cf. Osterhammel & Petersson (2005). As Pitts & Versluys note (Chapter 1, this volume), many contemporary theorists seem happy to disassociate themselves from an exclusive concern with the literally global, and to talk of 'globalisation' whenever the accretion of social networks is observed, at whatever geographical scale.

11. On modernity, Wagner (2008) and Morley (2009).

12. These are not, strictly speaking, economic ideas, but rather ideas (taken from geography and sociology) with clear economic implications; as Nederveen Pieterse (Chapter 10, this volume) notes, economic studies of globalisation have tended to concentrate on measuring the progress of a taken-for-granted development, for example by gathering data on price convergence at the global level, rather than seeking to understand or question the process itself.

13. Harvey (1989, 240).

14. On time–space compression, Harvey (1989, 201–307, esp. 240–83).

15. Horden & Purcell (2000, 123–72; 342–400).

16. Summary in Morley (2010, 70–101); see also the relevant chapters in Scheidel, Morris & Saller (2007).

17. e.g. Greene (1986); Peacock & Williams (1986); Tchernia (1986); summary of recent work in Wilson (2009).

18. Nicolet (1991); Romm (1992); Clarke (1999). Obviously the idea of 'Greco-Roman' or 'classical' culture is itself a reflection of these changes, both in terms of the actual exchanges of ideas on which it was founded and in terms of the conception of a unified culture spanning and drawing together previously separate regions.

19. Aelius Aristides Or.6:12–13. See also Sommer (Chapter 8, this volume), for further discussion.

20. cf. Hopkins (1978a); Saller (2005); Scheidel (2009a).

21. Summary in Morley (2007a, 55–78).

22. Duncan-Jones (1990).

23. The fact that most Roman historians and archaeologists have turned to globalisation theory as a means of addressing issues of cultural change may explain why they have a tendency to conflate or confuse the physical and the socio-cultural

aspects of globalisation – as I suggested above, two closely related but quite distinct phenomena – and hence to refer to 'time–space compression' when the development of a global consciousness is being discussed (e.g. Laurence & Trifilò, Chapter 5, this volume).

24. Hence – to make an obvious point – Rome's reliance on delegated military and political authority, not only in the process of imperial expansion but also when the empire came under pressure in the third century.

25. cf. Braudel (1944).

26. Woolf (1998, 194–202).

27. cf. de Ligt (1991) on rural production.

28. cf. Andreau (1999) on Roman business organisation.

29. Morley (2010, 38–69).

30. Smith (1976, IV.vii.a-b).

31. Robertson (1992, 8). Note that Giddens' account is based on an explicit contrast between modernity and earlier societies, which tends to imply that he at least would be uncomfortable with the idea of applying his ideas to classical antiquity.

32. Giddens (1990, 38). See also Giddens (1991).

33. This is seen above all in writings of the Second Sophistic; see for example Whitmarsh (2001) and Sommer (Chapter 8, this volume).

34. Graham (2006); Woolf (2011) on the development of Roman ethnography.

35. On religious change, Webster (1997); de Blois, Funke & Hahn (2006).

36. Woolf (1998, 1–23, 169–205); Morley (2007a, 46–52).

37. Millett (1990a); Woolf (1997). Brief summary in Morley (2010, 107–15).

38. Gill (2008) on modern resistance; Hingley (1997) on the equivalent arguments for 'Romanisation'.

39. Definitions in Grewal (2008, 18–43).

40. See, for example, Edwards (1993); Habinek (1998); Rosenstein (2006); Farney (2007).

41. cf. Morley (forthcoming).

42. Grewal (2008, 71–88 on language, 106–40 on power and choice).

43. Morgan (1998).

44. Grewal (2008, 4): 'It is simply [a phenomenon] that has become more visible in the contemporary world'.

4

GLOBALISATION, CIRCULATION AND MASS CONSUMPTION IN THE ROMAN WORLD

Martin Pitts

In popular media, globalisation is frequently conflated with the consumption of foreign goods and styles. In academic discourse, consumption is seen as a major indicator and symptom of present-day globalisation. This view increasingly extends to the study of the past, and it is becoming common to view world history through the lens of consumption.[1] In Roman archaeology and history, consumption has only recently become established as a major subject of inquiry.[2] In a short period, its study has been arguably subordinate to other topics such as the contested notion of Romanisation,[3] the long-standing debate over minimalism versus modernism in the ancient economy (e.g. the 'consumer city')[4] and recent concerns with social identity and ethnicity. It is against this backdrop that I consider whether concepts of globalisation offer any merit to the study of consumption in the Roman world.

The implicit focus of this chapter is mass consumption, which has particular relevance to theories of globalisation. I define mass consumption as the deep social dispersal of widely available and relatively cheap standardised objects. The term is especially applicable to relatively low-cost standardised ceramics (including *terra sigillata*), which collectively constitute the largest surviving class of archaeological evidence of consumption in the Roman world. For clarity, mass consumption should not be confused with *consumerism*. This is an important distinction as extreme consumerist behaviour is a recurrent trope of modern globalisation, as summarised in John Brunner's 1968 dystopia, *Stand on Zanzibar*,[5] which presents a familiar trope of the agency of objects in an imagined globalising era:

> The objects we possess weren't made by ourselves (unless we're fortunate enough to display strong creative talents) but by an automated factory, and furthermore and infinitely worse we're under pressure every week to replace

them, change them, introduce fluidity into precisely that area of our lives where we need most stability.

Defined as a societal condition in which the *majority* prioritise the ongoing acquisition of goods not needed for subsistence or traditional display,[6] consumerism is not thought to have widely existed before the eighteenth century.[7] While less extreme consumerist behaviour may indeed have occurred in the Roman world, especially within urban communities, the term 'mass consumption' is preferable as it makes no prejudgement on the motivations for the acquisition of things, nor on the specific role(s) of artefacts in the maintenance of social status and hierarchy.[8]

CONSUMPTION AND 'ROMAN' MATERIAL CULTURE

Consumption has become an attractive topic for a generation of Roman archaeologists seeking new approaches to the interpretation of material culture.[9] A common approach within this discourse involves a mixture of anthropological works such as Appadurai's *The Social Life of Things* and Douglas and Isherwood's *The World of Goods*, combined with received wisdom on Roman cultural processes, including Romanisation, Creolisation, 'becoming Roman' and discrepant experience/identity.[10] Although this has led to new insights on a subject traditionally overlooked in favour of production and exchange, the studies in question are often brief explorations.[11] In spite of sections of major works helping to develop more substantial and historically sensitive models for consumption,[12] there still exists a gulf between largely synthetic grand narratives and discrete archaeological case studies.

The dearth of extensive studies of the mass consumption of everyday artefacts since the explosion of interest in the subject in the 1990s is not entirely surprising. Despite enthusiasm for this approach, difficulties in accessing, gathering and re-processing data of sufficient quality for broader comparison form a major obstacle to further progress. Even in regions considered data rich for reasons of preservation and/or high standards in the recording and publication of material, historical problems in the application of different (and often incompatible) recording standards and approaches to typology and quantification often reduce the possibilities for the synthesis of wider patterns between areas of the Roman empire.[13] If mass consumption in the Roman world is to be understood through theories of globalisation, the legacy of national (and regional) descriptive languages presents major hurdles to this kind of artefact-driven research.[14]

Interpretations of the meaning and significance of consumption patterns are similarly problematic. The persistence of 'representational' understandings of material culture remains implicit amongst much scholarship. A basic example of this is the mass consumption of standardised red-gloss *terra sigillata* pottery in the Roman provinces. A common view is that *terra sigillata* can be used as a universal indicator of 'Romanness', and even the desire to acquire a Roman identity. However, this contradicts the writings of theorists such as Appadurai and Thomas, who stress that the meaning of objects is never fixed but context dependent.[15] The problem is intrinsically bound up with differing understandings of the term Romanisation. In the 1980s, Romanisation was often understood as a process of material homogenisation (or acculturation),[16] which may or may not have been driven by deeper cultural changes. Defined in this way, it is understandable, if limiting, to regard the spread of *terra sigillata* as 'as one of the most obvious signs of Romanizing'.[17] Conceptualising Romanisation as a series of purely material changes problematically frames the interpretation of mass consumption within the confines of container-thinking – the acquisition of, or resistance to 'Roman' culture.

One of the most influential accounts of the relationship between Romanisation and mass consumption is found in Woolf's *Becoming Roman*, concerning the spread of *terra sigillata* in early Roman Gaul. Woolf identifies two principal patterns. First was a 'consumer revolution' in the adoption of Roman-style ceramics shortly after conquest, being assimilated within Gallic feasting traditions and the needs of local elites to demonstrate their cultural competence. Second, the use of Roman-style ceramics by non-elites of later generations is explained by the emulation of the diverging lifestyles of local elites, which is further evidenced in the development of distinct regional cultures of consumption. In both cases, the acquisition or maintenance of Roman cultural *mores* by elites has precedence, and non-elites are pulled along either by a desire 'to transform themselves into new kinds of people suitable to inhabit a new world',[18] or to emulate their social betters and create distance from their perceived inferiors.

Although Woolf's synthesis of ceramic consumption patterns is compelling, it is not without problems. The notion of emulation has been extensively critiqued in early modern studies of consumption,[19] on the grounds that non-elites lacked the wealth, property, education and knowledge to truly emulate the lifestyles of the affluent. Furthermore, the explanations of non-elite mass consumption and the appearance of regional patterns of consumption among later generations are in need of further elaboration. Such hypotheses require further testing via analysis of patterns of pottery deposition in rural locations, which might shed light on whether patterns of 'elite' pottery usage were being emulated. More importantly, the focus on the adoption of *Roman* culture effectively stifles an explanation of the full range of patterning in material culture. Changes in consumption are effectively one-way, with innovation filtering from the top-down. Whereas this approach provides an important example of measuring the influence of 'Roman' culture in provincial societies, it offers a skewed analysis of consumption conceived outside the frame of reference to Rome.

The need for a new theoretical model is hinted at in Woolf's account of the initial popularity of *terra sigillata* and the proliferation of everyday material culture that marked out the Roman period from the Iron Age in Gaul:

> These changes cannot be ascribed to deliberate policy on the part of the conquerors, and they are too widespread and rapid to be the work of the new Gallo-Roman elites, who would in any case have disdained many of these new goods. Equally, although some innovations may have immediately been seized on as a means of realizing existing goals, the advantages of all of them were not self-evident and had to be learnt.[20]

Woolf thus acknowledges that while neither state intervention nor 'trickle-down' emulation of elites explain the widespread changes taking place throughout Gallo-Roman society, elements of uniformity and the acquisition of new forms of cultural knowledge are strongly implied:

> If material culture is viewed as a sign system ... the regimes of value manifested in this sign system were no longer local, nor even regional, but those of the entire Latin West.[21]

Woolf therefore credits early homogenising changes in material culture to the formation of an imperial society, defined as more than a single state ruling over conquered territories, but crucially involving the possibility for the sharing of culture by both provincial and Italian. Shifts in mass consumption are explained through local 'regimes of value' being replaced by those of the new imperial culture.[22] However, ascribing such patterns to a common 'imperial culture' is problematic. 'Imperial culture' risks association, conscious or not, with the direct machinations and ideology of the Roman state, whereas viewing material culture as a 'sign system' comes dangerously close to imbuing artefacts with fixed meanings. Judging by the first quote above, this is not Woolf's intention – the changes being neither the result of imperial intervention nor the emulation of local elites. Therefore, even in sophisticated accounts of cultural change such as this, it is apparent that a new framework is required to explain the wider spectrum of consumption practices drawing on both state and non-state models. Tantalisingly, Woolf's chapter on consumption uses several headings that evoke globalisation such as 'a new world of goods', 'the consumer revolution' and 'mass consumption and regional traditions', but the connection is not made explicitly.

In contrast, Wallace-Hadrill's consideration of consumption in *Rome's Cultural Revolution* places emphasis on luxury and fashions at the 'heart' of the empire rather than mass consumption in the western provinces.[23] This study addresses universal changes in standardised ceramics, including the widespread shift away from black-glazed Italian wares in the second half of the first century BC to red-glazed *terra sigillata*, a change also credited by Woolf to the transformation of 'imperial culture' in this period.[24] Describing *terra sigillata* as a consumer good with wide social penetration that evoked the world of elite luxury, Wallace-Hadrill's conclusions on the consumption of this material ultimately echo Woolf's:

> The 'romanisation' process of the provinces is not, except in its initial stages, about the importation of Italian manufactures, but about learning to generate their own consumer goods only originally derived from a Roman model ... Imitation does not exclude invention or independence. 'Becoming Roman' does not imply ceasing to be Gallic.[25]

In framing the discussion of mass consumption in the terms of Romanisation (although within inverted commas), a picture of blanket change driven by Italian models is perpetuated. Invention and diversity are acknowledged, if portrayed as secondary and inconsequential. The example given, of Lezoux *terra sigillata* developing barbotine decoration independently of Italian manufacture, creates the impression that such developments were mere exercises in expressing local distinctiveness. By not addressing the local meaning of this change, its significance is underplayed. What remains (of implied greatest importance) is the original Italian model. Although this may be correct, the passage demonstrates how little understandings of 'provincial' mass consumption have developed in the decade following the publication of *Becoming Roman*. Instead of privileging small stylistic changes (that should be understood within the context of the community of practice of pottery production at Lezoux), Wallace-Hadrill's analysis would be more effective if it explored the role of the new *sigillata* for provincial communities through its practical use and disposal.

In summary, the study of mass consumption in the Roman world has stalled due to a lack of substantial empirical studies and the persistence of outdated interpretive models. The potential of consumption to reveal complex social patterning cannot be realised until it is conceptually unshackled from notions of acculturation, Romanisation and 'Romanness'. Current models excel at explaining mass consumption directly relating to imperial expansion (e.g. army supply), urbanisation or the incorporation of local elites into the Roman empire, but they are less well suited to account for broader changes that affected the lives of the more numerous non-elite and non-urban populations of provincial regions. However, if current explanations are flawed, it is because they are unbalanced, not completely wrong. Herein lies the continued seductiveness of Romanisation.

In what follows, I suggest three perspectives in which theories of global-isation have the potential to bring something new.[26] The first concerns providing a more holistic framework for describing the basic consumption patterns that create the familiar paradox of unity and diversity in the Roman empire. The second involves a reappraisal of the role of artefacts in such patterns, in which I use an early modern comparison to highlight similarities in the use of standardised ceramics exchanged over long dis-tances and the resulting impact on regional cultures of mass consumption. The third perspective is to advocate a focus on networks as a structural means of conceptualising geographies of Roman consumption,[27] instead of privileging container-thinking (e.g. the Roman-Native dichotomy) and representative understandings of material culture (e.g. *sigillata* as a carrier of 'Romanness'). This approach acknowledges that some styles of con-sumption were related to networks independent from the core infrastruc-ture of the Roman state, and that such styles can be regarded as globalising, but not always Romanising.

GEOGRAPHIES OF MASS CONSUMPTION: EXPLAINING HOMOGENEITY AND HETEROGENEITY

My first experience of dealing with the effects and paradoxes of global-isation was as a researcher on a project examining the changing role of food in contemporary society.[28] My task was to analyse data to show how consumption patterns and practices had changed in the previous 50 years. The annual figures provided for each nation-state by the United Nations Food and Agriculture Organization formed a suitable starting point. This database provides recent historic information on the production, consump-tion, imports and exports of most imaginable bulk food commodities. To investigate the relationship between food and culture, I chose to examine the changing consumption of oils and fats. Edible lipids are essential for human life, but also permit insights into changing global cuisine, as rough proxies for regional cultures of consumption.[29] The study revealed two

Table 4.1: Convergence and divergence in global lipid consumption, 1961 and 2003. Data from Pitts, Dorling & Pattie (2007).

	Top 5 oils and fats available for food (convergence)					Imports of 'premium' oils and fats (%) (divergence)		
	Industrialised	%	Rest of world	%			Industrialised	Rest of world
1961	Animal fats	25.2	Groundnut oil	20.3	1961	Butter	10.8	4.8
	Butter	23.5	Butter	12.1		Cream	0	0
	Soyabean oil	11.3	Animal fats	11.0		Olive oil	4.1	2.6
	Sunflower oil	7.6	Cottonseed oil	10.7		Fish oil	15.6	0.5
	Cream	6.9	Coconut oil	9.7		Rape oil	0.6	1.9
2003	Soyabean oil	28.2	Soyabean oil	25.3	2003	Butter	4.4	1
	Animal fats	14.4	Palm oil	22.7		Cream	2.2	0.3
	Sunflower oil	13.9	Animal fats	9.3		Olive oil	5.2	0.4
	Butter	10.5	Groundnut oil	7.9		Fish oil	3.2	0.4
	Rape oil	9.5	Butter	7.6		Rape oil	8.6	1.6

principal trends. First, in terms of consumption, the previous half century showed an overwhelming tendency towards *convergence* or homogenisation of diet, with diverse regional produce giving way to a single variety (soyabean oil) (see first half of Table 4.1). Regions resisting this pattern included areas producing oils that could only be grown within a narrow climactic range such as the Mediterranean (olive oil), and poorer parts of Africa and southeast Asia that were less integrated into the global economy due to war, famine and political instability. Second, and in contrast to the general availability of edible oils and fats, data specifically relating to imports showed greater heterogeneity (*divergence*), with wealthy industrialised regions (e.g. North America, Europe, Australia and Japan) choosing to import an increasingly diverse range of oils from around the world (see lower half of Table 4.1), typically healthy oils (olive, rape and fish) or luxury fats (butter and cream). In contrast, the less wealthy regions (e.g. Latin America, Central Africa and the Middle East) tended to import comparatively fewer of these in contrast to mass-produced oils (such as soyabean oil), the latter ostensibly corresponding to US food aid programmes.

What was most intriguing about the results of the oils and fats project were the similarities with my doctoral research on ceramic consumption in southeast Roman Britain. Different scales of analytical resolution not withstanding, the principal trend had a familiar quality – a simultaneous convergence in the overall availability of a global commodity, combined with a divergence in access to imports. The overarching trends from the Roman period study were threefold, comprising (1) a general consumer *convergence* on a general range of pottery forms (e.g. dishes, bowls and beakers) across all settlement types after conquest (see the upper half of Table 4.2); (2) a *divergence* in consumption by settlement type, with the better-connected urban centres and smaller settlements attracting a greater diversity of imported ceramic material than rural areas (see the lower half of Table 4.2); and (3) greater evidence for the continuity of pre-Roman patterns of consumption and pottery use in the less well-connected settlements.[30]

Both studies reveal fundamentally similar trends in terms of the effects of increased connectivity and economic integration with more distant areas. They show a movement towards a universal template for consumption, yet with increased hierarchy in access to scarcer imported items and commodities. Such heterogeneity appears to be linked to underlying relations of power and inequality, which are spatially manifest in terms of differing degrees of connectivity and network membership. If the effects of globalisation on consumption are modelled in pure statistical terms, relatively speaking, Roman London (Londinium), as the most prosperous and well-connected Romano-British city, behaves in a somewhat analogous way to late twentieth-century Western nations. Both imported the largest quantities of long-distance trade goods, and both set a template for the availability of material to be loosely followed by other settlements/regions in their respective networks. Conversely, both Roman rural settlements and modern developing countries were strongly susceptible to the consumption of mass commodities of a consistently universal character (if *not* more luxurious products obtained from further afield).

In both cases, what 'global' amounts to is a seemingly universal quality that no longer has a particular affinity to a given locality or form of cultural expression tied to a geographical area. This does not presuppose ideological engagement with the aims of the Roman state or Western capitalism. Crucially, the effects of globalisation in so-called marginalised areas often result in the local production of mass commodities in forms or varieties with recognisable 'global' currency, be this favoured oil types such as soya, palm oil and rapeseed, or coarse ware pottery vessels in more characteristic 'Roman' shapes. Here I argue that the necessity for producers and landowners to integrate into larger networks for economic reasons (subsistence, profit, paying taxes, etc.) can to a large extent override questions of cultural choice and stylistic expression for non-elite mass consumers.[31] Hand-made Iron Age vessels are out, standardised wheel-thrown vessels preferred by urban markets are in. Of course, while changes in available consumer goods

Table 4.2: CONVERGENCE AND DIVERGENCE IN POTTERY SUPPLY IN THE ENVIRONS OF LATE IRON AGE AND EARLY ROMAN COLCHESTER (CAMULODUNUM) AND LONDON (LONDINIUM). DATA FROM PERRING & PITTS (2013).

Top 5 serving and display vessels (convergence)					Imports and selected wares (%) (divergence)		
	Major urban	%	Rest	%		Major urban	Rest
25 BC–AD 80	Flagons	19.4	Platters	4.5	25 BC–AD 80 Amphorae	40.3	1.1
	Globular beakers	8.3	Butt-beakers	4.3	Terra sigillata	7.7	0.1
	Cups	5.0	Bowls	3.6	Gallo-Belgic ware	0.1	1.1
	Bowls	4.8	Globular beakers	2.9	Other imports	0.7	0.1
	Platters	4.7	Beakers	2.0	Lids (local)	5.3	1.9
AD 140–250	Flagons	18.9	Dishes	15.1	AD 140–250 Amphorae	31.2	1.3
	Dishes	12.3	Beakers	9.2	Terra sigillata	3.4	2.5
	Bowls	11.7	Bowls	4.4	Black-burnish ware	12.7	2.8
	Beakers	4.8	Flagons	3.4	Verulamium ware	12.3	0.4
	Mortaria	4	Platters	1.3	Lids (local)	10.8	0.6

may constrain the basic materials for cultural expression, they cannot dictate it. This is most notably evidenced today in the continued existence and reinvention of regional cuisines in 'globalised' Western countries despite the large-scale industrial processing of staple ingredients. Likewise in the Roman Britain case study, the persistence of pre-Roman drinking practices is evident over a century after conquest, notably involving the use of vessels of supposed 'Roman' character that are imported *and* locally produced.[32]

Large-scale homogenisation of consumer goods in the Roman world, as today, must have had some underlying economic rationale. This did not necessarily override the cultural preferences of consumers, as seen in less integrated areas (e.g. northern Roman Britain, and parts of contemporary Africa and southeast Asia in the lipids study) that either resisted or were slow to converge on a universal model, but nor did it signal the wholesale consumer acceptance of foreign values, be they 'Western' or 'Roman'. Widespread homogenisation in ceramic consumption in parts of the Roman empire can only really be described as 'Romanisation' in a techno-material sense (i.e. the basic vessel shapes and fabrics being used). While such physical attributes may often provide clues to social use, they do not presuppose particular forms of consumption practice or social meaning. Thus, it is important to identify and explain discrepancies in *practice* underlying broadly universalised patterns of circulation.

A good example of the need to look beyond homogenisation of style alone can be seen in the circulation of coarse wares in the hinterlands of Roman London and Colchester (Camulodunum). In this area, the two most common locally produced pottery fabrics, sandy grey ware (GRS) and black-surfaced ware (BSW) are described as 'Romanised' and 'Romanising', respectively the basis of their fabric make-up and the styles of their constituent vessels.[33] Despite appearing in a similar repertoire of forms after a relatively short period of time, the two fabrics have different circulation patterns. At its peak production, GRS had a wide distribution across all types of settlement, featuring prominently in urban assemblages, whereas BSW was widespread but completely avoided the major urban centres of London and Colchester (Fig. 4.1).

In the context of Roman pottery studies, the above patterns might be explained in terms of GRS outcompeting BSW for the urban market. However, instead of seeing this pattern in purely economic terms, it serves to illustrate how globalisation (conceived as increased social and economic integration) can create, maintain or exacerbate pre-existing inequalities and divisions. For whatever reason, BSW was apparently not desired by urban populations, despite occurring in a similar range of 'Roman' shapes to GRS.

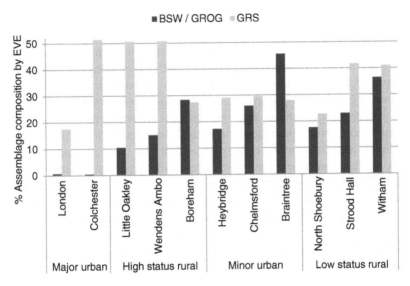

Figure 4.1: Percentage contribution by estimated vessel equivalent of so-called Romanised sandy grey wares (GRS) and Romanising grog-tempered (GROG) and black-surface wares (BSW) at sites in the hinterland of Roman Colchester, c. AD 140–250.

While it is impossible to know whether rural consumers were stigmatised for using BSW, its materiality (the colour difference, which perhaps signalled its Iron Age cultural biography) seems to have rendered it more suitable for rural as opposed to urban social settings.[34] Therefore, while both fabrics indicate the proliferation of a universal global style, BSW likely served as a receptacle for local memory, while potentially marginalising the people that used it. This example shows how the seemingly blanket spread of universal styles of ceramics in provincial contexts did not correlate with universal cultural outcomes, with striking asymmetries in the social distribution of different products in an essentially 'global' repertoire of pottery forms. In a crude sense, the words 'global' and 'Roman' are somewhat interchangeable here. A clear advantage of globalisation, however, is in providing a less culturally value-laden label for the material outcome of such large-scale phenomena.[35]

Although Hingley comments (Chapter 2, this volume) that studies of Roman globalisation risk overemphasising plurality and inclusiveness to the point of reinforcing the view that globalisation has an 'enabling influence' in the contemporary world,[36] I contend it is possible to present a view that reconciles increased consumer choice and mobility for some with the outcome of fostering of deeper overall socio-economic inequality.[37]

Although theories of Roman imperialism offer insights into the exploitation of provincial resources and people (e.g. precious metals, slaves and taxes) to fund the garrisoning of Rome's frontiers and the construction of urban infrastructure,[38] the impact of imperialism on regional patterns of mass consumption is arguably less direct, and to a strong degree dependent on pre-existing cultural geographies and economic systems. In such scenarios, it is more compelling to describe changes in consumption in terms of globalisation, which provides a decentred perspective on relations between producers and consumers, thus transcending the logic of centre–periphery thinking. In terms of applying globalisation thinking to material culture, it is especially helpful to regard the Roman empire as a 'polycentric periphery', which reflects the multiplicity of influences and flows that were often not directly related to the centre (Italy/Rome).[39] To enhance understandings of mass consumption, we must therefore move beyond the fascination with identifying sources of power. As Thomas puts it in his analysis of material culture and colonialism in the Pacific:

> Although the ultimately exploitative character of the global economy can hardly be overlooked, an analysis which makes dominance and extraction central to intersocial exchange from its beginnings will frequently misconstrue power relations which did not, in fact, entail the subordination of native people.[40]

Power relations clearly mattered in provincial societies, especially in the immediate aftermath of violent conquest, but they were not necessarily so pervasive to make mundane aspects of daily life a conscious (or even subconscious) statement of political ideology. The next section explores such matters pertaining to the contextual significance of mass consumption in greater detail.

HISTORIES OF MASS CONSUMPTION: MOVING THINGS, CHANGING MEANINGS

> we have to follow the things themselves, for their meanings are inscribed in their forms, their uses, their trajectories. ... from a *methodological* point of view it is the things-in-motion that illuminate their human and social context.[41]

As Romanisation as acculturation poses problems for the understanding of overarching trends in mass consumption, the notion of 'Roman material culture' presents similar difficulties with site-based and regional studies. While the label can be used as a convenient shorthand for material culture produced in the Roman period, it risks perpetuating an implicit connotation of objects embodying 'Romanness', as both a primary social characteristic and principal meaning to the consumer. Greater emphasis is required on the cultural biographies of commodities and things,[42] in which meaning often changes according to context, as opposed to notions of passive objects carrying fixed meanings (implicit or not), which remain embedded in much scholarship. Recent approaches to contemporary globalisation as 'circuits of culture' or 'commodityscapes' provide a helpful framework for explaining the role of things and commodities as they moved between different cultural contexts in the Roman world.[43] Such literature highlights the fractured nature of globalising processes by establishing the relationships between consumption in localised contexts with larger politico-economic networks, thus demonstrating the 'cultural materialization of the economic'.[44] These approaches reject the oft-perceived link between mass consumption, global homogenisation and the erosion of cultural difference.[45] Indeed, even the most ubiquitous of contemporary global brands such as McDonalds fast-food chains and Coca-Cola soft drinks have been demonstrated to be subject to significant localised adaptation.[46] Despite the obvious advantages of the circulation approach, it requires adaption to become a workable approach in archaeology. Although the geographer is able to 'follow the thing' through the real-time ethnographic observation of producers, merchants and consumers, the static archaeological record offers more partial insights. Similarly, while cultural geographers and anthropologists studying globalisation are typically less inclined to address issues of time-depth, or look beyond individual biographies, the opposite is true for the archaeologist interested in the changing composition of assemblages over several centuries. It is thus desirable for Roman archaeologists to investigate what Appadurai terms the *social history* of consumption to examine longer-term shifts in demand and usage, in addition to the *cultural biography* of specific things in given moments.[47]

In essence, archaeologists familiar with the work of Appadurai and others will find little new in the way that globalisation scholars have approached consumption.[48] However, as already discussed, it is not at all clear that these ideas have fully penetrated Roman archaeology. To make the case more forcefully, I draw upon another historical analogy, that of the mass importation of Chinese porcelain to Western Europe by the Dutch and English East India Companies in the seventeenth and eighteenth centuries.[49] Ironically, this cultural scenario has already been used by Romanists seeking historical parallels to explain the adoption of *terra sigillata* and related wares in the pre-conquest and early Roman periods in Britain and Gaul.[50] The comparison is revealing in several respects. Despite the effective political and economic role-reversal of northwest Europe, both scenarios were borne of globalising circumstances: in the Roman period, the annexation of large parts of Western Europe into the growing network of the Roman empire; in the seventeenth century, the expansion of European trading companies that led to the forging of commercial connections and colonies in the Asian Pacific. Despite obvious discrepancies in the speed, scale and economic underpinning of connections, patterns in the mass consumption of long-distance exchange ceramics between the two periods show remarkable consistency from the perspective of object biographies. Indeed, where differences in the social history of consumption do emerge, these help to clarify the defining characteristics of Roman and early modern globalisations, respectively.

The earliest *terra sigillata* and porcelain mass imports to arrive in northwest Europe were comparatively few. In biographical terms, they had been diverted from the pattern of their expected life cycles and were introduced into contexts lacking the cultural value systems that they had been produced for. In both periods, the exchange of such goods arose through the creation of new interfaces between previously (directly) unconnected cultural systems, and was often of a diplomatic character involving social elites. In the sixteenth century, a classic example is the appearance of blue and white porcelain vessels in the painting of Bellini's *Feast of the Gods* (1514), which is supposedly explained by a visit from Bellini's older brother to the court of Sultan Mehmed II where similar vessels would have been available.[51] Analogous to this example is the similarly jarring archaeological appearance of sets of typologically rare *terra sigillata* vessels in 'barbarian' contexts, many of which must have represented diplomatic gifts to friendly tribes from Roman officers.[52] In time, Roman imported ceramics and porcelain established themselves as tokens of aristocratic identity in their recipient European societies, in part due to their relative scarcity and the inability of local potters to create satisfactorily adequate equivalents, but perhaps also due to the special context in which they were exchanged. Crucially, there appears to have been little transfer of associated knowledge from the producer culture concerning the 'correct' use of such vessels. In both periods, once the taste for imported ceramics had set in, they were used predominantly for conspicuous display or gift exchange with other elites rather than being regarded as everyday utensils. Whole rooms were often set aside to show off large aristocratic collections of Chinese porcelain, the pyramidal ceiling of the De Santos palace (Lisbon) being a classic example.[53] Although there is limited archaeological evidence for the in situ domestic display of imports in pre-conquest and early Roman indigenous contexts, the frequent discovery of princely graves featuring large quantities of intact and often unused imported vessels suggests that a roughly analogous value system was in operation.

The biographical pathway of standardised Roman and Chinese ceramics entering northwest Europe to become markers of elite status did not remain unaltered for long. In both periods, change came through an intensification of connectivity with the producer areas. By the start of the first century AD, Rome's conquest of Gaul and the establishment of client kingdoms in southern Britain provided a more stable setting for the movement of a greater volume of goods, but also ideas, as seen in the development of *sigillata* industries in southern Gaul at locations such as La Graufesenque, and the production of Gallo-Belgic *sigillata* derivatives to the north focusing around Reims (Durocortorum). Conversely, at the beginning of the seventeenth century, the waxing power of the Dutch East India Company (Vereenigde Oost-Indische Compagnie, hereafter VOC) and the collapse of the Portuguese maritime empire meant that the large-scale shipping of Chinese porcelain directly from East Asia to north-west Europe was now possible.[54] As a result, the increased quantities of imported material enabled much wider social access than in previous generations. In the lead-up to the Roman conquest of Britain in AD 43, Gallo-Belgic and to a lesser extent *terra sigillata* fine wares appeared at most settlements in the territory of the dominant pre-Roman polities in southern Britain, with wide dispersion in funerary contexts in some areas indicating that imports were no longer restricted to elites.[55] Similarly, Chinese porcelain was first made available to a broader cross section of Dutch society after the contents of the captured Portuguese vessel *San Jago* were publicly auctioned in 1602.[56]

Determining what the imported ceramic material signified to the average consumer has provoked a wide range of views. The VOC records show that until the mass importation of tea from 1637,[57] the majority of Chinese porcelain imports were dish and plate forms, which could have been used as tableware as well as for display.[58] However, it is the smaller quantities of imported drinking vessels and bowls that potentially shed more light on the mass consumption of porcelain in the formative years of the trade. Analysis of the VOC records shows that the principal Chinese porcelain cup forms imported to the Netherlands in the first part of the century were kandeelskoppen (caudle cups) (Fig. 4.2, top, and Fig. 4.3).[59] Caudle was diagnostically European, a sweet, viscous alcoholic beverage made of various ingredients including eggs, milk, wine, sugar and cinnamon.[60] Likewise, the most popular Chinese porcelain bowl forms ordered at this time were klapmutsen (resembling upside-down hats with an everted rim) (Fig. 4.2, bottom, and Fig. 4.4). The klapmuts is considered the 'most un-Chinese' of the early seventeenth-century imports, and was better suited to the European consumption of soups and stews with a spoon than the

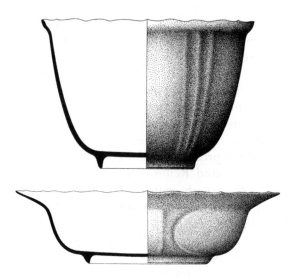

Figure 4.2: The so-called kandeelskoppen or crowcup (top) and klapmuts (bottom). Not to scale. After van der Pijl Ketel (1982, 104, 119) © Christine van der Pijl Ketel. Reproduced with permission.

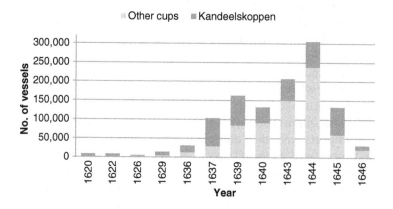

Figure 4.3: VOC imports of Chinese porcelain cup forms in the seventeenth century. Note that other cups became more popular than the so-called kandeelskoppen after the mass import of tea began in 1637.

equivalent Chinese practice that required drinking straight from a bowl with steeper sides.[61] These examples suggest the early mass consumption of porcelain in the Netherlands involved incorporating vessels from a universal global porcelain repertoire into local value systems in which use was dictated by pre-existing food consumption practices rather than a desire to

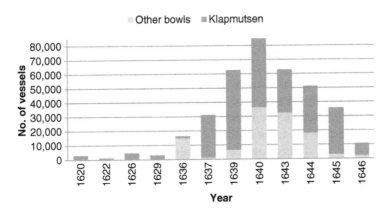

Figure 4.4: VOC imports of Chinese porcelain bowl forms in the seventeenth century. Note continued popularity of klapmutsen.

adopt Chinese cultural practices. This phenomenon can be aptly termed 'glocalisation' or the 'particularisation of the universal'.[62]

While many of the first mass porcelain imports in the Netherlands became popular for fitting into local cultures of eating and drinking, it is probably for similar reasons that so-called Gallo-Belgic imports appear to have been favoured over *terra sigillata* at the start of the first century AD by some communities in southeast Britain. This occurred in terms of the quantities of imports used and their relative influence on locally produced pottery. Despite Gallo-Belgic pottery featuring many vessels similar to the stock elements of the *terra sigillata* range, the most popular Gallo-Belgic forms in British contexts were often large drinking vessels, notably butt-beakers. Such types had no analogue in *terra sigillata* and must have reflected a similar northern Gallic predisposition for the consumption of local beverages (e.g. 'Celtic' beer) which required larger drinking vessels, as opposed to the smaller cups more suitable for wine consumption.[63] Whereas the increased use of standardised wheel-thrown ceramics is undoubtedly symptomatic of changing consumption practices and new ways of signalling status, there is little indication, especially amongst non-elites, that the use of imported vessels somehow reflected a desire to acquire Roman culture. The main point to emerge is that early mass consumers had greater input to the selection and use of imports and did not simply acquire them in order to 'become Roman' or imitate exotic Chinese practice. This is not to say that awareness of the biographies of these new commodities had no bearing on their popularisation. While the capacity for new products to evoke exotic and fantastic foreign lands in the imagination of the European consumer undoubtedly played some part in their mass proliferation, this did not necessitate or assume a wholesale shift in the identity of the consumer.

So far I have painted a picture of the mass consumption of long-distance traded ceramics as being ultimately subject to local value systems, and not simply the spread of a single global (or Roman) culture. Thus, what in strict material terms might be viewed as a process of homogenisation or convergence, is often in cultural terms a re-appropriation or re-purposing of commodities to suit local needs. However, culture is not static, and while useful for describing the short-term effects of particular globalising moments, this model is less useful to address longer-term trends in consumption under the conditions of more prolonged connectivity. Returning to the early modern period, it did not take long for local practices to become altered as a consequence of establishment of more expansive global networks. A craze for imported commodities (especially tea, coffee and chocolate) prompted a shift towards vessels geared to the polite consumption of such beverages. At the same time, many of the popular Chinese porcelain types imported at the beginning of the seventeenth century witnessed significant declines by the start of the eighteenth century due to competition from local imitations (caudle cups) or ceasing to be in fashion (klapmutsen).[64] Whilst the global replaced the local in terms of the commodities being consumed, the etiquette of consumption developed independently from Chinese practice. The direct trade with China via Canton initiated by the English and then Dutch East India companies at the start of the eighteenth century afforded much greater European control over the shapes of imported vessels and services. The basic Chinese export tea cup thus acquired handles, and was produced in a range of standard sizes and patterns to European specifications – a classic case of the 'particularisation of the universal'.[65] By the early–mid-eighteenth century, porcelain began to be produced in Europe, although the products of major factories such as Meissen, Sèvres and Chelsea were largely orientated to the aristocratic market.[66] The leading role of Chinese mass exports in fostering the development of new tastes, markets and industries is undeniable.[67]

Despite the intensity of connections between Europe and China in the early modern period, a degree of cultural distance was more strongly maintained throughout the seventeenth and eighteenth centuries, in contrast to the early Roman west.[68] Changes in the consumption of imported material culture that took place in new provinces such as Britannia thus developed in the context of more direct cultural exchange with the rest of the Roman empire, which is given primacy in most accounts of mass consumption as Romanisation (i.e. the desire to acquire 'Roman' practices). Unsurprisingly, it is in the longer term that the early modern case study begins to diverge from patterns of mass consumption in the western Roman provinces. Despite short-lived experiments in the production of *terra sigillata* in Britain, production did not take off in the same way that it did in Gaul, or that porcelain did in early modern Europe. Although this might be attributed to insufficient demand, broader changes in local and regional pottery production followed the general functional characteristics of *terra sigillata*, with a greater relative emphasis on dining (plates and dishes) as opposed to drinking vessels. In the southeast, the pre-conquest and early Roman period focus on Gallo-Belgic wares and drinking vessels such as butt-beakers subsided by the late first century AD, in a similar manner to the decline in klapmutsen in late seventeenth-century Holland.

Reconciling this apparent lack of sufficient mass demand for the universal 'global' product (*sigillata*) with the sweeping 'globalisation' of styles of local and regional pottery production and consumption is not straightforward. Considering the depositional profile of *sigillata* in Britain, which is quantitatively focused at the bastions of imperial infra-structure (i.e. military sites and new urban centres) planted as far as Exeter (Isca Dumnoniorum) in the West and the northern frontiers,[69] it is tempting to conclude that demand was largely confined to colonial communities. However, it is unclear whether or not such patterns are merely by-products of connectivity, with imports focusing at primary nodal locations and decaying with distance by road or river.[70] The broader changes in the functional emphasis of ceramic assemblages affected all pottery users – the majority of society. Such widespread changes may have represented a reorientation of production to supply urban markets in response to the stimulus of taxation, perhaps to raise cash through sales of pots or their edible contents, or to pay taxes in kind. Thus, whereas local value systems in eighteenth-century Europe appear to have been willingly altered in response to the expansion of global networks and the parallel demand for new commodities, in Roman Britain the political and economic impact of incorporation into global networks often involved changesagainst the grain of pre-existing cultural preferences. Although general changes in pottery shapes fit a broadly 'Roman' model, regional distinctiveness and agency were nevertheless maintained in the development of local styles, as Woolf similarly observed in Gaul. For example, a general transition in dining vessels from plates to deeper dishes by the end of the second century AD seems to have occurred more quickly in local and regionally produced pottery in the southeast than it did in imported *sigillata*.[71] In the prevailing imperial system, global changes were still mediated and reinterpreted in regional and local forms rather than imitating a distant metropolitan culture.

The striking similarities in the nature and pace of change between the mass consumption of ceramics in early Roman and early modern northwest Europe highlight the benefits of describing such patterns in terms of globalisation rather than imperialism or Romanisation alone. Each phase of consumption is intimately related to the impact of changed or prolonged connections with bigger 'global' networks, from the initial conspicuous display of imported ceramics by elites, to their early mass consumption within the context of local foodways, followed by the development of regional trajectories in local imitation. The initial adoption of mass imports was heavily dependent on how well they fitted into local consuming cultures, as well as their capacity to evoke a distant exotic culture, whereas in the longer term both imported *sigillata* and porcelain had a less important role in dictating the long-term development of local consumer cultures than is often assumed. Of course, not all of the patterns discussed were closely mirrored across both historical contexts. Unlike porcelain in eighteenth-century Europe, *terra sigillata* was not successfully produced in Roman Britain in quantity, and broader changes in pottery styles were arguably more a product of fulfilling the demands of imperial taxation as opposed to representing a genuine consumer revolution or true consumerism. Beyond the initial reorientation of elite consumption patterns in the first generation after Roman conquest, 'becoming Roman' has as much relevance to explaining changes in Romano-British pottery use and consumption practices as 'becoming Chinese' did in early modern Europe (i.e. none). However, while pottery vessels did not carry fixed meanings, they could still evoke exotic 'cultural concepts' to their consumers (e.g. of 'China' and 'Rome'), that undoubtedly enhanced the initial mass desirability of such commodities.[72]

NETWORKS AND MULTIDIRECTIONAL CHANGE

A major strength of conceptualising globalisation as a process of expanding and intensifying connectivity is that it encourages understandings of how individuals and communities came to be affected by larger-scale phenomena. Indeed, tracing flows of objects and commodities and the resultant impact on the formation of local and regional cultures provides an invaluable means of illuminating how bigger networks impacted on everyday life. In Roman provincial archaeology, a great deal of research has focused on networks embodying the reach of the Roman state, most notably the military (forts and frontiers) and civilian (cities and roads) infrastructure that accompanied annexation. This infrastructure needed to be maintained, and had its own distinctive consumption signature.[73] Under the agenda of Romanisation, the logical emphasis of studies of 'provincial' consumption is to explore the extent to which colonial styles penetrated broader hinterlands. However valid this approach may be for understanding Romanisation, it cannot provide a truly holistic view of consumption without acknowledging the existence of networks that operated independently from the Roman state.

A good example of the potential of studies of consumption to reveal complex alternative networks that operated in parallel to the more recognisable effects of Roman imperialism can be seen at Camulodunum (Colchester), the initial stronghold of resistance to the Claudian invasion of southeast Britain in AD 43. Analysis of pottery assemblages from various locations around Colchester dating to the 20 or so years after the Roman conquest reveal two consistently different patterns of consumption. On the one hand, at locations associated with a known Roman military presence (the fortress and later Colonia Claudia Victricensis), it is possible to isolate 'suites' of recurrently deposited material featuring an emphasis on imported *sigillata*, flagons, mortaria and dining vessels. In contrast, at locations associated with the continued occupation of the pre-conquest Camulodunum *oppidum*, including the Sheepen settlement and the Stanway aristocratic cemetery, the equivalent 'suites' included some *sigillata* but were dominated by Gallo-Belgic imports (which were negligible at colonial locations) and featured a relative emphasis on drinking vessels (Fig. 4.5).

At face value, this entangled and distinctive patterning highlights the micro-geography of cultural difference between colonist and colonised in the immediate post-conquest generation. As both sets of material are notionally 'Roman' in style and form, any other differences were originally overlooked in traditional narratives of Romanisation. Nevertheless, further investigation reveals that the pattern of use of Gallo-Belgic imports was replicated in the deposition of distinctive brooch types and the remains of particular animal species both within Colchester and at several other prominent centres in southern and eastern Britain, as well as northern Gaul.[74] Although this network was based upon several former pre-Roman tribal kingdoms, the evidence of consumption suggests it continued to exist 20–30 years after conquest. The essential characteristics of this regional network seem to have revolved around the needs of the communities and the remaining leaders of the pre-conquest generation to maintain a semblance of power andshared culture in the wake of the destabilising effects of colonisation. Although on a much smaller scale and lacking the overt monumentality of Roman provincial infrastructure, this network may be described as

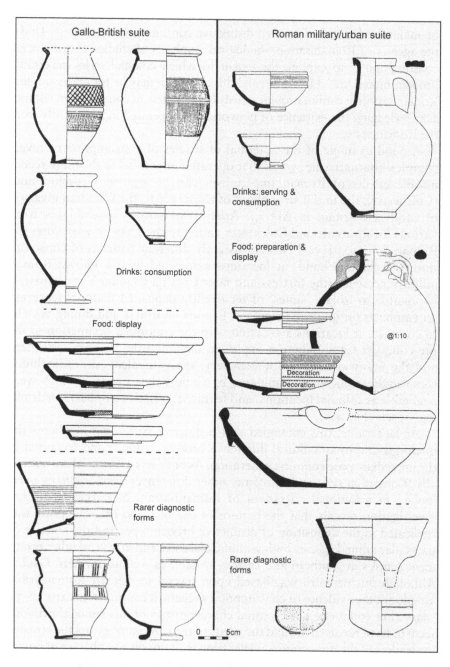

Figure 4.5: The composition of 'Gallo-British' and 'Roman urban/military' suites of ceramics at Sheepen, Camulodunum, c. AD 49–61. From Perring and Pitts (2013), drawn by Fiona Griffin © Archaeology South East. Reproduced with permission.

'globalising' and 'globalised'. In material terms it was characterised by a distinctive collage of vessels that particularised a universal style associated with Roman military and colonial foundations, by favouring vessels more suitable for local needs (drinking vessels), and incorporating (and updating) distinctive vessel types drawn from north Gallic and southern British repertoires. So-called Gallo-British combinations of pottery thus formed an alternative to consumption patterns favoured in urban and military centres, whilst simultaneously incorporating many of the same stylistic elements (Fig. 4.5).

Another potential benefit of studying Roman consumption within the framework of theories of globalisation is to shed new light on uneven geographies of consumption, within and between different networks. This topic has already been broached in Roman archaeology under the general heading of studies investigating the extent of urban hinterlands.[75] However, such studies have been predominantly concerned with the characterisation of the underlying economic logic of provincial urbanism, as opposed to the dynamics of cultural change. Of particular interest here is addressing the impact of expanding networks and the development of new nodes in pre-existing settlement landscapes. The example of Colchester given above highlights the sensitivity of consumption to cultural differences resulting from the cannibalisation of an existing pre-Roman centre or node into the dominant imperial network. Using the same principles, patterns of consumption could illuminate the extent to which some nodes served to extend 'global' space and culture at the expense of the unfamiliarity of newly conquered territories.

Not unlike the patterns observed at post-conquest Colchester, the nearby settlement at Chelmsford exhibited a similar disparity relating to ongoing tensions between global and local. As a new settlement established after Roman conquest, Chelmsford (Caesaromagus) acquired a *mansio* (an official stopping point on a Roman road as part of the *cursus publicus*). Shortly after the building of the *mansio*, the pottery assemblages at Chelmsford took on a much stronger universal or 'urban' character, probably to cater for the needs of travellers who would be unfamiliar with the more local styles of pottery in regular use. However, pottery assemblages from the temple site at Chelmsford, located outside what would become the walled area of the town, did not change at the same rate, retaining a distinctly local/non-urban character. It is thus likely that the settlement took on a dual character, with the *mansio* serving the needs of passing travellers rather than providing a model for the 'Romanisation' of the local populace, who appear to have continued to consume in their own fashion at the temple and surrounding settlements. This scenario recalls Tomlinson's writings on time–space compression and the cultural experience of visiting an airport in the late twentieth century: a distant place is made to feel more culturally close and familiar by minimising the cultural difference that would have been otherwise experienced in the wider landscape.[76] In this sense, approaching Roman consumption through the lens of globalisation helps to promote understandings of the day-to-day experience of the Roman empire without recourse to the unhelpful binary opposites of 'Roman' and 'Native' that ceased to have much relevance as discrete cultural categories by a generation or so after conquest.

Conclusions

Globalisation matters a great deal for the study of Roman period (mass) consumption. Most importantly it encourages a paradigm shift in the understanding of material culture – that there is a disconnection between objects and social practices, and moving goods have neither fixed meanings nor uses. For phenomena such as the mass uptake of *terra sigillata*, thinking in terms of globalisation is inherently more effective to describe changes that have been traditionally considered under the headings of Romanisation and acculturation.[77] Despite the strong case for globalisation concepts, however, there are risks involved in the adoption of a new '-isation' paradigm, especially one with substantial baggage. Rather than substituting the word globalisation for Romanisation, Roman archaeologists and historians need to create new frameworks for exploring the implications of globalisation, connectivity and time–space compression for moving scholarship forward. In terms of understanding Roman mass consumption, I identify three areas in which this may be done:

1. New perspectives

Globalisation encourages the identification of networks and styles of consumption separate from (or indirectly connected to) the infrastructure of Roman imperialism. By placing greater emphasis on consumption patterns in relation to variable degrees of connectivity, globalisation provides new ways of modelling the effects of Roman imperialism that acknowledge the unevenness of power, knowledge and economic resources, rather than taking recourse to simplistic notions of emulation. Indeed, by identifying but not over-privileging the inequalities and power relations underlying patterns of consumption, notions of globalisation as a benign enabler of plurality (i.e. 'a good thing') can be challenged. This is explicitly illustrated in southeast Roman Britain by pre-Roman coarse wares (discussed above) that were stylistically transformed after conquest to fit a universal global template of shape and functionality, yet whose distribution was largely confined to non-urban settlements. While inherently globalising, the distribution of such fabrics highlights a diverging experience of global culture at rural settlements, potentially signalling the marginalised and local status of its users.

2. *Privileging consumption*

To take globalisation seriously as a focus for research in Roman archaeology, mass consumption needs to be given more prominence, especially relating to the study of everyday artefacts and commodities. Following the methodological implications of studying consumption in terms of circulation and entanglement, this approach has the potential to provide detailed insights into degrees of global consciousness, participation and exclusion from aspects of global culture, and the general experiences of living in the Roman world for all social groups, especially non-elites. Pursuing an approach to globalisation demands that consumption is studied from a perspective which allows communities connected in the past (but often separated by modern national boundaries) to be examined at a combination of local, regional and interprovincial scales.

3. *Historical comparison*

Theories of globalisation bring the potential for new insights into Roman period consumption by providing a framework to contextualise parallel episodes of mass consumption and long-distance trade in other historical periods. At the same time, adopting globalisation concepts can provide an avenue for archaeological studies of consumption to contribute to broader historical and sociological debates. The Romanisation debate is tremendously unhelpful in this regard. Pursuing a comparative historical approach involves acknowledging and explaining the similarities and differences with other periods and civilisations. Although increased connectivity seemingly promotes parallel effects in the histories and geographies of mass consumption – notably the 'universalisation of the particular' hand-in-hand with the 'particularisation of the universal' – this does not presuppose a universal logic behind such processes.

ACKNOWLEDGEMENTS

This contribution was significantly reshaped by conversations arising and following the workshop held in Exeter in 2011. I am grateful for discussions with Stephen Mitchell, Elena Isayev and Barbara Borg that helped to refine the argument. I thank Elena Isayev in particular for introducing me to 'china' via Brook (2008). I am especially indebted to Astrid van Oyen, Miguel John Versluys, Tamar Hodos and the two anonymous Cambridge reviewers for their discussions and comments on the text. Any errors and omissions remain my own.

NOTES

1. For example, Trentmann (2012). A chapter on Roman consumption is conspicuously absent from Trentmann's extensive survey of consumption in global history.
2. See review articles of Ray (2006) and Greene (2008).
3. For a recent example, Morley (2007b, 574) directly links the process of cultural change under the umbrella heading of 'Romanisation' to the creation of new demand for mass-produced ceramics.
4. For example, Finley (1985), cf. Parkins (1997). The 'consumer city' model is based on the underlying assumption that the Roman urban economy was parasitical on wealth generated in the countryside, especially in the form of rents paid to elite landowners who conspicuously consumed such income in the urban environment. Although various alternatives (Whittaker 1995) and exceptions (Mattingly et al. 2001) have been proposed and identified, the model remains firmly entrenched in current understandings (e.g. Kehoe 2007).
5. Brunner was heavily influenced by the communication theorist Marshall McLuhan, who coined the term 'global village' (e.g. McLuhan 1964) and became an influential figure in the establishment of theories of globalisation.
6. Stearns (2006, vii): 'They become enmeshed in the process of acquisition – shopping – and take some of their identity from a procession of new items they buy and exhibit'.
7. Although notably, Greene (2008) argued for the existence of Roman consumerism. Greene (2008, 66) sees consumption simply as a means of fulfilling biological needs, with consumerism occurring on a larger scale driven by culturally determined desires. However, his definition of consumerism is too broad, focusing more on luxury consumption (versus necessity) than true consumerism. As Stearns (2006, 2–4) notes, luxury consumption in premodern societies should not be taken as a priori evidence for consumerism.
8. With reference to Roman pottery, Greene (2008, 74) argued that the rate of changing styles could be classed as consumerist, following Woolf's (1998)

account of ceramic consumption in Gaul. However, while pre-modern fashions in the uptake of new goods can appear rapid, the extent to which such societies indulged in high rates of *discard* is less clear. In contrast to modern consumer goods, the lifespans of Roman ceramic styles are rarely short enough to permit dating closer than 20-year units. Evidence for the long use-lives of *sigillata* vessels (Wallace 2006) does not support the notion of a truly consumerist society. True consumerism also requires the social order to be altered. This is possible for the urban (and military) minority constituting the principal markets for *sigillata*, but not necessarily the case for the widespread yet more infrequent penetration of such material outside the urban sphere, where new vessels were often incorporated into local forms of practice and ritual (e.g. feasting and mortuary ritual).

9. See especially the proceedings of the Theoretical Roman Archaeology Conference (TRAC), reflecting the work of largely Anglo postgraduate and early-career scholars, e.g. Ferris (1995); Meadows (1995); Hawthorne (1998); Eckardt (2000); Hawkes (2001); Fincham (2002); Carr (2003); Gardner (2003); Swift (2003); Cool (2004); Monteil (2004); Pitts (2005b); Ray (2006); Egri (2007). Outside TRAC in the same vein, see Cooper (1996); Hill (2001); Greene (2008).

10. Appadurai (1986b); Douglas & Isherwood (1996). On Roman theory see Millett (1990a; 1990b) on Romanisation, Webster (2001) on Creolisation, Woolf (1998) on 'becoming Roman', Mattingly (1997) on discrepant experience and Mattingly (2004) on discrepant identity.

11. Note, however, the development of some approaches in more substantial publications, e.g. Eckardt (2002), Cool (2006) and Gardner (2007a).

12. Notably Woolf (1998, 169–205) and Wallace-Hadrill (2008, 315–440). In contrast, Dietler (2010) provides an impressive narrative of consumption and colonial entanglement in Mediterranean France during the first millennium BC, in which material culture is given more adequate treatment from an anthropological perspective.

13. For Britain, Cool (2006) effectively summarises the problems and potential of using the wealth of published finds data. Allison (2004) presents a similar discussion of the evidence for Pompeii.

14. cf. Laurence & Trifilò (Chapter 5, this volume), who argue that 'global' and inter-provincial comparisons of material culture are vital for the study of globalisation in the Roman world.

15. Appadurai (1986a); Thomas (1991). For a similar view regarding visual culture, see Versluys (Chapter 7, this volume).

16. As defined by Reece (1988, 11).

17. Reece (1988, 33).

18. Woolf (1998, 174).

19. e.g. Weatherill (1993).

20. Woolf (1998, 174).

21. Woolf (1998, 181).

22. Woolf (1998, 185).

23. Wallace-Hadrill (2008, 315–440).

24. Woolf (1998, 187).
25. Wallace-Hadrill (2008, 437).
26. Here I draw examples from my research on ceramics in Britain, although the ideas are applicable elsewhere in the Roman world.
27. cf. Morley (this volume) for a complementary perspective in regard to networks.
28. Jackson (2009).
29. Pitts, Dorling & Pattie (2007).
30. Pitts (2008); see also Perring & Pitts (2013) for the analysis of a larger dataset incorporating Roman London and settlements to the north. Roth (2007) outlines similar patterns of structured heterogeneity underlying homogeneity in the spread of black-gloss wares in Central Roman Italy.
31. See Morley (Chapter 3, this volume), on cultural choices in relation to integration into economic and political networks.
32. Pitts (2008, 501; 2010b).
33. Going (1987); Perring & Pitts (2013). Here, 'Romanised' means made locally but introduced in direct association with Roman colonial communities, and 'Romanising' means the adoption of 'Roman' stylistic traits by pre-conquest potting traditions.
34. Black-surface wares derived from the pre-Roman local tradition of grog-tempered coarse wares, which may account for the reluctance of the more cosmopolitan urban populations to use it. If so, this stigma was not present in first-century London when large quantities of grog-tempered pottery found their way into the city before more adequate coarse ware supplies could be obtained (see Perring & Pitts 2013).
35. Pitts (2008).
36. Hingley (Chapter 2, this volume).
37. Pitts (2008). Pitts & Griffin (2012) highlight a potential link between low settlement connectivity (i.e. rural locations), poor health determined through the analysis of skeletal remains, and inequality in the distribution of grave furnishings within late Roman cemeteries in Britain. These results describe the human consequences of being forced into a largely localised existence in a globalised world (e.g. Bauman 1998), and mirror similar relationships between health and income inequality that are increasingly prevalent in contemporary globalised society in both affluent and impoverished regions (Wilkinson 2005; Wilkinson & Pickett 2010).
38. e.g. Hopkins (1978b); Cunliffe (1988).
39. Jan Nederveen Pieterse (pers. comm., April 2011, also Chapter 10, this volume).
40. Thomas (1991, 83–4).
41. Appadurai (1986a, 5).
42. Kopytoff (1986) provides a thoughtful discussion of this concept, although cf. the more careful discussion of Appadurai (1986a).
43. Foster (2006).
44. Cook & Crang (1996, 134).
45. Miller (1995a,1995b).

46. Foster (2006, 291).
47. Appadurai (1986a, 34, 36), cf. Kopytoff (1986).
48. Peña (2007) provides a thorough overview for the possibilities of modelling the life cycle of Roman pottery vessels from a biographical perspective.
49. See Versluys (Chapter 7, this volume), for further discussion of 'china' in the context of the wider interpretation of Roman material culture.
50. e.g. Reece (1988, 8); Cool (2006, 157–8). Pitts (2013) provides a detailed critique of these brief analogues.
51. Carswell (2000, 132).
52. Willis (1996, 202) discusses a notable example of the occurrence of rare *sigillata* types at the stronghold of Stanwick in northern England in the mid-first century AD. On a larger scale, a similar kind of mechanism (i.e. gift exchange) could account for the initial importation of ceramics in Roman client states, such as the Atrebates and Catuvellauni in Britain (Creighton 2000).
53. Carswell (2000, 129).
54. Volker (1954); Rinaldi (1989).
55. Pitts (2008).
56. Volker (1954, 22).
57. Volker (1954, 48–9).
58. Pitts (2013); Pierson (2007).
59. There is some debate whether the original VOC documents used by Volker say 'caudle cups' or 'camel cups' (Volker 1954, 22–3; Christine van der Pijl-Ketel, pers. comm.). Either way, the likelihood that such vessels were used for local beverages is reinforced by their relative decline in favour of new cup forms that coincided with the mass introduction of tea in 1637.
60. van der Pijl-Ketel (1982, 119).
61. Rinaldi (1989, 118–19); Brook (2008, 75–6).
62. Robertson (1992, 97–114), cf. Witcher (2000) and Versluys (Chapter 7, this volume).
63. Hill (2002); Pitts (2005a).
64. Jörg (1982, 164–80); Pitts (2013).
65. A similar phenomenon of porcelain being ordered to specification existed from the early seventeenth century, but was much less reliable due to the dependence on the middlemen (independent Chinese junks sailing to Dutch colonial bases such as Batavia).
66. Godden (1979, 15); Kerr & Mengoni (2011).
67. Sombart's (1967) influential thesis attributes the rise of capitalism and associated social changes in Western Europe to a burgeoning desire for new global luxuries.
68. Although (imagined) cultural differences were nevertheless still played out in the early Roman scenario.
69. Such patterns are described in detail by Willis (2011).
70. Indeed, Weatherill's (1996, 76) analysis of the frequency of china ownership in probate inventories at the beginning of the eighteenth century shows a similar decay in quantities down the settlement hierarchy from London and lesser towns to villages and rural areas.

71. Pitts (2013).
72. See in particular Versluys (Chapter 7, this volume) cf. Rujivacharakul (2011) on the distinction between culture, cultural concepts and material culture.
73. See, for example, King (1999) for animal bones, Evans (2001, 2005) for pottery, van der Veen et al. (2008) for plant remains and Eckardt (2002) for lighting equipment.
74. Pitts (2010a; 2010b).
75. Perring (2002); Gaffney et al. (2007).
76. Tomlinson (1999, 7); Pitts (2008, 500).
77. cf. Versluys (Chapter 7, this volume).

5

THE GLOBAL AND THE LOCAL IN THE ROMAN EMPIRE: CONNECTIVITY AND MOBILITY FROM AN URBAN PERSPECTIVE

Ray Laurence and Francesco Trifilò

The Roman empire covered a significant proportion of the globe,[1] therefore, the discussion of Roman culture through a geographical perspective, plotted and studied with distribution maps of different classes of evidence, can be legitimately made via theories of globalisation.[2] The global–local relationship provides the key focus for this chapter, first within Romanisation theory developed in the 1980s, and second through a series of data-led case studies. Fundamental to our approach is the realisation that to study globalisation in the Roman empire is to shift the academic focus of the disciplines of Roman archaeology and history from a focus on region/single province study to a wider viewpoint accounting for more material, either through projects on a larger scale or via scholars specialising in different regions or types of evidence working together. The collaboration between Ray Laurence, Gareth Sears and Simon Esmonde Cleary from 2005 through to 2010 provides a model based around weekly discussion of their views of the Roman city. The outcome was the monograph *The City in the Roman West*.[3] This book does not especially engage with theories of globalisation discussed in the editors' introduction, but it is ultimately about the globalisation of Roman urbanism. In particular, one of the preoccupations of the book was to explore the local adaptation of a global conception of urbanism, including how a 'way of life' was produced and a 'city form' was adapted. This opposition established one way of contributing to our understanding of globalisation which we analyse further in this chapter. The closest to a specific conception of globalisation we came to can be seen as:

individuals engaged or disengaged with the dominant culture of Romanness in quite different and even undefined ways to produce a physical manifestation of their identity. This approach allows us to envisage a *global* idea of Roman culture that was viewed differently according to the perspective of the individual.[4]

Yet, embedded in the book is the theme that will be pursued more explicitly in this chapter:

The use of the fabric of the city does not coincide with the spread of Roman citizenship, and indeed the city in the Roman Empire appears at once a global phenomenon and at the same time as a local adaptation of that phenomenon.[5]

What we might be seeing in this 2011 book is the influence of globalisation on our thinking that is derived from reading in the social sciences. Research on globalisation is extensive. The tip of the iceberg can be seen in two publications from 2012: a five-volume Wiley-Blackwell *Encyclopaedia of Globalisation* and a four-volume Sage *Encyclopaedia of Global Studies*.[6] Both of these volumes contain entries on 'Architecture', but neither contains a reference to 'Archaeology' or to 'History' – a sign of the disengagement with (or a reluctance to engage with) 'globalisation' within these disciplines.[7] However, many of the entries in the encyclopaedias will be familiar to those within Roman archaeology: 'postcolonialism', 'connectivity', 'spatiality', 'space of flows/space of place', 'time–space compression'.[8] This causes us to view globalisation not so much as a single coherent theory to be applied, but as a key academic discourse to engage the study of the Roman empire with, and to endeavour to learn from, as well as to contribute to.

In focusing on the relationship between the 'local' and the 'global' in this chapter, we wish to look back into Romanisation theory to see how the relationship was then articulated, prior to presenting a series of case studies that are explored with reference to cities. This is not to return us to 1990s-style Romanisation, but to recognise that within Roman archaeology the relationship between the local and the global has been fundamental and needs to be recognised as the prehistory of globalisation and the Roman empire. Our case studies focus on the use of Latin in inscriptions principally in Italy and in North Africa, but with a wider view of usage in the other provinces of the Latin West. The evidence that is studied in this chapter places in question the very concept of the relationship between the *centre* of the empire (geographically defined as Italy) and the provinces. The very notion of multidirectional change, discussed by the editors in their introduction, comes into question, when the evidence used in this chapter points to a cultural fracture between Italy and even the most connected regions of the Mediterranean. As a result, instead, we suggest that the global should be seen as not produced in Italy and exported, but produced by the empire as a whole to be developed locally in both the provinces and in Italy, to produce quite different versions of something that could be defined as globally 'Roman'. At this point in time, we can observe relationships between local and global contexts and can begin to investigate the patterns in the rich data of Roman archaeology. However, any conclusions are preliminary – since a far wider range of evidence needs to be studied for a full appreciation of the nature of variation in Roman culture, and needs further documentation and large-scale studies to fully realise the potential of Roman evidence to contribute to a better understanding of the time-depth of globalisation.[9] The chapter seeks to open up the possibility of articulating the local–global dialectic in the Roman empire, but is only a first step towards that goal.[10]

THE INTERSECTION OF THE GLOBAL WITH THE LOCAL IN ROMANISATION DISCOURSE

The study of the Roman empire is still dominated by academic concepts developed in the intensely creative period associated with the late 1970s through to the end of the 1980s – a period which precedes the rise to prominence of globalisation as a major research theme (discussed by Pitts and Versluys in Chapter 1). Interestingly, scholars at that time were seeking models and universals with which they could then interpret the data provided by archaeology. For the study of Roman Britain, this meant engagement with contemporary thinking in ancient history and, in particular, the concepts used to interpret societies and the economy of antiquity developed by Moses Finley. Martin Millett's book *The Romanization of Britain* was a contrast to previous books on Roman Britain, which, as an 'essay in archaeological interpretation' sought a wider engagement with developments in the empire as a whole.[11] This work provided archaeology with a synthesis of the evidence and a 'modern commentary on the social and economic development of the province' of Britannia.[12] More than 20 years on, it might be hard to imagine quite how different this book was from what students had read before: Frere's third edition of *Britannia* and Salway's *Roman Britain* engaged with quite a different conception of the global 'Roman' culture of the empire.[13] That is not to say that there was an absence of any concept, however poorly articulated it may have been.

A striking feature of the *Romanization of Britain* is that it is a book that in its first chapter drew on the ideas of ancient historians, in most cases Moses Finley and his students, to create an overview of the Roman economy and relate this field to that of Roman imperialism.[14] The emphasis on acculturation as a two-way process causes Millett's conception of Roman imperial rule to be decentralised and at a low level of control, with the consequence that the material gain to Rome was also relatively low. The empire was, therefore, 'a federation of diverse peoples under Rome, rather than a monolithic and uniformly centralized block'.[15] This viewpoint shapes the argument, so that the discussion of the import of Roman goods into pre-Roman Iron Age Britain is rejected as a tool for the social leaders of southeast Britain to maintain power through the mono-polisation of the use of exotic imports and other raw materials. This is not argued on the grounds of the type of material evidence but on that of the documented scale of supply: 'a highly exploitative economic network is inappropriate in the Roman empire'.[16] This coincides with some of the nuances associated with globalisation, and it is an attempt to read Roman culture as a fractured whole that is further disjointed via the consideration of gender and the migration of 40,000 soldiers that altered the gender ratio in society.[17] The picture of Roman Britain presented is a pattern of inconsistent cultures reacting to the new presence of Rome or, if not a presence, a new relationship to an established concept of Rome as a 'global' concept.

In summary, *The Romanization of Britain* is a book with a vision driven by a 'global' conception of the Roman empire derived from the model-building of ancient historians active in the 1970s and 1980s. There is, however, an important adjustment. The *civitates* of Britain may have had some public buildings, but this did not mean that the late pre-Roman Iron Age economy was necessarily developed or transformed by the conquest by Rome.[18] The local (or archaeological, as it is expressed in terms of material culture) is set in contrast to the global and ancient historical (focused, as it was, on larger scale and *longue durée*). The economy of Roman Britain appeared embedded in the pre-conquest social system, but stimulated by the global presence of taxation,[19] and adoption of Roman forms of elite competition via office holding.[20] This opposition generated a number of different regional outcomes. Some developments would be classified as 'entirely indigenous', 'stimulated by passive encouragement' or failed as 'Roman presence was socially disruptive'.[21]

Ultimately, it is the connection to a 'Rome' that is in question in this discussion – that 'Rome' might be expressed by a state institution such as the army or taxation, but also a complex body of global concepts such as city, toga or forum that underpins the landscape of 'Romanisation'. It is at points of connection that the global concepts of 'Romanness' can be seen to have been put into practice.[22] Those points of connection are where space–time compression occurs and it is here that the global becomes local. Interestingly, it is in the discussion of the development of towns in Britain that Tacitus in the *Agricola* (19–21) identifies the toga, Latin, *fora*, temples, baths, porticoes and dinners as the transpatial signifiers of Roman culture.[23] We might even suggest that urbanism is dependent on these signifiers to create something that is globally recognised as Roman, and it is with the spread of urbanisation to the countryside (villas, mosaics, wall painting, pottery distribution) that we can begin to consider the towns as nodes of cultural change for a wider region.[24] The extent of variation in this town-led cultural change, over centuries rather than decades, is yet to be fully established. This important point of the local–global relationship underpinning *The Romanization of Britain* simply got lost in the debate that followed about resistance and imperialism.[25]

BETWEEN THE GLOBAL AND THE LOCAL: ROME AS A WORLD EMPIRE

Richard Hingley was to become a key critic of Millett's *The Romanization of Britain*, and, perhaps not surprisingly, published a strong critique of globalisation in the first decade of the twenty-first century.[26] However, in an earlier work he developed a conception of the relationship between the global Roman empire and its inhabitants locally that effectively conceived of the global and the local interplay in a model of an administered economy.[27] Like Millett, he drew on Keith Hopkins' model of taxation and trade in the Roman empire combined with Immanuel Wallerstein's world systems analysis of the modern world.[28] At the heart of this argument was the idea that the *civitates* of the province and other administrative infrastructures were an imposed system that lay over the top of the existing Iron Age societies. The infrastructure connected the global to local societies to exploit resources in the form of taxation. At a local level, towns administered (collected) the tax from the countryside and controlled inter-regional trade. The economic transactions associated with trade were seen as both unequal and monopolistic, as trade and the monetary economy were centred on the towns.[29] Although the countryside is seen in this model to be subsistence based, money was needed for the conversion of produce into tax and for the purchase of luxuries.[30] Connectivity is located in the model through an imposed infrastructure focused on London (Londinium) and the southeast that created a new geography of exploitation or economic domination.[31] Fundamental to the explanation of the relation between any place (the local) and the Roman empire (the global) was the mediating role of the infrastructure of the Roman state. Where the state was connected, the global was present – where it was disconnected, it was absent.

With an approach proposing a role reversal between the local and the global, Greg Woolf published a paper discussing the validity of using world systems analysis as a framework for the study of the Roman empire.[32] This article revealed how an infrastructure of empire could integrate elite cultures to create a series of 'independent mini-systems' that had been taken over and incorporated by the centre – Rome. There is a primacy given in this piece of analysis to the political, but Woolf departs from Wallerstein's conception of the global empire with an account of the texture of interconnectedness in the Roman empire that varied from those who were 'separated and segregated' to others who were unified and integrated. This implies also that although we may find examples of global products (e.g. amphorae), their presence will be found to be greater at points of integration than at points of separation. These observations on the relationship of the local to the global have implications for the study of the evidence that is discussed below. The long distances over which trade could take place point to a level of time–space compression and, indeed, it could be argued that through objects and consumption, rather than economics, a concept of the global could have been developed from local action. The universal nature of the 'Roman' (i.e. as identified by a modern archaeologist looking at objects, images, plans or built forms) could be conceived of as an aesthetic of signification. This is to shift the debate away from the economic and the political which, at least in modernity, is fundamental to many articulations of globalisation theory. Here there is a view to locating the global within the realm of the everyday or at the level of the artefact.[33]

THE DISTRIBUTION OF A GLOBAL PHENOMENON: AGE IN EPITAPHS IN THE WESTERN MEDITERRANEAN

The wealth of artefacts available from the Roman period allows for the possibility of a full mapping of the uptake of particular cultural practices. Within the category of artefacts, we would include for example simple epitaphs that are seemingly global phenomena in the Roman empire (or at least the West). The carving of Latin letters and use of Roman numbers to record age at death provide a record of the place of burial and commemorate the identity of the deceased. There are vast numbers of epitaphs from the Roman west and it is therefore possible to analyse the use of a universal or global system of writing in the context of local commemorative practices. We selected the use of age in epitaphs as a global practice to analyse how it varied at a regional level. Our sample consisted of 24,000 epitaphs that mention the dedicatee's age at death.[34] It follows that if we are looking at a global phenomenon (the use of age in epitaphs), we can relate its variation to patterns of connectivity and begin to see how the 'global' was taken up at a local level.

Commemoration of age at death does not occur on all epitaphs, and thus when studied is an index of the uptake of this phenomenon across the Latin west. The use of numbers is the thing to focus on here, rather than a whole series of biases, that included age rounding to the Roman numerals ending in V and X, which cause the pattern of commemorative practice to have little relationship to the actual demography of any region of the Roman empire.[35] To minimise the basic bias and smooth out the abruptness of age-rounding variation, we have utilised age groups (children, young adults, mid-life and the elderly). Another notable bias is represented by the gender ratio of commemorated males and females (c. 60% males: c. 40% females). To allow for a more effective comparison between males and females commemorated, we have calculated the percentage within each category of the total males and total females to establish the patterns of age of commemoration. In theory, at least, the use of chronological age could, like other numeric systems (e.g. coinage or measurement of distance in miles), transfer from its point of production to other parts of the Roman empire. The fact that the use of chronological age is a more fuzzy concept than, for example, the measurement of distance means that it has a greater analytical value as an indicator of cultural practice. Therefore, the dataset can be evaluated to establish whether the patterns for males were so significantly distinct to suggest that gender may have been constructed in a very different way in Italy from the provinces, or in a manner that was convergent.

The overall pattern for Italy, divided into the age groups children (0–15 years), younger adults (16–30 years), adults in mid-life (31–60 years) and the elderly (61 years and over), shows a strong emphasis on the commemoration of the younger age groups over the elderly (Fig. 5.1). Given the thinking of demographers on the subject, this is a pattern of commemoration that is (in part at least) convergent with the pattern we expect of the

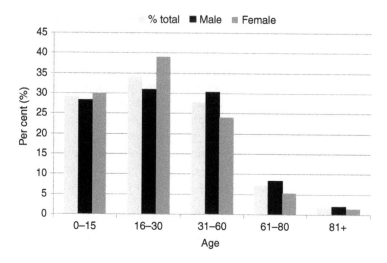

Figure 5.1: Age commemoration in epitaphs: Italy.

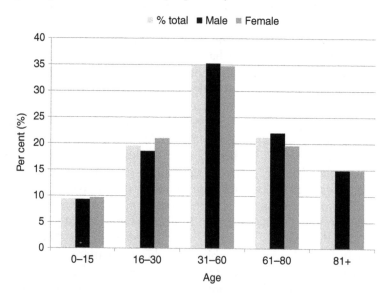

Figure 5.2: Age commemoration in epitaphs: Numidia.

Italian population of antiquity.[36] It is also notable that there is no strong variation in the pattern between genders according to age, except that younger females have a higher rate of commemoration than younger males.

The total and absolute contrast between the pattern of commemoration found in Numidia (Fig. 5.2) and that found in Italy (Fig. 5.1) is staggering.

The early stages of the human life course are commemorated rarely in the former, whereas those of mid-life dominate with a greater emphasis on commemoration of the elderly. This pattern found in Numidia is repeated across the North African provinces, and slightly more moderately in Baetica. The only province that begins to resemble the patterns of age commemoration found in Italy is Gallia Narbonensis.

The differences in patterns of commemoration set out here can be drilled down into, producing a series of explanations.[37] The family structure in Italy was fundamentally forward looking, with the commemoration of deceased children forming a preoccupation, whereas in Numidia the family was focused on the commemoration of parents and the past. The overall pattern found in Numidia has no convergence with that of Italy and is an indicator of a disjuncture between the cultures of the two connected regions of the Roman empire. This divergence, however, does not indicate that we cannot identify aspects of globalisation – both regions are utilising Latin formulae engraved on stone to commemorate the dead. The particular pattern found in Numidia is, in fact, convergent with the use of age in epitaphs by soldiers and appears to suggest that the military, as an institution, was the means of dissemination of the practice of representing age at death on both male and female epitaphs.[38] As a result, it is not geographical connectivity (the Mediterranean) that promoted a global concept of the use of age in epitaphs. Instead it was the connection with the global institution – the Roman army – that resulted in the dissemination of this particular practice. Interestingly, in Italy, the pattern produced is unlike that of either the North African provinces or the military, which suggests the need to identify other factors, including a different cultural formation, for the peninsula. This causes Italy, the heart of the empire, to be defined as culturally quite different to the provinces and places into question any process by which the culture of Italy was replicated in the provinces (that underpins concepts of acculturation/ Romanisation). Hence, globalisation needs to be conceived as a decentred cultural discourse in which the concept of Romanness exists as much in the imagination, and has little to do with the tangible or empirical mapping of cultures onto one another.[39] In other words, Rome is an unseen centre that is imagined to exist in a way that may conform to a localised conception of the manifestation of the global conception of Romanness.

LOCAL SYMBOLS OF A GLOBAL CULTURE: PUBLIC MONUMENTS

Building on the observations on the use of age at death in epitaphs, we looked for another sample to verify whether such a pattern could be located in a quite different class of material evidence. As a result, a similar statistical approach was applied to the artefact that can be considered central to discussions of Roman culture and globalisation – the city and its monuments. However, while a city building a new monument, say an amphitheatre, was engaging with a global phenomenon, we cannot say that anywhere without an amphitheatre was unengaged with global phenomena.

There were several forms of monuments, effectively high-cost manifestations of the global culture of the Roman empire, in which investment was possible. The priorities of that choice varied a little from region to region, and make a good comparison to the regional variation in the adoption of age commemoration discussed above. Figures from Hèlene Jouffroy's catalogues of monuments found in Italy and North Africa are expressed as raw data – i.e. the number of monuments of what type at what time.[40] If we look at the production of monuments within the cities of Roman Africa and Italy as the object of analysis, we can compare the two patterns once the figures for each monument type are expressed as a percentage of the total in each region. The patterns are divided broadly by century of construction to facilitate a sample sufficiently large to make the comparison work.

Figures 5.3–5.5 present patterns over three centuries of construction that display a very limited variation through time. It could be said that the

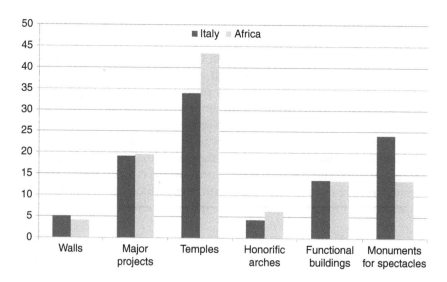

Figure 5.3: Numbers of public buildings and monuments constructed in Italy and Africa in the first century AD.

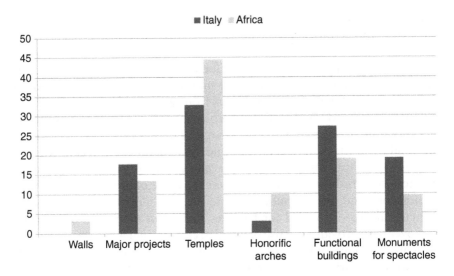

Figure 5.4: Numbers of public buildings and monuments constructed in Italy and Africa in the second century AD.

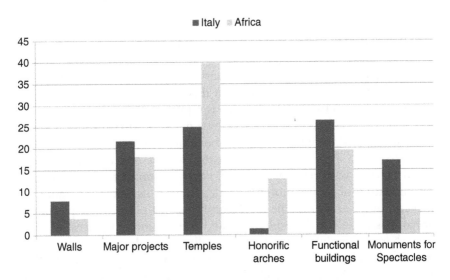

Figure 5.5: Numbers of public buildings and monuments constructed in Italy and Africa in the third century AD.

two urban systems produced monuments in the same way across the three centuries of the Roman empire. In Africa, there was a much greater emphasis on temple building and the construction of honorific arches, whereas in Italy there was a greater focus on the building/restoration of theatres and amphitheatres. There is a shift towards a greater proliferation of functional buildings (including baths) from the second century. However, we might be able to say that the two urban systems do produce monuments in a very similar way and with little change at the regional level. Obviously, the building of one monument in any one city had a very significant effect on that city, but little impact on the overall system. What these two urban systems do is produce monuments. There is a sense of predictability to these monuments and they would seem to be the global manifestation of Roman culture – provided for by elites that spent money on monuments that over time provided a sense of a global culture, which we can also locate in Aelius Aristides' oration, *On Rome* (Or.26).[41] This does not mean there was no local variation; the global concept was mediated in the context of the place of monumentalisation to produce a pattern that was divergent in Africa to that of Italy. In the long term, the patterns do not converge but continue to reproduce their divergence in the same way over time.

CONNECTIVITY AND TIME–SPACE COMPRESSION

The very mediation of monumentalisation, as well as any other Roman cultural practice spreading throughout this global empire, brings us to the question of connectivity (whether this is represented by the Mediterranean and changes in sailing technology or by a network of roads and improved traction animals), in which we should explore the presence of time–space compression.[42] Time–space compression was a concept developed by David Harvey with reference to post-1970s postmodernity within which the circulation of capital (goods) speeded up and disrupted the significance of place. In other words, the local significance of place was replaced by a global existence, which resulted in the better-connected places increasing their share of mobile capital (thus traditional industrial cities, such as Detroit, shrank).[43] In time–space compression, it is the 'space of flows' that alters the 'fixity of place'. For the Roman empire, we contend that there is a sense by which places on a named highway or at a coastal location had a greater level of connectivity than those at a distance from such routeways across the empire. These were places that were travelled through, whereas Reate in the Sabina would be recalled as a place of rusticity[44] – these cities on roads and sea routes were seen as locations of Romanness and potential places to stop at as a person planned their travel – a process that involved the linking of time taken to travel to the measurement of distance on the major roads by milestones. There is a sense by which those places that lay on routes that were measured with milestones were the locations at which time–space compression might occur, for the very reason that these were locations of measured distance – whereas much of the empire lay outside the remit of travel found for example in the Antonine Itineraries. There is a certain predictability of travel by land, in contrast for example with the unpredictability of travel by sea – as seen in the journey of St. Paul across the Mediterranean. That ability to predict time taken to travel from a to b is a measurement that we simply call speed and was a concept disseminated through the measurement of distance by milestones on the major roads.[45] A precursor to time–space compression is the measurement of space from which speed can be calculated, and only then can journey time become predictable. Our familiarity with the temporal speed of journeys causes us to underestimate the impact of the dissemination of measured distance in the Roman empire – perhaps the equivalent in importance to, say, the development of clock time for factory work in the nineteenth century. Interestingly, the speed of a journey could be increased through the improvement of the road surface, as made clear in Statius's poem 'Via Domitiana' (*Silvae* 4.3). The result was a time–space compression (or speeding up) for a journey from one day to just two hours (*Silvae* 4.3.36–9).[46] Paved roads of this type were also associated with the exceptionally fast journeys of antiquity: 100 miles per day for four days in a row, whereas the fastest journey in the second century BC was recorded at fifty-eight miles per day for four days in a row.[47] Messengers travelling fifty to eighty miles per day may have been the norm, whereas travel for others at a more leisurely pace can be recorded on paved roads at thirty-five miles per day.[48] The friction of distance is reduced as time–space compression occurs. This affects not only the traveller or transporter of goods, but also allows the possibility of the transmission of ideas, perhaps seen in the distribution of new innovative building types such as theatres across the West within a century of the construction of the theatres of Pompey, Balbus and Marcellus in Rome, but at the same time looking to their Greek origins in the experience of Pompey gazing at the theatre in Mytilene.[49] The patterns of such distributions reveal that time–space compression was not a universal experienced by all, but subject to patterns of connectivity.[50]

Taking our cue from Peregrine Horden and Nicholas Purcell's *Corrupting Sea*, we might expect that coastal cities were more likely to build monuments than non-coastal cities in Italy, using Hélène Jouffroy's

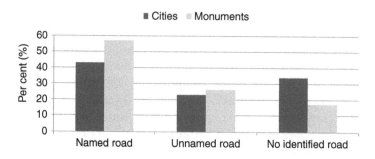

Figure 5.6: Monument construction in relation to city location on roads.

catalogues of inscriptions and monuments.[51] The analysis showed that 20% of all cities in Italy lay on the coast and that 22% of all public monuments were constructed in these cities (see fig. 5.6). There would seem to be a convergent pattern that did not identify a coastal location as preferential for the building of public monuments over the building of cities inland. What was shaping the distribution pattern of public monuments was something quite different, the position of cities in relation to land transportation – most notably major long-distance roads that were named (e.g. Via Flaminia). Cities on these major roads displayed a far greater incidence of monument building than those that were outside the major routes across Italy. It should be noted that these major roads were maintained by the state and can be seen as infrastructure invested in by the state – more often than not paved at an earlier date and with paving that was wider than that found on other roads.[52]

In Italy, at a macro level, the materiality of Romanness was disseminated more effectively in the cities that were located on the major roads, associated with infrastructure and maintained by the Roman state. Hence, what we are seeing here is that the state as an institution facilitated the spread of a Roman culture expressed in the format of monument building in those locations that were integrated by the state's infrastructure and experienced a degree of time–space compression.

There is an implication for this observed pattern in the evidence. It is that cities on roads, rather than at ports, have a greater incidence of monument building. This implies that land transport was a greater facilitator of cultural integration than the phenomenon of sea transportation.[53] It returns us to Richard Hingley's ideas about Roman Britain, in which Iron Age society was overwritten by a system of road transportation to create an administrative or, even, an imperialist geography.[54] The convergence (between the building of long-distance roads by the state in Italy and monument building in cities on those roads at a greater incidence) highlights the interrelationship between the global (movement of people and goods) and the direction of the global through cities that engaged locally and built monuments to be seen by travellers. The monuments allow a traveller to be familiar with the form of urbanism, because these are structures that were universal and engaged with a series of global ideas and imagery – not dissimilar to the ideas and imagery that can be read on Roman coins. What is relevant to the discussion is not so much the technological speed of movement in space–time compression, the key feature associated with the development of a global culture in modern history,[55] but the symbolic familiarity of Rome's global culture of cities. Travel time would have been reduced on major roads, but, more importantly, travel featured a not unfamiliar set of buildings and images – even in towns not yet experienced.[56] Travel became very different outside of the geographical space associated with the connected empire – it became effectively barbarian and with a different set of symbols (that can be found to be set out in Tacitus's *Germania*). Interestingly, disconnection and non-engagement with urbanism can be seen to have had symbolic as opposed to economic value and it is perhaps in the realms of the symbolic and the aesthetic, as opposed to the temporal (speed of travel or temporalities of economic development) and economic, in which we may locate globalisation or, at least, the intersection of the global with the local in the Roman empire.

The geographical thinking and conception of Rome's empire can be found in the Antonine Itineraries that connect places to Rome, and is calibrated through measured distance, which could have been cross-referenced locally to milestones.[57] Movement through space was the underpinning principle and created a linear network overlying a global surface, on which cities were positioned and broke up or punctuated movement on a journey across geographical space. The distance between cities varied and was lower in Italy than in the provinces, perhaps creating a subjective experience to index the level of development. Obviously, the closer spacing of cities would have caused the incidence of magistrates and the intensification of government to increase over a geographical area – since all cities had similar government forms. The absence or wide spacing of cities stretched the space of government thinly across space. What this implies is that, where cities were closely spaced, the distance between citizens and the state (devolved to the level of the city) was reduced or even compressed. Combined with a major named road, provided and maintained by the state, the relationship of these cities to the global phenomenon of the Roman state was different to that of cities in the provinces. However, we should note that the Roman state invested in transport infrastructure in the provinces, as well as in Italy, to replicate a geographical form that included key transport nodes such as Lyon (Lugdunum), Paris (Lutetia Parisiorum) and London (Londinium). Underpinning the Roman empire as a global entity was an infrastructure of communication onto which cities were built with monuments that symbolically represented ideas and concepts of Romanness, which had been developed at a distance in time and space from their location of display. This space–time compression is a feature of globalisation, but, perhaps at the same time, it is not the 'cultural change' searched for in the discussion of Romanisation of the 1990s, nor the type of time–space compression identified in the discussion of globalisation in the modern world. Yet, we should be clear, it is a form of time–space compression and it allows Roman archaeology to bring these forms of time–space compression into the discourse of globalisation, alongside the technology-driven changes in speed of travel.

LOCALLY ON THE FRONTIER, BUT CULTURALLY ON THE BAY OF NAPLES

So far the discussion has focused on the city and on regional distribution patterns that reveal the geographical position of a city, which in terms of connectivity altered the nature of the relationship between a place and the form of globalisation that we can locate in the Roman empire. It is now worth evaluating the relationship between seemingly disconnected places that perhaps need to have their connectivity asserted. The case study here focuses on bathing in Flavian forts on Hadrian's Wall and seeks to suggest that there was a global connection between social practice there and developments in architectural form on the Bay of Naples. The argument takes us in a quite different direction to the existing interpretation of cultural practice that has focused on frameworks derived from Romanisation theory.

The ability to bathe and to cleanse the body of dirt would seem to be essential in the context of both Hadrian's Wall and the Bay of Naples, but provides a means also to see the distinctions between settlement forms. Louise Revell examined the nature of military bath-houses in Roman Britain in a short note, establishing a fundamental dichotomy between those in legionary fortresses and those in auxiliary forts.[58] The former, such as Chester (Deva) and Exeter (Isca Dumnoniorum), had much in common with the bath-buildings found in cities across the empire, for example the Stabian Baths at Pompeii, whereas the latter, such as Chesters on Hadrian's Wall, were quite

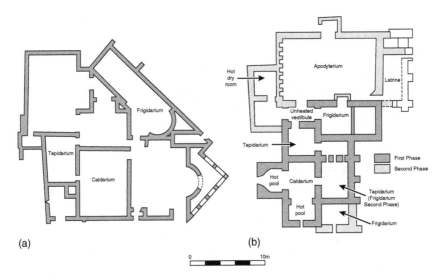

Figure 5.7: Comparison of the bath-house at the Villa of San Marco (Stabiae) (a) and that at Chesters, Hadrian's Wall (b).

different with far less emphasis placed on public space for display and social interaction (see Fig. 5.7). The spaces for bathing for legionaries (i.e. Roman citizens) were similar to those found in Roman cities, whereas those provided for auxiliaries (non-citizens) tended towards the functional need for cleanliness in a Roman manner without the spaces for social interaction that were prominent in baths in cities in Roman Italy. This leads one to suppose that the auxiliary bath-houses are derived from a different building tradition from those provided for legionaries.[59] This is a good, clear explanation. However, the earliest bath-buildings built at auxiliary forts in the Flavian period are architecturally congruent with private bath-buildings preserved by the eruption of Mount Vesuvius in AD 79 in Campania.[60] These private bath-buildings found at villas in Campania were designed for use not just by the owner and his family, but also by others such as guests and visitors.[61] Importantly, bath-house construction is associated with the earliest phase of the fort at Vindolanda, meaning that the structure was an integral element of living in the fort.[62]

Travel and periods of residence outside the comforts of Italy was an expected experience of the Roman elite and needs to be written into our conception of globalisation within the Roman empire. The implications in terms of agency need to be taken on board here, as the Roman elite could literally command human resources to enable construction of facilities ensuring that, wherever they were, their way of life was maintained. In contrast, those they commanded, in this case Batavians, may not have commanded sufficient resources to, or simply did not see the advantage of, constructing a bath-house of such a size that all in the fort might utilise – a contrast to the priorities of legionaries, who had access to much larger bath-complexes.[63] The global experience and mobility of the elite commander of auxiliaries may therefore be contrasted with the limited mobility of the Batavian recruit to the Roman army.

THE LOCAL AND THE GLOBAL TOTALS 200%

The discussion in this chapter has focused on the way in which globalisation can be used to interpret a selection of 'typical' features of Roman culture found in Italy and the western provinces: the use of Latin letters and Roman numerals in epitaphs, the construction of public monuments, and bath-buildings on the frontier. The local and the global were reflected upon as these examples were discussed with a focus on how the local intersected with the global. Obviously, the reverse could be stated, as others have done, that the global, such as the achievements of Augustus (the *Res Gestae*) can on inscription in Ankara became a local document.[64] Moreover, recent interest in localism points to the veracity that globalisation was a condition of existence in the Roman empire.[65] Whatever the objections of using globalisation theory, we need to recognise that the development of a concept of empire without end in space and time, the construction of transportation routes – roads, the exportation of forms of local government for cities – city charters, the development of a portable form of finance – gold coins, and elite mobility, all add up to a form of globalisation with a variation that can be defined as the incidence of connectivity.[66] What we hope to have shown in discussion of the case studies is not whether globalisation existed in the same way as it is conceptualised in the modern world, but to utilise globalisation as a heuristic device or model to allow us to reinterpret key features of culture within the Roman empire.[67] In so doing, there is a shift back and forth between the local and the global in a discussion that cannot unpick one from the other.[68] This is, in part, deliberate – since it is too easy to identify the global as alien/negative and dominant Roman culture and the local as the normative/positive and resistant to Roman culture that has underpinned late twentieth-century discourse on Romanisation.

In many ways, the local and the global cannot be separated from one another – they are part of a whole or two parts of a dialectic. Rem Koolhaas and his students at Harvard articulated this point in discourse on architecture and globalisation.[69] Underpinning this analysis by his graduate students was a very simple philosophy, a city is 100% local and 100% global – it is both things at the same time and, hence, must be 200%. This counter-mathematical logic encapsulates and draws on an understanding of the city as a generic form that is both local and global. A commander on Hadrian's Wall knows he is not in Italy (he is in a locality), but seeks to bathe in the manner that he was used to in Italy (he is undertaking a global practice). The less mobile, an archaeo-historical imagined 'local' elite, might engage with global attributes of Roman culture (e.g. Tacitus *Agricola* 19–21) and reproduce elements of it. In so doing, they are local but are acting globally. Discrepant experience, as articulated by David Mattingly, points the way here to the variation of outcomes within the Roman empire, in which we may see a relationship between the local and the global.[70] The use of age in epitaphs is another example as discussed above, where we find quite different patterns locally but an adherence to a set of formulae and commemorative practices that is global. Interestingly, the local may have a greater importance in the current literature produced by archaeologists on the Roman empire. This trend can be traced back to the Romanisation discourse that is present in Martin Millett's volume on this subject in relation to the province of *Britannia*.[71] This is not to deny the importance of forms of material culture that were not shared, but it is to point out that we have yet to understand the patterns of the global or the shared forms of material culture associated with the Roman empire.[72] The shared forms of material culture (or ways of living with objects and architecture) proliferated in locations of greater connectivity to state institutions and state-built infrastructure, particularly those of transportation – roads and low-weight/high-value gold coinage, including the mobility of tax revenues. What is so neat about a theory of 200% (100% local plus 100% global) is that it provides us with the means to resist dichotomies and recognise that contradictory trends are the very substance of the archaeological record of the Roman empire.[73] The stable conception of discretely defined archaeological identities read-off from material culture becomes more difficult and even impossible.[74] Critics of the application of globalisation to Roman material culture have pointed to the differences between modern and ancient, but perhaps underplay the changes to connectivity (as opposed to speed of transport) and opportunities for movement that were present in the Roman empire, when compared with earlier periods, as well as being associated with a proliferation of a 'sameness' in material culture and urban form.[75] The latter is a fundamental aspect of globalisation in any period of history and is deserving of attention.[76] More importantly, to date, material culture has not been incorporated into the discussion of globalisation with the exception of localised case studies.[77] The global, in many ways, can only be defined through digitisation of material evidence in the manner of the case study of epitaphs and age of the deceased discussed above. The data are there, but at present are inaccessible due to the fundamental scale and richness of the body of evidence. Roman archaeologists have an opportunity to make a major contribution to our overall understanding of phenomena relevant to our own human existence in the modern world that are today described by the shorthand – globalisation.[78] The alternative is to continue to produce studies of the local that have little understanding of the global, and an inability to develop a framework for those working on evidence from the Roman empire.

ACKNOWLEDGEMENTS

Both authors thank the reviewers and editors for their comments that have aided the process of articulating what might be said on this subject. Ray Laurence wishes to thank Martin Pitts for reminding him of his views expressed in Laurence (2001a) and the relevance of globalisation to his own subsequent research, as well as for his persistent persuasion to take part in the Exeter workshop that resulted in this chapter.

NOTES

1. Nicolet 1988 provides an overview of the Roman world view, and Dueck (2012, 16–19) on the distinctiveness of Roman geographical thought from that of Greek writers. Our focus here is on globalisation and culture, in contrast to Neville Morley's focus (this volume) on globalisation and economic history.
2. Pitts & Versluys (Chapter 1, this volume) set out the theoretical basis for the application of globalisation theories to antiquity and a context for discussion in this chapter of the relationship between the local and the global contexts within the Roman empire. We do not re-rehearse those arguments here, but acknowledge our debt to their articulation of globalisation theory and its applicability to antiquity.
3. Laurence, Esmonde Cleary & Sears (2011).
4. Ibid., 3, to find further references see index under Romanisation.
5. Ibid., 105–6, derived in part from Williamson (2005, 23).
6. Anheier & Juergensmeyer (2012); Ritzer (2012). For explanation of the 'jargon' of globalisation, these volumes prove their worth – but note entries written by different authors can be quite contradictory in pointing to the

creativity of the current debates in globalisation theories. Compare the earlier Encyclopaedia of Globalization edited by Robertson and & Scholte (2007).

7. It might be observed that this non-engagement or reluctance to engage is not unique to globalisation; it also characterised the late twentieth-century non-engagement between Roman archaeology and postmodernism. In some ways, the current debates on globalisation are an extension of debates within postmodernism in the 1980s and 1990s. Harvey (1996, 14) comments on the matter, in a book on globalisation that has a reference to Rome (ibid., 10).

8. Interestingly, acculturation is omitted from the Wiley-Blackwell encyclopaedia, but included in the Sage encyclopaedia.

9. The relationship of the local to the global is fundamental to the thinking of Henri Lefebvre; see analysis by Soja (1996, 29–32), and it is Lefebvre's thinking particularly in *The Production of Space* that is fundamental to Laurence's earlier work (1994), (1999) and (2007), as well as in Laurence, Esmonde Cleary & Sears (2011). The clearest conception of Lefebvre's work remains Soja (1996) and his development of the concept of thirdspace – the impact of Lefebvre's thinking on Roman archaeology remains quite limited when compared with Foucault, Bourdieu and Giddens, and would appear to be a missed opportunity to engage with the spatiality of Roman culture. Interestingly, Lefebvre's critique of Foucault is concerned with pinpricks on the periphery rather than the global, yet Foucault could emphasise the spatial in some of his work – see Soja (1996, 146–9) for discussion. However, the key to analysing space and the global rests on the work of Lefebvre that has obvious applications for Roman archaeologists and shifts our understanding towards the 'everyday'.

10. See Harvey (1996, 48–57) for a description of the principles of dialectics.

11. Millett (1990a).

12. Millett (1990a, xv).

13. Frere (1978); Salway (1981).

14. Millett (1990a, 2–8). See Pitts (2008) on the relationship of the global to the local in discussion of earlier studies of Roman Britain.

15. Millett (1990a, 8).

16. Millett (1990a, 38).

17. Millett (1990a, 60).

18. Millett (1990a, 65–101).

19. Following the model of Hopkins (1980).

20. Revolving around Hopkins (1983).

21. Millett (1990a, 101).

22. Revell (2009, especially 191–3).

23. Hillier & Hanson (1984, 40–2) define the transpatial as having a 'conceptual relation between local systems' in their delineation of all human social formations exhibiting a 'duality of spatial and transpatial, of local group and category'.

24. Revell (2009, 2) stresses Roman was a 'discourse' based around a shared identity that was 'less absolute' than in the modern world, due to an 'absence of globalising technologies'.

25. See, for example, Webster (2001).
26. e.g. Hingley (1997, 82–6); Hingley (2005). See Naerebout (2006/7) and Prag (2006a) for discussion of Hingley (2005); also Hingley (Chapter 2, this volume).
27. Hingley (1982).
28. Hopkins (1980) for the influential model; discussed further in Pitts and Versluys (Chapter 1, this volume).
29. Hingley (1982, 24–6).
30. Hingley (1982, 26).
31. Hingley (1982, 23).
32. Woolf (1990).
33. e.g. Pitts (Chapter 4, this volume). It may also be seen in the regional use of the Latin language documented by Adams (2007), which begs for an explanatory framework derived from globalisation theory.
34. The full project and dataset is described in Laurence & Trifilò (2011).
35. For example, Duncan-Jones (1990, 79–92).
36. Parkin (1992); Scheidel (2001).
37. The project as a whole is being written up and will be fully published by Laurence & Trifilò in the near future. For now, see Laurence & Trifilò (2011).
38. Laurence & Trifilò (forthcoming).
39. Revell (2009: 2). Soja (1996, 1) fully explores the concept of 'real-and-imagined' in relationship to Los Angeles and seeks to 'encourage you to think differently about the meanings and significance of space and those related concepts that compose and comprise the inherent *spatiality of human life*'. Harvey (1996, 77–95) sets out 'The dialectics of discourse' that can extend Revell (2009) to a wider range of Roman material culture.
40. Jouffroy (1986).
41. For which see Sommer (Chapter 8, this volume).
42. See discussions elsewhere by Pitts & Versluys (Chapter 1, this volume). Note that Morley (Chapter 3, this volume) argues against time–space compression on the basis of travel time by sea, based on analysis of Duncan-Jones (1990, 7–29), but does not fully consider the significance of time–space compression in relation to land transportation. Morley's point of comparison being the last two centuries, perhaps, misses the subtleties of change in the Roman empire associated with the size of draught animals (especially mules) and improvements to road surfaces through paving. The productivity of metals (evidenced by analysis of the Greenland ice core data) in the Roman empire may be an indicator of time–space compression or an alteration in mobility – proof, of course, is elusive in connecting these two phenomena.
43. Harvey (1989; 1996, 242–7) is key to the development of this key concept. For a brief summary of time–space compression see Ritzer (2012 volume 4, 1976–7). See earlier discussion in Laurence (1999, 78–94). Because we focus on time–space compression in land rather than sea transportation – our conclusions are at odds with those of Morley (Chapter 3, this volume) in his analysis of time–space compression.
44. See Dench (1995, 2005).

45. Tomlinson (2009, 2–5) defines speed both as measurement and as a 'matter of cultural value'. Harvey (1996, 207) emphasises that 'time and space are social constructs' and are historically/culturally specific to a particular context.

46. Accepting the probability of literary exaggeration, the discourse on speed is significant in itself as an indicator of the presence of such discussion in the first century AD.

47. Laurence (1999, 81–2) for discussion and references.

48. Ohler (1989, 101); Laurence (1999, 82).

49. Plutarch, *Pompey*, 42; Sear (2006, 48–53); Laurence, Esmonde Cleary & Sears (2011, 238–9).

50. Harvey (1996, 429–30). Urbanisation in the context of globalisation is and was in the Roman empire a pattern of uneven development.

51. Horden & Purcell (2000); Jouffroy (1986). For a discussion of Mediterreanism, see papers in Malkin (2005b) and Harris (2005). Lucy Titmus undertook the number crunching behind these figures for her BA dissertation at the University of Birmingham, and we gratefully acknowledge her willingness to re-crunch the numbers, because new geographical paradigms occurred over the course of the 9 months of supervision.

52. See Laurence (1999) on road construction. For parallels of changes in maritime technology, see papers in Harris (2011).

53. On limitations of the Mediterranean paradigms in relation to religion, see Woolf (2005).

54. Hingley (1982).

55. See discussion by Morley (Chapter 3, this volume).

56. cf. Pitts (Chapter 4, this volume), on the use of 'familiar' and global technologies of consumption associated with *mansiones* in Roman Britain, in contrast to the local ceramics and practices found immediately outside the global space of the *cursus publicus*.

57. Laurence (1999, 2001b).

58. Revell (2007). See De Haan (2010) for further examples of baths found in houses.

59. Revell (2007); Bidwell (2009).

60. Compare examples in Bidwell (2009) with those in Fabbricotti (1976) – for comparison see Figure 5.7 of this chapter.

61. *Tab. Vindol.* II. 292–3 for visits to Vindolanda by an equestrian woman to the commander's wife; Allason-Jones (1999, 41–2).

62. Birley (2001, 11–12).

63. Revell (2007).

64. Cooley (2007).

65. van Dommelen & Terrenato (2007); Whitmarsh (2010a); Woolf (2010). However, the trend towards localism was noted by Witcher (2000, 223).

66. See Gilhus (2008) for exploration of a different range of variables suggesting that globalisation is a concept for historians of antiquity.

67. See Gilhus (2008) for discussion of applicability of globalisation to the Roman empire.

68. What the editors of this volume refer to as 'glocalisation' in their opening chapter.
69. Koolhaas et al. (2001). Ray Laurence had the privilege of being a critic for the Masters in Architecture programme at the Graduate School of Design at Harvard in 2001.
70. See Mattingly (2004, 13–22) for a succinct encapsulation of his thinking on this concept.
71. Millett (1990a). It could be said that the discourse on Romanisation has an implicit relationship to the development within the present of a better understanding of globalisation and its effects on the lives of writers in the last decade of the twentieth century and the first decade of the twenty-first century.
72. See Revell (2009, 2) for application of the globalisation in Roman archaeology that can produce material cultures that are shared and those that are known but not shared and those that remain local. See also Pitts & Versluys (Chapter 1, this volume).
73. Drawing on Witcher (2000, 215–18).
74. See Pitts (2007) for analysis that shows that the relation of objects to a 'cultural' identity can have primacy in archaeological discourse over all other foci of identity studies. See chapters in this volume by Pitts & Versluys (1, 4, 7).
75. Morley (Chapter 3, this volume); Naerebout (2006/7).
76. It is possible that the archaeological contrast between the local and the global takes place without the production of any actual substance or evidential basis.
77. An exception is Pitts (2008).
78. It should be noted that globalisation would seem to be implicit in recent work by Mattingly (2004), Revell (2009) and, perhaps, is even present in Millett (1990a) – in that there is an attempt to relate the local (Britain) to the global (the Roman empire as studied by Finley and Hopkins – see discussion earlier in the chapter).

6

POLYBIUS'S GLOBAL MOMENT AND HUMAN MOBILITY THROUGH ANCIENT ITALY

Elena Isayev

Human mobility, along with circulation of commodities and ideas, is seen as one of the defining features of globalisation today. If Rome was truly globalising, we might expect a sharp increase in such movement following its political and military dominance of the Mediterranean from the second century BC. However, the distribution of people of Italian origin around the Mediterranean prior to the second century BC is difficult to ascertain from the remaining evidence. The overriding perception is that, on the whole, only a small number of Italians chose to venture beyond the shores of the peninsula until the rapid expansion of Roman power in the wake of their victory in the Second Punic War. This setting coincides with, and is perceived as the catalyst for, the *global moment*. In essence, with increasing connectivity not only would we expect a substantial increase in the rate of movement, and especially free movement, in contexts deemed globalised, but also a lower rate in the periods preceding them. It is in part the effects of such an assumption that I would like to test in this chapter, and to suggest that what most people take as the *global moment* may have involved a shift in thinking about the nature of connectivity, as outlined by Pitts and Versluys in Chapter 1 of this volume, rather than a significant break from what had gone before. The following discussion also forms the starting point for an investigation into whether there was a substantial change in the nature of that movement and its agents, which in part may have been what prompted the shift in perception.

As concerns any recognition in our written sources of an increased out-migration of individuals from the Italian peninsula at this point, outside of colonising and military endeavours, it is largely lacking. Ancient authors seem uninterested in the presence of Italians abroad, whether from Magna Graecia or the hinterland, nor are they distinguished from any other foreign group. Their movements did not constitute a migration phenomenon. That does not mean that Italians were not a significant part of the mobile community, but rather that their presence as individuals of Italian, and particularly Roman origin, rarely appeared on the radar, and en masse only in special circumstances. One such incident that drew the attention of ancient commentators occurred in the first century BC, when Mithridates ordered the authorities of cities in Asia Minor to massacre their Roman and Italian residents, resulting in the death of 80,000 people, according to some reports.[1] For historians of migration it is not just the cruelty of such an act that is shocking but the figure itself. As we will see below, our evidence, primarily from inscriptions of the second century BC onward, gives no indication that such a high number of foreigners from Italy had taken up residence in this corner of the Mediterranean.

The episode of the massacre in 88 BC, and the epigraphic evidence in the eastern Mediterranean (considered below), give rise to two key questions concerning mobility from Italy: (1) Is the second century BC the beginning of Italian emigration? (2) If not, is there evidence for an earlier more persistent presence of Italian settlers abroad that stretches back centuries? The pressure to answer the first question in the affirmative comes partly from the identification of the second century BC as the *global moment* for the Mediterranean. Such a reading of the period is not simply made by current scholars, who see it in conjunction with the expansion of Roman power, but also by those who were there to witness the transformations. Most notably Polybius, observing his contemporary world from his perch in Rome, noted in the *Histories* that from his time on, previously distinct local historic trends were intertwined and all history became an organic whole, a universal history based around Roman hegemony.[2] While the passage raises the possibility of something that comes near to contemporary global consciousness – a criterion of some definitions of globalisation,[3] the motivations of Polybius in presenting Rome's rise as coinciding with, or even being responsible for, globalness can be questioned.[4] Not least because Herodotus too presented the Persian Wars as just such a shift, when previously separate histories were intertwined.

The ancient historian Polybius, in much the same way as our own generation, labelled what he was witnessing as an evolutionary moment. Even if not defining it as *globalisation*, he stressed that it was a break from the past and a move from separate entities into a large interconnected whole. The fact that he perceived it as such is interesting in itself, but can we trust this identification which implies that what had existed before was very different? Horden and Purcell's *Corrupting Sea* and numerous other studies have successfully shown the intensely interconnected nature of the

Mediterranean throughout the last millennium BC. Hence, the identity of a *global moment* only towards the end of the millennium cannot be wholly accurate, and Versluys's punctuation of connectivity section highlights precisely this point.[5] As concerns the second century BC specifically, while Versluys is right in indicating that archaeological findings, especially shipwreck data, suggest a substantial increased connectivity between the third and first centuries BC,[6] more appropriate is his earlier point that it is intensification that we are dealing with, and a strengthening of certain vectors of the network, rather than an increase as such. As concerns Italy, it would also be difficult to believe that Italian communities, and especially Rome, were unique in the Mediterranean by remaining largely static until this point, although that is the image of Rome that Polybius puts forward. It is one of the aims of this chapter to make explicit the fragility of any historic moment identified as *global*, or rather the problematic implication that the periods before it were not. The question, which perhaps this volume as a whole attempts to answer is: when is connectivity perceived as globalisation?[7]

MIGRATION AND MOBILITY

Globalisation is one volatile term, *migration* is another, which is why mobility is a more preferable neutral expression. The difficulty of applying *migration* to the ancient context becomes evident when we consider the history of how the concept came into being in American English, and the way it is used in such key works as Manning's *Migration in World History*.[8] Our current usage of *migrate* and its derivatives, meaning to move *across* an international border or boundary, in a *permanent* way with the purpose of *residence*, is very recent, with roots in the eighteenth-century context of North America.[9] The novelty of its use was noted at the time by the philologist John Pickering, who included the terms *to immigrate*, *immigration* and *immigrant* as neologisms in his 1816 work, *A Vocabulary or Collection of Words and Phrases Which Have Been Supposed to Be Peculiar to the United States of America*.[10] By 1828 the new definition appeared in Webster's *American Dictionary of the English Language*: 'Migrate – To pass or remove from one country or from one state to another, with a view to permanent residence, or residence of some continuance'.[11] The result was that space, time and purpose became fundamental characteristics of migration. This new construction of migration, with a focus on permanent residence, encouraged a fear of displacement and overcrowding by new arrivals into America at the time.[12] The reality of cyclical or circular mobility was ignored once migration came to be defined more narrowly, as a one-way relocation, moving along a single trajectory. It fuelled a particular view of the foreigner as threatening, and hence also a protectionist migration policy by autonomous states, a policy which has been projected back into history as the norm.[13]

Such a definition of migration would not have been possible in a world prior to the Treaty or Peace of Westphalia of 1648. It created sovereign states with territorial integrity, and hence the notion of an international border, which could, or could no longer, be crossed.[14] Both the idea of a territorial state border, as opposed to a particular status or state membership, and also the sense of a permanent residential relocation, as distinct from the enduring nature of one's birthplace, are therefore not suitable for the earlier historical contexts. Human mobility in the ancient world is more ephemeral, without the same interest in physical border crossings, and it is therefore difficult to answer directly questions such as: Who migrates? How many? For how long? How far? And into what state? In part this is because such questions assume that migration is an isolated identifiable phenomenon which has a beginning and an end, and that the move is in one direction only. The lack of such one-way trajectories makes it difficult to capture the extent of emigration or immigration in the ancient context, but we can get the sense of the rate of mobility which appears to have been high throughout the last millennium BC.

THE 88 BC MASSACRE OF ITALIANS IN ASIA MINOR

On a pre-determined day in 88 BC, the residents of some cities in Asia Minor responded to Mithridates' command and murdered the *Rhômaioi* – the Romans and Italians, who lived among them.[15] Appian, writing some two centuries later, provides a gruelling narrative of women and children being torn away from their refuge at sacred sanctuaries, only to be massacred with the rest.[16] The total number of those killed was substantial.[17] Ancient authors writing in a period closer to the events, Valerius Maximus and Memnon of Heraclea Pontica, both record 80,000 deaths.[18] Plutarch goes even further and almost doubles the figure to 150,000.[19] Can we believe such high numbers?[20] Were there even 80,000 *Rhômaioi* available for execution in the early first century BC in this part of the eastern Mediterranean? The figures had to be believable on some level, but even if they were to be reduced by a multiple of ten or even one hundred for this episode, the total still alludes to the magnitude of Italians overseas, easily numbering in the thousands if not tens of thousands.

These Italians were dispersed across numerous cities, they were not in Asia Minor as part of any Roman state-initiated mass resettlement project. They came as individuals for a variety of reasons and over a long period of time, stretching back at least two generations. These types of private or independent movements leave little trace in the archaeological record, and hence those who moved are almost invisible. Inscriptions provide the most direct evidence of their presence overseas, but they too have limitations. Iasos, for example, a prosperous coastal town, has a particularly well-preserved epigraphic record of foreigners in the second century BC.[21] The eighty inscriptions mentioning foreigners reveal that they arrived from forty different locations, including sites as far away as Scythia, Sicily and Jerusalem (Hierosolyma).[22] Iasos was a cosmopolitan hub where no single alien group appears to have dominated. No Italians are recorded as part of this mixed community until the first century BC. This is not surprising, as the total number of inscriptions mentioning inhabitants with Italian origins in Asia Minor, prior to the massacre of 88 BC, is little more than a handful. In part this may be due to the writing habits among communities in Italy. For the whole of the peninsula the total number of Latin inscriptions known from the third century BC is some 600, of which only about 146 are from the city of Rome.[23] In the following two centuries the total Italian figure rises to over three thousand, and most of these date to the final 160 years,[24] precisely the point at which Italians overseas become epigraphically more visible. We do know of a substantial community of Italians in Delos already from the third century BC, and a sprinkling of inscriptions make reference to Italian craftsmen who were scattered around the Mediterranean. But even with this increase spurred on by the changing epigraphic habit, the numbers of settlers from Italy who are attested directly are in the hundreds, not tens of thousands.

Studies focusing on the epigraphic evidence for the spread of Italians in the Greek world, such as that of Müller and Hasenohr, confront some of the constraints of this type of material. In particular they note the difficulties in establishing the provenance of individuals through the record of names alone. Members of a family carrying a *gens* name may have moved between places within a lifetime and over several generations. For example, the successful family of *negotiatores*, the Castricii, could have originated from Campania, but throughout the second and first centuries BC they are mainly known to us from their activities in Boeotia and Delos.[25] The earliest record of their name appears overseas, and only later in Italy, where they may have moved to once such ports as Puteoli became major trading hubs.[26] Could we not see them then as Boeotians or Delians coming as foreigners to Italy? How long the label persisted would in large part depend on what incentives were in place to keep it, such as Roman citizenship that allowed access to privileges and networks, although perhaps not in Asia Minor in 88 BC. The characteristic cyclical nature of individual mobility that conveyed people around the Mediterranean in search of opportunities may have deposited them in a place only fleetingly or for the remainder of their lifetime. In capturing their presence on records, whether of death, patronage, honours or memberships, we are left with a static snapshot of a small element of one mobile community. As already noted, the material does not provide evidence of immigration or emigration trends, since such single trajectory movements from point A to B are difficult to trace in the ancient evidence. For these reasons it is not surprising that we hear little of the Italians who met their fate under the hands of Mithridates. Beyond the evidence of epigraphy, other forms of material culture, while excellent for connectivity, tracking the movement of goods and spread of knowledge, are less suitable for tracking migratory trends of specific communities for contexts in which the mobile are integrated into existing settlements, the net migration is zero and the form of mobility is cyclical.

MOBILITY BEFORE THE GLOBAL MOMENT

To get a sense of the nature and rates of human mobility through Italy in the period prior to the second century BC we rely heavily on the material evidence. Archaeological remains can show us moments of creation and growth of a site and its collapse in larger networks. Within Italy itself these have been used to consider the process of colonisation, or the formation of emporia, in the early part of the first millennium BC, with a focus on connectivity and the influx of people into the peninsula. One of the best known sites, often presented as the earliest Greek settlement in Italy, is Pithekoussai, which was situated not on the mainland but on the island of Ischia just off the Campanian coast. Its situation is particularly useful for investigating early circulation of goods and people, which has also been used to question whether colonisation is a relevant term for the processes occurring in this early period.[27] At the beginning of the eighth century BC, the site of Pithekoussai was probably a centre for exchange, an island emporion that linked the maritime traders with the producers of metals on mainland Italy. From the material objects at the site, which have multiple provenances representing a variety of cultural trends, it is clear that there were diverse communities who participated in its creation, including those 'indigenous' to the island, the Phoenicians and the Greeks. The population mix was not the result of any single state programme but was due to the opportunities at this particular node of the ancient Mediterranean network. For it to have been successful, which it was, with a rapid gathering of a population estimated at some 5–10,000 at its height, we must imagine a context where there is constant high mobility of groups and individuals with wide knowledge, who are looking for opportunities. A site offering considerable potential encourages individuals to pause there for a significant amount of time to create a substantial settlement, or increase an existing one. Pithekoussai is one example of a site, the populating of which could only have been the result of an environment that was intensely interconnected.

This perspective from the archaeological material does not sit comfortably with the myths of early migrations narrated by later historians, which include scenarios of mass influx of ethnic groups into new lands as a result of land hunger, leading to takeover and expulsion of local populations. The Gauls appear in various narratives, such as that of Dionysius of Halicarnassus,[28] as the perpetrators who force out indigenous inhabitants and Etruscans from the north of Italy. However, the archaeological evidence from the sites around the Po valley shows ongoing contact between these groups over centuries. In the Veneto and in Liguria, archaeological evidence points to the presence of these groups within Italic settlements visible already from the seventh century BC.[29] The scenario of the threat of a mobile barbarian incomer, taking over civilised sedentary communities, is a literary trope that suits the perspective of individuals based in densely populated urban environments, or territorial states. My point here is not to negate the violence that was exercised by one group over another, often culminating in the expulsion of local communities or their enslavement. Polybius's *Histories* are full of such episodes. Rather, it is to question the scarcity of land as the catalyst for takeover of communities, and the scenario of en masse migrations as a key factor. The long-term study of Italy carried out by Lo Cascio and Malanima, even taking into account reservations about the difference in opinion of the low and high count of the Italian population in the period,[30] shows that for two millennia the peninsula sustained a population fluctuating between seven and sixteen million until the industrial period.[31] Population growth rates fluctuated but did not reach such high proportions as to outgrow the resource base. Demographic studies show that if there was a migration 'crisis' in the ancient context it was due to emigration or out-migration and not overpopulation. The difficulty was trying to keep people in one place. Italy was most likely underpopulated not overpopulated.[32] Such urban environments as Rome, although appearing crowded, needed an ongoing influx of people to sustain themselves.[33] It is this influx into both Rome and Italy that most of our literary evidence focuses on for the period before empire. The problem is that except for military ventures, we have very little evidence in the literary texts for Italians at sites outside of Italy before the second century BC, and as we saw at the start of the chapter, they are also largely invisible in the material record as individual foreign settlers. They are, however, visible as being active players in the network of connectivity that animated the Mediterranean.

PLAUTUS, FOREIGNERS AND INSTRUMENTS OF CONNECTIVITY

One piece of material evidence that attests to the mobility of individuals from Italy is the small and rare object known as the *tessera hospitalis*, or *symbolum*. It could be in a myriad of shapes and designs, such as a fish, a boar or a lion, and made out of a variety of materials, including ivory and metal. It consisted of two parts, each of which was kept by the parties whose names it recorded. We are fortunate to have surviving examples of *tesserae* from Italy and from other parts of the Mediterranean (Fig. 6.1). One half of

Figure 6.1: *Tessera Hospitalis*, ivory boar *Tessera* found in a cemetery at Carthage. The inscription, in Etruscan, is as follows: *Mi puinel karthazie els q[–]na* (I (am) Puinel from Carthage ...). Drawn by Antonio Montesanti after E. Peruzzi, *Origini di Roma: La Famiglia*, vol. 1, Florence: Valmartina 1970, Tav. I and Tav. II.

such an ivory plaque, carved in the shape of a boar, proclaims in Etruscan: *Mi puinel karthazie els q[-]na*; 'I (am) Puinel from Carthage ...'.[34] This *tessera*, found in a cemetery in Carthage dating from the sixth century BC, is a testament of a link between a Carthaginian and his Etruscan speaking guest-friend. It could also be used as proof of identity at a reunion years or decades later. The hospitality to which these objects attested stretched across vast distances and over generations.

This instrument of connectivity appears in the earliest extant Latin texts of the late third – early second century BC. The characters in Plautus's comedy *Poenulus* exhibit how such a device may have been used and the forms of mobility implied by its very existence.[35] The Carthaginian protagonist of the comedy, Hanno, having travelled around the Mediterranean in search of his stolen daughters, lands in Calydon. He proceeds to the house of his guest-friend, who unbeknownst to him is dead, and is instead greeted by his friend's heir Agorastocles. As Hanno presents his half of the *tessera*, which attests to his official tie and also acts as proof of his identity, Agorastocles recognises that it is the other half of the one his adoptive father has stored in the house.[36] This leads to a happy reunion of family friends – who turn out to be relations, but that is another story. We have no way of knowing how many such *tesserae* Hanno, or others on the move, would have carried on their journeys, or brought with them when they changed their place of residence. These objects would have formed part of a wider system of private contracts on which the Mediterranean network was based.

The scenario described above is exemplary of the world portrayed in Plautus's comedies, which is full of highly interconnected and internally diverse communities.[37] Every play has foreigners in it, many of whom are the main protagonists. There is no sense that this is somehow a new cosmopolitan environment or different to one that had preceded it. While we do find cultural stereotyping, occasions when appearance, language and exotic destinations all provide opportunity for comic interludes, there is no indication of xenophobia. Undoubtedly foreigners had a different status, which is expressed in the comedies through such episodes as the attempt by foreigners to bring criminals to justice, which they explicitly note is more difficult than for locals. Yet, the very fact that they can do this shows frameworks of understanding and shared reciprocal inter-state agreements. A less favourable status did not prevent characters coming from abroad or going to foreign shores, which they do for a myriad of reasons – love, wealth, escape – mostly personal, as we would expect in the comic genre. It is such individual mobility which appears most prominently. The large en masse migrations that are the foundation for demographic studies are hardly visible in the comedies, although we do see some of their effects. There are soldiers returning from battle, parents searching for their enslaved children, prisoners of war and recruitment for colonial endeavours. Although Plautus's work is based on earlier Greek originals, the environment he depicts in the comedies, and especially in his meta-theatrical prologues and comments, is that of his contemporary Italy – an Italy that is perfectly comfortable with its cosmopolitan, or *globalised*, state already in the third century BC. While the Plautine corpus in itself may not be concrete evidence for a highly mobile Italian environment, it does provide a sense of the context that was prevalent at the end of the third century. The comedies portray an open attitude to foreigners in their midst, and also to mobility, especially for those at particular points in their life cycle, the youth and the middle-aged. The choice to move to another place or to set out on a journey was one option that was commonly taken, seemingly, with little regard for distance or the dangers of travel.

POLYBIUS AND THE GLOBAL MOMENT

Polybius was a near contemporary of Plautus, writing several decades later, but reflecting on the same period of the late third – early second century BC. While in Plautus the interconnected environment is portrayed as an ever present norm, Polybius instead chooses to identify it as the *global moment*, a historic shift into a newly transformed state of being for the world as he knew it. To what extent can we trust this astute historian's assessment? It is true that Polybius is not specifically talking about mobility and connectivity, as such, but displaying a new perception of these phenomena and their agents. The first thing to note is that such a perspective was part of the rhetoric of the age that saw itself as a new beginning. As part of this rhetoric, and for the purpose of his *Histories*, which was to show how a little known place like Rome rapidly took over the known world, it meant that Polybius needed to have Rome as small, and as isolated as possible at the beginning of his narrative. This would then allow him to narrate her rapid rise and expansion in the second century BC, leading up to becoming the head of empire by the end of his work. However it may be defined, the rapid rise of Roman imperialism in the second century BC is uncontested. What interests me is rather what Polybius does to create the image of an infant Rome at the start of his narrative, and the way he chooses to identify a point of transformation bringing Rome into the wider sphere of connectivity within the Mediterranean. For Polybius this moment of engagement is when Rome first took to the sea.[38] It is for this reason that he gives such prominence to what he calls the first Roman crossings into Sicily in 264 BC, and then Illyria in 229 BC.[39]

To emphasise the rapidity of Roman progress, he highlights the fledgling state's initial incompetence at sea, not simply in military terms and through the inability to construct warships,[40] but also in relation to any seafaring venture.[41] The resulting image of Rome prior to this period of engagement, as one of insularity and ineptitude, does not stand up to scrutiny. There is enough evidence from other sources, and within Polybius's own narrative, to show that he must have been aware not only that Rome's aggression spilled over outside the peninsula well before that memorable crossing to Sicily in 264 BC, but also that Roman trading ships had been plying the Mediterranean coasts for some time.[42] The Roman treaties with Carthage that pre-date this venture, which Polybius discusses in some detail,[43] outline rules and constraints on Roman trading practices in the fourth century BC and include a ban on the foundation of cities in those areas that were under Carthaginian control, specifically Libya, Eastern Sicily and Sardinia. An agreement about the restrictions on such activities would have been unnecessary unless they were already being practised by both powers in each other's area of influence. Polybius's Second Treaty between Rome and Carthage, which is believed to date to 348 BC,[44] may have been prompted by a Roman attempt at what appears as a colonising venture in Sardinia as early as 378 BC (or 386 BC).[45]

The crossing to Illyria and that part of Europe in 229 BC is highlighted as another major event in the Roman spread of power into areas previously unchartered by them.[46] Yet, the explanation of the grievances that provoked the expedition suggests that the Romans could not have been wholly unfamiliar with the region. Polybius describes how Illyrians had been in the habit of maltreating sea merchants from Italy *for a long time*, and that recently such a clash had resulted in the robbery, imprisonment and death of many Italian traders.[47] These few clues need to be seen in connection with the activities of other Italian trade hubs outside of Rome, such as for example the ports of Caere and Tarentum, where Romans had a presence. We also need to add into the mix the image of mobility presented in Plautus and the strong evidence for shared international frameworks of understanding. This broader picture suggests that we need to treat Polybius's turning point not as a break from what had gone on in the past,[48] but rather as an intensification and a shift in the nature and perception of connectivity, especially for Italy and Rome.

COUNTING THE MOBILE

Up to this point there has been little consideration of any specific numbers for mobility rates or the demographic studies for which Polybius's narrative is of importance, especially his account of the mobilisation for the Roman campaign against the Gauls in 225 BC.[49] The evidence that informs demographic investigations is gleaned from recorded figures for the Roman census, and state-initiated events that include: colonisation; veteran and viritane settlement; enslavements; mass transfer of populations – such as the Ligurians or Picentines; repatriation of prisoners of war; and military recruitment. There are ongoing debates about the total population of Italy from this period, with both low and high counts continuously being reassessed.[50] The human flows tend to be considered in the context of a total free population of Italy in the range of at least three to four million, the low count, with some preferring to see the figures closer to seven million or higher.[51] For this population, Scheidel estimates that the total number of individual movements in the last two centuries BC, excluding slaves, was in the range of two to two and a half million.[52] The statistics for slave imports into Italy for the same period Scheidel calculates at some two and a half million, cautiously using figures such as those recorded by Polybius of the 150,000 enslaved in Epirus in a single campaign led by Aemilius Paullus in 167 BC.[53] These figures, while not measuring precisely like for like, fall considerably short of the theoretical extreme of forty million movements that Erdkamp estimates if we were to apply Osborne's method in his studies that use comparable trends from the early modern period.[54] The difference between the two ends of the spectrum is determined by how much weight is given to the rate of individual mobility, as compared with that which is initiated by the state. While Scheidel leans towards a relatively low figure for individual or personal movement, it would be a mistake to presume that what he suggests is a low overall rate of mobility, his calculations for a more specific period reveal otherwise. He estimates that at the time of Augustus, for which we have better data, some 40% of male Romans over the age of forty-five would have been born in a different location from their current place of residence.[55] Scepticism of such high figures is a common knee-jerk reaction, especially if compared with official statistics for mobility today. While these do not measure identical forms of mobility, they give a sense of the trend: the UN estimated that by 2002 some 185 million people lived outside their country of birth for at least twelve months, which is just over 2% of the world's population.[56] Despite such a seeming contrast, and our scepticism, there is good evidence for a context of high mobility in, from and through ancient Italy.

Understanding the extent of individual or personal movement is central to predicting the nature of the mobile elements of communities. Although this type of mobility is difficult to quantify, Broadhead's study of a series of episodes, which are included in Livy's narrative of the second century BC, highlights the potentially large figures that were involved in such movement.[57] In a well-known episode of expulsion, dated to 187 BC, Livy records that Latin communities pleaded with the Romans to help them restore their citizens to their colonies by tracking them down.[58] Roman authorities gave in and some 12,000 Latins were sent out of Rome to return to their own cities. Ten years later, in 177 BC, once again Italian communities came to Rome and this time included the complaints of Samnites and Paelignians that some four thousand families had transferred to Fregellae.[59] Both of these instances suggest that individuals are constantly on the lookout for opportunities to improve their quality of life, whether in economic or in other ways. We may be less surprised that Rome attracted so many people, but the popularity of Fregellae may at first appear difficult to comprehend in terms of economic or political advantage alone. Although once we start looking for signs of its appeal, we get glimpses of its popularity from some unexpected sectors, such as for example the Carthaginian hostages who were requesting to be moved from Norba. Their request was met, and they were moved to Signia, Ferentinum and also Fregellae.[60] Whatever may have been the reasons behind the movement of these individuals and their families, and even if their numbers were lower than those recorded by Livy, the implication is that many chose to relocate and there were no barriers to prevent them from doing so. Such an observation does not sit comfortably with the supposed *ius migrandi* – an exclusive law allowing privileged free mobility between Rome and the Latin communities, which until recently appeared alongside other rights that the Latins shared. Through contextualising the Livy passages dealing with these migratory moments in 187 and 177 BC, Broadhead has successfully shown that the *ius migrandi* never existed.[61] The institution of a 'migration law' is the fabrication of modern scholarship that does not fit the evidence and institutional developments, which point to the free and anticipated movement of individuals in ancient society.

Conclusions

In relation to *ius migrandi*, what allowed the interpretation of the ancient evidence to be skewed in the first instance is the assumption of modern migration-as-threat mentality, which assumes that states would have wanted to prevent immigration. If that was the case we would not have thousands of Italians in Asia Minor or circulating around the Mediterranean, as do the majority of the Plautine characters. In earlier periods, non-state initiatives such as Pithekoussai would also be difficult to explain, as well as the thousands who wanted to make Rome or Fregellae their new home. Instead, what these episodes show is that there was: a mobile population seeking opportunities; a knowledge system that directed it; sites and communities that were keen to draw in groups and individuals; and institutions and bordering practices that did not inhibit such mobility. This highly interconnected environment existed well before the transformations that were noted by Polybius. What he observed was not a shift from a less globalised to a more globalised state, but a re-centring of trajectories around Rome, the new facilitator of this interconnected environment. The Roman state fostered a global consciousness, which in turn is what most likely prompted the Polybian reflection in his *Histories*, a perspective which we may choose to term globalisation.

To characterise such a development as globalisation, however, does not necessarily tell us very much about the ancient context, but rather the way that contemporaries perceived it.[62] Where its application is useful is in a comparative context, and when considering the *longue durée*. Looking at early periods of history through the lens of globalisation makes explicit our explanatory frameworks. At the same time it highlights the assumptions made in some contemporary globalisation discourse, which tend to be evolutionary minded, by providing alternative episodes and fluctuations that force a rethinking of globalisation as a one directional phenomenon.[63] Our community of the twenty-first century considers itself globalising (if not strictly fully globalised) by assuming a preceding non-globalised state of being, in the same way as did Polybius, presumably. Between these two historic points of alleged globalisation there must have been periods when society was, or felt itself to be, or wanted to be, less globalised. There would have been phases of perceived or real de-globalisation and fragmentation and, as Pitts and Versluys emphasise, it is a relative concept.[64] We may wonder whether one such point of de-globalisation is captured in the fourth-century AD poem *Mosella* by Ausonius from Gaul, as Rome's centrality is undermined. Through the long lens of history we need to ask whether there are patterns that enhance or prevent what may be termed globalisation, or whether it is an ever present phenomenon that we *perceive* as rising and receding.

Acknowledgements

The workshop that has resulted in this publication was a truly thought-provoking experience, and I would like to thank Martin Pitts and Miguel John Versluys for all their suggestions and patience in bringing this volume together and their astute comments on this chapter, along with that of the readers, which have made it a much better and more coherent piece than it would have been otherwise.

NOTES

1. See discussion below.
2. Polybius, *Histories*, 1.3. As also noted in Pitts & Versluys (Chapter 1, this volume).
3. e.g. Robertson (1992, 8), and others building on his ideas have shown that globalisation is not modernity: see Pitts & Versluys (Chapter 1, this volume).
4. See Morley (Chapter 3, this volume).
5. See Versluys (Chapter 7, this volume).
6. Ibid.
7. See Versluys (Chapter 7, this volume), esp. the section on 'punctuating connectivity', and Sommer (Chapter 8, this volume).
8. Manning (2005).
9. For a discussion of the term's new meaning in this period, see Shumsky (2008).
10. Pickering, J. (1816, 108); *The Oxford English Dictionary*; Thompson (2003, 195 n. 21); Shumsky (2008, 132).
11. Webster (1828). Offering a second definition of *migrate*, Webster acknowledged that the word has an alternative usage – 'to pass or remove from one region or district to another for a temporary residence: as the Tartars *migrate* for the sake of finding pasturage' (Shumsky 2008, 130).
12. Shumsky (2008, 131–4).
13. The 2010 UK immigration policy, and the introduction of a cap on immigrants, is just one example of this phenomenon, which is fuelled by the kind of stereotypical image of the immigrant that is presented in one of the many articles on this issue in the *The Guardian Newspaper* on 25 September 2010, concerning Sweden's tightening immigration policy, as a key issue in the political election. For statistics and data currently used to inform UK government policy, see the material provided by the *Migration Observatory* of the *Centre on Migration, Policy and Society (COMPAS)* at the University of Oxford: www.migrationobservatory.ox.ac.uk.
14. For the liberty and control of movement in the Imperial period and the role of territory, which depended on political structures and degrees of centralisation, see Moatti (2004, 1–24, esp. 4–7); Moatti & Kaiser (2007).
15. Only Appian distinguishes the victims as Italians and Romans, all the other sources speaking of *cives romani*, and post-89 BC the distinction had little meaning since all Italian communities south of the Po were enfranchised in the wake of the Social War. For a discussion of the terminology and the events, see Wilson (1966, 94); Amiotti (1980, 137–8).
16. Appian, *Mithridates* 4.22–24.

17. Cicero does not provide specific figures but notes they were substantial in his *Pro Flacco*, 25.60, and also mentions that the massacre of Roman citizens spread across numerous cities in his *Pro Imp. Cn. Pomp.* 3.7.
18. Valerius Maximus 9.2.3 (ext.); Memnon of Heraclea Pontica 31.9 (= FGH III B, p352, lines 16–21).
19. Plutarch *Sulla*, 24.4–7, with comments by Wilson (1966, 126).
20. Hind (1994, 148) suggests that such high numbers were probably an exaggeration as Dio, fr. 109.8, believed that the mutual pogroms of Marius and Sulla were far worse. Wilson (1966, 123) indicates that the figure may have only entered circulation in the last decades of the republic. For discussion of the figures see also Magie (1950, 216); Brunt (1971, 224–7).
21. Mastrocinque (1994); Delrieux F. (2001).
22. Delrieux (2001, 154), for details.
23. Gordon & Reynolds (2003, 219–20).
24. Note also the increase in inscriptions following the Social War, documenting euergetism, an obligation which directly stimulated the growth in epigraphic commemoration, with further references in Gordon & Reynolds (2003, 219–20 n. 37, 227–8).
25. Wilson (1966, 98 n.3, 131–6); Müller & Hasenohr (2002, 18–20).
26. For the importance of Puteoli as a draw for international traders, see Cébeillac-Gervasoni (2002).
27. Osborne (1998); Horden & Purcell (2000, 347–8, 399); Bradley & Wilson (2006); Cuozzo (2007, 246).
28. Dionysius of Halicarnassus 7.3.2. Livy 5.24, 5.33–35, presents a couple of alternative versions of migrations into North Italy, including a long and a short version.
29. Häussler (2007, 45); Lomas (2007, 36). For example in Padua a mixture of Celtic and Venetic names, such as Tivalos Bellenios, appear on inscriptions (Prosdocimi 1988, 288–92), and in the funerary sphere, stelai exhibit Celtic motifs in the iconography (Fogolari 1988, 102–3).
30. For more about the debate, see discussion below.
31. Lo Cascio & Malanima (2005, 227). With discussion in Scheidel (2004, 1); Scheidel (2006, 209).
32. For debates about demography in Italy, de Ligt & Northwood (2008), de Ligt (2012).
33. Edwards & Woolf (2003).
34. Rix (1991, Af 3.1); with discussion in Prag (2006b, esp. 8–10, 24); Messineo (1983, 3–4); Acquaro (1988, 536).
35. Plautus, *Poenulus*, 958; 1047–55. Plautus's comedies, dating to the end of the third – early second century BC, are some of the earliest Latin texts surviving from Italy.
36. Plautus, *Poenulus*, 1047–55.
37. For aspects of mobility in Plautus see Isayev (forthcoming).
38. Polybius 1.5.1.
39. Sicilian crossing: Polybius 1.5.1, Illyrian crossing: Polybius 2.2.1, with notes for the date in Walbank (1970, Vol. II, 47, 153, respectively).

40. Polybius 1.20.
41. Polybius 1.37.10, comments on the destruction of Roman ships due to ineptitude and arrogance.
42. For a discussion of the development of Roman sea power, see Thiel (1954); Steinby (2007), with comments in Leigh (2010).
43. Polybius, 3.22–5.
44. Diodorus 16.69.1 and Livy 7.27.2, see discussion in Walbank (1970, Vol. I, 346); Serrati (2006, 119).
45. Diod. Sic. 15.27.4, provides the main evidence for this venture, but the reliability of this passage and such early Roman colonisation overseas has been questioned; see Thiel (1954, 54–5); Serrati (2006, 118, n. 17), contra Momigliano (1936, 395–6), who questions the authenticity of the Diodorus passage.
46. Polybius 2.2.1; 2.12.7.
47. Polybius 2.8.1–4.
48. For notions of mobility that long predate the Punic Wars, and the mistaken belief that the earlier the period the less mobility, see Purcell (1990).
49. Polybius 2.23–4.
50. For the figure of four million, Scheidel (2006, 209). Most recently, however, Scheidel (2008) has expressed reservations about the low population count, and has now moved toward a middle ground. The high count of fourteen to twenty million, he still sees as extremely flawed, and more so than the low count. The collection of papers by de Ligt & Northwood (2008) provides the latest debates on the demography of ancient Italy. For the figure of ten million in Augustan Italy, the mid-point between low and high counts, see Hin (2008). For debates of what constituted the census figures, and how that affects the overall population count, see the contributions in de Ligt & Northwood (2008).
51. Lo Cascio & Malanima (2005, 227); Scheidel (2006, 209, 2004, 1). See also previous note for references.
52. The figure is made up of an estimate of 1–1.25 million individuals who were settled in colonies or viritane settlements in the last two centuries BC, and adding to that a similar number of centripetal movements from the countryside to urban centres (Scheidel 2004).
53. Scheidel (2005). Polybius 30.15 (16) as cited by Strabo 7.7.3.
54. Osborne (1991) with a cautionary note by Erdkamp (2008), who questions the reliability of the comparison.
55. Overall he concludes that even if his figures need tweaking – there is no arguing for the massive demographic effect of the different movements and especially the relocation programmes (Scheidel 2004, 13–20; Scheidel 2006, 223–4).
56. Castles & Miller (1993, 4). Additional figures cited by Hollifield (2008, 185) show that at the end of the twentieth century 125 million people lived outside of their country of birth (the figure does not take into account illegal movement).
57. Broadhead (2001, 2002, 2004, 2008).
58. Livy 39.3.4–6.
59. Livy 41.8.6–12.

60. Livy 32.2.3–5. Nepos, *Hann.* 7.2–3 states they were moved to Fregellae; with further discussion in Allen (2006, 89, esp. n. 70).
61. For the historiography of *ius migrandi*, see Broadhead (2001).
62. That from this point on there was a sense of Rome as a global city according to those living at the time, may be in line with that of modern standards, as suggested by Robertson & Inglis (2006), and allows us an insight into the social imagination but not necessarily about the historical circumstances that led up to it.
63. As discussed by Pitts & Versluys (Chapter 1, this volume).
64. Ibid. See also Jennings (2011) in his discussion of multiple globalisations.

7

ROMAN VISUAL MATERIAL CULTURE AS GLOBALISING KOINE

Miguel John Versluys

> the actualities of the *longue-durée* . . . always produce specific geographies, both real and imagined. If the genealogy of cultural forms is about their circulation across regions, the history of these forms is about their ongoing domestication into local practice.
>
> (Appadurai 1996, 17)

INTRODUCTION: CHINA, *CHINA* AND CHINA

In the tomb of a Ming dynasty prince, who died in China in 1603, archaeologists found a porcelain serving plate made in the European style amongst Chinese-style grave goods.[1] How can this mixing of two such different cultural components in the same tomb be accounted for? Most scholars would routinely – although implicitly – use the concept of 'methodological nationalism' to provide some clear answers.[2] Europeans were present in China during the period and the coming together of cultures resulted in this particular 'hybrid' situation. Thus, the object could testify to the ever-growing presence and importance of 'European' culture and imperialism in Asia; or, alternatively, the will of local Chinese elites to 'become European'. Many interpretations of 'Romanisation', and of the presence of 'Roman style' material culture in a 'Native' context constitute a parallel for such reasoning.[3]

However, concerning the 'European' plate in the 'Chinese' tomb, the story really goes as follows.[4] What is called china ('a species of earthenware of a fine semitransparent texture originally manufactured in China and first brought to Europe in the 16th century by the Portuguese who named it porcelain', *OED*) was a late development in the history of Chinese ceramics, and the effect of blue on white was borrowed aesthetics from the Persian world. At the time Chinese potters began firing true porcelain, in the thirteenth century, China was under Mongol rule. Mongol dominance over Central Asia resulted in a direct link between the Chinese and Persian pottery industries. Through proscriptions in the Koran, wealthy Persian elites were prohibited from serving their food on gold and silver plates and they wanted something precious and expensive as an alternative. Porcelain was perfectly suited to fulfil this need, and the Chinese therefore started manufacturing forms and decorations to Persian tastes. This intercultural crossover of material and aesthetic factors would transform ceramic production worldwide. Not only the Mongols and the Chinese developed a liking for china: by the fifteenth century, Syrian potters were producing china as well. This process continued worldwide throughout the sixteenth century, when china was even produced in Mexico – although not always with satisfying results as far as quality was concerned. To profit from this now worldwide demand – and, at times, lack of expertise – Chinese potters started to produce for export markets all over the globe. Most of what they produced was so-called carrack or kraak porcelain, an export product that was considered vulgar and by no means 'the real thing' in China itself. The European elites, however, did not care about these Chinese aesthetics and actively bought the product. This made carrack porcelain a marker of elevated social standing and identity in Europe. In due course, it also came to be found further down the social ladder, which, in turn, made the European elites look for different articulations of social distinction.[5]

In the seventeenth century, (carrack) porcelain thus functioned as a European elite (or mostly not-quite-so-elite) marker while, in fact, it was a Chinese re-appropriation of a 'global' consumer good called china that developed from a Persian concept made and appropriated by the Chinese in the context of the Mongol empire. And it is as such that it ended up, probably, in the Ming dynastical tomb: as a foreign elite marker profiting above all, or so it seems in this context, from its social exoticism. The convergence, as Brook notes, is intriguing that 'the upper classes at the opposite ends of the Eurasian continent were both acquiring carrack porcelain. Chinese, because they thought it embodied an exotic Western elite style and Europeans because it seemed to them quintessentially Chinese'.[6] And none of these assumptions were really true.

The example of China and china is especially illuminating for this chapter, as the same word denotes both the 'culture' itself and the 'concept' associated with it as it expresses itself in material culture. This essay is about the relation between cultures on the one hand and material culture stylistically associated with those cultures on the other hand, in the Roman world. I argue that globalisation theory and that 'thinking in terms of globalisation' are particularly helpful and useful when we want to understand the relationships and disconnections between Greece and material culture we call Greek, or between Egypt and material culture we call Egyptian (etc.) in the Roman Mediterranean. It is interesting that scholars such as Tonio Hölscher have proposed hypothetical models to understand the use of styles and types of material culture in a semantic way – that is, as cultural concepts having developed independently from their original cultural background – already a quarter of a century ago.[7] However, the question what kind of world-system one would actually need to account for such a semantic system has hardly been explored. Here, I bring these two elements together and try to build on the idea of a semantic system by theoretically anchoring it within the social sciences, using globalisation theories as a hermeneutic device. I argue that it is from the period of around 200 BC onwards that a *koine* of shared cultural symbols is present and functioning all around the *oikumene*, and that, hence, we cannot but understand the cultural system as a globalised one from that period onwards.

In her recent essay, Vimalin Rujivacharakul has coined China as *cultural connotation* and china as *materiality*.[8] When following these definitions it becomes clear at a glance that China and china are not at all directly related and that to understand the relationships and disconnections between China and china one must always ask about their specific cultural conditions. The book, *Collecting China* presents a wide array of examples illustrating that disconnections (and re-appropriations and processes of inventing authenticity, etc.) between cultural connotations of China and china-materialities are the norm – as the example of the Ming dynastical tomb likewise illustrates. It is only a 'global history of collecting', *Collecting China* demonstrates, that can bring these relationships and disconnections in sharp focus. The main point of this chapter is that the same holds true when we want to better understand relations between the main three ingredients making up the history of the Roman Mediterranean: (1) cultures, (2) cultural connotations and ideas on those cultures and (3) objects with their stylistic and material properties as they are associated with those cultures and their cultural connotations.[9]

In the present situation it is important to explain why the concept of globalisation is evoked and 'made to work' to solve problems in the first place, in this case within the archaeology of Roman (visual) material culture.[10] I therefore start by outlining and illustrating what I consider to be the main problem – the concept of acculturation dominating archaeological interpretation – and explain why Roman archaeology is in need of a framework 'beyond container thinking'. As an example, current understandings of the Aegyptiaca from the Roman world are discussed to illustrate why Roman archaeologists should stop doing 'transfer studies'. I then focus on the field of Roman visual material culture studies in particular and show how alternative approaches – implicitly undermining acculturation thinking – have already been developed: be it without much attention to Romanisation issues and other aspects of historical anthropology.[11] As an addition to the part dealing with Egypt and Aegyptiaca, here the examples focus on Greek style material culture. A final section deals with the chronological punctuation of globalisation and argues for substantial change from the period around 200 BC onwards.[12] There is a difference between the 'international style' of the Bronze Age Mediterranean and the Hellenistic *koine* from the Roman Mediterranean, and I argue that there are good reasons for talking about the former in terms of connectivity and about the latter in terms of globalisation. The conclusion argues that globalisation indeed provides a good thought perspective when analysing Roman visual material culture, and that pushing the globalisation analogy more strongly is a fruitful way forward. There are two important reasons for this in theoretical terms. Firstly, a globalising perspective helps us to envision Rome, in (material) culture terms at least, not as a specific geographically located culture, but as what one perhaps could call an 'aggregative cultural praxis'. Secondly it adds, by means of its focus on how meaning is (primarily) constructed through things in networks, to recent debates on the agency of material culture and human–thing entanglement in the Roman Mediterranean.

OUTLINING THE PROBLEM: WHAT'S WRONG WITH ACCULTURATION

Contact between different cultures in the ancient world was first studied from a unilinear, diffusionist perspective. This was the context in which Romanisation and Hellenisation were initially formulated, with Rome and Athens functioning as historical predecessors to the culturally and morally superior centres of civilisation that the new (European) nation-states of the nineteenth century imagined themselves to be. From this perspective Romanisation was a *mission civilisatrice*. This view continues within popular imagination, but it has now been thoroughly deconstructed and historiographically contextualised.[13] Thinking in terms of acculturation initially provided an important step forwards from this point of view, because acculturation as a process is *not* unilinear. Acculturation allows for changes to the original cultural patterns of *both* groups involved in culture contact. Thus, cultural change is clearly perceived as a *dialectic* between cultures, resulting in outcomes that can differ in substance. Stereotypical generalisations of the most frequently occurring results are assimilation and fusion of cultures on the one hand, and separation and marginalisation on the other. In historical reality, of course, borders between the different outcomes are not so clear cut and, moreover, temporality has an important role to play. Marginalisation in the first generation, for instance, might develop into separation of subsequent generations, but also in fusion via assimilation.[14] Acculturation thus invites us to see culture contact along the lines of a kind of 'Christopher Columbus scenario', with a boat full of people from culture *x* landing on the shore of a culture *y* that is totally alien to them. This is understandable given that the model was developed in the context of ethnology. However, it makes the concept problematic for an analysis of culture contact in the Roman world, for the simple reason that due to the immense connectivity that characterised the pre-Roman Mediterranean and Near East, there were very few genuine 'Columbus moments' left. This critique has been succinctly summarised by Ulrich Gotter:

> For societies as we encounter them within historical disciplines, the use of the cultural-anthropological concept of acculturation is absurd. The development from 'first-hand contact' to 'subsequent changes' is, in fact, simply impossible to pursue when contact is a permanent phenomenon ... The history of societies that are engaged in endemic exchange with one another is therefore acculturation from beginning to end ... With this conclusion, however, the concept loses any real heuristic value.[15]

A second critique is that through its nature of thinking in distinct cultures, acculturation has as its basic premise the existence of a distinct Self and Other. Acculturation reasons, in other words, in terms of identity *contra* alterity. This is highly problematic in the context of the Roman Mediterranean. 'Roman' was, in principle, a political and juridical term alone and its meaning in terms of culture and identity is notoriously slippery.[16] What is more: distinctions between Self and Other seem to have been contextually constructed in the Roman world to the point of being interchangeable. One could 'be Roman by going Greek' in one particular moment and context; in another, Roman culture can be seen almost 'nationally' defined *contra* things Greek. The same applies to Roman and Egyptian. In some contexts, Orientalising strategies evoked Egypt as the non-Roman Other par excellence; simultaneously the emperor (and supreme symbol of Roman power) functioned and was displayed as Egyptian pharaoh. We cannot understand these as acculturation processes between distinct cultural containers. Self and Other are not oppositional categories in the Roman world, nor indications of relative degrees of acculturation: Self and Other are cultural concepts having to do with identity and social experience. They are, in other words, part of the *same* cultural container.

A third important critique is that – even if acculturation might help describe the outcomes of culture contact in very general historical terms – it is not at all well equipped to understand (styles and types of) material culture. Acculturation sees styles and types of archaeological material characteristic of culture *x* as an indication of (people belonging to) culture *x*. Thus, in archaeology, acculturation thinking has resulted in the (often implicit) assumption that there is a direct link between style and ethnicity or identity – as with the example of the Ming dynastical tomb discussed above. Greek material culture, in other words, may do and mean very different things but always has something to do with Greece or Greeks. However, already from the Bronze Age onwards different styles of material culture were distributed and adopted by people from very heterogeneous cultural backgrounds all around the Mediterranean. Thus, these styles acquired meanings and developed patterns of association *independent* of the cultures they originally belonged to. Phoenician material culture is probably the best example of how, already in a very early stage, specific styles are not tied up with (ethnic) identities, and how style *becomes* content. Below it is explained how, with the establishment of Roman political dominance over the largest part of the known world from around 200 BC onwards, this developed into a truly semantic system spanning that entire *oikumene*. Returning to the example used at the start of the chapter, acculturation, therefore, always puts China central to its analysis, has little attention for cultural concepts of *China* and ignores the existence of an independent category of china altogether.

To sum up: acculturation is not suited to understanding the cultural complexities of the Roman world as it is necessarily concerned with culture *x* and *y* and the linear relations between them. However, when studying the use and functioning of different cultural elements in the Roman world, always 'one is confronted with the logic of the network and not with a linear flow'.[17] What we need, therefore, is a concept that has *x* and *y* as relative categories that are part of the *same* cultural container. We need, in other words, a concept in which not linear relations are central, but continuous circularity is.

ILLUSTRATING THE PROBLEM: ROME AS THE OTHER

The previous section details why acculturation is not a useful concept to analyse culture contact in the Roman Mediterranean; especially not for archaeologists. Of course that does not mean there is something *inherently* wrong with it. One could look at Roman Egypt, for instance, and conclude that what we see there, after some time, is assimilation and fusion.[18] But that is a very general conclusion, applicable, so it seems, to the largest part of the Roman empire, especially during the second century AD. Moreover, it does not help us to explain why Roman and Egyptian elements occur where they do. It is clear that the Roman world, at least in cultural terms, functioned very differently from the nineteenth-century nation-states (and their colonial Others) for which the acculturation model was developed. The main specific characteristics that have been indicated are (1) the existence of 'Roman' and 'Other' as relative concepts having to do with identity and social experience in the first place; and (2) the functioning of styles and types of material culture as quasi-independent concepts with their own stylistic and material properties. This section provides some more background on these characteristics by discussing a specific example – the so-called Aegyptiaca or Egyptiana: 'Egyptian' and 'Egyptianising' artefacts from the Roman world – also to illustrate the need for a framework 'beyond container thinking' more practically.[19]

The meaning of the many Egyptian-style artefacts that have been preserved from the Roman world is heavily debated. Aegyptiaca are most often divided in two categories: 'Egyptian' (which is meant to indicate: coming from the Nile valley, sometimes already centuries old and 'authentic') and Egyptianising (meaning: made outside Egypt after the Egyptian style and 'less authentic'). The scholarly creation of this dichotomy as a fundamental premise, for interpretation is characteristic of methodological nationalism and container thinking as described above. In the same vein, contacts between the two political entities – the Roman republic on the one hand and Ptolemaic Egypt on the other, starting off in the third century BC – are routinely evoked to account for the historical context in which Aegyptiaca could emerge. In the Roman empire the 'real Egyptian' material would have been functioning – referring to Egyptian realities and mainly having to do with (Isiac) religion – *versus* the unfaithful, 'Egyptianising' copies that would testify to exoticism or 'Egyptomania'.[20]

In reality, however, the Italic peninsula and Egypt had been part of the same Mediterranean context for a long time. Both actively took part in the formation of common practices in the Mediterranean from the period of the Iron Age onwards, and probably even earlier. Moreover, through its distinct stylistic and material properties, 'the Egyptian style' established itself soon as an important component of the *koine* from those periods. It is in this way, through surfing the Mediterranean Web,[21] that Egyptian scarabs, for instance, become popular in Sardinian tombs from the eighth century BC onwards. Already at that time, scarabs made in Egypt and scarabs made locally can both be found; often being interchangeable and probably serving the same purposes.[22] It is true, therefore, that people, ideas and goods surfed the Mediterranean Web from a very early period in Mediterranean history onwards; but it is crucial to realise that they could do so *independently* from one another. Their speed and distribution was uneven and so was their contextual appropriation and meaning. This implies that if they are found together in the same historical or archaeological context, they do not necessarily have something to do with each other.

From the third century BC onwards, Rome conquered the Mediterranean and as a result its material culture looked, in the end, like a blend of Egyptian, Greek, Etruscan, Italic and 'Oriental' elements and styles. All these foreign influences changed Rome and Roman cultural identity, or perhaps one could better say that all these elements *made up* Rome and Roman identity in a process of cultural innovation. What does this imply for our understanding of foreign styles and elements in a Roman context? Probably that these were less foreign than we describe them to be by calling them Egyptian, Greek, Etruscan, etc.

The 'Egyptian' goddess Isis and the role of the cults of Isis in the Hellenistic and Roman world serves to underline this point.[23] As a Hellenistic goddess venerated all over the eastern Mediterranean, Isis became part of the Roman pantheon in the later Republican period and quickly established herself in all kinds of social strata. Becoming Roman apparently was quite easy and on the Italic peninsula we see Isis often being equated with, for instance, Fortuna (Fig. 7.1). However, in the context of the civil war with Mark Anthony and Cleopatra at the end of the Republic, the (now) 'Egyptian' goddess Isis was banned by Octavian. She was made quintessentially Egyptian (in the sense of: 'being representative of the cultural container Egypt') *at that particular time*, even though she was worshipped by Roman (elite) families before and would develop into one of the principal deities of the Flavian dynasty thereafter. If we follow this trajectory and look at the cults of Isis in Rome at, for instance, the beginning of the second century AD, the same contextual and relative understanding of the category 'Egyptian' becomes clear. The official opening of the Roman seafaring season is now intimately linked with a large and public Isis ceremony (the *navigidum Isidis*) and its celebrations, up to a point where 'Egyptian' and 'Roman' apparently have become synonymous. Simultaneously we see the goddess being (re-)Egyptianised – and hence explicitly un-Romanised – in the religious domain, where, in this period, she is presented as a quintessentially Egyptian/Oriental mystery goddess

Figure 7.1: Bronze figure of Isis-Fortuna found in Herculaneum, around 70 AD, now housed in the Museo Archeologico, Napoli (5313).

who is everything what the Roman state gods are not. What makes the case of the 'Egyptian goddess' Isis so exemplary for the subject of this essay is that, in fact, she was a Hellenistic, Mediterranean innovation of the old-Egyptian Isis and, moreover, that Egyptian priests themselves played a crucial role in establishing this innovative 'translation'. We can thus not talk about an *interpretatio graeca* or *romana* from something 'Egyptian', as Egyptians themselves played an active part in the *interpretatio*.[24] The Hellenistic and Roman Isis, therefore, cannot be explained by thinking in terms of acculturation processes between cultural containers like 'Egypt', 'Greece' and 'Rome': *all* players are involved in creating something new. Therefore the relation between Egypt and Isis is similar to the relation between China, *China* and china. These *seem* to be intimately and directly linked but, in fact, they are not: we must investigate specific cultural conditions and historical contexts to understand their relation, expecting disconnection to be the norm.

We begin to understand this even better when we look at what happened in another geographical part of the same cultural context: Roman Egypt. There, the Roman emperor was displayed as an Egyptian pharaoh in the visual language that had developed to do so over millennia. Even Augustus, the 'imperialistic' conqueror himself, used this cultural scenario. These practices are visible in other domains of society as well. It is clear, for instance, that 'Egypt owned the afterlife': when it came to burial, Egyptian concepts of life and death were used together with the distinctly Egyptian visual language. In the course of time almost all ethnic groups living at the Nile were buried in the Egyptian way. The well-known Fayum portraits, for instance, displaying the deceased in a 'realistic', veristic style, were considered as a normal part of a distinctly Egyptian-style mummy (Fig. 7.2). The people buried this way were neither ethnically half-Roman/half-Egyptian, nor were they looking for a Roman and/or Egyptian identity. They had themselves portrayed the way elites had themselves portrayed all around the Mediterranean (veristic), and they were buried the Egyptian way. In the same period, an ethnic Syrian living in the Fayum could be buried like this.[25]

Again we end up with the image of continuous circularity in which cultural containers like 'Egyptian' and 'Egyptianising' make little sense: methodological nationalism does not work when studying cultural processes in the Mediterranean. In the Roman world 'Egypt' served as a marker of some distinct 'Roman' things, like the civil war that ended the republic. In the city of Rome, real 'Egyptian' things may serve to (re-)Egyptianise and make exotic a Hellenistic goddess who had become part and parcel of the Roman system. At the same time 'Egyptianising' things may originate from Egypt: the Hellenistic and Roman Isis as we have her might very well be said to be 'Egyptianising' and was an innovation largely designed at the Nile. The traditional dichotomy between 'Egyptian' and 'Egyptianising' therefore makes no sense.

The meaning of *Egypt* as *cultural connotation* was already relative and context dependent – as has been illustrated for Isis whose 'Egyptianness' was re-appropriated (and invented) when the circumstances made this desirable. The meaning of Egypt as stylistic and material concept can perhaps be expected to be even more relative and context dependent due to its long history of development in so many different contexts from the Bronze Age onwards.[26] And besides all the 'ideas of Egypt' as cultural connotation (*China*) and Egyptian-looking materialities (china) floating around, there also was the country at the Nile itself (China) actively producing and consuming both categories. In appears that these three have actively and innovatively made use of one another in the Roman Mediterranean.

Be that as it may, I hope the examples above show that to understand 'Egypt' in the Roman world we should stop doing transfer studies. I use the term transfer studies on purpose in concluding this section to bring the

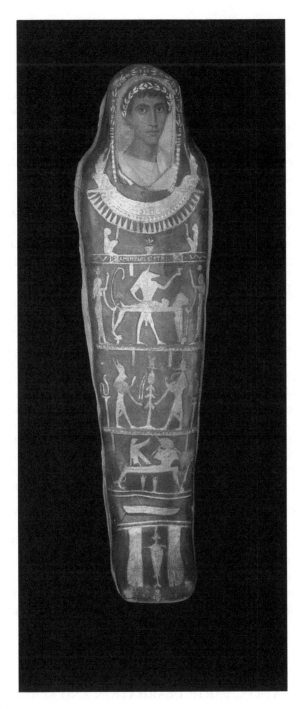

Figure 7.2: Mummy case and portrait of Artemidorus, Hawara, 100–120 AD, now housed in the British Museum, London.

discussion back to the feasibility of the concept of globalisation. I have argued above for an understanding of the Roman world, in cultural terms, as a circular system with many different (inter-)connections in which the various European, Mediterranean and Near Eastern cultures, ideas about those cultures and stylistic and material properties associated with them all constitute one another. Can we arrive at an understanding of such a system by adding re-flows to the flows and thus building in circularity? Probably not. The concept of transfer studies was coined and elaborated in the 1990s by Michael Werner and Bénédicte Zimmermann who, in a recent, self-reflexive article, clearly identify its weak spots. 'Thinking in terms of culture contact', they concluded, has 'through a sort of boomerang effect' in fact resulted in strengthening the borders it set out to undermine:

> Thus, if on the level of relationships between national units, the initial purpose of a transfer study was to show that borders were more permeable in order to undermine the myth of the homogeneity of national units, the result is that the categories of analysis reintroduce, through a sort of boomerang effect, the national references that were to be put in question. The study of exchanges does lead to a richer approach of the culture of reception: it underlines foreign contributions and helps to historicize the concept of national culture. But the representation itself of this culture is not really called into question. Thus, rather than softening the national grounding of historiographies and human and social-science disciplines, research into transfers paradoxically often leads to strengthening it. More generally, to the extent that the reference points of the analysis are not questioned as such, transfer studies run the risk inherent in any approach that overlooks its self-referential dimension: they only reinforce the prejudices that they seek to undermine.[27]

In my opinion, we see exactly the same thing happening within Roman studies, in terms of a strengthening of the Roman–Native dichotomy through the (post-colonial) realisation that the boundaries between them were highly permeable.[28] Transfer studies alone will not suffice to move beyond Roman and Native and to make us understand the relations, in the Roman world, between what we should distinguish as three different categories: cultures (China), cultural debates (*China*) and material culture (china).

ROMAN VISUAL IMAGERY AS SEMANTIC SYSTEM: UNIVERSALISATION, PARTICULARISATION AND *KOINE*

So far I have shown how 'things Egyptian' could amount to very different things in very different contexts, and how Egypt on the one hand and

Egyptian-style material culture on the other hand might not be as directly related as usually thought. Aegyptiaca, therefore, had multiple meanings. This is not surprising as meaning is, in fact, always constructed in a specific historical context and situation: meaning is a function of use. What *is* surprising, perhaps, is the enormous dynamic. Already from the short and very general summary above, it becomes clear that both cultural connotations of Egypt and Egyptian materialities had distinct 'cultural biographies' that were part of all kinds of pan-Mediterranean and Near Eastern developments. Moreover, Egypt itself existed along with something of an Egyptian diaspora: people from the land of the Nile are to be found everywhere in the Mediterranean and Near East during the Roman period. The variety of meanings, associations, uses and users was therefore potentially enormous, as were the intersections. It is a dynamic similar to what Arjun Appadurai has phrased as 'moving images meeting deterritorialized viewers', and its results are comparable to what Daniel Miller has described as 'the local contextualization of a global form'.[29]

For the Roman period it is possible to study this dynamic – and relations between all kinds of moving images and all kinds of deterritorialised viewers and their local contextualisations – in more detail from an archaeological perspective due to the fact that the 'cultural biographies' of some of the styles and elements that make up Roman visual imagery are known.[30] That the Roman world is a 'stew', a 'melting pot' with all kinds of borrowing and translation processes and thus 'hybridity', should not surprise us; we should explain how Roman visual imagery functions within and as a result of it.[31] Later on in this chapter I attempt to summarise the debate in these terms, using universalisation, particularisation and *koine* as its key words and mainly focus, as an addition to the former paragraph that discussed Egyptiana, on Greece, cultural concepts of Greece and Greek (style) things.

In the field of Roman visual material culture, the problematic nature of the container 'Roman' was realised and commented upon long ago.[32] 'Roman art' is clearly not a recognisable nation-state culture style, as most of the time it looks distinctly Greek, or Etruscan, or Egyptian or otherwise. Apparently Rome used the Other(s) – that is the cultures and styles of the people it had conquered – for its own identity formation. One could perhaps argue, therefore, that the field of Roman visual material culture studies in particular should have been engaged with deconstructing methodological nationalism. We will see that to a certain extent this is indeed the case, although only seldom theoretically explicit and rarely, unfortunately, in relation to wider debates on Romanisation.[33]

The initial reaction, however, was very different. To understand the Greek stylistic and material properties of Roman visual material culture, scholars simply took 'Greece' as the cultural container-*explanandum*. As a consequence, Roman art was mainly studied in relation to Greece and to Greek art as culture style – and validated as inferior in art historical terms. The formula *Roman copy after Greek original* was the interpretative crux of this framework of interpretation, as thoroughly deconstructed in recent years.[34] Even at the beginning of the twentieth century, however, scholars had developed alternative approaches, taking their cue from ancient sources that indicated that there was a style or subject deemed appropriate for every genre or context. When Cicero writes to Atticus (*Atticus* 1.6.2) about visual decorations to be acquired for his gymnasium, he uses the word *gymnasiode* ('appropriate for the gymnasium') without further elaboration. We thus deal with a kind of 'formulaic visual culture', where manner follows matter and where appropriateness (*decorum*) seems to be the main instrument for the application of a certain subject or style.[35] Roman visual material culture, therefore, has eclecticism as its defining characteristic: calling it 'hybrid' is therefore no explanation whatsoever. Tonio Hölscher tried to describe this practice in terms of a truly semantic system in which specific themes and styles were used to evoke specific associations.[36] In his view, styles were taken from a 'reservoir' of possibilities at hand to express contemporary concepts and associations. A style characteristic of the Greek sculptor Phidias, for instance, would have been necessary for the display of gods in freestanding sculpture because the subject 'god' was associated with the concept 'majesty' – and concepts like that were displayed through the style of Phidias. Important for our discussion is that the original meaning and historical background of the styles and elements that were used played no (real) role with their application.[37] These were early stages in their 'cultural biography', not necessarily of any relevance any more but, of course, ready to be evoked when needed. It is debatable whether one can really speak about a system in the rather 'rigid' way Hölscher imagines it.[38] I, however, leave that discussion and focus on two (uncontested) points from his model that are crucial to the argument of this chapter: (1) the existence of a common repertoire of types and styles of material culture available all around the Mediterranean and Near East – a *koine* or 'common language' used and supplied and further developed by all participants; and (2) the characterisation of these types and styles of visual material culture as semantic – in opposition to 'realistic' in the sense of being a direct expression of the social and political realities of its time – from around the period of 200 BC onwards. The latter point is important because, as indicated above, it is their semantic character that enables these styles to function as china unrelated to *China* and China. The former is important as it shows that these shared cultural symbols are present and working all around the *oikumene*, and that, hence, we cannot but understand the cultural system as a globalised one.[39]

To further explain the functioning of a Hellenistic *koine* – and a world in which moving images were constantly meeting deterritorialised viewers – the terms universalisation and particularisation are most useful.[40] *Universalisation* indicates that styles and elements that originally belonged to a specific culture are detached from that specific culture in order to play a role in a larger system. One could say that they now enter a distinctly new phase in their 'cultural biography', and in that process their original function and meaning changes. This is how a (Hellenistic) *koine* is built up. Through increasing connectivity, all kinds of elements (for the Hellenistic repertoire: mostly Greek, but also Egyptian, Etruscan, Persian, etc.) can be found in ever-widening contexts, acquiring new meanings there and changing in character. The conquests of Alexander the Great and their results are, of course, most important for how this *koine* came into being – the Hellenistic world, in my view, was an era of 'cultural globalisation' as much as the seventeenth and eighteenth centuries were (see below). With this common repertoire of universal (global) elements available, we subsequently see *particularisation* in local contexts. Elements from the Hellenistic *koine* were only made to work and got their specific interpretation through contextual application. This does not mean, of course, that they were blank: earlier meanings and associations could play an important role, as is discussed below. It is also clear that not all areas or groups in society had equal access to the Hellenistic *koine* (although *koine*, it is certainly not about elite material culture alone; also pottery styles and decorations, for instance, fit the framework), or that the repertoire looked everywhere exactly the same. As with present-day cultural globalisation, a farmer in Nubia in 50 BC, for instance, had less access to the *koine* than a well-educated citizen from Rome; and at the Nile the *koine* looked different from how it looked in the centre of the western Mediterranean. But the point is that they were both part of the same system, as is clearly testified by the occurrence of the same types and styles of material culture all around the Hellenistic and Roman world. The so-called Second Pompeian style serves well as illustration.[41] Second Style wall paintings are decorations of (mainly) upper-class houses that show architecture and architectural elements. Although best known from Rome and Pompeii, the Second Style was a global Mediterranean phenomenon that was popular from around 80 to 20 BC (Fig. 7.3). Each time, forms and materials from all over the Hellenistic world were combined in novel ways. Nowhere, therefore, do Second Style wall decorations look the same and there are certainly differences between (local) particularisations over the (global) Mediterranean. But the elements are all taken from

Figure 7.3: Second Style wall painting from the villa of Oplontis, room 15, eastern wall, 60–40 BC, in situ.

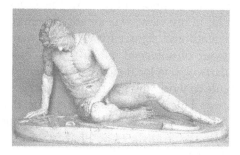

Figure 7.4: The dying Gaul, Rome, now housed in the Capitoline Museum.

the same reservoir. Through their particularisation, moreover, new combinations are made that, in their turn, are added to the *koine* with the possibility of being particularised (etc.). Through processes of universalisation and particularisation the 'Second Pompeian style' is globalised and globalising.

Of course these elements, even when looking similar, did not at all mean the same thing in all these different contexts. Even a global, seemingly uniform 'American' cultural concept like Coca Cola is, amongst myriad other ways, locally contextualised as 'a black sweet drink from Trinidad'.[42] The famous Ludovisi barbarians (known today as 'the dying Gaul' and 'the Gaul killing himself and his wife'), now in the Capitoline Museum (Fig. 7.4) and the Palazzo Altemps (Fig. 7.5) in Rome, respectively, provide a good example of how this process works in practice.[43] These statues in a distinct Pergamene style were always thought to be Roman copies of a Hellenistic

Figure 7.5: Gaul killing himself and his wife, now housed in the, Palazzo Altemps, Rome.

victory monument dedicated by the Attalid kings of Pergamon (Pergamum) after their victory over the Celts. Miranda Marvin, however, has convincingly argued that neither this specific meaning nor their Pergamene context played an important role in the Roman 'copying'. Within the Hellenistic *koine*, the Pergamene style had acquired two major functions: it was associated with 'good' Greek monarchs (the Seleucids and Ptolemies being the 'bad ones' for the Romans) as well as with a major theme of Attalid propaganda: a grand victory over the Barbarian. This latter idea had a meaningful historical background: the Pergamene rulers had selected it, as the clash between civilisation and barbarism had been one of the most important defining metaphors for Classical Athens. The stress, in Roman visual material culture, on the conquered made this theme and style an excellent candidate for local particularisation in (probably) the second century AD. The Ludovisi barbarians then 'reveal distinctly Roman ideas about victory, join a long line of Roman images of the conquered and fit into a known pattern of adoption of Greek predecessors'.[44] From realistic

Celts they had been universalised into semantic barbarians to be particularised as 'conquered by Rome'. It is the triumph of empire that is displayed here, in a 'Greek' style that had nothing to do with Greece, and only slightly with the idea of Greece as conquering the uncivilised. Another example, which I draw from the work by Annetta Alexandridis on female statues, underlines the importance of these stages in the life histories of styles and themes.[45] For Alexandridis the Greek style of these female statues is not relevant for their interpretation ('perhaps they would not even have been recognised as "Greek", but were only perceived as a sign of belonging to a broader elite culture'[46]): she thus sees the statues as china unrelated to *China* (or China). Originally portraying individual women with exceptional earnings for the community, these portraits were universalised into a portrait type within the Hellenistic *koine*. Combined with the guise of goddesses, such portrait statues were a privilege of the imperial entourage during the very first part of the first century AD. Through this particular contextualisation this type of portrait statue was, somewhat later under Claudius, also attractive for imperial freedmen, which resulted in a rather general use of them as theomorphic images at the end of the first century AD. Statues of exceptional, individual women were thus universalised into a general, female portrait type, to be particularised as imperial goddesses and therefore, consequently and again one stage further in their 'biography', as status symbol for a specific social group of freedmen – to end up as rather general theomorphic images (Fig. 7.6). It thus is, every time again, mainly the direct previous stage in the 'life history' of this theme that determines the next; other previous stages perhaps played a role; original ones most probably not.

In the process of universalisation, styles and elements lost part of their original meaning. Through their subsequent particularisation they acquired new meanings and understandings as well. As such they built up a distinct 'cultural biography' – and with that undoubtedly also some form of agency. The understanding of types and styles of visual material culture in the Roman Mediterranean therefore lies at the intersection of their 'cultural biography' on the one hand and their 'contextual application' on the other. Their meaning, therefore, is, to quote Appadurai from the beginning of this essay, all about 'the actualities of the *longue-durée*'.

PUNCTUATING CONNECTIVITY

We have seen that the system of Hellenistic *koine* – which could be called the software of Roman visual material culture – came into being through a

Figure 7.6: Statue of Athenais from the nymphaeum of Herodes Atticus in Olympia (small Herculaneum woman type), around the middle of the second century AD, now housed in the Olympia Museum.

process of much increased connectivity that spanned the whole known world, and that it functioned remarkably similarly to our present-day globalising culture in terms of universalisation and particularisation. I argue that it is through the Roman political and military dominance over the whole *oikumene* that this system was distributed on an unprecedented scale to include an unprecedented amount of participants and to become a truly globalising *koine*. Indeed Rome is globalised and is globalising.[47] Culturally speaking, in the Roman world 'things Greek' become the empire's most leading 'global' commodity. The previous section explains why, in the Roman republic and empire, things Greek were *not* mere materials representative of a culture ('things') any more, but possessions that carried socio-economic and cultural values within a world-system (what we then perhaps could call 'subjects'). In an important article, Robin Osborne has shown how similar 'semantic' principles already played a role in earlier periods.[48] For Osborne, the much discussed distribution of Athenian black and red figure pottery throughout the Mediterranean in the Classical period *presupposes* rather than transmits cultural knowledge. This is to say that he considers the pots and their images to be functioning as 'cultural concepts' in a circular system. Greek pottery had been universalised earlier – not in the least by the fact that in the eighth and seventh centuries BC large amounts of, for instance, Corinthian pottery were transported throughout the Mediterranean. The contextual particularisation of that pottery in the Classical period, therefore, often will have had little to do with its original meaning (and cultural baggage). But of course the fact that they were 'Greek' pots may have played a role. What we have to understand by 'Greek', however, depends on the development of this concept over time whereby the stylistic and material properties of this distinct category of material culture should not be overlooked – this chapter has drawn the same conclusion on Aegyptiaca. Be that as it may, it seems to be clear that the network as such, with a common (global) culture characterised by circulating 'subjects', was already in place during what we call the Archaic and Classical period. Tamar Hodos has clearly shown to what extent this period is about shared practices and common bodies of knowledge, and therefore characterises it as the 'Global Mediterranean Iron Age'.[49]

I have used the opposition of 'things' versus 'subjects' on purpose in reference to Michel Foucault's *L'Archéologie du savoir* (1969), as the distinction might be useful to clarify the punctuation of connectivity that is explored in this section. Can we pinpoint a transition from types and styles of material culture as 'things' towards these same types and styles as 'subjects'? Of course we cannot in absolute evolutionary terms, but still it is interesting and useful – even in a very general and impressionistic way (as in this section – to try and validate different 'moments' in the history of the Mediterranean and Near East in terms of relative connectivity.[50] Hölscher's model for understanding Greek-style sculpture in the late republic and Roman empire shares characteristics with Osborne's reconstruction of the functioning of Greek-style pottery in the Archaic and Classical period and with Hodos's analyses of Iron Age Sicily; but are they talking about the same thing? I think there is an important difference in scale. The ancient historian Paul Veyne, a friend of Foucault's, already noted the importance of that difference in his famous article from 1979 when he analysed 'the two Hellenisms'. As an example of the first – which he calls 'international Hellenism' – Veyne mentions the Etruscan artisan working in a 'Greek' style. This happens, Veyne argues, as a matter of fact, without much value judgement (or inkling) on 'Greekness'. Strong value judgements do play a crucial role, however, in the 'second Hellenism' when, from the end of the third century BC onwards, cultural definitions on what is (and is not) 'Greek' give shape to Rome in a period when it 'had to teach itself world civilisation'.[51] *Contra* Veyne, I would argue that this has little to do with acculturation, but everything with the cultural concept of Greece as that had been developed in the post-classical and Hellenistic world and now served an important purpose for Roman *ethnogenesis*. Apparently something had changed quite dramatically. But what?

Justin Jennings has recently distinguished 'eight hallmarks of global culture' in order to characterise what he identifies as multiple periods of globalisation.[52] We could start by applying them to see whether they help to explain the difference Veyne alludes to in terms of globalisation. Jennings's characteristics can be summarised as follows: (1) time–space compression (the impression of living in a smaller world); (2) deterritorialisation (culture becomes increasingly abstracted from a local, geographically fixed context); (3) standardisation (the emergence of a common 'language'); (4) unevenness (the existence of a power geometry); (5) cultural homogenisation (people coming into contact with widely shared ideas and products); (6) cultural heterogeneity (the blurring of boundaries results in a need to stress those boundaries); (7) re-embedding of local culture (things come into sharper relief and hence locality is stressed); and (8) vulnerability (places become increasingly dependent on actions that are occurring in other places). The identification of these hallmarks is most useful, as it forces discussions on understanding ancient societies in terms of globalisation to be much more specific than they usually are. On the other hand, a lot of cultures from the ancient world fit these characteristics as being global, which do not explain, for instance, the difference Veyne talks about. Jennings himself identifies the Uruk-Wara culture (Mesopotamia, around 4200–3100 BC) as global, which is an obvious candidate as Algaze had already described Uruk as the first 'world-system'.[53] This would probably characterise the great Near Eastern empires following that period (Babylonian, Assyrian and, perhaps most particularly, Achaemenid) as truly global; while also other political and social structures of, for instance, the first millennium BC (the Phoenicians and their diaspora; the Greek city states with their pan-Hellenic cultural vehicles) match the criteria in one way or the other. Could one be more specific?

The development of mankind has been described as a long-term trajectory that started with diversification ('out of Africa', 150,000 BC) and changed into convergence from the Neolithic period onwards. Beginning with the Neolithic and the globally spreading process of Neolithisation, therefore, convergence is the dominating trend, although of course with many breaks and interruptions.[54] The Bronze Age is an important punctuation: scholars have talked about a world-system for this period and it is clear that there existed something resembling a Bronze Age *koine*, no matter whether we define this as an 'international style' or not.[55] An important role here is played by what historians have called the 'commercial revolution' that started with trade diasporas from around 1,000 BC onwards. The circulation of goods amongst elites, characterising the Bronze Age, is now, in the Iron Age, supplemented by a circulation of people.[56] Growing convergence and interconnectedness resulted in what is considered to be another crucial new punctuation: the period around 600 BC. It is around this time that we see the definition by cultures of themselves as 'cultural containers' and, with that, the creation of distinct (Greek, Egyptian, Persian, Jewish, etc.) cultural traditions.[57] The fact that we witness this kind of grand-scale self-definition occurring worldwide can only be the outcome of living in a highly interconnected world. It is only in confrontation with the other that one defines its own culture and the 'Axial Age' *ethnogenesis* thus testifies to (and seems to be the outcome of) a process of long and intense intermingling. As a result of this process of identity formation, so it seems, 'things' more and more start to become 'subjects'. It is only with Alexander the Great and the Hellenistic period, however, that slowly a system emerges in which, in the Mediterranean and Near East, all these highly interconnected 'cultures' develop something of a common (Hellenistic) culture.[58] Hellenistic kingship is an example hereof; and in the religious and cultural spheres we witness a profound process of 'translatability' between the different cultural traditions. As nodal points, cities are crucial for the emergence of this 'global culture' and it does not surprise therefore that they were one of Alexander's main instruments of empire – and that Rome eagerly absorbed this principle. However, I argue that it is only through the Roman conquest, and the institutionalisations it brings with it, that we have the time–space compression in the real sense, which characterises globalisation to a significant degree. A new punctuation in the history of the Mediterranean and Near East seems to begin after the Second Punic War, around 200 BC, with 'intensification' as its defining characteristic. Shipwreck data, for instance, display a threefold rise in the number of shipwrecks from the third century BC to the first century BC. Survey data from all over the Mediterranean world show a multiplication of sites in the last two centuries BC. The economy grows exponentially. We are therefore not simply dealing with increased connectivity (again), but with what seems to be the result of increasing connectivity over a sustained period.[59] Perhaps this punctuation must also be connected to the fact that 'the developments in the second and the first centuries BC marked a decisive stage in the integration of the Mediterranean, Indian and Chinese spheres, and in their interconnection', as Philippe Beaujard maintains.[60] The institutionalisation of the Hellenistic system over the whole *oikumene* resulted in an unparalleled circulation of goods and peoples and common practices. Along with that came the stress on local identities that is characteristic of a globalised world. The global culture itself was Hellenistic, but it was only through the Roman conquest of the known world that, from a contemporary perspective, the world also literally became global.[61] From the period of 200 BC onwards, therefore, the whole *oikumene* is one 'hyper-network', which we should call 'global' to better indicate the degree of connectivity and time–space compression we are talking about.[62] From this period onwards, also, the semantic system of Hellenistic *koine* wherein 'things' really have become 'subjects' begins to take off.[63] It is only against the background of a globalised world that we can understand the functioning of such a system.[64] Of course there still were a lot of cultures in the Mediterranean from 200 BC onwards – that is not the point when calling it a globalised world – and these cultures still implied difference. These differences, however, were no longer taxonomic, but largely had become interactive and refractive.[65]

CONCLUSION: ACTUALITIES OF THE *LONGUE-DURÉE*

There are many issues within the field of Roman (visual) material culture studies that our current paradigms fail to effectively address. In this respect, this chapter has analysed acculturation thinking and, emanating from that framework, transfer studies as a major problem. For the Roman world these models are insufficient to account for the dynamic of worldwide circulating material culture and – sometimes with them but often also independent from and without them – people and ideas. This was illustrated by discussing the functioning of material culture we call 'Egyptian' and 'Greek' in that period. It shows that these were often much more 'subjects' than 'things', and that to arrive at a reconstruction of their meaning we should look at the actuality of their *longue-durée* development. The geographical unit proper and its inhabitants (Egypt/Greece and Egyptians/Greeks), ideas about those cultures as they circulated throughout the (Mediterranean) world and, thirdly, the stylistic and material properties associated with these cultures influenced and constituted each other in processes of cultural and social formation. In the Hellenistic and Roman period these 'subjects' had been thoroughly universalised and had become part of a *koine*, from where they could be taken and be particularised for a next stage in their cultural biography. Hölscher realised the fundamentally different nature of this system (and hence Roman 'art') from what came before and he therefore described it as semantic. He identified the period of around 200 BC as its beginning.[66] Looking at some important punctuations of connectivity in Mediterranean and Near Eastern history suggests a reason for this watershed. From around 200 BC onwards Hellenistic culture, in itself already 'global' in nature, was brought to dramatic time–space compression through the Roman conquest of the *oikumene* and its institutionalisations. It is for this reason that Polybius (Histories 1.3) writes, only some decennia later, about the world from that period onwards as an 'organic whole'.[67] And that indeed should be our perspective to understand it.

Do we need globalisation theory to arrive at these kinds of analyses? The answer to such a question is, of course, always 'yes and no'. Drawing on the conclusion of a recent important book, however, illustrates well, I think, why that trying to push the globalisation analogy more strongly – and for now preferring the 'yes' over the 'no' in answering the question – is a fruitful way forward. Andrew Wallace-Hadrill's *Rome's Cultural Revolution* (2008) has rightly been reviewed as a landmark publication that has established the new *communis opinio* on how to understand the transformation of Roman society in the late republic and early empire. Its main innovation lies in the fact that it understands processes called 'Hellenisation' and 'Romanisation' – earlier distinguished as markedly binomial and understood in nation-state terms – as related and relative. Against fusion, hybridity and other terminology rooted in acculturation thinking and cultural container conceptualisations of the Ancient World, Wallace-Hadrill proposes to think in concepts like code switching. The metaphor he advances for his alternative understanding of cultural interaction is the drawing and pumping of blood to and from the heart. The first, diastolic, phase sees Greek culture being drawn into Italy; in the systolic phase Greco-Roman culture is pumped away to the provinces; etcetera. The image immediately makes clear where the strength of Wallace-Hadrill's model lies, and that is in the *continuous circularity* it puts central to its understanding of culture contact. Still, the metaphor is a rather crude one and leaves important questions unanswered.[68] What about the earlier period of the 'first, international Hellenism'? What about 'cultures' and cultural concepts other than 'Greek'? And what about the stylistic and material properties of so-called culture styles? Perhaps one could place *Rome's cultural revolution* on the brink of moving towards concepts of 'cultural globalisation' while not speaking that language.[69] Be that as it may, the dynamics Wallace-Hadrill tries to understand are better described, for instance, in terms of Arjun Appadurai's 'global ethnoscapes' than by means of a diastolic/systolic metaphor which, despite its circularity, retains the cultural containers Greek and Roman.[70]

Approaching the Roman world – and Roman material culture especially – through globalisation studies therefore seems to be an excellent way to arrive at important new understandings and perspectives. This counts in particular for the main subject of this chapter: the connections and disconnections between cultures, cultural concepts and material culture stylistically indicated by these names. The study of the meaning of Aegyptiaca, the important scholarly discussion on Roman 'copies', their 'Greek' originals and the semantic functioning of Roman visual material culture, our understanding of Rome's cultural revolution, Romanisation: all these discussions would profit immensely from including insights and theories from the globalisation debate.

Lastly, how can we define the advantages of understanding the Roman *oikumene* as a global ethnoscape characterised by continuous cultural circularity in somewhat more general, theoretical terms? From the case studies discussed above two points come to the fore. The first is that cultural concepts and material culture routinely studied under nation-state headings (Greek, Roman, Egyptian, etc.) do not so much express (some kind of 'original') meaning having to do with these headings. On the contrary, they provide the capacity to *make* meaning. What we call Roman culture was therefore not integrative (as cultures are usually imagined to be and sometimes are) but, in fact, *aggregative*.[71] And through its specific characteristics as a successor culture – globalised by and globalising through the system of Hellenistic *koine* – Rome was immensely aggregative. The second point brings us back to the Ming dynastical tomb and the difference between China, *China* and china. The existence of an independent category of china with its own stylistic and material properties has the potential to provide important alternative interpretations for the Roman world. It has long been realised that objects are not just passive carriers of meaning but constitute people (and history) as well.[72] If we want to understand (visual) material culture from the Roman world we should get *beyond representation* and not solely focus on what something *meant* in a certain context and for a certain viewer but also what it *did*. It is clear that, in the Roman Mediterranean as in all societies, objects were perceived as having agency. Many literary sources testify to these kinds of viewer responses towards things.[73] Also with Hölscher's ideas on 'the language of images' (see above), agency of material culture was shown to play an important role, as certain subjects or styles were able to evoke certain associations with the viewer.[74] Talking about agency, therefore, is not about saying that things were alive, but rather saying that people ascribe characteristics to things that they normally ascribe to human beings alone. As such, objects become agents functioning in a network of social relationships. As Ian Hodder (2012) recently schematised it: humans depend on things; things depend on other things and things depend on humans.

The important question then is: How did objects in the Roman Mediterranean acquire their specific form of agency? What did this form look like and where did its power come from? What, in other words, was the strength of their language about and what specific impact did their agency have? In beginning to provisionally answer that question it seems that the notions of universalisation, particularisation and *koine* should (again) play an important role. As described above, it is through these continuous appropriations over time that styles and themes build up their own 'cultural biography'. I suggest that it is this cultural biography or, in other words, the cultural memory that has condensed in these objects that gives them their specific form of agency. The archaeological parameters of the perception that the object evokes through its cultural history are *style* on the one hand and *materiality* on the other.[75] It has been described above how, for the Ludovisi barbarians, their Pergamene style made them into something of an ultimate symbol for 'the conquered' in the second century AD. That this style evoked this association so strongly was a result of its cultural biography: it arrived not blank in the second century AD but imbued with a lot of cultural memory circling around concepts like Hellenistic monarchs, Pergamon, Athens/Persia and the Other. The marble itself might well play a role in strengthening the agency of these associations-through-style. How these two (can) work together becomes clear when looking at the Aegyptiaca discussed in this essay. Often Aegyptiaca in Rome have very specific stylistic and material properties: not only do they stand out by their style but also by their materiality of being made from hard, dark stones like granite or greywacke. Style and materiality thus seem to have worked together in evoking, in the case of Egypt, associations with Mediterranean cultural concepts like, amongst other things, (deep) historical time, religion and the (Oriental) Other. Aegyptiaca came with a lot of cultural memory and will thus have had a particular and strong form of agency. However, in order to understand this agency in a particular historical context it is important to look at what had happened to this potential in the previous phase of the cultural biography and to focus on specific styles and types within the category, as Marvin (2002) did in her case of 'Graeciana'.

I have not dealt in depth with the agency of (visual) material culture in the Roman world; elaborating on it here only served to underline the importance of distinguishing an independent category of china that is functioning as an actant in a network where also ethnic categories (China) and cultural categories (*China*) can be found circling around. This essay concludes that in cultural terms the Roman *oikumene* was a global ethnoscape characterised by continuous cultural circularity. If we see objects as actants in this circular system – and if we think about how humans depend on these things and how these things depend on other things – a rather different picture of the Roman world emerges than usually imagined. A picture fundamentally characterised by objects in motion. In quantitative and qualitative terms there is an explosion of forms and styles and types and combinations of material culture in large parts of the Mediterranean and Near East from around 200 BC onwards.[76] Thus, many more actants than ever before were added to the hyper-network we call the (globalised) Roman world. As things with agency these objects would indeed strongly influence the people around them. If we decide to place most emphasis in our understanding of the Roman world on these objects in motion, we could perhaps even say that all political and social developments traditionally employed to describe it are just structures built around these circulating things.[77]

Be that as it may: if we look at the various scholarly debates on Roman (visual) material culture as they have been briefly presented in this chapter, it could well be argued that (ultimately) they all are looking for a theoretical framework that sees Roman archaeology primarily as understanding objects with their agency in motion.[78] Globalisation studies are crucial in building such a framework.

NOTES

1. See Brook (2008, 76) for a discussion of this example; I have used his account as my primary source of information. The find itself is published and commented upon in *Wenwu* (*Cultural relics*), a journal published by the Institute of Archaeology from the Chinese Academy of Social Sciences, (1982: 16–28) and (1993: 77–82).

2. The term 'methodological nationalism' is meant to indicate that due to nationalism as the dominant paradigm for writing history since the nineteenth century, cultural achievements have been routinely claimed for nations. As a result, culture has often been 'nationalised' and 'territorialised' (Nederveen Pieterse 2009). The practice is summarised by Rowlands (2010, 237): 'We are used to names and things being mutually constitutive as part of a modern nationalist ideology'. See further critique in relation to Roman archaeology in Pitts & Versluys (Chapter 1 this volume).

3. Compare, to take just one example, a tomb that was found in 1988 at Mušov in Moravia, 60 kilometres north of the Danube frontier, and that contained 'both

Roman imports and significant objects of local manufacture' (Wells 1999, 120–1). In his interpretation, Wells sees the 'local' objects as referring to the traditional position of the elite warrior in European prehistoric society, while the 'Roman' objects would refer to knowledge of Roman dining customs or the Roman system of client kingship. I use this example to show that (even) a theoretically refined book like Wells (1999) reasons from a direct relation between material culture that is stylistically 'Roman' (or 'Native') and a 'Roman' (or 'Native') meaning. I am not concerned here with the validity of his argument in this case, but with his method of interpretation.

4. Also here I largely follow Brook (2008, 54–83). Further background to the development and meaning of china is provided by Finlay (1998; 2010) and Rujivacharakul (2011).

5. See, for example, (Pitts, Chapter 4, this volume), on the European adoption of porcelain as a comparative model for Roman period mass consumption.

6. Brook (2008, 76).

7. Hölscher (1987/2004).

8. Rujivacharakul (2011). For materiality see further below.

9. For reasons of proper historical analysis, I therefore add a geographical unit to Rujivacharakul's model: there is China (the country with its 'culture'); there is the cultural concept *China* and there is china as materiality. Thinking in terms of globalisation does not imply that culture areas can no longer be used as units of historical analysis; for this discussion, see Lederman (1998).

10. I refer here to the critique from scholars who maintain that the concept of globalisation is *not* going to help us to better understand the Roman empire; the most thoughtful and wide-ranging being Naerebout (2006/7). See also the final paragraphs of Pitts & Versluys (Chapter 1, this volume): if our field is really at the beginning of what for other disciplines has been described as a paradigm shift, it is useful to underline at this stage what the problems with current concepts are, or, in other words, why we take the risk of evoking the buzz word globalisation.

11. Be that as it may, it is interesting to note that 'Roman art', a branch of classical archaeology often thought about as 'old-fashioned and under-theorised', has, in fact, developed important perspectives for the field as a whole.

12. See Isayev (Chapter 6, this volume), for a somewhat different perspective on this period.

13. See, for instance, the many publications in this domain of Marchand (f.i. 1996) and Hingley (f.i. 2001a).

14. The foundation charter is the article by Redfield et. al. (1935, 145–6), with the definition: 'Acculturation comprehends those phenomena which result when groups of individuals having different cultures come into continuous firsthand contact, with subsequent changes in the original cultural patterns of either or both groups'. See more extensively, for the concept of acculturation (in relation to archaeology and the ancient world), Cusick (1998); Flaig (1999); Naerebout (2006/7); Naerebout (2007) and Späth (forthcoming).

15. Gotter (2001, 286): 'Für Gesellschaften, wie wir sie in den historischen Disziplinen begegnen, ist bereits der Versuchsaufbau des kulturanthropologischen

Akkulturationskonzepts unsinnig. Die Entwicklung von einem "first-hand-contact" bis zu "subsequent changes" ist nämlich schlichtweg nicht sauber zu verfolgen, wenn Kontakt ein Dauerphänomen ist ... Die Geschichte von Gesellschaften, die endemischen Austausch mit anderen pflegen, ist also geradezu von Anfang bis Ende Akkulturation ... Mit dieser Feststellung aber verliert das Konzept jegliche heuristische Prägnanz'. The fact that later on in his text he tries to 'save' the concept as he sees no alternative, does not make this critique less true.

16. For Roman identity and the usefulness and application of the concept of identity in the study of the Roman world, see Pitts (2007); Wallace-Hadrill (2007); Versluys (2008, 2013); Whitmarsh (2010b). See Cordier (2005) for a more extensive critique on acculturation in this respect.

17. 'on est confronté à une logique de réseau, et non à un flux linéaire'. Quote from Bonnet (2009, 70), when she summarises one of the main general conclusions of the German project 'Römische Reichsreligion und Provinzialreligion: Globalisierungs- und Regionalisierungsprozesse in der antiken Religionsgeschichte' (for which, see Rüpke 2011).

18. For this in itself valuable conclusion, see Naerebout (2007).

19. I draw here on my own previous work (Versluys 2010a and forthcoming; I refer to those articles for full bibliography) and on current research that is undertaken as part of the NWO (The Netherlands Organisation for Scientific Research) VIDI research project 'Cultural innovation in a globalising society: Egypt in the Roman world'.

20. From a theoretical point of view Tanner (2003) is one of the best analyses of 'understanding the Egyptian'; unfortunately the article is only seldom referred to, which might have to do with the fact that its subject proper is 'finding the Egyptian in early Greek art'. Against what he calls 'the ethnic paradigms of art history', Tanner argues for 'connectivity and incorporation'. Illustrative for the view underlining original religious backgrounds is the interpretation by Quack (2005) of the meaning of Aegyptiaca and temples for the Egyptian gods in Italy. For the very problematic term 'egyptomania', see the review article by Curran (1996).

21. I owe this metaphor to Crielaard (1998).

22. For this material (and the meaning of Aegyptiaca in this period more in general) see Hölbl (1986) and Gordon (1996).

23. See in general, with many examples and full bibliography, the volumes of Isis studies as published in the last decade: Bricault & Versluys (2007; 2010; 2013).

24. As, through his identification of Egyptian 'priestly bricoleurs', Frankfurter (2000) has so well shown to be the case for Late Antiquity.

25. For this view of Hellenistic and Roman Egypt as a cultural Renaissance actively looking back (and around), see Versluys (2010a) (with bibliography). For the success of the cultural scenario *Egypt* in contexts of death and burial, see Riggs (2005). Note that, in line with what has been argued at the beginning of this paragraph, this particular use and understanding of *Egypt* also was established as a common practice in the Mediterranean long before the third century BC as

testified by, for instance, by 'Egyptianising' symbols and elements in Etruscan tombs.

26. The fact that the cultural concept of Egypt, the ideas on the country at the Nile and its civilisation, had been actively discussed and developed in the Mediterranean already from the Archaic period onwards is important with the first aspect. For these ideas on Egypt in Antiquity (and the consequences of this large and important cultural debate), see most recently Moyer (2011). Concerning the second aspect: in a recent article Eva Mol (2012) has taken this approach even one (radical) step further by deconstructing the notion of 'Aegyptaica' as a useful category of (-emic) perception in a Roman context altogether.

27. Werner & Zimmerman (2006, 36–7). Note also the (similar) critique by Gotter (2001).

28. See also Pitts & Versluys (Chapter 1, this volume). This observation ties in with a point made by Waters, who wrote (1995, 111): 'Material exchanges localize, political exchanges internationalize and symbolic exchanges globalize'. Roman (visual) material culture is mostly about symbolic exchange but still is often studied in terms of material exchange alone.

29. Appadurai (1996, 4); Miller (1998, 185).

30. I use the term 'cultural biography' in reference to the body of archaeological theory that has grown from Kopytoff (1986). For its relevance in the study of Roman (visual) material culture, see more extensively Versluys (2013).

31. In her introduction to the edited volume *Collecting China*, Rujivacharakul (2011, 15) states: 'When material objects are circulated in multicultural contexts, their cultural definitions always change. The challenge is to locate the criteria that alter or maintain those definitions'. I put 'hybridity' between inverted commas as I consider it to be an unhelpful term: it leads back to container thinking (see Pitts & Versluys, Chapter 1, this volume) and, for the Roman world, has very limited explanatory power (see below).

32. I use the term 'visual material culture' in order to by-pass the discussion on the existence of a separate category of 'art' and its usefulness as a category of historical analysis. For this discussion, see the recent volume of *Arethusa* 43 (2010).

33. Probably for that reason as well, the huge advances within this field are not always sufficiently taken up in larger debates. A book like Wallace-Hadrill (2008) could be said to laudably bridge that gap.

34. See for critique and a new approach, Gazda (2002) and Perry (2005).

35. See Perry (2005, 49) for this terminology; her book is probably the best, general introduction to the subject and presents many examples.

36. Hölscher (1987/2004).

37. Hölscher (2004, 125–6): 'In such conditions, what mattered was not necessarily the origins of the forms, in terms of the history of style, and doubtless even their connection with values frequently came to be loose. The received forms were allowed to become value-free elements in a language of imagery, which one simply used'.

38. Hölscher (1987/2004). Hölscher has elaborated on his ideas in various publications, specifically focusing, so it seems, on the concept of 'roles' in recent

years (see Hölscher 2008). A proper and wide-ranging evaluation of his groundbreaking work is still lacking. Contextualisation and (some) criticism can be found in the Foreword to Hölscher (2004) by Elsner, and in Strocka (2010). For another, more applied description, see Zanker (2007), who characterises the system as 'Schlagbild-Repertoire'.

39. Rightly, therefore, Alexandridis (2010, 253) discussed 'copying as a global practice' in this respect.

40. For the notion of Hellenistic koine (and its historiography), see Colvin (2011). For *koinoniai* as 'global' networks bringing together people from different backgrounds in the Classical period, see Vlassopoulos (2007). For its functioning in terms of universalisation and particularisation, see the important article by Witcher (2000) that I elaborated upon in Versluys (2013).

41. For this example, see Versluys (2013) with earlier bibliography.

42. Miller (1998). Note that his plea *not* to focus on production and consumption contexts but on the different *conceptualisations* is highly relevant for a better understanding of Roman (visual) material culture. I have tried to apply such a perspective in Versluys (2013).

43. I follow here the analysis and interpretation of Marvin (2002) and refer to that article for detailed information and bibliography.

44. Marvin (2002, 223).

45. Alexandridis (2010). Note her plea for an approach 'that follows the statue types over time and focuses on the meaning they adopted through use'.

46. Ibid., 259.

47. See Nederveen Pieterse (Chapter 10, this volume).

48. Osborne (2007).

49. Hodos (2009, 2010b).

50. For Foucault there are three important stages in the formation of 'subjects' out of 'things': their emergence, the development of their power to influence social institutions and the social order and taxonomy they result in. Here I am mainly concerned with the first stage. For a long-term perspective of Mediterranean connectivities more in general, see Sommer (Chapter 8, this volume).

51. Veyne (1979, 8). Veyne borrowed the idea of this distinction from Eduard Fraenkel. On the concept of acculturation Veyne commented (4): 'Décidément l'acculturation n'est qu'un mot, qui désigne les conséquences variées et subtiles de situations historiques qui sont autant d'intrigues variées et compliquées. A vrai dire, l'acculturation est un phénomène incessant et universel' ('Ultimately acculturation is just a word, indicating the varied and subtle outcomes of historical situations that are all both varied and complicated. To be sure, acculturation is a constant and universal phenomenon'). His phrasing hints at a similar critique on acculturation as expressed in this essay. For the friendship between Veyne and Foucault (and an interesting view on Foucault's work), see Veyne (2008).

52. Jennings (2011, Chapter 7). Jennings rightly sees globalisation in ancient societies not as a long-term historical trend leading to modernity. Fundamental for his definition are the existence of a leap in interaction in combination with the creation of a global culture; identifying these results in 'multiple globalisations'. cf. also Pitts & Versluys (Chapter 1, this volume).

53. It is one of his three examples; the other dating to 600–1000 AD (Huari, Peru) and 1050–1300 AD (Cahokia's peak, Mississippi).
54. See Manning (2005); Lucassen (2007). For Neolithisation as a global process, see Louwe Kooijmans (1998).
55. The work by Algaze (1993) on Uruk has been mentioned. Note that the recent discussion (and elaboration) by Stein & Özbal (2007) uses the word *oikumene* as main characterisation. For the Bronze Age world-system, see Beaujard (2010, 1): 'For the late Bronze Age one can acknowledge the existence of a multi-centred Western world-system encompassing the Mediterranean basin, Egypt, and western Asia'. For the 'international' stylistic *koine* of the period, see Feldman (2006) in particular.
56. See Sommer (2007), who concludes that, for the Iron Age, thinking in terms of 'Greek' and 'Phoenician' networks does not really work and proposes to speak of a 'composite Mediterranean network to which Phoenicians, Greeks and "indigenous" populations, settled and mobile groups, traders and producers of commodities, mercenaries and slaves each contributed to a specific extent'. cf. also Hodos (2010b).
57. Karl Jaspers' ideas on these canonizations, originally published as *Vom Ursprung und Ziel der Geschichte* (1949), are still useful, although now best approached through the volumes edited by Eisenstadt (1987–1992) and the recent volume edited by Bellah and Joas (2012). I will not deal here with the discussion and critique on the concept of the 'Axial Age'. Beaujard (2010, 15) talks about 'the key period of the sixth century' and notes a change of scale in interconnections going hand in hand with a new phase of integration of (what he calls) 'the Western World-System through the Achaemenid empire'.
58. From Jennings's analyses it is clear that the emergence of a 'global culture' is one of the main defining characteristics of 'a globalisation'; and rightly so. Beaujard (2010) describes the period from around 350 onwards as also witnessing growing interaction between the three world systems.
59. cf. Hodos (2010a, 24): 'The movement of goods, styles and ideas led to developments, accommodations, and assimilations of practices, goods and ideas'.
60. Beaujard (2010, 34).
61. Literary sources quoted throughout this book testify to the fact that, also from a contemporary perspective, drawing a line around 200 BC makes sense: people really thought of themselves as living in a new era, see, in particular, Pitts & Versluys (Chapter 1, this volume).
62. cf. Rutherford (2007).
63. See Zanker (2007, 12): 'Im Laufe weniger Generationen kam es zu einer Umfassenden Neugestaltung aller Lebensräume. Funktion und Bedarf an Bildern änderten sich dadurch grundlegend, und in der Folge entwickelten sich die Strukturen eines neuartigen, spezifisch römischen Bildersystems'. ('There was an allcompassing redesign of all domains of life within only a few generations, Through this, the function of and the need for images fundamentally changed, and subsequently the structures of a novel, specifically Roman system of images were developed'.)

64. Wells (2012) draws very similar conclusions as I do here, also arriving at his interpretations through a combination of globalisation-thinking and material culture studies. For his area (western temperate Europe) and his subject (the so-called La Tène style) he defines the period around 200 BC as the major transition, strengthening my ideas about the importance of this period as watershed from his perspective.

65. I paraphrase Appadurai (1996, 60) here when he remarks on his context: 'Culture does imply difference, but the differences now are no longer taxonomic, they are interactive and refractive'. Almost all case studies presented in Whitmarsh (2010b), for instance, illustrate this.

66. A conclusion now to be compared to Wells (2012).

67. For the importance of these conceptualisations of the world as a single sphere in terms of globalisation, see Sloterdijk (2004). Polybius's 'global moment' must, of course, be understood from the context of his *Histories*, see Isayev (Chapter 6, this volume) and, more in general, Smith & Yarrow (2012) with an earlier bibliography. This watershed is also visible, perhaps, in how scholars (implicitly) deal with culture contact before and after, as the papers in Hales & Hodos (2010) might illustrate. Scholars talking about the pre-Hellenistic Mediterranean generally develop their ideas well in thinking in terms of connectivity and 'hybridity' to make the point that foreign objects are not the same as foreign ideas, but that interpretations should be about the own, local *habitus*. In Hales & Hodos (2010), it is only the paper by Alexandridis that moves from connectivity towards globalisation, as it deals with the system of inherent pluralism of the period after 200 BC described in this chapter. Perhaps for the same reason, van Dommelen & Knapp (2010a), although dealing with, mentioning and using globalisation as a concept, do not put it central to their analyses – or their title.

68. See also the important review by Osborne & Vout (2010).

69. It is interesting to note that Geiger's (2009) review of *Rome's Cultural Revolution* starts off by saying that: 'To realise how much this book reflects present-day concerns one should read it alongside Keith Thomas's wonderful and exactly contemporaneous *The Ends of Life. Roads to Fulfilment in Early Modern England*: for instance their discussions of the spread of consumer goods, luxury wares and fashions show one of the most amazing historical parallels one is ever likely to encounter'. Note that Veyne (1979) draws parallels with contemporary society throughout his article to arrive at his conclusions.

70. See Appadurai (1996, 48) for a definition (when talking about why this is a proper neologism for an ethnography to understand modernity): 'The landscapes of group identity – the ethnoscapes – around the world are no longer familiar anthropological objects, insofar as groups are no longer tightly territorialized, spatially bounded, historically unselfconscious, or culturally homogeneous. We have fewer cultures in the world and more internal cultural debates'. This is exactly what we see accelerating from around 200 BC onwards. Describing the late republic and early empire as a global ethnoscape helps considerably to easily contextualise all the processes Wallace-Hadrill describes.

71. For this distinction, see Cohen (1985).
72. Material culture has agency – something that within archaeology is often discussed under the heading of materiality. Debates on its meaning and usefulness often go in very different directions and it seems that many scholars are working on the same thing under different headings and with (sometimes) a very different emphasis: materialty, human–thing entanglement, agency of material culture, thingness, 'matter striking back', etc. I use the term materialty here in a very general way to refer to this growing body of theory and to emphasise that (1) materiality is an integral dimension of culture; social existence cannot be fully understood without it, and (2) especially for archaeologists, materiality should be a starting point in studying cultural processes; they should not see objects as passive carriers of meaning imbued on them by historical subjects and/or periods from the outside (alone). Particularly useful (and with an overview of the debate and key terminology) are Gell (1998), Pels (1998), ter Keurs (2006), Tilley et al. (2006) and Hodder (2010; 2012). For more detail see Versluys (2014).
73. For which, see Bussels (2012).
74. Hölscher (1987/2004). Note that the title of the book is about images having a language (and thus agency from their part to speak to viewer and context).
75. One could also understand the style and the stylistic properties of an object as part of its materiality. Here I retain the two categories as, throughout the chapter, 'stylistic and material properties' have been mentioned. Materiality is understood here, then, in a rather practical way as the material from which the object is made with its specific colour and other material characteristics.
76. And Europe, see Wells (2012).
77. cf. Appadurai (2001, 5) on our present-day globalised world: 'It has now become something of a truism that we are functioning in a world fundamentally characterised by objects in motion. These objects include ideas and ideologies, people and goods, images and messages, technologies and techniques. This is a world of flows. It is also, of course, a world of structures, organizations, and other stable social forms. But the apparent stabilities that we see are, under close examination, usually our devices for handling objects characterised by motion'.
78. See Versluys (2014) and, in general, Foster (2006). I think other fields of Roman studies show comparable developments. When, for instance, Rüpke (2011) writes on a new conceptual framework for the religion of the Roman empire that we should understand as 'a process by which religious symbols were connected to ever-changing nets within a homogeneous space', I think he is very much pursuing the same intellectual agenda. The same holds true for literary studies; see, for instance, Späth (forthcoming).

8

OIKOYMENH: LONGUE DURÉE PERSPECTIVES ON ANCIENT MEDITERRANEAN 'GLOBALITY'

Michael Sommer

> What was said by Homer, 'The earth was common to all', you have made a reality, by surveying the whole *oikoumene*, by bridging the rivers in various ways, by cutting carriage roads through the mountains, by filling desert places with post stations, and by civilizing everything with your way of life and good order ... And now indeed there is no need to write a description of the world, nor to enumerate the laws of each people, but you have become universal geographers for all by opening up the gates of the *oikoumene* and by organizing the whole *oikoumene* like a single household.[1]

This euphoric praise of the Roman empire's civilising mission, written in the middle of the second century AD by the Greek orator Ailios Aristides, is arguably the single most striking piece of evidence confirming that contemporaries, at least at the apogee of Roman power, were aware of the fact that they inhabited a shrinking world: a world unmistakably affected by the integrating effects Roman imperial rule had on the Mediterranean basin and the adjacent areas, from Britain to the Nile, from the Euphrates to the Strait of Gibraltar. This essay attempts to trace the ingredients of what Aristides calls the *oikoumene*: what made possible the rise of a 'global' society two thousand years before period we call the 'age of globalisation'? How did 'globality' evolve across the centuries?[2]

To be sure, it was Aristides' intention to please and even to flatter his Roman audience. This was the very purpose of panegyric speeches such as *Eis Rhomen*, which were commissioned by, and delivered in, the cities they praise. Yet in essence the Greek-speaking eastern Mediterranean intellectual's assessment is surprisingly accurate. It is in three areas that, according to Aristides, the effects of Rome's civilising power could be felt. Firstly, space – and the blessings of infrastructure and geographical knowledge helping people to come to terms with it: Roman geometers had surveyed every bit of the world; they had erased the last remaining white spots from the map and made geographical knowledge, previously an arcane lore of the few, accessible to the many; in addition, the Romans had built roads and bridges, they had dug tunnels, drained marshes and made steppes and deserts arable; the Roman *cursus publicus* had facilitated communication to a degree unheard of; commodities, people and ideas had become more mobile than ever before in history. Secondly, law: the Roman state had, in addition to, and partially superseding, indigenous laws, established a set of universal norms binding for everybody living or travelling within the empire's perimeter; Roman lawyers had developed their profession to a scientific perfection and Roman citizenship had become a protective shield throughout the provinces – as well as a hallmark of status and prestige. Thirdly, ways of life and 'identities': while Roman rule certainly had not levelled cultural difference and diversity altogether, Greco-Roman architecture, furniture, garment, cuisine, bathing and dining culture, theatrical spectacles, religious customs and concepts of the divine had, by the time of Aristides, changed the provincial world for good, certainly in the West, but increasingly also in the Semitic-speaking east. Still more importantly, this was a change that not only affected, but actively involved almost every single inhabitant of the Roman empire; it was not brought over the provincials, but, to a substantial degree, brought about by them.

This chapter shall investigate the fields set out by Aristides and attempt at tracking, in an extensive – although by no means comprehensive – *longue durée* survey, the changes in geographical knowledge, infrastructure, law and mentality that brought about the integrated, well-connected and, as it were, 'global' *oikoumene* or the Roman world: Aristides' 'single household'. The focus is on the Mediterranean, but occasional excursions into Rome's northwestern provincial universes of Gaul, Britain and Germany exemplify the civilising pull the Mediterranean exerted in Classical Antiquity at all times. In order to allow for a certain degree of comparability, the survey concentrates on the material clustered around three chronological 'thresholds': the time around 800 BC at the beginning of Karl Jaspers' *Achsenzeit*, shortly after the foundation of Carthage, but before the Greek Mediterranean settlement diaspora came into existence – at a time when Phoenician merchant adventurers explored the distant coasts of the Aegean, Italy, North Africa and the Iberian Peninsula; the period of the classical polis of the fifth and fourth centuries BC, when the Mediterranean had become Plato's proverbial pond, around which the Greeks were sitting like frogs; and the early imperial period, when Ostia was the hub of

Mediterranean maritime trade and Roman citizenship became common all over the ancient world.[3]

SPACE

When the great Alexander's army marched across the mountain ranges of central Asia and through the forests and marshes of India, the warriors were followed by flocks of geographers, *bematisteis* (land surveyors) and ethnographers, who supplied Alexander with vital information, mapping at the same time the unknown and thus expanding their contemporaries' geographical knowledge. Furthermore, Alexander had at his disposal the Achaemenid empire's infrastructure and the geographical data it has collected. Yet the Macedonian leadership's knowledge about the part of the world they were operating in was startlingly limited. Only from scouts and locals did the army learn that they were nowhere near the eagerly awaited end of the inhabited world.[4]

Five hundred years before Alexander, the seafarers and traders who, coming from the Levant, had cruised the Mediterranean and settled on far-flung shores could not resort to any geographical data stored by anybody who had ploughed the seas before them. The people who founded Carthage and the ones whom we meet in the Greek myths having *nostoi*, homecomers, as their protagonists, travel through unchartered territories: a mysterious space, full of (mostly negative) surprises and exotic encounters.[5]

The stories the Greeks told about the Mediterranean and Black Sea adventures of their ancestors, their encounters with 'natives' and all kinds of adversity explain the reality of an ethnically diverse, at least partially hostile space the Greeks were about to discover. The wandering of such tales' protagonists, from Odysseus to Iason, from Herakles to Diomedes, is of course emblematic for the unknown these heroes were penetrating: 'charter myths' in the true sense of the word, the stories were part and parcel of the mapping of this alien world beyond the relative safety of the Greek homeland. Sending Greek heroes on 'odysseys' to distant shores transformed a vast, alien and a priori meaningless 'space' into 'place': through myth, the Mediterranean's geography became loaded with significance.[6]

A slightly different perspective is added by the myth centred upon Elissa, Dido for the Romans, the Tyrian princess whose destiny it was to become the founder of Carthage. Conspicuously, of the many cities the Phoenicians founded, only Carthage has a foundation myth of its own. The story survives, in its most complete form, in Justin's epitome of Pompeius Trogus', an Augustan historian's, world history. The narrative's outlines are well known: following the death of her father and the murder of her husband, Elissa escapes from her greedy brother Pygmalion taking, with her crew and companions and after a brief stop on Cyprus, refuge in North Africa. The newcomers are welcomed by the indigenous population and by their Phoenician kinsmen from nearby Utica. Through trade, Elissa and her group establish a friendly relationship with their neighbours, which turns hostile only when the king of the local Maxitani, Hiarbas, starts courting Elissa.[7]

The place of origin of this myth is as mysterious as the time of its creation. The story can be traced back to Timaios of Tauromenion, a historian from Sicily who lived in the third century BC. Yet in all likelihood at least parts of it are much older. The myth has a complex narratological stratigraphy: its core, the story evolving around Elissa's landing in Africa and the foundation of Carthage, appears to evoke an environment in which 'colonisers' and 'colonised' meet on an equal footing: a setting best matched by the Iron Age Mediterranean, when seafaring migrants from the east – Levant and Aegean – first encounter 'natives' in various western 'middle grounds'. There are only very subtle allusions to the Phoenicians' technical head start and their more complex social organisation. Nothing seems to suggest here that the stereotype of the 'barbarian' had fully evolved when this part of the story was first created.[8]

At first glance, the Elissa story seems to share a common stage with the Greek myths of the *nostoi* and of explorers like Iason: a strange new world through which the protagonists sail, populated by non-Greek, non-Phoenician strangers; middle grounds, where the newcomers settle along these strangers, thus creating small local and regional networks and attracting inward mobility from neighbouring zones. But while Odysseus and Diomedes are subjected to erratic, aimless wanderings through an unchartered, seemingly limitless wilderness, Elissa's migration is targeted at a specific point on the African coast, where people from the Phoenicia have settled before, at Utica. Her cruise follows a straight line, via Cyprus, from the Levant to Cape Bon, which corresponds to the first sections of the Phoenician maritime trade route to the far west of the Iberian Peninsula.[9]

Read in context, the Elissa story and the Greek *nostoi* myths represent two asynchronous realities of the Iron Age Mediterranean: the reality of the Aegean, where people were just about to embark on their 'colonial' adventure, and the reality of the Levant, which had dispatched its seafarers and traders on the journey westward since at least the early first millennium

BC. Accordingly, the Greeks' geographical world view was running behind the Phoenicians' mapping of the Mediterranean by more than a century. While Phoenician settlers around 800 BC were still pioneers in the West, they had available the geographical knowledge collected by the peripathetic traders who had travelled Cyprus, the Aegean, Italy, Spain and North Africa long since, at a time when Greeks were still recipients of the Levantine long-distance trade.[10]

Probably back into the eighth century dates a Phoenician text which, somehow, has found its way into the biblical book of Ezekiel: the so-called Lament over Tyre, describing in detail the trade of the metropolis in the Levant: 'Tarshish was your customer because of all kinds of wealth; with silver, iron, tin and lead they paid for your wares. Javan, Tubal and Meshech, they were your traders; with the lives of men and vessels of Bronze they paid for your merchandise'. Thus the text carries on, effectively drawing a map of Tyre's (Tyrus's) commercial network across the Near East and the Mediterranean. On this map, the text confidently locates places known to the Phoenicians: Tarshish (Andalusia), Javan (Ionia), Tubal (the Iberian Peninsula?), Meshech (Cappadocia). The 'Lament over Tyre' clearly indicates that, by the eighth century BC, the Near Eastern and Mediterranean world's geography was familiar to the Phoenicians, whose cutting-edge shipbuilding technology, navigational skills and geographical knowledge were superior to any of their neighbours.[11]

The Mediterranean around 800 BC was hence a space of enormous disparities in technology, development and knowledge. Seafaring groups (the 'Phoenicians') explored areas with populations participating in maritime trade mainly (the Aegean) or totally (the coasts of the Mediterranean west) passively or not at all (the respective hinterlands). Broadly speaking, social complexity and active involvement in commercial exchange decreased from east to west, with mountain ranges and deserts as marginal peripheries.[12]

In the fifth century BC, disparities still divided the Mediterranean basin, but the gap between east and west was closing. From a Greek perspective, the sea between Europe, Asia and Africa had by now become Plato's proverbial pond: the 'Great Colonisation' – certainly no colonisation in the modern sense of the word[13] – had created a Greek diaspora around the Mediterranean; Athenians, Corinthians and many other natives of the southern Balkans and Aegean had settled in the Levant, North Africa, the Iberian Peninsula, southern Gaul, in Sicily and southern Italy. Greek mercenaries were deployed on countless battlefields from the Persian empire to Sicily, and the market was growing since Greek hoplites had excelled at Marathon. The *periplus* written by the Carthaginian admiral Hanno after his expedition along the coast of West Africa was soon translated into Greek: strong evidence that the Phoenician monopoly of geographic knowledge had given way to a sphere in which geographical data could easily travel from one civilisation (and language group) to another and was hence available to those with a vested interest.[14]

Only in such a world could Athens, by far the largest city on the Greek mainland, for its subsistence depend on the continuous importation of large quantities of grain. While the degree of Athens' dependency is disputed since August Boeckh's *Staatshaushaltung der Athener* was first published in 1817, the extent of the city's commercial network certainly is not: grain came from places as far away as the Bosporan Kingdom, Magna Graecia and Sicily. The organisation of such a trade required, obviously, the geographical knowledge of the areas and routes in question as well as a sophisticated infrastructure, of which Athens' maritime hub, the Piraeus, was the centrepiece.[15]

Not just goods, but people as well travelled the Mediterranean with increasing frequency and speed: pilgrimage, oracles and the pan-Hellenic games all implied the mobility of many people. The religious delegations (*theoriai*) dispatched from and to sanctuaries of supra-regional importance such as Delphi or Delos created arteries between cities and sanctuaries: connectivity over distances became thus institutionalised; 'theoric networks' linked one city to others, from the Hellenic motherland to the colonial diasporas of the West and the Black Sea.[16]

Not only for Hellas, but for the Mediterranean at large, the sudden increase in spatial mobility was a watershed: by the end of the sixth century BC, the Greeks had not only physically penetrated the Mediterranean, they had also embarked on an intellectual journey which led them to a profoundly changed understanding of the world they were living in. Still in the sixth century, Hekataios of Miletus wrote his *periegesis*, a remarkably exact description of the world known to the Greeks. At the time when Hekataios wrote, not only the Mediterranean, but also its Celtic fringe was, from a Greek point of view, a *terra cognita*, which was expanded and further filled with meaning by later generations: Herodotus's world encompassed Mesopotamia as well as North Africa, Spain as well as the steppes of southern Russia. Even where Herodotus's account is evidently overgrown with myth and legend – as is the case with the exotic peoples dwelling in the midst of the Saharan desert – the geographical accuracy of the text betrays relatively reliable sources: for places Herodotus had not travelled himself, he could at least obtain some information from hearsay. Yet, for Herodotus, the Sahara was a territory sufficiently unchartered to populate it with the most strangely behaving tribes. By the time of Herodotus, mythical narratives required as their settings exotic places: separated from reality either through an enormous gap in space or in time – or indeed both. In order to create a mythical, extramundane place, Plato had to locate his Atlantis in a distant past in the Atlantic Ocean, far beyond the Columns of Heracles. Analogously, India, Ethiopia and the country of the Hyperboreans were such exotic wonderlands where the realities of the Hellenic world could be defied, their rules and customs easily turned upside down. Between such outlandish places lay the enormous and continuously growing *oikoumene*.[17]

All this suggests that the decisive breakthrough in geographic knowledge, which made possible the stunning increase in integration and connectivity the Mediterranean saw in the Classical and Hellenistic periods, had happened by the middle of the fifth century. If there was a trend towards 'globality', this was a *longue durée* process; and the first stage of this development was the period when the bulk of the geographical information that Greek and Roman – and Phoenico-Punic – societies could rely upon was collected and first processed: the age of exploration and 'experiment', the years between 800 and 450 BC, roughly the first half of Jaspers' *Achsenzeit*. It was in this period that the *oikoumene* of the Phoenico-Greco-Roman world was forming: a universe of explored, mapped territory with a high level of connectivity and accelerated mobility of people, commodities and information.[18]

The later Classical and Hellenistic periods added substantial data to this stock of information, but they did not expand the *oikoumene*: As did Hanno the Navigator in Africa, Alexander with his campaigns on the Danube and of course in Central Asia and India went beyond the known world, but only to establish the limits of the world that mattered to the Greeks. Roman soldiers took their legionary standards, under the Egyptian prefect Aelius Gallus in 25 BC, to the southern tip of the Arabian peninsula and, under Domitius Ahenobarbus in 3 BC, across the River Elbe; Roman rulers, from Caesar to Domitian, conquered a large portion of north alpine Europe, including Britain; Trajan added Dacia to the empire – without, however, altering in substance the mental universe that had been originally established in the Iron Age.[19] And while the commercial ventures linking the Mediterranean basin to the Indian Ocean – from the Hellenistic and early imperial Red Sea trade based to the Incense Road on the Arabian peninsula and Palmyra's oriental trade across the Syrian Desert, Mesopotamia and the Persian Gulf again expanded the geographical knowledge of the world, they did not incorporate the Indian Ocean into the *oikumene*.[20]

Impressive as these achievements may seem, still more important was another contribution Rome made towards a 'globalised' ancient world.

Roman soldiers and administrators did not only conquer and map the Mediterranean world; they also transformed its physical shape to an extent unheard of, thus giving their presence in the conquered territories a totally new degree of intensity. The Romans' approach to newly conquered territory can best be understood from the considerable effort they put into surveying and cadastrating. While they were measuring the land and breaking it up into regular lots, Rome's surveyors performed an act of appropriation: the conquered territory was literally 'Romanised' by depriving it of its original character; instead it was submitted to the Roman system of land registry, which showed only minimal respect to natural features and previous ownership. In the Roman world, the surveyor's *groma* was no less a tool of conquest than the soldier's *gladium*.[21]

Yet, the land survey was merely the overture to a whole range of building activities. The surveyors were followed by engineers and builders, who constructed the infrastructure of roads, bridges, tunnels, drains and aqueducts, which put a distinct, durable Roman stamp on the landscape. And after them came, from Augustus onwards, the personnel who manned and maintained the *mansiones*, the relay stations of the imperial postal service, the *cursus publicus*. Some marginal areas, like the Hauran in Syria, were made accessible to agriculturalists only owing to the skills or Roman engineers.[22]

While the *oikoumene* thus became more Roman, Rome, the capital, was in turn becoming increasingly 'provincial'. In a manner of speaking, the empire struck back – peacefully, not confrontationally[23] – with all the power of its cultural diversity: not only did men from Gaul, Spain, Africa or Greece enter the epicentre of power, becoming senators and, later, even emperors. Romans had become dependent on imported grain and begun to prefer imported wine, oil and *garum* over local products; some started to wear *braccae*, trousers from Gaul, instead of a *tunica* or *toga*; and 'imported' provincial art was on display everywhere in the capital, most notably in the *Templum Pacis* built by the Flavians, where artefacts from across the empire were piled up for the capital's populace to admire.[24]

By the second century AD, when Aristides wrote, Roman soldiers, land surveyors and engineers had indeed left their mark on the wider Mediterranean world – as had the provinces on Rome, which was now firmly intertwined with its empire. The agents of empire had, as had the seafarers, merchants and colonists of previous ages, shrunk this world; the vast, savage and seemingly empty expanse of Homer's Mediterranean had given way to Aristides' 'household', a familiar universe through which even an infamous ignorant like Petronius's Trimalchio could wander, despite a somewhat jumbled geography, with some degree of confidence:

> I don't have to buy [my wine], thanks to the gods. Everything here that makes your mouths water, was produced on one of my country places which I've never yet seen, but they tell me it's down Terracina and Tarentum way. I've got a notion to add Sicily to my other little holdings, so in case I want to go to Africa, I'll be able to sail along my own coasts.[25]

LAW

When Trimalchio made his fortune with maritime trade, his investment was relatively safe. Not only did his ships cross waters with which their captains and crews were familiar, they could also rely on Roman laws and jurisdiction giving them protection, in particular if they were Roman citizens. To be sure: the Roman empire was no constitutional state; there was no absolute rule of law – the emperor became soon the source of all justice and hence of legislation. But the Roman institutions did provide a standard of legal security that was unique in the ancient, if not in the entire pre-modern world.[26]

Throughout the vast empire, the emperor was ultimately responsible for the enforcement of law – whatever law. By no means did Rome impose its own legal framework on the communities it had conquered. Cities and tribes retained their own laws; men and women in the provinces sold their possessions, leased their land, sued their neighbours, passed on their property in line with the laws their ancestors had adhered to. The Roman authorities did not interfere with such legal traditions. Instead, they made sure they were observed. In the first century AD, the empire was still a conglomerate of different legal systems – *Reichsrecht* (imperial law) coexisted with *Volksrecht* (the people's law) everywhere between Britain and Egypt.[27]

But the domain of imperial law was expanding, while the niches in which the (traditional) law of the people was observed were becoming fewer and fewer. This development was owing to two main factors. First, the overwhelming prestige of Roman law prompted local communities to follow the Roman model. Perhaps the most striking example is the *lex Irnitana* from the tiny city of Irni (*municipium Flavium Irnitanum*), near Seville (present-day El Saucejo). The statute from the Flavian period not only follows the patterns of Roman law in almost any detail, it also reserves a provision for such cases which are not explicitly covered by local law: 'for all those matters let them use the civil law which Roman citizens use and shall use among themselves', states chapter 93 of the statute.[28]

A second reason for the decline of local law lay in the spread of Roman citizenship. We have, of course, no reliable date indicating how 'Romanised' the imperial population was, from the point of view of citizenship, in the mid-first century AD. But the evidence suggests a sharp growth in the number of Roman citizens between the Augustan period and the reign of Claudius. Claudius was not only criticised for admitting members of the local élite of Gaul to the Senate; he was also notorious for giving away Roman citizenship without getting much for it in return.

Dwindling numbers of peregrine, non-Roman inhabitants contributed to the empire's creeping juridical unification. Being a Roman citizen was about legal security – Paul famously invoked his status as a Roman citizen and was spared being lynched by a Jewish mob; he had his case also heard by the governor and, ultimately, by the emperor himself. Being Roman entailed valuable privileges, which could turn out crucial if one wanted to survive in critical situation. Besides and perhaps still more importantly, Roman citizenship carried an enormous prestige, particularly in the cities of the eastern provinces, where usually only the upper crust could boast the *tria nomina*.[29]

Because citizenship was a reward for loyalty and, to a degree, assimilation, it was also a formidable push-factor towards 'Romanisation'. Had the rebellious inhabitants of Italy, following the Social War, been forcefully enfranchised, in the imperial period Roman citizenship became a valuable prize. However, its overall value could not be inflated ad infinitum: when the emperor Caracalla, with the *constitutio Antoniniana*, in AD 212 enfranchised the bulk of the empire's free population still of peregrine status, he effectively did away with citizenship as a criterion of distinction. But still in the early second century AD, the historian Tacitus pointed to the crucial role citizenship – and the Romans' generous practise of awarding it – had played in the success of Roman imperial expansion: whereas the Athenians and Spartans had treated the populations subjected by them as *alienigenes*, the wisdom of Romulus had turned Rome's enemies into loyal supporters.[30]

Tacitus was right: the Greek *poleis* failed to turn their citizenship into a tool of integration; on the contrary: the more democratic they were, the more suspiciously they controlled access to their civic body. Hardly surprising, the Spartans, whose Lykourgian community was the most exclusive and, in many respects, the most egalitarian of all political systems of Greece, featured the most severe system of scrutiny. The requirements for full Spartan citizenship included descent from full Spartan citizens, both on the mother's and on the father's side, having run through the *agoge*, and contributions to, and participation in, the *syssitia*. Somewhat less strict, but still exclusive, was the Athenian law of citizenship, which was tightened at the initiative of Pericles in 451 BC, making full citizenship of both parents a requirement.[31]

The polis's civic body, the *politeia* (meaning citizenship, civic body and political system at the same time), was and remained, in contrast to Rome's *civitas*, a collectivity of 'shareholders' in what was literally a 'common-wealth'. With such a practice of 'an der Polis teilhaben' ('participating in the polis')[32] it was impossible to universalise the idea of citizenship. Inevitably, any attempt of doing so would sooner or later collide with the material interest of the shareholders. Hence Aristotle's appeal to restrict the growth of the civic body of a polis: the upper limit was, even in Athens, the urban society which could perform its civic rights and obligations directly. Hence also the Hellenistic empires' incapacity to create 'imperial' civic bodies. There was no such thing as a Seleucid or Ptolemaic citizenship.[33]

In the world of the fifth century, individuals moving or settling outside their hometown were foreigners. And foreigners were, generally, rightless. If they were resident in a foreign polis, they could at best, as did the metics in Athens, expect some guarantees in return for a special tax they had to pay: the *metoikion* in Athens. Due to the Greek *politeia*'s intrinsic inability to evolve into something more universal, legal security for foreigners had to be guaranteed, in the wider Hellenic world, by means of, bilateral agreement or, individual or collective, privileges.[34]

How this could work is illustrated by a document from the mid-third century BC, an Athenian honorific decree for Straton, the king of Sidon. In return for the assistance Straton has provided for an Athenian embassy to the Persian king, Straton is declared *proxenos* of the Athenian people. This honour for the king and his successors entails a number of fairly practical privileges for Straton's subjects: (1) the parties agree on the exchange of *symbola*, which identify their bearers as *proxenoi*; and (2) Sidonian citizens staying in Athens are exempt from the duties of metics; they are liable neither to the *metoikion* nor to irregular contributions.[35]

The document illustrates the integrating power of bilateral accords. First, the basis for such accords is *proxenia*, the practice of individuals representing foreign states that evolved in the fifth century BC. Second, Sidonians resident in Athens are no longer individual metics deprived of most civil rights, but citizens of their home town and hence under the protection of both, the Athenian state and the Sidonian king. Third, the Greek institution of *proxenia* and mutual agreements based on it are not restricted to the Hellenic world; it can be extended to communities which are, from a socio-political perspective, compatible to the Polis model, as was the case with the Phoenician cities in the Levant. The concept of citizenship was known to the Sidonians; hence they qualified for *proxenia*.[36]

Proxenia had its roots in another institution, which predated inter-polis agreements and even the polis itself: *xeinosyne/xenia*, the time-honoured, highly ritualised bond of reciprocal hospitality. For the Greeks, the foreigner was protected by Zeus Xenios, and caring for strangers was an essential social commandment. Without even being asked for his name, a foreigner in the world of the Homeric epics would receive fresh clothes, a bath and a gift as a token of hospitality; he would have been admitted to the community of the *oikos* of his host, whose table he shared. Accommodating a guest created a reciprocal relationship, which could last over several generations. The Homeric *xeinosyne* is a bond of mutual loyalty stronger even than political opportunity. When Diomedes, the Achaean, and Glaukos, the Trojan, meet in battle, they discover that, through their ancestors, they are tied to each other by hospitality.[37]

In a world that was anarchic as far as inter-state relations were concerned, unregulated by international law and state authority that stretched over more than a few square miles, reciprocal institutions like *xeinosyne* provided a quantum of reliability desperately needed by those who travelled and traded. If one thing was 'global' in the Iron Age Mediterranean, it was the rule of reciprocity. Without observing such institutions and relying on others to observe them, no traveller would get very far. When Odysseus and his comrades reach the island of the Kyklopes, he decides to first explore the area and get some intelligence on the locals: 'I want to see if they are barbarous bandits and immoral savages, or friendly to foreigners (φιλόξεινοι) and honouring the gods'.[38]

A millennium lies between the Iron Age norms of reciprocity to the principle of universal citizenship established by the *constitutio Antoniniana*. This millennium witnessed the rise of the polis, of territorial monarchies and finally of the Roman empire. In the course of these thousand years, matters which had been 'private' became 'official', regulated by law. While in the age of Homer everybody had to see to his own safety, the personal integrity of every single inhabitant of the Roman world had, by AD 212, become the responsibility of the state. In the same time span, contacts between different parts of the Mediterranean world multiplied, the geographical knowledge increased exponentially and there was a massive surge in mobility and connectivity. One questions remains: how did this affect the *imaginaire* of the people involved? Did integration and the mechanics of, as it were, 'globalisation' forge an awareness of belonging to a 'global' community?[39]

BELONGING

Reconstructing historical identities is a delicate undertaking, especially if the period in question is remote and the evidence scant. If we accept that collective identities do not exist a priori, but only as social constructions, in the lofty space of peoples' *imaginaire* rather than in the material world of sherds and bones, we unavoidably need *Selbstzeugnisse*, ego-documents: narratives in which the people we study explicitly tell us who they are and how they feel about being what they are. Such documents will normally be texts; in exceptional cases they can be images complex enough to tell a story.[40]

The frustrating conclusion from this is that a history of Mediterranean identities in Classical Antiquity cannot be written. Even for the better-attested parts of this period, our stock of ego-documents relevant to their authors' identity is ruefully small. By far the bulk of such documents comes from Latin or Greek authors, reflecting either the point of view of the Roman state's Italian centre or of the Greek-speaking world. Most of the remaining narratives we owe to biblical and rabbinic Judaism, which opens one window onto the alternative reality of a community at the margins of the classical *oikoumene*. The other peripheries, as seen from a Greco-Roman point of view, remain disconcertingly silent: the whole Phoenico-Punic diaspora, the Celts in transalpine Europe, the inhabitants of the western and northern Balkans, the entire Aramaic-speaking eastern fringe of the Hellenistic-Roman world and, despite the linguistically interesting evidence from the papyri, Egypt. Classicists and archaeologists meditating on cultural identities in the ancient Mediterranean can hardly live comfortably with this situation.[41]

However, for the purpose of this chapter, holistic 'cultural' or 'ethnic' identities, which risk appearing static and monolithic, are not that relevant anyway.[42] Whether people from Sidon and Tyre shared, besides their respective civic identities, a sense of belonging to the same 'Phoenician' community (which they probably did), or the inhabitants of Roman Gaul had 'become Roman' down to the most humble stableman (which they probably had not), is not pivotal to our quest for a *longue durée* 'globalising momentum' in the history of the ancient Mediterranean. What is decisive for such a momentum to be unleashed is the availability of (elite) groups ready to become the spearheads of globality: groups sharing the same patterns of behaviour and consumption and at least a similar yardstick for value, prestige and, ultimately, ethics.[43]

Such groups' behaviour and the material culture associated with it can be traced in countless texts and, more importantly, archaeological records. One paradigm, which has met much attention in recent scholarship, across the disciplines, is the culture of aristocratic banqueting. In the context of this chapter, the convivial ritual is so interesting, because it was both a catalyst of intercultural exchange and a cultural technique spreading through intercultural exchange. Aristocratic banquets required specific utensils and, as preconditions, a degree of social complexity as well as certain social norms, among which hospitality, conspicuous consumption and reciprocity ranked very prominently. You needed all this in order to perform, understand and appraise the convivial ritual properly.

What makes the banquet so valuable for an investigation of ancient Mediterranean globality is its extraordinary diffusion over both time and space. Practised between the Iberian Peninsula and Iran, banquets in elite contexts are attested from the Iron Age through to Late Antiquity. As 'Eucharist' they enter Christian liturgy, with a continuity stretching well into our own global present.[44]

This is not to imply that aristocratic banquets had one single origin from where they spread, or indeed that all the different banquet cultures of the classical world were genetically related to each other. But it means that elites practising convivial rituals, whether in Spain or Etruria, in Iran or Palmyra, were behaviourally compatible to each other. They would, despite many differences in detail, mutually understand and respect their performances and values. This generic concordance then facilitated the emergence of a canonised version of the banquet, with standardised sets of utensils and obligatory codes of conduct. In order to spread, these items presupposed a 'zone of intense contact': an existing network of exchange with dense interaction and 'high degrees of reciptivity'.[45]

In Homeric Greece, the *symposion* was part and parcel of the new lifestyle of a new aristocracy. In an ideal manner, it combined the ostentatious display of wealth through conspicuous consumption with leisure, 'availability' (*Abkömmlichkeit*) in the terms of Max Weber, the second pillar of aristocratic exclusivity, and refined taste, its third pillar. Wealth was displayed by means of selected food and drink in enormous quantities, which was served on luxurious tableware. All these ingredients feature time and again in the Homeric epics. One impressive example for the esteem in which precious drinking vessels were held is the *krater* set out by Achilleus as a prize in the *agon* held in honour of Patroklos: 'a mixingbowl of silver, richly wrought; six measures it held, and in beauty it was far the goodliest in all the earth, seeing that Sidonians, well skilled in deft handiwork, had wrought it cunningly, and men of the Phoenicians brought it over the murky deep, and landed it in harbour, [745] and gave it as a gift to Thoas; and as a ransom for Lycaon, son of Priam, Jason's son Euneos gave it to the warrior Patroclus'.[46]

Not incidentally, this *krater* was the work of 'Sidonian' craftsmen, brought to Thoas by 'Phoenician' seafarers as a token of hospitality. In the Levant, *symposia* were held long before the Greeks created that word. We know from texts from late Bronze Age Ugarit that exclusive aristocratic table communities, so-called *marzēaḥ*, indulged in the consumption of large quantities of wine. In the Iron Age, this custom continued to flourish: *marzēaḥ* (vocalised *mirzaḥ*) were celebrated throughout Judah and Samaria in the eighth and seventh centuries BC.[47] *Marzēaḥ* were also practised across the wider Phoenico-Punic world. The term is attested in the mid-third century BC Piraeus inscription, a text belonging to the environment of Sidonians resident in Athens' port, and the so-called Marseilles (Massilia) tariff, a fourth or third century BC inscription probably originating from Carthage and listing duties payable to a temple and its staff.[48]

By this time the custom of consuming food and drink at symposiastic gatherings had already reached beyond the Phoenician and Greek worlds. With the formation of aristocratic elites in Etruria, the use of painted tableware and of other equipment needed for a *symposion* spread across Italy – and soon beyond. Prestigious items circulated in elite networks. By doing so they often transcended cultural boundaries. Deprived of their original contexts, they were often – creatively – misunderstood, assuming as a result new significations. The classical, historical parallel is the story told by Columbus in his logs about the glass beads the Spaniards traded for food and which turned to prestige goods in the hands of their native recipients.[49]

Erich Kistler tells the story of such an artefact in his *Objektbiographie* of an Achaemenid glass bowl found at Ihringen near Freiburg in 1993. The bowl had been buried, around 500 BC, in a *Fürstengrab*, the tomb of a local warlord, who was then still young, in his 30s. In the Achaemenid empire, 'cups', a collective name for objects like the Ihringen glass bowl, were used as hallmarks, *symbola*, of the Great King's favour: high-ranking members of the imperial aristocracy would receive such gifts at the 'table du roi' on the occasion of convivial banquets at the royal palace at Persepolis. From them, they would then move further down the line, passed on from host to guest as tokens of the highest esteem.

Some of these 'cups' found their way into the Greek cities of the Ionian coast: the Achaemenid far west. From here, they entered the exchange networks of the Mediterranean, where they could circulate for several generations, sometimes for over a century. The modalities of exchange were those described by the Iliad for the Patroklos *krater*. The occasion for passing on such a precious, exotic gift was, as in the vessels' Achaemenid county of origin, still the round table of the convivial gathering. But the hierarchy between the donors and the recipients was less steep here.

Through such a Mediterranean Odyssey, and in all likelihood via Etruria, the Ihringen glass bowl finally reached the slopes of the Kaiserstuhl in southwest Germany, in the core area of the Iron Age Hallstatt Culture. Here, a stratified society with 'elders', who were buried with rich grave goods, had been developing since the eighth century BC. Soon, the forms of communication between the 'Big Men' and those of inferior rank echoed the ones known from the Mediterranean: patterns of a symposiastic culture emerged, with excessive feasting, the conspicuous consumption of large quantities of food and drink and 'streams of gifts' running downhill to keep the Big Man in place.[50]

The *symbolon* of the Persian 'table du roi' had thus become the 'new symbol' of a 'new elite' in what was to become Celtic Europe. Aristocratic societies were about to mushroom everywhere, from North Africa to Gaul, from Britain to the western Balkans. The new aristocracies developed forms of aristocratic conviviality compatible, but not identical, to those known from the Mediterranean. Kistler points to the contextual isolation in which the glass bowl and similar items were found: no material remains of kraters, symposiastic furniture or indeed alphabetic graffiti on tableware have ever been found in the regions to the west and north of the Alps.[51]

Some five hundred years later, symposiastic culture was still thriving in the ancient world which was now Roman. Our survey ends at Palmyra, where, in several inscriptions from the city's epigraphic record, the time-honoured term *marzēaḥ* sees a revival. We know numerous personalities who were honoured with inscriptions while they served in the presidency of a *marzēaḥ* (*brbnwt mrzḥwt*). It seems clear that each of them was attached to one of the major sanctuaries of Palmyra, the most important and prestigious being that associated with the Temple of Bel. That membership was restricted to priests is unlikely, because in some cases dignitaries, who were clearly no priests, seem to have held a *brbnwt mrzḥwt*. The position was undoubtedly prestigious: In one case, admittedly very late (AD 272), a certain Hadudan, head of the Bel *marzēaḥ* was a Roman senator; another individual, Septimius Vorod, a Roman citizen with procuratorial rank, was '*symposiarches* of the priests of Bel' (AD 267). The importance of this 'confraternity' is further highlighted by the enormous dimensions of the banqueting facilities found in the temenos of the Temple of Bel: a hall measuring thirty metres across and ten metres high, located prominently vis-à-vis the main temple.[52]

Much about the *marzēaḥ* in Palmyra remains still mysterious. The fact that Palmyrene bilingualism translated the function of presiding over a convivial fraternity with the Greek word *symposiarches* is as revealing as it is confusing. Did the Palymyrenes simply copy symposiastic culture from their Greek neighbours? Was it western influence that made the oasis dwellers turn towards convivial indulgence? Or was the *marzēaḥ* part of a cultural memory going back to a common Iron Age heritage, of which the actors in the first and second centuries were, somehow, still aware? The quest for obscure origins is pointless, as usual. What matters is that the Palmyrenes of the early imperial period, when they needed to find a terminology and a canonic form for whatever had evolved in their midst, had no choice but to adopt Greek concepts and a Greek vocabulary.

They owed this stunning lack of options to the tide of 'globalisation' that had swept – in the course of a millennium – across the ancient world and had left behind the *oikoumene* their contemporary Aristides was praising so much; they owed it to the integrating powers of the 'single household' into which expanding geographical knowledge, the institutional framework of Roman law and modular, easily adaptable cultural techniques like symposiastic feasting had transformed a previously chaotic, essentially anarchic world. When reflecting about this dramatic change, one is tempted to have the protagonists of this chapter – the Phoenician merchant adventurers, Homer's aristocratic warriors, the Big Man from Ihringen, Plato's frog pond dwellers, Trimalchio, the members of the Palmyrene *marzēaḥ* and the orator Aristides himself – all join the same symposiastic celebration of the *oikoumene*. That none of them, despite dramatic differences and enormous asynchronisms, would probably step too badly out of character is sufficient proof that Aristides' vision of globality was not just wishful thinking.

NOTES

1. Arist. XXVI. 101–2 (καὶ τὸ Ὁμήρῳ λεχθὲν 'γαῖα δ᾽ ἔτι ξυνὴ πάντων' ὑμεῖς ἔργῳ ἐποιήσατε, καταμετρήσαντες μὲν πᾶσαν τὴν οἰκουμένην, ζεύξαντες δὲ παντοδαπαῖς γεφύραις ποταμοὺς, καὶ ὄρη κόψαντες ἱππήλατον γῆν εἶναι, σταθμοῖς τε τὰ ἔρημα ἀναπλήσαντες, καὶ διαίῃ καὶ τάξει πάντα ἡμερώσαντες. [...] οὐδέ γε δεῖ νῦν περιήγησιν γῆς γράφειν, οὐδ᾽ οἷς ἕκαστοι χρῶνται νόμοις ἀπαριθμεῖν, ἀλλ᾽ ὑμεῖς

ἄπασι περιηγηταὶ κοινοὶ γεγόνατε, ἀναπετάσαντες ἀπάσας τῆς οἰκουμένης τὰς πύλας καὶ παρασχόντες ἐξουσίαν αὐτόπτας πάντων τοὺς θέλοντας γίγνεσθαι, νόμους τε κοινοὺς ἅπασι τάξαντες καὶ τὰ πρόσθεν λόγου μὲν διηγήσει τέρποντα, λογισμῷ δ᾽ εἰ λαμβάνοι τις, ἀφόρητα παύσαντες, γάμους τε κοινοὺς ποιήσαντες καὶ συντάξαντες ὥσπερ ἕνα οἶκον ἅπασαν τὴν οἰκουμένην).

2. This chapter, despite addressing in very broad terms the *problématique* of globalisation, avoids the term, more or less consistently. The reason for this is that, to the mind of the author, an explanans should not be confounded with an explanandum. Occasionally, the reader will stumble across old-fashioned concepts such as 'Romanisation' – used in the continental, not Anglo-Saxon fashion. The somewhat idiosyncratic and solidly monoglot English/American discussion (for which see the footnotes of Hingley, Chapter 2, this volume and now Versluys (2014)) has so far failed to appreciate the dynamism of continental scholarship applying modified variations of the concept, cfr., for instance, Desideri (1991); Torelli (1999); Veyne (1999); Stephan (2002) and the contributions in Schmidt-Colinet (2004) and Schörner (2005). On globalisation and how it relates to complementing concepts such as hybridity and connectivity, see Nederveen Pieterse (Chapter 10, this volume). The 'inherent pluralism' that Nederveen Pieterse sees in the Roman world was at work in all ancient Mediterranean societies (as it is, indeed, historically ubiquitous) and is, in manner of speaking, the other side of the coin of 'globalisation'. Fundamental on Aristides' speech *eis Rhomen* are Klein (1995) and Zahrnt (1995). See also Oliver (1953); Klein (1983).

3. 'Achsenzeit': Jaspers (1949). See Eisenstadt (1987) and now Bellah & Joas (2012). All historiography which has the Mediterranean as its protagonist owes much to Braudel (1949). Less ecology-centred, but still very selective and hence unduly narrow in its thematic approach is Horden & Purcell (2000), the most ambitious (perhaps overambitious) and widely read synthesis of recent days. For a 'human', yet not entirely satisfying, history of the Mediterranean see now Abulafia (2011).

4. On the logistics of Alexander's army, Engels (1978); Sonnabend (2007, 115–23).

5. On the geographic world view of Homer's Odyssey see Hübner (2000); Wolf (2009). The *nostoi* and the Archaic Greeks' constructions of the 'Sea of Returns' have been the subject of Malkin (1998: esp. 62–93). On the rise of scientific geography in Greece in general terms Gehrke (1998).

6. Malkin (1998, 178–209) (Odysseus in the west); Moreau (1994); Thalmann (2011, 25–52) (Argonauts in the Back Sea); Bonnet-Tzavellas (1983); Bonnet (1988); Bondì (2005); Malkin (2005c) (Herakles-Melqart); Malkin (1998, 234–257) (Diomedes). On the transformation of 'space' into 'place' through mythological constructions see Tuan (2002, 85–100).

7. Iustin. XVIII. 3–6. On the Elissa myth and its narratological in more detail, see Sommer (2013). See also Kowalski (1929); Panaro (1951); Svenbro & Scheid (1985); Horsfall (1990); Haegemans (2000).

8. In contrast, the second half, focusing on the Maxitani king Hiarbas and his courting of Elissa is soaked with the topos of the antagonism between barbarianism and civilisation. On the 'middle ground' as a heuristic tool see

Malkin (2002, 2004 and 2011, 45–8). For the application of the concept to the Iron Age Mediterranean see Hodos (2006).

9. See Aubet (2001, 159–64) for trade routes.

10. On the organisation of the Phoenician long-distance trade with the West see Niemeyer (1989a, 1989b, 1990a, 1990b, 1995, 2002); Bondì (1995); Aubet (2001, 163–84). On the interaction between eastern newcomers and indigenous populations in the West see van Dommelen (1998, 2002, 2005) (Sardinia); Bondì (1977); Hodos (2006, 89–157) (Sicily); Ben Younès (1995); Hodos (2006, 158–99) (North Africa); Aubet (1990); Schubart (1995); Rodriguez (1997); Aubet (2001); Belén Deamos (2009); Celestino Pérez (2009); Sanmartí (2009).

11. Ezek 27:12–13. On the passage see Liverani (1991, 2003c, 188); Block (1997: vol. 2, 28–86); Sommer (2004a, 239–40; 2005a, 164–5; 2007, 102–3).

12. For an attempt to understand the social and economic disparities of the Iron Age Mediterranean as expressions of a pre-modern 'World System' see Sommer (2004a). This attempt has only been partially successful and has met some justified criticism (Scheidel 2009c, 415).

13. For a typology of 'colonial' expansions see the classic Finley (1976); Osterhammel (1997, 7–18) and for the author's personal point of view, Sommer (2011c). The specifications of modern 'colonialist' expansion have been set out in Osterhammel (2009, esp. 465–672).

14. This despite the Greeks' unwillingness to engage with other cultures by learning their languages, as stated by Momigliano (1975). Others were not reluctant to learn Greek. On the repercussions of colonisation on the Greek world view Gehrke (1986, 39–41). One by-product of the colonial experience was Greek ethnography, in which the encounter between Greeks and others was, from the later Archaic period onwards, systematised in a proto-scientific way (Müller 1972, vol. 1, 58–9; Bichler 2007, 69–88). On mercenaries: Trundle (2004, 132–64). How the experience of mercenaries could enhance the Greeks' geographical knowledge is best shown by Xenophon's *Anabasis* (Sonnabend 2007, 111–15). For the *Periplus* of Hanno: Blomqvist (1979); Picard (1982); Porter (2003).

15. For Athens' grain trade, still valuable is Boeckh (1817, vol. 1, 85–99). Garnsey (1985, 75) has argued that previous scholarship has 'inflated' Athens' dependency on imported grain. But see now Oliver (2007, 15–47) for a differentiated discussion of late classical Athens' 'economic vulnerabilities' caused by its dependency on imported grain.

16. For 'theoric networks' Rutherford (2007, 24–6). See also Kowalzig (2005).

17. Hekataios: Bertelli (2001). On geography in Herodotus see now Harrison (2007) and Engels (2008). The trans-Saharan route described by Herodotus IV. 168–94 has been the subject of some controversial discussion: while Swanson (1975) believes the narrative to be a myth, the majority of scholars (Law 1967; Liverani 2000a, 2000b, 2001, 2003a, 2003b; Sommer 2011b) accepts the existence of a trans-Saharan trade route in the Classical period. Atlantis: Plat. *Tim.* 20d-25c; *Krit.* 108e-121c; see Gisinger (1933); McKay (1980); Görgemanns (2000); Nesselrath (2002: 27). For the Greek image of India see Arora (1996).

Hyperboreans: Herod. IV. 13–15 and 36; Strab. VII. 3, 1; see Bridgman (2005, 27–98). On exoticism in Greek literature, Sonnabend (2007, 68).

18. For the Archaic period as an *'age of experiment'* Snodgrass (1980).

19. On Aelius Gallus see Sidebotham (1986); Marek (1993); on Domitius Ahenobarbus now Johne (2006, 120–8); on India Parker (2008, esp. 72–8) with Versluys 2010b.

20. Young (2001) is a useful introduction. On the relationship between the Mediterranean see now Seland (2010) and the contributions in Seland (2007).

21. Cantor (1875); Dilke (1971); Schubert (1996, esp. 103–5).

22. Cursus publicus: *Di Paola* (1999); Siegert (2003). Land melioration in the Auranitis region: Millar (1993, 426–7); Butcher (2003, 157–61). Key to the 'spread of sedentarisation' was, in the Hauran and elsewhere in the arid areas of Syria, irrigation, the infrastructure for which the Romans expanded on a large scale (ibid., 161–6).

23. The flaws and limitations of binary concepts are highlighted by Pitts & Versluys (Chapter 1, this volume).

24. On the world of images in the *Templum Pacis* and Flavian Rome, see Bravi (2006, 2010) and Versluys (forthcoming).

25. Petr. Sat. 48, 2 (*Deorum beneficio non emo [vinum], sed nunc quicquid ad salivam facit, in suburbano nascitur eo, quod ego adhuc non novi. Dicitur confine esse Tarraciniensibus et Tarentinis. Nunc coniungere agellis Siciliam volo, ut cum Africam libuerit ire, per meos fines navigem*).

26. For the emperor's role as the ultimate source of law, see *Dig.* I. 4, 1 (Ulp. inst. 1) and *Pomp.* D. I, 2, 2, 11–12. However, Mommsen (1907, 192) views the emperor as 'durch Gesetze gebunden' ('binded by laws'). On aspects of constitutional government and judicature in imperial Rome, see Bleicken (1981, 130–2); Johnston (1999, 8–9). The importance of law and legal government for the emperor's legitimacy has been discussed by Sommer (2011a, 162–7).

27. Still immensely valuable on the problem of imperial and indigenous legal traditions in the eastern provinces is, after 120 years, Mitteis (1891, esp. 85–142). The question of competition between legal systems has been treated by Wolff (1979). For a contemporary discussion, with respect to the Babatha and Salome Komaise archives from the Dead Sea, now Oudshoorn (2007, 25–31). On the emperor's role in jurisdiction: Millar (1977, 228–52); also discussing the working of the 'petition and response' system (507–49).

28. For an authoritative edition and translation of the *lex* now Wolf (2011). See also González (1986); Crawford (2008). Specifically on the relationship between local and Roman law Simshäuser (1992); Kränzlein (1993); Lamberti (1993).

29. On St. Paul's arrest and trial Acts 22–25. See Garnsey (1966, 182–5); Millar (1977, 511). On Roman citizenship as a prime prestige resource in the Near East, with particular respect to the middle Euphrates-Khabur region, Sommer (2004b, 166–76; 2005b, 305–29). In order to understand the criteria of enfranchisement, the Tabula Banasitana (CIL XIII 7335 = ILS 7096), an inscription from Banasa in Mauretania Tingitana (present-day

Morocco) dating from AD 177, is an instructive document. Iulianus, a member of the local tribe of the Zegrenses, and his family, were made Roman citizens because (1) he is one of the leading men of his tribe (*de primoribus esse popularium/suorum*); (2) he had been always loyal to the Roman cause (*nostris rebus prom[p]to obsequio fidissimum*); and (3) due to his enfranchisement, Iulianus would serve as a role model for other tribesmen to emulate (*cupiamus ho/nore a nobis in istam domum conlato ad aemulationem Iuli/ani excitari*).

30. See Tac. *Ann.* XI. 24, 4: There is some debate as to the universalisation of citizenship through the *constitutio Antoniniana* and its impact: while Buraselis (2007, 120–57), points to the edict's integrating and legitimising effects, other scholars see the *constitutio* more in a different light (Hekster 2008, 45–55 distinguishes between intended and contingent effects). At any rate, the constitutio Antoniniana did not level the legal disparaties between different groups inhabiting the empire. On the contrary, the distinction between citizens and non-citizens was, already from the mid-second century AD onwards, replaced by a new differentiation between (legally privileged) *honestiores* and *humiliores* (ordinary people). For the long and complicated history of research see Rilinger (1988, 13–33). On citizenship as a (supposed) aim of Rome's Italian allies in the Social War, see Keaveney (1987, 63 and 126), but especially Mouritsen (1998, 87–109).

31. Perikles' law was targeted at the aristocracy. It led to a further erosion of aristocratic power, rendering the Panhellenic marriage policy of Athenian upper class obsolete (Schubert 1994, 158–61). From the law, Perikles emerged as Athens' dominating political actor. Sparta: Walter (1993, 173–5); Athen: (ibid., 185–210); see also Sainte Croix (2004) and, for an overview, Westhead (1991).

32. Walter (1993).

33. Aristot. pol. 1278a, 26–34; on Aristotle's conception of the *politeia* see the valuable discussion in Piepenbrink (2001, 67–77). For a case study in citizenship in Seleucid Babylonia, see Spek (2009, 114).

34. Two or mere Greek city-states could, on a mutual basis, agree on a joint citizenship, while maintaining their respective autonomies (*isopoliteia, isoteleia*), or they could merge into a new political unit (*sympoliteia*). On this relatively late development in Greek law Gawantka (1975, esp. 21–46).

35. Tod GHI II 65 (Austin/Vidal-Naquet 71).

36. Gschnitzer (1974); Habicht (2002).

37. Hom. *Il.* 6, 215–31.

38. Hom. *Od.* 9, 175–176 (ἤ ῥ' οἵ γ' ὑβρισταί τε καὶ ἄγριοι οὐδὲ δίκαιοι, ἦε φιλόξεινοι, καί σφιν νόος ἐστὶ θεουδής). The fundamental work on the integrating power of reciprocal norms of behaviour is Mauss (1923/24), who first described the rationality behind reciprocal 'règles de la générosité' of pre-modern societies. According to Gouldner (1960), reciprocity creates a climate of confidence, because you help and do not harm those, who have previously helped you.

39. For further details see Pitts & Versluys (Chapter 1, this volume).

40. The concept of collective identity as a social construct goes back to the seminal work by Berger/Luckmann (1966, 194–200). See also Müller (1987, 121–44); Assmann (1997, 130–44). That archaeological cultures cannot be equated with historicial (ethnic) identity groups has been argued conclusively by Jones (1997). On the use of *Selbstzeugnisse* as historical sources, see Redlich (1975).

41. For an up-to-date overview see the contributions in Gruen (2011). To be sure, each of the areas mentioned here has been thoroughly scrutinised by scholars, and with considerable intellectual yield. Israel/Judaism: Stemberger (1983); Gruen (1998, 2002); Stemberger (2009). Phoenicians and Carthaginians: Sommer (2009). Celtic Europe: Woolf (1998); Hingley (2005, 91–116). Balkans: Mócsy (1974, 53–79). Aramaic-speaking east: Millar (1993); Ball (2000); Butcher (2003); Sommer (2005b, 2006). Multilingualism and identity in Egypt: Frankfurter (1998); Torallas Tovar (2010).

42. See Versluys (2013; Chapter 7, this volume) on the fallacy of the nation-state perspective and holistic concepts of ethnic/cultural/national identity. See also Pitts & Versluys (Chapter 1, this volume) on the pitfalls of modern, national perspectives on the Roman world.

43. On the role of elites in processes of globalisation Luhmann (1971, 1997, vol. 1, 145–6); see Rehbein/Schwengel (2008, 130–42).

44. This final section owes much to the research of my Innsbruck colleague Erich Kistler, who has investigated aristocratic banqueting cultures across the Mediterranean in a series of important studies: 'banquet ideology' in the Iliad and the Odyssey (Kistler 1998, 78–141); in Persia at the Achaemenid court (Kistler 2010a); in archaic Sicily (Kistler 2009); in Celtic Europe (Kistler 2010b). On classical banquet culture and the Eucharist, see Smith (2003, 1–12).

45. The terminology has been borrowed from a typology proposed by Ulf (2009, 93–101 and 110–16), who distinguishes zones of 'open' from those of 'intense contact', the latter of which constitute spheres of high 'receptivity'.

46. Hom. Il. 23, 741–7 (ἀργύρεον κρητῆρα τετυγμένον· ἒξ δ᾿ ἄρα μέτρα χάνδανεν, αὐτὰρ κάλλει ἐνίκα πᾶσαν ἐπ᾿ αἶαν πολλόν, ἐπεὶ Σιδόνες πολυδαίδαλοι εὖ ἤσκησαν, Φοίνικες δ᾿ ἄγον ἄνδρες ἐπ᾿ ἠεροειδέα πόντον, στῆσαν δ᾿ ἐν λιμένεσσι, Θόαντι δὲ δῶρον ἔδωκαν· υἱὸς δὲ Πριάμοιο Λυκάονος ὦνον ἔδωκε Πατρόκλῳ ἥρωϊ Ἰησονίδης Εὔνηος). Abkömmlichkeit: Weber (2005, 1053–4).

47. For Judaea see the polemic against symposiastic culture in Amos 6: 4–6. The word *marzēaḥ* can be traced back to late third millennium Ebla-Tell Mardikh. On the Eblaitic texts and on occurances of *marzēaḥ* in the documents from Ugarit-Ras Shamra see McLaughlin (2001, 9–34). *Marzēaḥ* are also mentioned in Jewish diaspora environments: in the Cairo Museum Ostracon 35468a from Elephantine (ibid., 35–6) and, repeatedly, in rabbinic literature (ibid., 61–4).

48. Piraeus inscription = KAI 60; Marseilles tariff = KAI 69. Greenfield (2001, 907) wrongly assumes that the *marzēaḥ* 'originated in all likelihood in Carthage'.

49. On creative misunderstandings and cultural transgressions Ulf (2009, 116–17). Columbus: Reichert (2001, 214). For what follows: Kistler (2010b, 66–86).

50. Kohl (2000, 66) ('Gabenfluss').
51. Kistler (2010b, 87–8).
52. PAT 1358; PAT 2812 (Hadudan inscriptions, see Gawlikowski 1971: 412–21). PAT 0288 = CIS II. 3942 = Inv. III. 7 (Vorod inscription). On the Palmyrene *marzēaḥ* Teixidor (1981); McLaughlin (2001, 48–61); and above all Kaizer (2002, 220–34).

9

GLOBALISATION AND ROMAN CULTURAL HERITAGE

Robert Witcher

INTRODUCTION

This chapter explores the intersection of contemporary globalisation and Roman cultural heritage and, specifically, tangible heritage in the form of archaeological landscapes, sites, monuments and artefacts. It works across a number of closely related disciplines in order to evaluate the distinctive position of Roman heritage and its diverse academic treatments, political appropriations and popular receptions. It takes the imperial frontier provinces and, in particular, the *Frontiers of the Roman Empire* World Heritage Site (WHS) as a case study. The starting premise is that, just as the intimate historical relationship between archaeology and nationalism had been clarified,[1] globalisation has undermined the nation-state and hence archaeologists are confronted with the renewed task of redefining the relationship between past and present.[2] The particularly close relationship which arose between Roman archaeology and nationalism during the nineteenth and early twentieth centuries raises questions about the continued relevance of this heritage for a post-national global order. In particular, the prevailing rhetoric of the globalised present asserts that borders and boundaries retreated with the nation-state and hence the study of Roman frontiers might therefore be perceived as particularly passé. Yet, one of the many paradoxes of recent globalisation is the resurgence of the nation-state. In such a context, might Roman cultural heritage be of renewed resonance? Not least, the revival of the nation-state has been accompanied by the resurgence of old as well as new borders, suggesting that the Roman imperial frontiers might assume a newly relevant role in contemporary mobilisations of Rome's cultural heritage. Advancing from this starting point, the aim of this chapter is to reinforce calls for archaeologists to reflect on the political positioning of their research and how they communicate it beyond the immediate discipline, and to consider the problems and opportunities of Roman cultural heritage at the intersection of archaeology, politics, tourism, economics and identity.

GLOBALISATION VERSUS GLOBALISM

In recent years, a number of scholars have suggested that globalisation might be a useful lens through which to understand the Roman world.[3] These contributions must be put into a wider context. Since the late 1990s, historians and archaeologists of many other periods and places have also employed the concept and/or the vocabulary of globalisation in their research, including studies of the Iron Age/Hellenistic Mediterranean[4] and the Germani of early Medieval Europe.[5] These contributions restrict themselves to single period examples and surprisingly few make explicit whether they believe globalisation is only of relevance to their particular case study or whether it is of broader value for understanding other periods and places as well.[6] All, however, are explicit in their use of the concepts and terminology of globalisation. In contrast, though Horden and Purcell's influential volume *The Corrupting Sea* (2000) has been characterised as a globalising narrative because of its emphasis on connectivity and flows,[7] this description is refuted by at least one of the authors.[8]

These examples, and the others discussed in the introduction to this volume, point toward one clear conclusion: scholars of the Roman empire do not have a monopoly on the use of globalisation for studying the past. Moreover, the chronological and geographical range of these examples is significant because it highlights the fact that the concept of globalisation can be deployed in extremely diverse contexts. One reason for its breadth of apparent significance and applicability is that globalisation is a term which simply *describes* generic processes of enhanced connectivity and cultural relativisation. The concept itself does not *explain* any of these specific developments; it is simply a description for periods of particularly intense connectivity and cultural change across the long term.[9] The Roman empire and the contemporary world are just two phases of globalisation amongst many, each of which requires specific explanation. Whilst there may be some cross-cultural similarities between the mechanisms used by complex societies to expand, interact and integrate, there are also likely be substantial differences in the specific explanations for the rise of, for example, Uruk, Rome, the Goths and the modern world. To explain why globalisation is particularly intensive today, it is necessary to consider neoliberal political and economic policies, and technologies such as telecommunications; these specific explanations for the contemporary world order have been labelled

'globalism'. Likewise, alongside descriptions of the Roman empire as globalised, we need to develop an explanatory theory equivalent to contemporary
globalism (as also advocated by Nederveen Pieterse in Chapter 10, this
volume) to explain the enhanced connectivity of the Roman empire.

During the late 1990s, I wrote a paper entitled 'Globalisation and Roman
Imperialism', which drew attention to some similarities between Roman impe-
rialism/Romanisation and contemporary globalisation.[10] Though I was careful to note the many differences between the ancient and modern worlds, I was
struck by the apparently easy slippage between the two and I subsequently
became increasingly concerned that globalisation was simply a fashionable
synonym for Romanisation and, worse, one which failed to address the many
well-documented conceptual issues associated with the latter. Distinguishing
between description and explanation now makes clear to me that the reason
Romanisation and globalisation can appear so similar, even interchangeable,
is because they are merely descriptions of enhanced connectivity and cultural
relativisation. For example, 'time–space compression' is simply a generic
description that can accommodate both the ancient and contemporary worlds;
the explanation for such compression may be as different as the circulation of
Roman coinage and the Internet (see also Morley, Chapter 3, this volume).

Making a distinction between explanation and description (or cause
and effect) also throws light on the debate about whether or not globalisation is universal or uniquely modern. For example, Dench states that
'"[G]lobalisation" is clearly an anachronistic concept, a phenomenon far
more aggressive, divisive and all-seeing than anything of which the Romans
were capable even in their wildest dreams'.[11] Pace Dench, I argue that
globalisation is not anachronistic; it is a long-term historical phenomenon.
The differences between the Roman and contemporary worlds lie not in the
existence of such processes, nor even in their scale, but in their specific
explanations. Moreover, the real task of the archaeologist and historian is
not simply to explain each of these different historical phases individually,
but also to explain why some phases were more or less intensive than others.

Recently, the historian A. G. Hopkins has suggested that the sudden
conversion of many of his colleagues to the cause of historical globalisation
was part of a dramatic academic shift following the terrorist attacks of
11 September 2001.[12] The gradual swell of archaeologists' interest in globalisation may or may not be attributed to this event, but from the particular
perspective of Roman archaeology there is arguably a more specific explanation. Around the turn of the millennium, there was a substantial shift in
perceptions of the character of contemporary globalisation. In the early
1990s, the dominant discourse concerned homogenisation and the levelling
of global difference. For the post-colonial generation of Roman scholars,

intent on the deconstruction of the universalising concept of Romanisation, this type of globalisation was anathema.[13] By the 2000s, however, understanding of globalisation shifted significantly in order to emphasise the diversity of local and regional identities that have proliferated alongside global economic interdependence and political integration. This reorientation towards diversity has had much greater resonance for the post-colonial generation, with its insistence on the heterogeneity of Roman identities. Arguably, it is this convergence of ideas that explains why scholars of the Roman world have, after initial hesitation, embraced globalisation, or at least its vocabulary, with some speed and enthusiasm.[14]

Whilst my thinking has inevitably evolved over the decade since my previous contribution, I maintain a strengthened belief that globalisation is of great relevance to studies of the Roman past. In part, this relates to my deeper awareness of, and concerns about, the cultural and political context of (Roman) archaeology. Hence, in this chapter, I approach the subject from a very different perspective compared with my previous contribution. Rather than considering if and how globalisation can help archaeologists to understand the Roman past, my aim is to consider the ways in which the Roman past may help contemporary society to understand the globalised present. How have the artefacts, monuments and landscapes of the Roman past been integrated or ignored in the most recent and intensive phase of globalisation?

GLOBALISATION AND HERITAGE

The intimate connection between the nation-state and heritage has been well studied.[15] During the nineteenth century, archaeological sites and monuments were constructed into discourses of inclusion/exclusion, as nations mobilised heritage to counter competing claims of sovereignty and to justify overseas colonial ventures. Their central objective was to replace a kaleidoscopic range of ethnic, cultural and religious identities with strong connections between national citizenship and territory through the promotion of shared historical genealogies. This territorial approach meant that heritage became, and remains, a particular focus of dispute; ownership by one state means that it is not owned by another – a 'zero sum game' approach to the past.[16]

Across the contemporary world, cultural heritage is implicated in a growing number of disputes and armed conflicts within and between nation-states. Historical sites such as the Preah Vihear temple on the border of Cambodia and Thailand, or the city of Jerusalem (Hierosolyma), are the subject of competing claims that attempt to assert one cultural, political or religious identity over another through territorial control of cultural heritage. Simultaneously, even paradoxically, there are increasing demands upon heritage to promote social cohesion, to stimulate economic growth and to generate tourist income. It is within this context that the theory and practice of heritage management have been completely transformed over the past 25 years. The discipline may have started with a focus on the physical conservation of historical sites, but it has reoriented to stress the symbolic value of heritage sites in the creation and contestation of historical and contemporary identities, their role in causing and resolving social injustice, in promoting what might, could or should have been and in building a better future.[17]

In the contemporary world, cultural heritage has therefore been seen to be both part of the problem (e.g. appropriation by nationalist and colonialist causes) and part of the solution (e.g. promoting social inclusion). Within this scenario, Roman cultural heritage holds an interesting position. González-Ruibal makes the striking point that whereas ancient Greece has been appropriated in *cultural* terms, ancient Rome has been appropriated in *political* terms.[18] Whilst this is a simplification, it effectively underscores the way in which the Roman past has been repeatedly and overtly used by political regimes to justify their actions[19] and thereby helps to explain why Roman archaeologists of the later twentieth/early twenty-first centuries have been more wary of engaging with political agendas than scholars of some other periods and places.[20]

Yet if archaeologists have been reticent to address the contemporary and political dimension of the Roman past, others have not. Heritage professionals, museum practitioners, novelists, journalists and TV producers all find the Roman empire a source of particular fascination. From the perspective of communicating with the public about the past and its resonance with the present, the Roman empire delivers an abundance of historical detail, monuments and personal artefacts such as writing tablets and tombstones which provide tangible insights into the lives of individual Roman subjects (Fig. 9.1). This fascination must be understood in terms of the deeply embedded ancestral status many Western European countries ascribe to the Roman past and both actively and passively inculcate through processes such as schooling and 'banal nationalism'.[21] In the Western imagination, the chronological remoteness of the Roman past has been bridged via engrained societal admiration for the technological superiority of straight roads, flushing toilets and underfloor heating, and the civilising gifts of language, law and art.[22] Even dystopic visions of Rome, particularly popular with Hollywood film makers, tend to contrast the corrupt Rome of the emperors with the lost and honourable ideals of the republic.[23] Given the historical

Figure 9.1: Tombstone of Regina (RIB 1065). D(is) M(anibus) Regina liberta et coniuge / Barates Palmyrenus natione/Catuallauna an(norum) XXX (to the spirits of the departed and to Regina, freedwoman and wife of Barates of Palmyra, a Catuvellaunian by tribe, thirty years old). Photo: author.

development of Roman archaeology and the centrality of Rome in the Western imagination, what changes if any of perspective and interpretation have occurred as a result of contemporary globalisation?

GLOBALISATION, MULTICULTURALISM AND PLURALITY

As observed above, globalisation in the 1990s was often understood as homogenisation ('McDonaldisation'), which was a threat to local, regional and national identities, and this remains a widespread belief. More recent work, however, has recognised the proliferation of identities that result from and accompany the spread of global consumer culture and increased inter-dependence. Some of these identities have resurfaced, as for example with the collapse of the Soviet Union; other identities have emerged due to the increased mobility of people via migration and diaspora. Heritage is increasingly central for the creation, maintenance and assertion of these identities. In their introduction to this volume, Pitts and Versluys argue that the main impact of globalisation on Roman archaeology to date has been through interest in the issue of identity in the past, paralleling a wider shift in the social sciences from class to race, ethnicity, religion and gender as the preferred categories for sociological analysis.[24] Mattingly's post-colonial concept of 'discrepant identities' in the Roman empire provides a particularly developed example, arguing that individuals and groups used identity to emphasise difference as much as to stress unity.[25]

If heritage is increasingly considered central to the assertion of identities, it is also seen as a means to manage these identities via policies such as multiculturalism which seek to recognise the value of, and to create respect for, cultural diversity. Significantly, different nations have their own specific multicultural aims and policies. Some require tolerance, others demand equality; some intend the retention of particularistic identities, others envisage the emergence of new hybrid, cosmopolitan societies. Strictly speaking, multiculturalism is therefore a series of nationally specific political strategies designed to address contemporary social issues.[26] All, however, impinge upon the issue of heritage and shared historical experiences and values.

As a political strategy, multiculturalism is contentious and is the subject of critique from both the Left and Right. The latter argues that multiculturalism leads to social balkanisation and is therefore a threat to community cohesion and national unity. In contrast, critique from the Left argues that multiculturalism fetishises diversity and therefore does nothing to radically rework social relations or to empower the excluded groups it purports to help; by defining cultures as stable and exotically 'other', it is has been seen as cosmetic and depoliticising rather than transformative.[27] Still others argue that the concept is useful, but that the terminology has become impractical.[28]

Notwithstanding such critiques of contemporary multiculturalism, there are growing numbers of references to historical multicultural societies in both academic contexts (e.g. the Caliphate of Cordoba,[29] Roman York (Eboracum)[30]), and in broadsheet newspaper articles and museum exhibitions.[31] These references to historical multiculturalisms find resonance in the past for a key contemporary issue. Most such uses of this term, however, appear to mean simply that two or more cultural or ethnic groups co-existed. In this weak descriptive sense – for which plurality is arguably more appropriate – all societies are multicultural. Empires are particularly multicultural, if not fundamentally so, because of their territorial expansion, strategies of deportation and military recruitment, and the inability to enforce cultural change across large and diverse subject populations; empires also create new opportunities for voluntary movement such as trade. The notion that societies might not be plural is a legacy of nineteenth-century nationalism. Dench considers multicultural Rome to be 'vague but politically resonant, and generally aspirational', but finds problematic an approach to ancient societies which are 'imagined to be like "us", as "we" aspire to be, or the opposite of "ourselves"'.[32]

The reinvention of Rome as a model of inclusiveness needs to be treated with caution. As well as concerns about the unqualified use of the term multicultural, there are many examples of national, colonial and neoliberal projects which have eulogised Rome's supposed tolerance as a means of incorporating others. For example, the French and Italians cited Rome's 'openness' with its citizenship to justify their colonial ventures in North Africa.[33] More generally, the representation of distinct ethnic and cultural groups by colonial powers is rarely a celebration of diversity for diversity's sake, but rather an assertion of power through the spectacle of varied and exotic conquered peoples. Indeed, the much wider focus on identity and multiculturalism across the social sciences has been critiqued as a smoke-screen for the ongoing political and economic project of globalism, obscuring the importance of underlying power asymmetries and inadvertently perpetuating the inequalities it aspires to address.[34]

In sum, multiculturalism is progressive, but may also have some regressive tendencies.[35] In applying this term to the past, or focusing more generally on identity, we should take care to consider the underlying issues of power in both past and present.[36] We must recognise historical diversity and explore its significance, but we must also avoid replacing one unsatisfactory model with another. The significant question is therefore not whether past societies were plural but the ways in which that plurality was constituted, its extent and its motivations. Were there mechanisms which promoted or repressed plurality? What were the social and political contexts in which identities were asserted? More specifically, was Rome more plural than any other society? Or was it was more important to emphasise plurality and consequently it is more visible in the archaeological record?

GLOBALISATION AND COSMOPOLITANISM

The intersection of proliferating identities and heritage is expressed through increasing dispute based on territorial claims to specific monuments or landscapes. To challenge such regressive and rooted appropriations of the past, a notion of a common human heritage has been promoted.[37] For example, sub-Saharan archaeology has concentrated on human evolution as the shared inheritance of all. But such a focus conveniently predates recent historical colonialisms which complicate the picture. Meanwhile Meskell, arguing that globalisation is implicated in neoliberal globalism, promotes a cosmopolitan archaeology which intends to encompass a single global community united by diversity and tolerance;[38] in particular, she stresses the ambition to elide past and present and to make political action the goal of the discipline. Such a cosmopolitan archaeology firmly closes any divide between archaeology and heritage.[39] Cosmopolitan archaeology, however, must navigate a precarious path between universalism and particularism. Not least, some ideals such as democracy, secularism and even some human rights may be perceived as new forms of Western colonialism.[40] In this context, González-Ruibal argues that the language of 'cooperation' which underpins cosmopolitanism can conceal existing inequalities whilst imposing essentially Western concepts such as choice and individualism.[41]

Such criticisms aside, from the perspective of Roman cultural heritage, the most significant issue with these attempts to link archaeology and heritage in common political cause concerns the apparent limits of their geographical and chronological scope. For example, the case studies in *Cosmopolitan Archaeologies* notably exclude one whole continent – Europe – and its southern colonial extension, North Africa.[42] The case studies also focus on recent colonial and contemporary examples and exclude any reference to classical antiquity, including the Roman empire. This raises the question of whether there are regions and periods which cosmopolitan archaeology cannot or does not wish to address. If this is the case, where does this leave the practice of politically engaged archaeology in Europe and North Africa, and where does it leave wider Roman cultural heritage? Here, we might discern an artificial divide between European 'public' or 'community' archaeology, which seeks to reconcile indigenous majorities with immigrant minorities, and 'cosmopolitan' or indigenous archaeology practised elsewhere in the world, which seeks to empower either indigenous minorities (e.g. the United States, Australia) or former colonial subjects (e.g. sub-Saharan Africa). In this scenario, Roman cultural heritage is ignored and the Roman cultural heritage of North Africa and the Middle East is left doubly so.[43]

In fact, despite the perceived centrality of the Roman past for Western Europe (and via colonialism, the wider world),[44] Roman cultural heritage is barely mentioned in wider debates by archaeologists and heritage professionals. For example, only one paper on Roman archaeology can be found in each of the volumes: *Cultural Identity and Archaeology* and *The Politics of Archaeology and Identity in a Global Context*.[45] Of course, with their global coverage, we should not expect many papers on Roman archaeology in such volumes; perhaps more telling is the recent issue of *Archaeological Dialogues* (2008, vol. 15.1) on European Archaeology, which scarcely mentions the subject (Breeze's two-page contribution on the *Frontiers of the Roman Empire* WHS is a welcome but late addition). Hence, despite developing an impressive post-colonial literature of its own,[46] Roman archaeology appears to be of marginal interest or relevance to the wider archaeological community. It seems that for other academic archaeologists, Roman cultural heritage is tainted by nationalism (Europe) and colonialism (North Africa and the Middle East). Past historical appropriations, combined with a misperception that the subject is theoretically uninformed and text driven, makes Roman archaeology appear irrelevant at best and toxic at worst. Yet, in sharp contrast to its marginalisation within academic archaeology, the Roman past remains as popular as ever within wider public discourse through television, film, tourism, museums and books.

Roman cultural heritage therefore occupies an interesting position, straddling not only historical, political and religious divides, but a major theoretical fault-line. More than ever, it is imperative for Roman archaeologists to grasp the full breadth of the empire – a global empire – and not to fragment it into East and West, in either the Roman or contemporary senses. It is the case study *par excellence* of the questions of value raised by a common heritage divided between nations of very different subsequent histories.

GLOBALISATION AND THE ROMAN FRONTIERS

During the 1980s and early 1990s, scholars of globalisation heralded the imminent demise of the nation-state and, concomitantly, international frontiers. For example, Giddens and others argued for a radical de-territorialisation,[47] with the nation-state and its sovereign borders receding under pressure from market and technological forces. Frontiers were out; networks were in. Within Europe, the fall of the Berlin Wall opened the way to recreate the European border as 'past' or heritage. The subsequent Schengen Agreement means that borders are now most often encountered as irritating queues at a city airport rather than as a peripheral and militarised border. During the early twenty-first century, however, resurgent nationalism has led to a process of *re*-territorialisation and (Schengen Europe aside) a proliferation of political frontiers, from Israel/Palestine, via United States/Mexico, to the Arctic.[48] Giddens et al. can now be seen to have overstated the imminent demise of the nation-state and are even viewed by some as apologists for globalism.[49] Against this shifting background, heritage has become more contested and arguably the Roman frontiers have acquired renewed resonance.

The city of Rome is traditionally seen as the cosmopolis, the world city where it was possible to experience the diversity of the empire as a whole.[50] In contrast, the frontiers were physically and culturally peripheral. Through imperial agency, however, the diversity of the empire was just as visible on the frontiers as at Rome itself. John Steinbeck captured this perfectly: '. . . one bicycle trip along Hadrian's Wall makes you know the Roman Empire as you never could otherwise'.[51] The remainder of this chapter therefore turns to the imperial frontiers and the frontier provinces as a case study to explore the intersection of archaeology, politics, economy, tourism and identity.

HADRIAN'S WALL

Given its high profile and protected status, it would be easy to imagine that Hadrian's Wall has always been culturally valued; much of this attention, however, is relatively recent.[52] A new phase in the monument's biography began in 1987 when the Wall was inscribed on the UNESCO list of WHSs in recognition of its 'Outstanding Universal Value'. Since then, the Wall has undergone a marked physical and symbolic renaissance. It has been made to serve as an international tourist destination but also to promote regional economic regeneration and social inclusion. Its primacy in these roles has been recognised more recently through the creation in 2006 of Hadrian's Wall Heritage Ltd, subsequently renamed Hadrian's Wall Trust in 2012; this organisation is charged with the dual task of managing the WHS and promoting regional economic regeneration. It may have been a marriage of convenience, but the choice of partner is no less significant. The agency's name signals that one heritage (Roman) is valued over others (e.g. coal-mining, shipbuilding, Northumbrian Christianity, Border Reiver). At the eastern end of the Wall, on Tyneside, the renaissance of Hadrian's Wall as a tool for economic regeneration has been characterised as a shift in values away from the recent post-industrial legacy of economic decline towards the more positive and inclusive opportunities offered by the Roman past.[53] Across the wider region, since 2009, major new museum galleries focusing on the Roman past have been opened at Carlisle, Newcastle, Vindolanda and York (Eboracum), as well as Glasgow in Scotland. Compared with the protracted and disputed proposals for Stonehenge, the political momentum and economic resource invested in Hadrian's Wall and the Roman heritage of northern Britain speaks volumes.

The Wall has long been implicated in English/British national identity,[54] a trend which continues. For example, the (now defunct) government-sponsored website www.icons.org.uk named Hadrian's Wall as one of a series of English icons for the twenty-first century, serving to reaffirm the Wall's significance for national identity. A particular trend has been to describe the Wall as multicultural; for example, a recent exhibition sought to transform the Wall from a monument of/to imperial might into an exemplar of cultural diversity.[55] For some Roman specialists, the recent attention given to the Wall's cultural diversity is something of a surprise, as the ethnic and cultural identity of the Wall's garrisons has long been a focus of enquiry.[56] The novelty of a multicultural Wall, however, is not in the discovery of diversity in the past, but rather a new sensitivity towards it and the political desire to act upon it by authorities, archaeologists and public alike.[57] Yet such re-imagining is not unproblematic. These appropriations of Hadrian's Wall tend to perpetuate the well-known tendency to recreate the past as better than the present. Unpleasantness, inequality, brutality, and evil do not serve the purposes of those attempting to reconcile social differences, to regenerate economies or to attract tourists.[58] If the past is to be a model for the future, it has to be made to reflect that aspirational state. Superficially, the pluralism of the Wall's population looks attractive for the idea of a model community of diversity and tolerance; but as noted above, 'multicultural' means different things to different people and in many cases is simply used as a synonym for plurality. Either way, there is limited attempt to explain why these different groups co-existed on the Wall and why they felt it important to express their different ethnic and cultural identities. What is missing in such accounts is the issue of power. In this Utopian society, each identity is placed on an equal footing. This may be politically desirable for presentist purposes, but it obscures the inequalities between legionaries and auxiliaries, military and civilian, men and women, colonisers and colonised in the past. More significantly, the wider political context of the Roman world is ignored. The population of the Wall did not live in a Western democracy; what brought these people together voluntarily or by force was an autocratic regime based on an expansionist military project. The integrative power of the Roman world was colonialism – hardly an aspirational model for the present.[59] This colonialism created and sustained a highly plural Roman society, but once the expansion of the empire slowed, so too did its power to disperse and mix populations. In other words, once we begin to explain the dynamic of the plural/multicultural Wall, rather than simply to describe its existence, its value as a straightforward model begins to unravel.

The problem with all of these narratives, as Morley has recently noted, is that those making these appropriations are frequently untroubled by 'academic' details such as context, and hence they are free to make highly selective use of the evidence.[60] Rome's cultural pluralism was not underpinned by any ideological respect for cultural difference (i.e. a policy of multiculturalism), but rather by the fact that it had limited power to enforce an alternative even if had so wished. Rome tolerated diversity as long as it was supplemented by acceptance of a limited set of core values (e.g. law, property) and political loyalty (e.g. the imperial cult, the military cult of *disciplina*). But further, Rome did not simply insert a set of core values amongst a diversity of existing identities; Rome's actions also served to create or even exacerbate cultural difference. For example, the strategy of recruiting garrisons of soldiers from one region and deploying them to another can be seen to have created the conditions in which the expression of ethnic and cultural difference might have become particularly important. Derks and Roymans note that ethnic identities are always constructed in association with power – and often colonial power.[61] Far from homogenising difference, Roman incorporation stimulated a wealth of new identities. In sum, current re-imaginings of the Wall as a model for the present and future are well meant, but one-sided. They achieve their goal by taking a selective approach to the evidence, static snapshots which describe but conveniently do not explain and which ironically reduces their resonance for the globalised present (see below) and also leaves them vulnerable to nationalist counter-narratives which assert parity on the grounds of equally selective use of the evidence. Instead of idealising the past, we need to find ways to accommodate ambivalent or troubling heritage and to acknowledge its inherent conflicts.[62] This should also make our interpretations more robust and therefore less vulnerable to ideological misappropriation.

In fact, the Wall offers a striking opportunity to communicate a story with real significance for contemporary identities in a globalised world. Just as we debate plurality and the extension of citizenship, so Roman society also reflected on the consequences of imperial expansion for its own and others' identities.[63] Just as neoliberal globalist policies have empowered some and marginalised others, so the Roman empire similarly created both opportunity and oppression. In this context, we should recognise that the characterisation of Hadrian's Wall as plural is simply an initial and descriptive step. It provides no explanation for that plurality. Indeed, the explanation (i.e. colonialism) might be seen to undermine the value of the Wall as an ideal for contemporary society. Yet, if we refuse to reduce the past to a simple model to be imitated, then explanation can add much more nuance and resonance to the story. In particular, it can address the complex ways in which individuals and groups were brought together in a colonial context and simultaneously empowered and marginalised. It is an approach in which Regina can be acknowledged as an example of a 'mixed marriage' but also as the former slave of her husband (Fig. 9.1); where African soldiers were deployed as auxiliaries against their will but whose military identity afforded them some privileges and powers denied to others; and where Britain was garrisoned by a 'Roman' army whilst British men were posted elsewhere as 'Roman' soldiers to garrison other peoples' land. In short, if archaeologists can claim a particular contribution to addressing some of the problems of the contemporary world, it is by demonstrating how identities are contextually and culturally constructed and how they have evolved over time.[64]

From Hadrian's Wall to the frontiers of the Roman empire

In 2005, the *Hadrian's Wall WHS* was renamed as the *Frontiers of the Roman Empire* and extended to include a stretch of the Roman frontier in Germany; in 2008, it was further extended to include the Antonine Wall in Scotland. The ultimate ambition is to extend this WHS to encompass the entire frontier system through Europe, the Middle East and North Africa in recognition of its 'Outstanding Universal Value'.[65] This is a highly ambitious, long-term project which intends to create a WHS that is not simply transnational, but trans*continental* – a WHS fit for the globalising times. Given the many and diverse countries involved, the official documentation is a powerful medium through which the conceptual unity of the frontiers is to be created and reinforced.[66]

Breeze's account of the *Frontiers of the Roman Empire* WHS nomination process catalogues some of the many challenges encountered.[67] Notably, his discussion is connected with the pragmatic issues of differing national approaches to Cultural Resource Management (e.g. legal, linguistic, procedural). There is limited consideration of the wider social and political dimensions that such an international site of Roman cultural heritage raise across the diverse nations of Europe, the Middle East and North Africa. Clearly, those involved are well aware of such issues, and it is no criticism to observe that in order to make progress they have focused on finding common ground; legal and technical standards are easier to agree than social, political and cultural values. But what *is* the 'Universal Value' of a Roman frontier for countries as diverse as Scotland, Bulgaria, Syria and Morocco?

Critics of the concept of World Heritage stress the way in which universalist rhetoric is used to legitimise *national* heritage discourses. For example, Long and Labadi note the wide international appeal of WHS status is not a 'shared and altruistic appreciation of cultural diversity', rather 'nations use the alleged universalism of the World Heritage Convention for their own nationalistic purposes'.[68] Indeed, 'it is this very universalised and de-politicised veneer that seems attractive to nation-states'.[69] Ironically, World Heritage has not only perpetuated nationalist agendas, but actually strengthened them. One effect may be to disenfranchise local expressions of identity beneath larger national formulations.[70] For example, beyond their state-sponsored value for tourism, Silberman notes the potential ambiguity of sites such as Ephesus, Baalbek (Heliopolis), Jerash (Gerasa) and Petra for local populations.[71] Transnational or even transcontinental WHS status may promote the language of *inter*national cooperation, but is susceptible to nationalist appropriation and may also lead to tensions with more local and regional expressions of identity.

Political authorities have repeatedly appropriated the physical and symbolic heritage of earlier regimes to legitimise their status. Some claim direct cultural or ideological connections, but the shared aim of all states is to secure the power which rests upon the preservation of the symbolic significance of heritage as signs of political authority. Indeed, nation-states are particularly adept at integrating and deploying disparate monuments, with which they may not claim any shared values, for their own nationalist ends;[72] when it comes to the past, it seems that territorial control trumps ideological affiliation. A journey along the Roman frontiers, starting in the UK, well illustrates this situation.

The markedly differing public profiles of Hadrian's Wall (England) and the Antonine Wall (Scotland) arguably relates to the very different contexts in which these monuments have been historically investigated and incorporated into political discourses. The successful nomination to UNESCO of the Antonine Wall as part of the *Frontiers of the Roman Empire* WHS in 2008 can be understood as a Scottish nationalist enterprise. Historically, as a relic of Roman (and by association, English) oppression, the Antonine Wall has played a limited role in Scottish history and identity. But within an increasingly autonomous Scotland, and with strong support from the devolved Scottish National Party administration, the Antonine Wall now forms part of an international WHS which commands national parity with not only the 'English' Hadrian's Wall, but also the Taj Mahal, Angkor Wat and the Pyramids.

In much of Western Europe, the centrality of Roman cultural heritage to national identities is long established. Through historical colonialism, the

Roman heritage of the Middle East and North Africa has also been appropriated to European national causes.[73] The 'value' of Roman heritage to Middle Eastern and North African nation-states may therefore appear doubly problematic, representing not simply one (ancient) Western occupation but also a number of more recent interventions justified by repeated reference to the first. What may appear as monuments to (repeated) colonial oppression, however, can be re-imagined by these states for their own nationalist purposes.

Unlike in much of Western Europe and in the Middle East, the Roman past forms just one part of a broader Classical heritage and is just one of many colonial experiences; the archaeology of these different periods is also crosscut by religion. In Jordan, pre-Islamic archaeology has been used to assert the historical legitimacy of the Jordanian people and their territory, tracing an indigenous Nabataean identity to the WHS of Petra, a site best known for its impressive Hellenistic architecture.[74] Jordan has also promoted Christian archaeology in support of its claim to be a crossroads of religions and cultures based on tolerance and plurality. Jordan's Jewish heritage, however, remains marginalised.[75]

Meanwhile, across the Israeli border, the site of Zippori (ancient Sepphoris) is promoted as a multicultural Roman city with a mixed religious population that lived in peace and respect.[76] But tourists will find no mention of the forcible depopulation of the Palestinian village which was removed in order to excavate and display the site.[77] Moreover, although the site is presented as a multicultural city, Bauman's research demonstrates that the majority of visitors leave with the message that it was a specifically Jewish city.[78] For Israel and its neighbouring states, the Classical/Roman past might therefore be seen as universally useful but with no agreement about its 'Universal Value'. It is not, however, simply religion and the Arab–Israeli conflict which complicates the value of such heritage across the Middle East and North Africa.

Silberman argues that post-colonial states in these regions have invested in archaeology as the tried-and-tested means of building national pasts for both domestic and international audiences.[79] In particular, many of states perpetuate the archaeological practices of former colonial regimes in order to assert equal status as sovereign members of the global community; this has led to a prioritisation of certain types of site with an 'emphasis on large-scale, impressive, masonry constructions. In the Mediterranean... that means sprawling, marble-column-filled classical sites'. It also means urban sites along the tourist coast rather than the military frontier sites of remoter inland areas.

This appropriation of Classical/Roman cultural heritage for national purposes has also been detected in Turkey. Here, Atakuman argues that the choice of candidate WHSs reflects Turkey's specific relationship with the West.[80] In order to signal its readiness to join the EU, Turkey promoted multi-period sites which stressed tolerance and plurality (e.g. The Old City of Istanbul, Byzantium). But following the most recent blockage to Turkey's entry into the EU, nominations switched to Classical/Roman sites such as Aphrodisias and Sagalassos. Atakuman interprets this as an assertion of the territorial possession of sites which historically have been appropriated into a Western genealogy. In other words, Atakuman argues that the nomination of Classical/Roman sites is not a request for recognition of their 'Universal Value', but a claim of nationalist control in a game of international diplomacy intended to mark out the distance between Turkey and the EU.

Meanwhile, in Tunisia, the World Bank and the former Ben Ali government used heritage and tourism to instigate neoliberal economic restructuring. The choice of sites for development was politically and culturally significant, such as the selection of Oudna (ancient Uthina) for $1.29m of investment; this prioritised a Roman site, attractive to Western tourists rather than sites of, for example, local Berber or Islamic significance.[81]

By inscribing the frontiers of the Roman empire as a WHS and promoting cooperation across international borders, UNESCO could be seen to be moving with the globalising times. Yet, any extension of this WHS across other European, Middle Eastern or North African countries is likely to be based on the national claims of those countries, just as in England, Scotland and Germany, to 'their' Roman cultural heritage. Hadrian's Wall has become an English monument and the Antonine Wall a Scottish monument, in the same way that the Pont du Gard is a French monument, and Lepcis Magna (Leptis Magna) is a Libyan monument. World Heritage designation, and the concomitant commodification and tourism which follows, epitomise the globalising tension between the universal and the particular.

Finally, in pondering the value of the Roman frontiers, it is instructive to remember that these are not the only problematic historical boundaries to cross Europe, the Middle East and North Africa. Some, such as the Moroccan Wall in the western Sahara are poorly known and little visited.[82] Others, such as the Berlin Wall and the Iron Curtain have been appropriated into new inclusive heritage discourses which stress German and European integration.[83] The Iron Curtain, in particular, has been creatively re-imagined as the European Greenbelt (*Das Grüne Band*), a corridor of biodiversity and ecological cooperation stretching from the Arctic Circle across central Europe to the Black and Adriatic Seas (www.greenbelteurope .eu; Fig. 9.2). Under the slogan 'Borders divide, nature unites', it seeks to promote international environmental cooperation across Europe, finding new meaning and resonance without losing sight of its unsettling history.

Figure 9.2: Map of Europe, North Africa and the Middle East showing the frontiers of the Roman empire (solid black line), *Das Grüne Band* (dashed line) and the borders of the European Union (solid grey line). (Based on BlankMap-Europe-v4.png, available under a Creative Commons Attribution-Share Alike 3.0 licence. © 2006 Roke.)

The *Frontiers of the Roman Empire* WHS might similarly take a line which once divided and re-imagine it as a line which connects.[84] But more importantly, it should value this line not for what it was, but for what it can tell us about the present and future. This must involve incorporating the full (i.e. pre- and especially post-Roman) biography of these landscapes and monuments in order to draw out the diversity of their local, national and international significance. Paradoxically, the *Frontiers of the Roman Empire* cannot be a uniquely *Roman* cultural heritage; if it is to have wide resonance, it must encompass the diversity of responses to the Roman past as well. In practice, this means reversing the usual process through which heritage is globalised. Typically local heritage supplies the unique and particular places which the market commodifies and sells as tourist destinations for global consumption; instead we need to take a 'global' Roman heritage and to reconnect it to local communities. This may also address the classic tourist problem of substitutability, that is, why visit a destination if you have already visited somewhere similar? The closely spaced and superficially similar forts of Hadrian's Wall are a case in point. By developing such sites as local and unique expressions of a global culture, with rich post-Roman histories, there is more scope to differentiate them and to encourage tourists to visit more than one of them.[85]

GLOBALISATION IN THE PAST VERSUS GLOBALISING THE PAST

One possible definition of heritage is: 'the use of the past as a cultural, political and economic resource in the present'.[86] It treats the past as a 'quarry of possible raw materials from which a deliberate selection can occur'.[87] Arguably, such presentism and selectivity are no less characteristic of archaeology. In this context, I question the premise that we can and should make a clear distinction between globalisation *in* the past and *globalising* the past. For example, it has been noted above that the universal values and international mechanisms espoused by UNESCO can be subverted for nationalist purposes. This observation seems little different from interpretations which argue that Greco-Roman models were adopted and adapted by non-Romans to reassert their local or hybrid identities – whether building a Hellenistic theatre at Pietrabbondante to declare Samnite identity,[88] or adopting the accoutrement of a polis in the Syrian desert to assert a distinctively Palmyrene identity.[89] Similarly, when Whittaker argues that the question is not *whether* the Roman empire was full of multiple ethnic identities, but what values or mechanisms underpinned this plurality, how far can his question be separated from our contemporary concerns about cultural cohesion and pluralism?[90] And to what extent can we distinguish the idea that foreigners have been written out of accounts of British national history,[91] from the observation that local German groups were written out of the history of Roman Xanten (Castra Vetera) and Cologne (Colonia Agrippina)?[92] Are we reading the present back into the past? Or has 'the classical world come back to us'?[93] I suggest that it is conceptually impossible to distinguish globalisation *in* the Roman past from *globalising* the Roman past.

Likewise, what or for whom is a multicultural Hadrian's Wall intended? Is it to explain the Roman past? Or to engage the public, especially those groups who may not previously have seen Roman cultural heritage as 'theirs'? Is it intended as a model of social cohesion for the present and an aspiration for the future? Is it a way of catching the media's attention, attracting more tourists and winning research grants? In the globalised world, where archaeology is at the intersection of politics, identity, tourism and market forces, all these uses and more blur together.

This does not mean that we can and should simply impose the present on the past, nor should we recreate the past as we would like it to have been. Rather, it recognises that the data we select, the questions we ask and interpretative frameworks we employ cannot be separated from our contemporary perspectives. Globalising heritage should not aim to find a universal history for all, nor should it accept the fragmentation of heritage into seven billion ancestry projects. Rather, it needs to develop an approach which acknowledges the tensions of global and local, and which blurs the distance between past and present without disregarding their real differences.[94] In practical terms, the development of more plural and inclusive histories is not predicated on finding individual sites to serve specific interest groups, but drawing out the full biography of multi-period sites, whether recognising mosques in the ruins of Roman towns in North Africa, or stressing the cultural diversity of 'Roman' soldiers on Hadrian's Wall in a wider colonial context.[95]

Conclusions

One reason that archaeologists and historians have been cautious about exploring globalisation in the ancient past has been the broader debate about whether or not contemporary globalisation represents a 'good thing'. And if it is not a good thing, does talk of globalisation in the Roman past provide legitimacy and historical pedigree to a Western version of global history? These are not debates which need to be resolved *before* exploring the value of the concept for the Roman past. Indeed, Rome's cultural heritage is one of the means *through* which we might explore such questions. Significantly, debate over whether globalisation is both good *and* bad can be seen to parallel discussion in the Roman past about the positive and negative effects of imperial expansion on Roman identity.[96]

Another specific issue about exploring ancient globalisations is the concern about the imposition of anachronistic ideas and terminology on the past.[97] In this context, it is useful to remember that, whilst the concept of Roman imperialism is now ubiquitous, its initial application to the Roman past provoked much controversy.[98] Terms such as imperialism and Romanisation have now become orthodox and their original controversial status has been eclipsed. A strong argument in favour of the use of terminology and concepts such as globalisation is that it is more obviously 'modern' and therefore we are more alert to the complexities of the debate (see also the introduction to this volume).

If we accept a presentist definition of heritage and archaeology, then different periods of human history will become more or less useful depending on the changing requirements of the present: promoting social cohesion, regenerating economies or boosting tourism. Yet, Rome has loomed large in the consciousness of European societies for centuries. It seems capable of continual reinvention for presentist purposes; this centrality speaks volumes about the ancestral value ascribed to it and, moreover, implicates Roman cultural heritage in the current global order. In this context, Morley has argued that the core task of the Roman historian is to expose Rome's centrality in order to critique the current global order.[99] Globalising the Roman past helps to relativise – or perhaps more appropriately, provincialise – Rome's cultural heritage so that it sits alongside other historical societies, within and beyond Europe. For example, by putting the Roman empire into comparative and long-term perspective, both Rome and contemporary Western dominance may be exposed as anomalous episodes in a longer process in which China and the East have been more dominant.[100]

Within academia, Roman archaeology has sought to de-colonise itself through explicit recognition of its past complicity; in the process it has addressed the legacy of colonialism through innovative post-colonial perspectives. But as we move into the wider domain of heritage, museums and the media, there are plenty of examples where old colonial categories are perpetuated or which promote well-meant but flawed visions of the Roman past which lack awareness of historical context and political misuse. This is not an argument for academic smugness. We must do more than simply write better post-colonial critiques as part of an internal dialogue; we also need to influence wider public discourse and to address popular (mis)conceptions. It is a call for a closer relationship between archaeologists, heritage professionals, museum practitioners, journalists and TV producers.[101] Archaeologists can no longer assert the objectivity of their data and interpretations in order to maintain a neutral position whilst blaming others for misusing their work.[102] We need to become more, not less, involved in communicating the Roman past and its relevance to the present.

Specifically, we need to tackle uses of the Roman past which promote entirely positive (or negative) visions; instead we need to promote more robust interpretations which engage critically with the data and all its complexity. We need to get past the use of Roman cultural heritage as a mirror, a model or a moral lesson and to communicate its subtleties. There are indeed strong similarities between the Roman past and contemporary world – and the most striking similarity is that it is simplistic to present either as inherently good or bad. Just as modern commentators struggle to reconcile the balance sheet of contemporary globalisation, so understanding of the Roman period has come to recognise that the Roman empire could both empower and marginalise simultaneously.[103] This does not mean, however, that we cannot or should not sit in judgement. But we should do so from a position informed by as much of the evidence as possible, rather than by highly selective samples; the same is true of the contemporary world. In this context, questions about identity asked in the Roman past, such as 'could a North African be Roman'? resonate with questions about identity asked today, such as 'is Turkey European?'.[104] The point is not to use the past to answer these questions decisively, but to give historical depth to the fact such questions exist and that different answers can and have been proposed. Despite its academic marginalisation, Roman cultural heritage is of central relevance to the globalised present precisely because it has inspired individuals, communities and states for centuries – for the very best and for the very worst of reasons.

ACKNOWLEDGEMENTS

My thanks to Martin Pitts and Miguel John Versluys for their invitation to contribute to the Exeter workshop and to the other participants for their comments and discussion. Thanks also to Alice Hiley and Richard Hingley for discussing some of the ideas included in this chapter.

NOTES

1. e.g. Trigger (2006).
2. Baram & Rowan (2004, 3).
3. e.g. Hitchner (2008); Pitts (2008); Sweetman (2007); Witcher (2000).
4. Hodos (2010b).
5. Heather (2010).
6. A number of collected case studies have begun to appear including LaBianca & Scham (2006); De Angelis (2013). Also, most recently, note the ambitious integrated comparative study of Uruk, Cahokia and Huari by Jennings (2011).
7. Morris & Manning (2005).
8. Nicholas Purcell, pers. comm. Morris's (2003; 2005) 'Mediterraneanisation' covers similar ground but explicitly acknowledges the influence of globalisation.
9. Nederveen Pieterse (Chapter 10, this volume), describes this situation as 'globality' rather than 'globalisation'.
10. Witcher (2000).
11. Dench (2005, 218).
12. Hopkins (2010).
13. Indeed, this perception is still powerful. For example, Mattingly (2006, 17) cautions about the use of globalisation because it may stress conformity rather than diversity.
14. e.g. Woolf has long argued for the need to juxtapose the 'diversity and unity' of Roman provincial culture (e.g. Woolf 1992) but has not formulated this explicitly in terms of globalisation until much more recently (e.g. Woolf 2010). Similarly, whilst Woolf's keynote paper at RAC2001 made cautious use of the language of globalisation, there were multiple and unequivocal

references to the 'global Roman empire' at RAC2010 and TRAC2011. See also Laurence & Trifilò (Chapter 5, this volume).

15. e.g. Hamilakis (2007); Trigger (2006).
16. Ashworth et al. (2007, 37).
17. Ashworth et al. (2007, 40).
18. González-Ruibal (2010).
19. See inter alia Hingley (2000); Munzi (2005).
20. Though Hodder (1991a) suggests this is a sensitivity for European archaeology in general.
21. e.g. Billig (1995); on Rome specifically, see Terrenato (2001).
22. In relation to Hadrian's Wall, see Witcher (2010).
23. Mattingly (2011, 5).
24. Ashworth et al. (2007, 28).
25. Mattingly (2004, 2010).
26. See Ashworth et al. (2007); Holtorf (2009).
27. See Ashworth et al. (2007, 19).
28. e.g. Ang (2005).
29. de Souza Briggs (2004).
30. Leach et al. (2010).
31. e.g. Higgins (2009).
32. Dench (2005, 9).
33. Dench (2005, 10–11); Lorcin (2002); Munzi (2005).
34. González-Ruibal (2010); Hopkins (2010); Tomlinson (2003).
35. Ashworth et al. (2007, 20).
36. These issues are certainly not incompatible, as Mattingly (2011) clearly demonstrates through his integration of identity with economy and imperialism. He does not use the term 'multiculturalism'.
37. Baram & Rowan (2004, 20).
38. Meskell (2009, 25).
39. See also Samuels (2008, 80–2).
40. Ashworth et al. (2007, 28); Holtorf (2009, 679).
41. González-Ruibal (2009, 2010).
42. Meskell (2009). The exclusion of North Africa seems to support Garcea's (2005, 111) observation that only sub-Saharan Africa is seen to contribute to sensitive issues of indigenous archaeology, leading to a general marginalisation of North Africa by archaeologists.
43. Mattingly's (1996) paper on Roman archaeology in the Maghreb is an early and important exception.
44. e.g. Hardt & Negri (2000).
45. Graves-Brown et al. (1996); Kane (2003).
46. e.g. Mattingly (2011); Webster (2001).
47. Giddens (1990).
48. Hazbun (2004); Kohl (2004, 298).
49. Ashworth et al. (2007, 55).
50. Edwards & Woolf (2003).
51. Steinbeck (1989, 709).

52. For a taste of the changing valuations and disputes, see Hutton (1802); Davies (1974); Norman (2008).
53. Usherwood (1996).
54. Hingley (2012).
55. Tolia-Kelly (2011).
56. See Hingley (2008); most recently, Swan (2009).
57. Ashworth et al. (2007, 45).
58. Ashworth et al. (2007, 52); Silberman (1995, 260).
59. See de Souza Briggs (2004).
60. Morley (2010).
61. Derks & Roymans (2009, 2). For similar arguments, see also Ando (2010) and Woolf (2009).
62. Copeland (2002); González-Ruibal (2010).
63. See Dench (2005, 5).
64. Jones & Graves-Brown (1996, 19).
65. Breeze & Young (2008).
66. e.g. providing multilingual documentation including Arabic; the integral discussion of sites in the Middle East and North Africa in the volume on the *European Dimension of a WHS*, Breeze & Jilek (2008).
67. Breeze (2007).
68. Long & Labadi (2010, 6).
69. Ibid., 9.
70. Salazar (2010, 134).
71. Silberman (1995).
72. The example of the Imperial Palace in Beijing is informative. The new Communist state recognised its central importance for stability and political legitimacy both at home and abroad. Rather than not destroy this monument to the former emperor's power, the Palace was transformed into an international symbol of feudal oppression shared by all, but simultaneously a monument to a specifically Chinese nation-state (Hamlish 2000, 150).
73. Silberman (1995).
74. Addision (2004, fn.74); Maffi (2009).
75. See also Addison (2004); Hazbun (2004, 326).
76. See Bauman (2004).
77. For an identical situation at Dougga in Tunisia, see Samuels (2008, 84–5).
78. Bauman (2004, 221).
79. Silberman (1995).
80. Atakuman (2010).
81. Samuels (2008, 76–8).
82. Brooks (2005).
83. Baker (1993).
84. UNESCO has recently published a manifesto on the contribution of World Heritage to global ethics (Albert et al. 2012). The *Frontiers of the Roman Empire* WHS is explicitly identified, if only with a single sentence, as a valuable example of the history and evolution of globalization, alongside other examples including the Silk Roads and pilgrimage routes such as that to Santiago de

Compostela (von Droste 2012). The Roman frontiers aside, a few individual Roman monuments have been appropriated for new causes, most obviously the Colosseum as a symbol of the campaign for the abolition of capital punishment, Hopkins & Beard (2005).

85. For some of the challenges of marketing Hadrian's Wall, see Warnaby et al. (2010). On the post-Roman biography of Hadrian's Wall, Hingley et al. (2012).
86. Ashworth et al. (2007, 3).
87. Ashworth et al. (2007, 40).
88. Wallace-Hadrill (2008, 143).
89. Sommer (2005b).
90. Whittaker (2009).
91. Tolia-Kelly (2011).
92. Derks & Roymans (2009, 8).
93. Mount (2010).
94. Samuels (2008, 88–9).
95. Witcher et al. (2010).
96. See Dench (2005).
97. Dench (2005, 218–19).
98. See Erskine (2009); Morley (2010).
99. Morley (2010).
100. See Mutschler & Mittag (2008); Scheidel (2009b).
101. e.g. Baram & Rowan (2004, 6); Samuels (2008, 72).
102. Jones & Graves-Brown (1996, 18).
103. Hingley (2010); Mattingly (2010).
104. For example, Suetonius's *Vita Terenti* preserves debate between Augustan writers about the identity of the playwright Terence. It is agreed that he was born at Carthage, but perceptions of his precise heritage are affected by the date and circumstances of his enslavement. Snowden (1970, 270) reviews contrasting modern perspectives. The identities of Septimius Severus and Tertullian as Roman and/or African have been similarly debated in the modern literature, Birley (1971); Wilhite (2007).

PART III

PERSPECTIVES

10

Ancient Rome and Globalisation: Decentring Rome

Jan Nederveen Pieterse

According to Haverfield, 'Greece taught men to be human and Rome made mankind civilized ... the form it took was Romanization'. This is a brief version of the Romanisation paradigm, which is now an old and weary narrative in Roman history and archaeology.[1] Romanisation is a diffusionist perspective, assuming Rome as the centre and standard, without necessarily much reflection on how this centre and standard came about. Some Roman archaeologists and historians are turning to globalisation as a possible alternative, which has sparked discussion.[2] Variables at issue in this discussion are *which* globalisation, which approach to globalisation, and which Roman history, which approach to the Greco-Roman world. In contrast to Romanisation, the globalisation take on the Roman world situates Rome in the stream of history; it decentres Rome. In this view, Rome is globalising by being globalised.

The first section of this chapter discusses approaches to globalisation and global history. The second section turns to different approaches in ancient Roman history and archaeology. The third section asks not what globalisation can do for Rome but what Rome can do for globalisation, and reflects on the importance of Greco-Roman history to the broader field of globalisation studies. The fourth section develops a two-way perspective of Rome being globalised and globalising. The concluding section formulates a timeline of globalisation in the light of revisiting ancient history, synthesising the argument.

Globalisation and global history

The theme of globalisation emerged first in business studies in the 1970s and then rose steeply in the 1990s. Hence much of the globalisation discussion is marked by 1990s flavour, themes and sensibilities. It is then that the dominant works on globalisation were written and global studies were occupied and colonised by 1990s perspectives. Thus, most globalisation studies suffer from presentism and eurocentrism. Presentism assumes that globalisation unfolds from 1980 or thereabouts. For many perspectives – such as economics, business studies, media studies and cultural studies – this may be effective for much of the relevant database dates from the 1970s or 1980s onward, such as the rise of multi-national corporations, followed by global value chains. Thus many disciplines date globalisation from the 1970s with the rise of multi-national corporations and accelerated communication (most economics, international relations, political science and media studies). Another periodisation refers to neoliberal globalisation, 1980–2000.

Eurocentric perspectives assume that globalisation stems from modernity, starting with the Enlightenment, the French Revolution, followed by industrialisation, from circa 1800.[3] Alternatively, Marxist views date globalisation from 1500, from the 'conquest of the world market'. Here globalisation is equivalent to 'modern capitalism' (as in Marx and in Wallerstein's 'long 16th century'). Thus, the capstone moments of occidental globalisation are 1500 CE and 1800 CE. Each links back to the Renaissance: the 1500 CE view via the age of reconnaissance and Columbus, and the 1800 CE view via the Renaissance humanists, the seventeenth-century scientific revolution and the Enlightenment philosophers. By implication, each eventually links to Antiquity so the conventional views on globalisation incorporate the Greco-Roman world, and do so via a thoroughly conventional historical lens and periodisation.

Some treatments in Roman history and archaeology discuss, criticise or take as yardstick the 1990s globalisation perspectives to understand the globalisation of the Roman world.[4] However, at this stage the question is not simply engagement with globalisation but with *which* globalisation. The globalisation literature now ranges over thirty years and has become increasingly diverse, sprawling according to disciplines (economics, sociology, international relations, ecology, etc.), theoretical leanings and historical timelines.

Historians used to view globalisation as a 'modern' or contemporary phenomenon and kept their distance from it. This changed with Hopkins' volume, *Globalization in World History* (2002), which has also prompted historians of ancient Rome to reconsider and to view the Greco-Roman world as part of globalisation history.[5] However, with this perspective on globalisation in the *longue durée* comes a timeline that adopts a caesura in global history in which globalisation unfolds from 1500 CE and that what goes before is 'archaic globalisation'. In other words, 'real globalisation' refers to 'modern globalisation', which is European, Western, and what come before are preludes to, infrastructures of globalisation. This view is widely shared,[6] also in wider globalisation studies.[7] This timeline restates the Eurocentric perspective – 'modern history' and modern globalisation start with Europe; the difference is that the new eurocentrism comes with a larger appetite and acknowledges wider, sprawling contributions to the European take-off from different eras and civilisations. This view both opens wider to the past and shutters it by means of the conventional rupture of modernity.[8] While the infrastructures become more visible, the 'product' remains European.

By one account, this is a semantic issue. Many historians have traced wide and deep infrastructures of global connectivity and mobility, without using the terminology of 'globalisation'. By another account, terminology matters and periodising globalisation is representing and negotiating world history. Looking beneath questions of terminology, what is essentially at issue is whether or not a caesura or rupture that privileges Europe (modernity, modern capitalism, modern world system, modern globalisation) is appropriate. Several contributions to global history, whether or not they use the framework of globalisation, question or reject this rupture.

The Chicago history tradition of McNeill and Hodgson is concerned with deep and broad civilisational lineages,[9] drawing on the anthropological history of Marshall Sahlins and others. 'Globalisation' does not figure in these accounts but neither does a rupture of 'modernity'. Frank and Gills trace the history of the world system back from 500 to 5000 years.[10] They follow David Wilkinson's argument of a 'central civilization' that emerged from the confluence of Egypt and Sumer around 1500 BCE.[11] Using economic criteria of 'interpenetrating accumulation', Frank and Gills argue that this confluence included the Indus Valley civilisation and the area of Syria and the Levant and occurred earlier, around 2700–2400 BCE. While their unit of analysis is the 'world system', not 'globalisation', their argument is critical of the Eurocentrism of Wallerstein's 'modern world-system'. Stavrianos's global history also starts from prehistory and does not privilege Europe.[12]

Abu-Lughod traced capitalism back to 1250, situated in Egypt and the Middle East.[13] Hobson's thesis of oriental globalisation traces the beginnings of globalisation further back to circa 500 CE.[14] Keynotes of oriental globalisation are the resumption of the Middle East caravan trade around 500 CE, and Asia emerging as the centre and driving force of the world economy from 1000 CE or 1100 CE, where it remained until 1800 CE.[15] A shorthand account of this phase of globalisation is 'the Silk Routes'.

In subsequent work Hobson distinguishes four historical phases, marked by varying relative strengths of oriental and occidental influences.

In the first phase, from 500 CE to 1450 CE, the extensity, intensity, velocity, and impact of Afro-Eurasian interactions qualify as 'proto-globalisation'.[16] In this phase orientalisation was dominant in the sense that the 'proto-global network was crucial for delivering Eastern resource portfolios into Europe'. In the second phase, 'early globalisation' (1450/1492 CE–1830 CE), 'the diffusion of "resource portfolios" from East to West' led to the 'fundamental re-organization of societies across the world including Europe', a period characterised as 'Orientalization dominant and Occidentalization emergent'. The third phase, 'modern globalisation' (1830 CE–2000 CE), witnessed 'Occidentalization in the ascendance, with the West being the dominant civilization', which was achieved by colonisation and neocolonial globalisation (i.e. Western capitalism). The current phase, 'postmodern globalisation', witnesses 'the return of China to the center of the global economy'. This account adopts a caesura between 'proto-' and early globalisation, times 'modern globalisation' from 1830 CE and adds postmodern globalisation after 2000 CE. Terminology aside, this account differs radically from more traditional narratives and gives much greater credit to oriental influences, past and present. I also view globalisation as a process of East–West osmosis and interplay: 'globalisation is braided',[17] and view the phase of globalisation after 2000 CE as an 'East-South turn'.[18]

GRECO-ROMAN HISTORY

Within Roman history and archaeology very different approaches exist, and each of these strands tends to hold different perspectives on globalisation.

In recent archaeological studies of the Greco-Roman world, mobility and connectivity loom large. According to Morris, a new model is taking shape in Mediterranean history: 'Where the old model emphasized static cells, rigid structures, and powerful institutions, the new one sees fluidity and connectedness'.[19] In its strongest form the new model links up 'the whole period from later prehistory to the eighteenth, nineteenth, or even twentieth century'.[20] 'The three concepts of mobility, connectivity and decentring are at the heart of recent historical/anthropological treatments of the Mediterranean', which 'sets it apart from many 1970s and 1980s accounts of ancient Mediterranean history'.[21] The principles of materiality, mobility, contact and identity inform a new archaeology and history of the Mediterranean; 'material connections' and 'processes such as long-distance and prolonged migrations, hybrid practices and object diasporas', as part of the 'social biography of objects', take centre stage.[22]

We find similar sensibilities in cultural studies of Greco-Roman history. Hybrid Rome, or the 'inherent pluralism' of the Roman world, is well established.[23] Other tropes are syncretism, Creolisation and multicultural antiquity.[24] The Roman world is an assemblage of diverse influences in every sphere – economic, cultural, political and symbolic. Greece and Egypt are prominent influences along with the Etruscans, Persia and the influence of the colonised lands and peoples. Egypt's influence, as Versluys points out, includes casting the Roman emperor in the image of the pharaoh.[25]

Both archaeological and cultural studies of ancient Rome tend to accept globalisation as a productive approach to Roman history, or at any rate, share sensibilities such as an emphasis on mobility, connectivity and mélange. In contrast, state-centric accounts of Roman history tend to adopt views that centre on Rome and the evolution of state institutions. Thus in Hitchner's view, the Roman super-state unified the fragmented world of the ancient empires and with the institution of Roman citizenship in 212 CE, this process of unification evolved at a further level, with a gradual process of decline setting in from the third century CE.[26] While Hitchner recognises push-back from Rome's peripheries in the first century CE, his is generally a Rome-centric account and a restatement of the Romanisation paradigm, in which the empire is the globalising force.[27] 'Romanisation', of course, matters and new archaeological and cultural accounts emphasise that they do not seek to ignore or marginalise the significance of institutions and empire. Rather, the emphasis falls differently. In state-centric accounts it is structures and institutions that unify the Mediterranean world, while in globalisation perspectives connectivity, mobility, objects, and knowledge networks do.

These and other strands of Roman history are criss-crossed by macrohistorical views – in which Greco-Roman history is more often a bystander than a protagonist. Thus, some historians of ancient Rome who adopt the globalisation perspective follow Bayly's and Hopkins' periodisation of globalisation,[28] while a wider periodisation would be more appropriate and relevant to understanding the Greco-Roman world (discussed below).

ASK NOT WHAT GLOBALISATION CAN DO FOR ROME, BUT WHAT ROME CAN DO FOR GLOBALISATION

Historians of ancient Rome may look to globalisation as an alternative perspective to overcome the limitations of Romanisation, while scholars of globalisation ask, rather, how can we learn from Roman history and archaeology to deepen and refine understandings of globalisation? Keynotes that emerge from Greco-Roman history concern the timeline of globalisation, the analytics and the unit of analysis of globalisation, questions of mobility, and lineages of cosmopolitanism.

First, Roman history matters with regard to the timeline of globalisation. If we accept that the Arab-Muslim world was the epicentre of early oriental globalisation (following Hobson's argument), we cannot understand it properly without taking into account both its Hellenic character and its role as a 'middleman civilization', brokering between wider civilisational worlds. Greco-Roman history shows that starting globalisation in 500 CE is inadequate; we must go further back in time. It draws attention to the contributions of the Greco-Roman world to globalisation both as a *nexus* between different globalisation phases and as a major accelerator of globalisation.

With regard to analytics, ancient history and archaeology confront us with the recurrent confusion between globalisation as process and as outcome or condition, or between globalisation and globality (or globalness).[29] Should globalisation be 'global'? Should globalisation be literally global and encompass the world; or else, should it refer to conditions that are 'sufficiently global'?

Economists prefer 'hard', quantifiable definitions of globalisation, such as the permanent existence of global trade, when all major zones of the world 'exchange products continuously ... and on a scale that generated deep and lasting impacts on all trading partners',[30] or price convergence across continents.[31] But oddly this measures not globalisation but globality; it concerns a condition or outcome, not the *process* through which it comes about. However, globalisation refers to a process, not a condition. A fundamental consideration is to distinguish between the *form* of globalisation in a specific era and globalisation as a process. As Robertson notes, we must distinguish between the forms and the trend of globalisation and should not mistake a specific form of globalisation (e.g. neoliberalism) for globalisation per se.[32]

A familiar form of this question is the idea of the *world economy* as the threshold of globalisation, in the sense of a trans-regional division of labour that is necessary for social reproduction (as in Wallerstein's world-system approach). A world economy in this sense does not apply to all ancient empires but does apply to the Roman world, which established and sustained an inter-regional division of labour that comprised olive–grape agriculture (Gaul, Spain), grain (Egypt, North Africa) and Mediterranean trades.[33] The map of Roman value chains matches the 'greater Mediterranean' argued in recent accounts, extending from Sumer to the Danube (and in the sixteenth century CE, to Antwerp).[34] This included significant trade with India and China (wine, silk, muslin). Silk was part of Roman culture and of Rome's foreign trade,[35] but was not necessary for social reproduction. However, ancient history and archaeology in their current guises also suggest an analytical shift to a less structuralist and more processual understanding of globalisation, a turn to globalisation as processes, to trade routes and nodes, migrations and interconnections.

Third, with regard to mobility, the Roman world breaks with stereo-typical representations of the past as immobile, fragmented, segmented, sheltered, closed off, which is belied by research on ancient mobility,[36] on migrations[37] and on the spread of religion and the travel of knowledge and technology.[38]

Fourth, the Greco-Roman world is significant in relation to globalisation as subjectivity, or world consciousness, and the evolution of cosmopolitan-isms.[39] The Stoics often figure as an early cosmopolitanism.[40] Polybius's *Histories* are often mentioned as a precursor of global sociology.[41] *Orbis terrarum* is an early world consciousness. Another consideration is that there was no racism in the ancient Mediterranean world in our modern understanding of the word, even if we consider the role and treatment of corsairs, slaves and prisoners of war.[42] The major ancient cosmopolitan-isms, Indic civilisation with Sanskrit and the Greco-Roman world with Greek and Latin, overlap in time.[43] After the Latin and Sanskrit worlds shrank and gave way to local vernaculars, Islamic civilisation with Arabic emerged as the next major cosmopolitan world, geographically bridging East and West, stretching at its widest expanse from Muslim Iberia to Muslim traders in China, and as subjectivity, while carrying Hellenic lega-cies.[44] The Ottoman millet system continued Mediterranean and Muslim cosmopolitanism.

If we explore how ancient Roman history can learn from globalisation, the key point is to decentre Rome. This concerns, first, the difference between inward- and outward-looking perspectives on the unit of analysis. Decentring Rome means viewing Roman history from the outside, as a regional subset of history embedded in the broad sway of Eurasia and the Bronze Age, which, in turn, is part of wider and, if one will, evolutionary history.

Jack Goody's work takes us back to the Bronze Age, ranges widely across Eurasia and offers articulate criticisms of Eurocentric views. In his view there is not one but 'many Renaissances' and the miracle is not Europe but Eurasia.[45] Bronze Age culture, stretching across Eurasia, was marked by the use of animal traction, plough agriculture, an urban revolution and the ongoing existence of urban culture. This perspective is profoundly relevant to the history of ancient Rome. From this viewpoint, the Hellenistic-Roman world was a western extension of Bronze Age culture, contemporaneous with the expansion of Han China in the east.[46] As part of Eurasian trade and culture networks, the Hellenic-Roman world is linked to the east, part of East–West osmosis and an East–West hybrid. The Greco-Roman world, then, emerges as a nexus and bridge in-between the Bronze Age phase of globalisation and the phase of oriental globalisation, starting c. 500 CE. The Eurasian perspective sheds light on the world of interconnected knowledge, religions and technologies; the world of Egypt, Mesopotamia, India, Persia, Phoenicia, ancient Greece and Rome; the world of Karl Jaspers' *Achsenzeit*, Martin Bernal's *Black Athena* and McNeill's *The Pursuit of Power*.[47] The Hellenistic-Roman Stoics are part of a wider cultural lineage. The Roman world, then, emerges as a Western extension of Eurasian urban culture.

The decline of the Roman empire meant the West losing urban culture and relapsing into rural culture, hence the long period of feudalism and the castle system. Most of Europe was forest and after Rome's decline it reverted to forest, making a gradual comeback only from the eleventh century onward. The decline and fall of Rome meant Europe gradually losing urban culture. The castle system ended in the late Middle Ages with the introduction of Chinese gunpowder and cannon.

ROME IS GLOBALISED AND GLOBALISING: A TWO-WAY PERSPECTIVE

First, Rome is globalised; witness the 'inherent pluralism' of the Roman world and Rome as an eclectic 'successor culture'.[48] Thus, the trope of multiple identities and 'multiple sources of the self' that is often viewed as characteristic of postmodern times,[49] we find in antiquity as well. To refer to a well-known example: King Herod, who was appointed King of Judea by the Romans, was 'by birth an Idumean (i.e. Edomite), by profession a Jew, by necessity a Roman, by culture and by choice a Greek'.[50] Multiple and intersecting cultural layers and overlapping jurisdictions, then as now, generate multiple identities.

Conversely, Rome is globalising, as a successor to and westward extension of Egypt, Persia, Macedonia, Greece, the Hittites, the Phoenicians, Carthage, enabled by precursors, building on their infrastructures – in criss-crossing the Mediterranean, wiring East and West, and as a westward extension of Eurasian culture. Part of Rome's western expansion was that it brought aqua and wine/grape culture to northwest Europe, as well as widespread olive oil consumption not seen again until the late twentieth century.[51]

Of course, Romanisation matters, but what does it mean? More precisely, how Roman is Rome? Rome is globalised and globalising. If we accept that Rome was globalised, it follows that *Romanisation is globalisation*. The peripheries define the centre as much as the centre shapes the peripheries. The peripheries are many and there is also travel between peripheries, before, during and after the Roman era. The Romans globalised their peripheries by bringing in their own influence and elements of *other peripheries*. Mesopotamians guarded Hadrian's Wall and legionaries from Africa served on the German frontier.[52] The Romans brought *garum*, fermented fish sauce, possibly from a recombination of Asian recipes, all over the empire. In early Roman London (Londinium), an emergent 'taste' for seafood seems to have contrasted with avoidance and possible religious reverence in Iron Age Britain[53]; in an early demonstration of the relationship between power, social formation and 'taste' within the British Isles, revered sea fauna became seafood. *Liquamen* or *garum* are in many respects similar to fermented fish sauces used in contemporary Thai and Vietnamese cooking and, in a coincidental continuity, they are one of the most widely available and used flavourings in east London today.[54]

The dialectics of empire and emancipation are that as the empire gobbles up the peripheries, the peripheries influence and reshape the centre.[55] In the endgame the frontiers often take over the centre.[56] Christianity becomes the religion of the empire like barbarian mercenaries guarding the imperial frontiers take over the empire itself. Part of fine-grain imperial history and the network approach to empire is the recognition that the peripheries polemicise with the centre; indeed, every point is a centre.

At the same time, the centre polemicises with the periphery. Tacitus's *Germania* blamed the decline of Rome on its absorption of foreign, alien elements: 'The German tribes are stronger because they are pure'. This theme was taken up by Edward Gibbon and influenced Europe's eighteenth- and nineteenth-century elites and their thinking about decay and decadence – as in Comte de Gobineau's thesis that mixture produces decay. Purity (of 'blue blood' and of 'race') thus became a key sensibility of Europe's declining aristocracy,[57] and exercised a profound influence on Nazism.[58]

Part of the nexus *Romanisation as globalisation* is that during Hellenistic-Roman times Europe was linked to the East. In time Latin Christianity, driving the Crusades, weakened Byzantium and contributed to the West-East split. Latin cosmopolitanism lingered in the Roman Catholic Church (the 'oldest international') and revived in Renaissance humanism. The Renaissance meant Europe resuming urban culture *and* its links to the East (via Venice, the Levant trade, the Silk Routes).[59] The infrastructure of the Greco-Roman world contributed to Europe's trade networks. Meanwhile, part of the subtext of 'modern' Europe, while explicitly neo-classical (Greco-Roman) in style and outlook, is that it rejoined Eurasia.

In aesthetics and symbolism the Roman empire framed imperial power in the West – in Napoleon's empire style and Napoleonic code; in the British empire's notions of law, citizenship and infrastructure modelled on the Roman example; and in Italian fascism, Nazism and American superpower.[60] To the East also, the Ottomans (adopting imperial-style architecture in the Topkapi Palace) and the Russian tsars echoed elements of the Roman empire. The American and French Revolutions, led by elites reared in the classics, were also steeped in Roman imagery.[61]

In this context, is empire a productive theme? Then, which imperialism? Relevant approaches are the pericentric theory of empire,[62] in which peripheries play a central, not just a marginal role, and multicentric and network understandings of empire. This generates multiple and layered understandings of the Roman world including the diversity, polyphony and dynamics of Romanness: unfolding across nine centuries, multi-centric Rome involves many actors, many different Romanisations and Roman identities.

While Roman history and archaeology involve accomplished methodology, large databases and impressive case studies, monuments, artefacts and texts defined the case. To the extent that archaeological data lead the argument, because the data are monumental (as traditionally studied in Classical archaeology) the argument takes on a monumental bend. The monumental bias in Roman history drives state-centric approaches. This formal framework may mistake the stage (monumental remnants of which remain) for the performance, which may have been more polyphonic than the monuments would suggest. By contrast, more recent archaeological and cultural studies of the Greco-Roman world are 'backstage inquiries' and shifted their focus from the centre to the peripheries, and from the monumental to the mundane.

Second, there is a Western bias in Roman history. Part of the 'the spell of Rome' and the Rome of Cecil B. de Mille and Walt Disney is a whitewash of Rome, as Bernal discussed in relation to ancient Greece.[63] While the eastward extension of Hellenism is extensively on record in the Gandhara civilisation, Rome's eastward extension is relatively little explored. Rome's links with the East, with Parthia, Bactria and Asia are understated and remain relatively under-researched.[64]

This includes the links with China and East Asia.[65] Chinese traders reached the Roman world, known as 'Da Qin', probably mainly as far as Syria. A Chinese embassy reached Da Qin in 130 BCE and a Roman envoy visited the Chinese emperor as alleged in Chinese records of 166 CE.[66] Second-century CE Chinese records discuss routes to Da Qin. The main overland route led via the 'Jade Gate' through central Asia, but sea routes were also used. Of Da Qin, first-century CE records note: 'they regularly make a profit by obtaining Chinese silk, unravelling it, and making *hu* ("Western") silk damasks. That is why this country trades with Anxi (Parthia) across the middle of the sea'.[67] Chinese descriptions of products of Da Qin show detailed knowledge: 'Gold-threaded embroidery, poly-chrome (warp twill) fine silk or chiffon, woven gold cloth, purple handker-chiefs, *falu* cloth, purple *chiqu* cloth, asbestos cloth, fine silk gauze cloth, shot silk, "clinging cloth" or "cloth with swirling patterns", *dudai* cloth, Wensu cloth, multi-coloured *tao* cloth, crimson curtains woven with gold, and small, round multi-coloured mosquito nets'. This research also brings the silk routes further back in time.[68]

CONCLUSION: RE-TIMING GLOBALISATION

The importance of Greco-Roman antiquity for global studies is fourfold. First, it establishes a clear link between Bronze Age cultures and later developments. Second, it sheds light on oriental globalisation taking shape in the Middle East. Third, it makes the entire sway from prehistory to the present more intelligible. Fourth, the plural, Creole, multicultural Mediterranean of recent historical and archaeological research debunks another Eurocentric myth, the myth of antiquity itself along with the misguided narrative of an East–West split (ranging from the battle of Troy to Huntington's 'clash of civilizations').

Assessments of the timing of globalisation range widely, from globalisation as a planetary evolutionary process, or as a long-term historical process going back to 3000 BCE (in historical anthropology and heterodox world system thinking); as a world economy, with dates ranging from 500 CE (Hobson), 1100 CE (Frank, Chaudhuri), 1200 CE (Abu-Lughod, Gunn, Braudel), to 1500 CE (Marx, Wallerstein); as modernity, 1800 CE (Giddens); and as a recent trend from the 1970s. A general principle is, the later the timing of globalisation the greater Europe's role and the more Eurocentric the perspec-tive (which changes again after 2000 CE).

According to a general, matter-of-fact definition of globalisation, global-isation is the trend of growing worldwide interconnectedness.[69] It refers to the growing scope and density of connections between distant lands and locations. Hence globalisation is spurred by technologies of transport and communication, which include the institutions and security conditions of an

Table 10.1: Phases of globalisation (after Nederveen Pieterse 2009, 125).

Phase	Start time	Central nodes	Dynamics
Eurasian	3000 BCE	Eurasia	Agricultural and urban revolutions, migrations, trade, ancient empires
Greco-Roman world	1000 BCE	Greater Mediterranean and west Asia	Hellenism
Oriental globalisation 1	500 CE	Middle East	Integration of the world economy
Oriental globalisation 2	1100	East and South Asia	Productivity, technology, urbanisation
Atlantic expansion	1500	Multipolar and Europe	Triangular trade, Americas
Industrialisation	1800	Euro-Atlantic economy	Enlightenment, colonialism, colonial division of labour
20C globalisation	1950	United States, Europe, Japan	Multi-national corporations, Cold War, global value chains
21C globalisation	2000	East Asia, BRICS, emerging societies, petro-economies	A new geography of trade, global rebalancing

imperial pax. Thus, the rhythms of globalisation follow the conditions and vicissitudes of connectivity, which are not always in forward motion; there are accelerations as well as breakdowns of connectivity. These dynamics frame the phases and periods of globalisation (Table 10.1).

Resuming the wider historical discussion, the sequence of early globalisation is that Bronze Age Eurasia sets the stage for the ancient empires, Egypt, Mesopotamia, Persia, Greece, Ashok India and Han China. Their common features include developed agriculture and urban culture. Hellenism, in turn, enabled the Roman empire and Greco-Roman Hellenism set the stage and the preconditions for oriental globalisation.

Turning to the timeline of globalisation, the disadvantage of taking contemporary times as cut-off and as start time of globalisation is presentism or ignoring history. The disadvantage of using modernity (whether from 1500 CE or 1800 CE) as cut-off in globalisation thinking is Eurocentrism, or cutting Europe off from global history. The advantage of taking the long view is that it embeds globalisation in the *longue durée*; the disadvantage is that globalisation becomes too wide and general a category. This disadvantage can be overcome by identifying different phases and shifting centres in global history, which poses the problem of identifying and labelling periods (Table 10.1).

Features of the periodisation in Table 10.1 are, first, globalisation starts with the Bronze Age and Eurasia. Second, Antiquity and the Greco-Roman world are an intermediary phase, a westward extension of the Eurasian momentum. Third, in oriental globalisation Mark 1, the direction of trade flows is on balance eastward, from the Middle East towards Asia, and in oriental globalisation Mark 2, the balance is westward, from East and South Asia towards the Middle East, resuming the early Silk Routes. Fourth, distinctive for the period from 1500 CE is the growing role of Europe, the addition of the Americas, and the triangular trade, in short the Atlantic turn, in addition to the ongoing central role of Asia. Fifth, characteristic of the phase from 1800 CE is industrialisation. I refrain from categorising the latter two phases as 'early modern' and 'modern' because of the Eurocentric associations of these terms.

To conclude on a general note: scholars often expect too much from paradigms, as if they could be an all-purpose elixir to serve their needs and wishes. Change the paradigm, say from Romanisation to globalisation, and the problems do not disappear, they just relocate. The question then becomes *which* globalisation, according to which approach? A further question is agency. Globalisation is often reified and treated as an agent – as if globalisation overwhelms other agents – the agency of sovereignty, empire, state, the nation, the local. Globalisation taken and used in this sense is disabling, not enabling. Thus, using paradigms means reworking them in the process.

NOTES

1. Haverfield (1912). For the Romanisation debate, see Mattingly (2004; 2006) and Pitts & Versluys (Chapter 1, this volume); also and Hingley (Chapter 2, this volume and Versluys 2014).
2. Hingley (2005); Naerebout (2006/7); for an overview of the debate so far, see Pitts & Versluys (Chapter 1, this volume).
3. Giddens (1990).
4. Naerebout (2006/7).
5. Pitts & Versluys (Chapter 1, this volume).
6. Bayly (2004); Hopkins (2006).
7. Robertson (2003).
8. A critique is Nederveen Pieterse (2005).
9. McNeill (1963, 1979); Hodgson (1974).
10. Frank & Gills (1993, 2000).

11. e.g. Wilkinson (2000).
12. Stavrianos (1998).
13. Abu-Lughod (1989).
14. Hobson (2004).
15. Frank (1998); Pomeranz (2000).
16. Hobson (2012).
17. Nederveen Pieterse (2006, 2009).
18. Nederveen Pieterse (2011a).
19. Morris (2005, 31).
20. Ibid., 31.
21. Ibid., 37.
22. van Dommelen & Knapp (2010b, 1, 6); van Dommelen (2006a).
23. Versluys (2010a); Hingley (2005).
24. e.g. Webster (2001). See also Witcher (Chapter 9, this volume) for further discussion.
25. Versluys (2010a).
26. Hitchner (2008).
27. Alternative perspectives are Witcher (2000) and Geraghty (2007); see also the various contributions to this volume.
28. Discussed further in Pitts & Versluys (Chapter 1, this volume).
29. cf. Pitts & Versluys (Chapter 1, this volume), and Morley (Chapter 3, this volume).
30. Flynn & Giraldez (2006, 244).
31. O'Rourke & Williamson (2002).
32. Robertson (1992).
33. cf. Woolf (1990).
34. Morris (2005, 36, 45); Horden & Purcell (2000).
35. Cohen (2000, 12).
36. Isayev (Chapter 6, this volume).
37. Hoerder (2002).
38. McNeill (1982).
39. Edwards & Woolf (2003).
40. Nussbaum (2006).
41. Inglis & Robertson (2006). After the Punic wars, between 160 and 120 BCE, Polybius wrote: 'Now in earlier times the world's history had consisted, so to speak, of a series of unrelated episodes, the origins and results of each being as widely separated as their localities, but from this point onwards [after the Second Punic war] history becomes an organic whole: the affairs of Italy and Africa are connected with those of Asia and of Greece, and all events bear a relationship and contribute to a single end' (*Histories* 1.3). For this text, see also Pitts & Versluys and Isayev (Chapters 1 and 6, respectively, this volume).
42. I refer here to the scholarly discussion that has shown the premise of Isaac (2004) that racism was invented in Antiquity to be not convincing.
43. Pollock (1996).
44. Hodgson (1974); Nederveen Pieterse (2007, Chapter 7).
45. Goody (2010a, 2010b); Nederveen Pieterse (2011b).

46. McNeill (1963, 1979).
47. McNeill (1982).
48. Versluys (2010a, 17).
49. Taylor (1989).
50. Quoted in Nederveen Pieterse (2007, 9). See, more in general, Pitts (2007), Versluys (2013) and Wallace-Hadrill (2008).
51. Pitts, Dorling & Pattie (2007).
52. Tolia-Kelly (2011).
53. On fish in Iron Age Britain, see Dobney & Ervynck (2007); on fish in Roman London and Britain, Cool (2006, 104–6).
54. Rhys-Taylor (2010, 165); cf. Kurlansky (2002).
55. Nederveen Pieterse (1989).
56. Wells (1999).
57. Nederveen Pieterse (1989, Chapter 11).
58. Krebs (2010).
59. Goody (2010a); Nederveen Pieterse (2011b).
60. Bondanella (1987); Hingley (2000); Murphy (2008).
61. Bondanella (1987).
62. Fieldhouse (1973).
63. Bernal (1987).
64. See Parker (2008) and Versluys (2010b). Ball (2000) is an important (and programmatic) exception.
65. Hill (2011a, 2011b).
66. Sitwell (1986, 130, 146–7).
67. From a translation of the Chronicle on the 'Western Regions' from the *Hou Hanshu*, composed in 107–125 CE compiled by Fan Ye, 398–446 CE.
68. Hill (2011a, 2011b).
69. Nederveen Pieterse (2009, 43). For (more) definitions, see the introduction to this volume.

11

GLOBAL, LOCAL AND IN BETWEEN: CONNECTIVITY AND THE MEDITERRANEAN

Tamar Hodos

INTRODUCTION

Globalisation is a concept considered by many to be relevant only to the modern world. This is evident from the emphasis, and impact, of works such as Tom Friedman's (2005) *The World Is Flat: a Brief History of the Twenty-First Century*, Naomi Klein's (2007) *The Shock Doctrine: the Rise of Disaster Capitalism* and Pankaj Ghemawat's (2011) *World 3.0: Global Prosperity and How to Achieve It*. Contemporary critics of globalisation point out that the impact of such wide-scale connectedness does not reach the entirety of the globe, and suggest instead that the term and its ideas serve as a synonym for Westernisation.[1]

Such criticisms are counterbalanced by a deeper delving into the processes of globalisation and the mechanisms behind its development and maintenance. Firstly, scholarship on globalisation acknowledges that the impact of global connectedness does not extend to all communities and individuals across the planet. Indeed, 'global' as meant by globalisation discourse is not intended to refer to a sense of all-encompassing. In other words, 'global' refers to a particular scale.

Secondly, scholarship is quick to point out that globalisation is not restricted to Westernisation. Tomlinson outlines the limits of Western globalisation,[2] Appadurai considers the structures that contribute to globalisation and how their limits might be overcome in analytical practice,[3] and Ghemawat illustrates numerous examples of how 'global' connectivity transcends individual cultures to create in practice a semi-globalisation.[4]

Finally, many scholars have argued for globalisation's longevity and cite numerous examples of past periods of global engagement.[5] Many of these only consider previous globalisations since the Enlightenment, which is often taken as the origins of modern (Western) society.[6] Thus, there are specialists of the ancient world who doubt that the concept can be applied appropriately to the more distant past, such as the Roman period, since the world was not wholly connected.[7] Furthermore, ancient world scholars object to the term's popular synonymity with Westernisation,[8] which is discordant with current trends in scholarly analysis that strive to deconstruct colonialist narratives as part of post-colonial/post-modern analysis, a point illustrated clearly in the introduction to the present volume by Pitts and Versluys.[9] Ancient scholar critics of globalisation also tend to regard it simply as a kind of uniformity, a point to which Witcher draws attention in this volume (Chapter 9) in his overview of how globalisation has been used in recent years with regard to the Roman world, both by scholarship and also with regard to the contemporary heritage industry.

Taking as their starting point how globalisation might be applied to the ancient world, many of the contributions presented here focus on the common characteristics suggested by the concept of globalisation. They draw particularly on contemporary analyses of the processes through which the world is regarded as a coherently bounded place, and the ways in which we are made conscious of this sense of one-placeness.[10] This enables us to examine the balance between the shared practices that gave rise to the notion of overarching cultures, such as that of Rome, while recognising and contextualising the diversities in their regional practices, the varied impacts they had on others and the diverse nature of engagement local communities had with them, which has been the emphasis of recent post-colonial scholarship.[11] My own contribution aims to extrapolate certain characteristics from the case studies presented in this volume to establish a methodology of applying globalisation theories to the past (for, as Hingley notes in the present volume (Chapter 2), a consensus is unlikely to be achieved, and, indeed, may not even be desirable, given the variabilities within any connected environment). This reflexive process responds to Nederveen Pieterse's emphasis here that such paradigms need reworking within the context to which they are applied.

UNDERSTANDING GLOBALISATION

How does one define globalisation? Morley, Witcher and Nederveen Pieterse note explicitly in the present volume (Chapters 3, 9 and 10, respectively) that the term itself is merely a descriptor of processes of enhanced connectivity and relativisation. These are widely regarded as transformative processes that spread economic, political, social and cultural relationships with increasing intensity and velocity, and transcend the ties between engaged communities.[12]

Are all of these features necessary in order to consider the essence of globalisation as relevant to what we see in antiquity? As has long been noted,[13] there are two key features to the processes of globalisation. The first is that what we think of as a global culture incorporates sets of loosely shared practices or bodies of knowledge that transgress national or cultural ideas.[14] What we see, therefore, are certain aspects that are commonly understood across cultural or social groups. It is this element of mutual understanding that creates a common discourse that operates at the global level between groups to foster and develop further links between them; at the same time, those aspects are also recognised within the social groups that participate globally, and permeate within and contribute to the social development of those groups.

The second aspect is that an important outcome of more intensive communication and collaboration at what we take as a global level is the stronger articulation of boundaries between the different groups engaged at that global level. Thus, with similarity comes a greater emphasis on difference as a direct reaction to and means of distinguishing groups and individuals from the increasing similarities. Instead of promoting cultural homogeneity, such processes can result in highlighting and reinforcing cultural heterogeneities. This paradox does not, and did not, come about passively but is, and was, an active (but not necessarily conscious) reaction to global engagement, as discussed by Pitts and Versluys in their introduction.

Both aspects are frequently overlooked by critics of globalisation, as is evident above.[15] Also often overlooked is that one result of any such engagement is the development of hybrid practices. This is not a simple fusing of practices originating elsewhere, but it is the creation of new social and material forms;[16] although the mix of origins may still be visible, this does not necessarily infer that the social meanings remained the same. Cultures are not static but constantly evolving, and not necessarily at an even rate. Similarly, cultural developments borne of shared practices will also evolve at an uneven rate, pace and take-up. In short, globalisation processes produce common and distinct practices and bodies of knowledge, as well as mixed ones and new ones. It is not a simple dichotomy of global commonality and local difference.

Furthermore, the elements that contribute to what we associate with globalisation are not uniform in time, place or impact extent, and the activities that arise from and contribute to globalising effects will differ from place to place, and from one aspect of social consideration to another. This is not merely a question of elite/non-elite identities, or other forms of us/them that often serve as the focus of a study through a globalising lens. This is one reason why aspects of network theories[17] have gained increasing importance in studies that consider multicultural interactions and social developments in the ancient world, especially those that examine globalising processes. Networks are one of the facilitators of the sense of connectedness and commonality that underpins the sensations of globalisation, and therefore they contribute to the processes of globalisation. However, networks alone do not promote globalisation. Agency, social competition and identities are other factors, for example, but they are all underpinned by the various networks maintained between people. It is the changing rates of flow in such networks over time that create the punctuated connectivities discussed by Versluys in the present volume (Chapter 7).

As noted above, several schools of thought have been identified in contemporary discourse on the longevity of globalisation.[18] The first argues that globalisation is a recent process.[19] The second argues that globalisation has a long pedigree;[20] such a view implies a linear development, of which today's globalisation is an acceleration. The third focuses on the processes of change in particular periods, and the paradox that globalisation concurrently encourages diversity while fostering convergence.[21]

Discussions of the ancient past have focused, understandably, on the second aspect – that there have been previous periods of globalisation in human history, especially when globalisation is taken to mean the world as known by a particular group in its time. This aspect is illustrated neatly by Hingley's contribution in the present volume, in which he highlights that a division between the past and present is impossible idealism. This is a very post-processual perspective, for it emphasises the fact that archaeology must be regarded critically, given that our understandings of the past are shaped by our present social circumstances.[22] It is for this reason that Hingley is able to explore our understandings of Roman globalisation alongside discussions of contemporary globalisation, acknowledging that each informs the other. This is also considered by Witcher, who examines how, within a globalised present, our perceptions of cultural heritage inform our understandings of the past. His challenge that multiculturalism is merely a synonym for the co-existence of cultures can go further, for the social groups that make up the multicultural spectrum are also regarded (externally) as static, which highlights the limitations and dualities encouraged by such terminology. His astute observations of the contrasting manipulation of the Antonine and Hadrian's Walls in the promotion of particular cultural heritages can be expanded to consider the fact that what we perceive as 'Roman' is already a hybrid concept that is locally constructed.

Globalisation is a process of continuous evolution, and not one of linear development,[23] and it can only be understood fully by appreciating that it is a multi-centred phenomenon that is jointly produced by all participating parties, and not a form of central domination over peripheries.[24] Nederveen Pieterse highlights this with his illustration of the interconnectedness of globalisation processes over time, especially between the east and west from the Roman period onwards. His illustration of the changes in flows and balances of the Roman world's participation in global networks, especially through scrutiny of its eastern connections, reminds us that there are different centres, or nodes of connectivity, where the influences of cultures upon each other served to foster respective notions of the 'Roman world'. Morley brings out another aspect of such connectivity by considering the networks themselves, which rely upon a common standard, such as speaking Latin or using Roman coinage. This emphasis provides a mechanism by which the network idea has a more broad social application, and one that is loosened from the more common class and status considerations.

Furthermore, that today's globalisation is not a linear development from past connections has led some scholars to advocate an archaic globalisation that is distinguished from modern times notably by the nature of past consumption habits and by the role of religion.[25] Pitts's study in the present volume of mass consumption in Roman Britain (and elsewhere at other times) carefully unpicks the apparent discrepancy between mass demand for *sigillata*, as a global Roman product, with the homogenisation of form in local and regional British ceramic outputs. In doing so, he demonstrates the role of regional identities and agency, alongside the political and economic progressions, in the uneven mediation, interpretation and performance of global developments. While modern notions of globalisation may be considered to encourage uniformity, the globalised aspect of consumption in antiquity partly derived from difference to locally available products.

UNDERSTANDING GLOBALISATION IN THE PAST

Many of the essays presented in the present volume contribute to dialogues of the third school of thought outlined above, namely the processes of change that arise from connectivity, and especially the balance between globally shared practices and localised differences. From these, we may begin to outline the variety of processes at play in ancient globalisation.

There are two overarching points that can be drawn from many of the contributions to this volume. The first is that any consideration of globalisation in antiquity must embrace issues to do with the intersection between local and global. In his discussion of time–space compression, Morley argues that production has been rationalised at the supra-regional level in today's world, whereas in the Roman world, inter-regional distribution in some contexts decreased as regional and then local production took over. He briefly cites a study by Woolf of *sigillata* pottery produced in France during the first centuries BC and AD that illustrates this very development (the same study is considered by Pitts with regard to mass consumption).[26]

There are two sub-points worth drawing out here. The first is that shared practices are not the same as identically replicated ones, and engagement at the global level is to emphasise the commonality, which is not necessarily identical, but overlapping and shared. This can be seen in modern examples, such as the omnipresent Starbucks, Gap and McDonalds, referred to in the present volume already. These are multi-national corporations with branches in different countries, and their internationally shared sense of sameness is expressed through features such as common products (particular burger or coffee types; casual clothes) and store décor. The second point is that global engagement concurrently emphasises locality and reinforces local practices, tastes, customs and habits. For example, accompanying food in a Starbucks in Turkey is predominantly Turkish in type, style and flavour, there are no milk varieties to cater to individual preferences, and tea is served black, with sugar, and in traditional Turkish tea glasses. McDonalds in the UK makes a point of emphasising the UK origins of its meat and eggs in its UK marketing campaigns because food miles and meat safety are significant social considerations in contemporary Great Britain, whereas the availability of salads is less important to most UK consumers, and hence they do not feature on McDonald's UK menu; in contrast, salads have been readily on offer in its US outlets for decades, and the origin of ingredients used by its US stores remain unmentioned for they are of less importance to most US consumers. Finally, Gap restyles the designs and colours of its (US) clothing for the European market.[27]

A similar balance may be seen in the Roman ceramics example above: Woolf notes that while a taste for the kind of pottery represented by *sigillata* spread throughout Gaul from c. 30 BC onwards, the actual ceramics themselves favoured in this consumption varied widely from region to region, with primary and secondary areas of consumption developing.[28] Initially, such material was likely used by individuals as part of their display of elite status, one that would be recognised more globally by other elites of the Roman empire, but also acknowledged locally as an indicator of that individual's ability to acquire luxury goods, thereby reaffirming their elevated status within their community. The increased diversity of ceramic forms throughout Gaul towards the end of the last century BC and first century AD may be interpreted as the generalisation or mass commoditisation of *sigillata* and other Roman styles within local Gallic societies, as such styles became less a marker of elite status and more a characteristic of social norms. We have the advantage of an extended time period in which to observe changes in consumption patterns, and thus to see changes in the balance between global and local: as Woolf says, 'if the cultures of Roman Gaul were once again regional, they were also provincial, a part of a greater imperially structured civilization'.[29]

This chimes with Pitts's discussion of ceramic consumption patterns in both Roman Britain and seventeenth- and eighteenth-century Europe. *Sigillata* was initially an imported product used in status display that influenced the development of local pottery vessels in standardised forms, and manufactured in many centres. At the same time, each centre produced its own styles of pottery – variations on the same theme, so to speak – that accorded with localised traditions, practices and tastes, which required particular forms. As a result, over time, regional consumption patterns altered. As Pitts notes, in the case of southeastern Britain, this included preference for specific forms of particular Gallo-Belgic shapes not in the *sigillata* repertoire, which better served local culinary practices than the *sigillata* forms. The development of the klapmuts in seventeenth-century Netherlands is another case in point. In short, the devil is in the detail: the significance of local practices continued to inform material choices over time, articulated in consumption decisions through more localised (or regional) mediation and reinterpretation rather than imitation of global ideas and forms.

By considering changes in pottery consumption patterns, we can see the global–local balance: social groups were globally engaged but in ways that were locally significant and appropriate to local needs and social values, which were constantly evolving, sometimes with dramatic effect over the long term. Such a perspective realigns consumption interpretations away from unidirectional views that emphasise cultural adaptation, such as Romanisation and all that the term implies, towards those that consider social values in a world of cultural connectivity. This is one of the key points made by Versluys's contribution: a globalising approach that emphasises balance and connections prevents us from assessing social identities within a static framework, and enables the component of time to be incorporated into our analysis and understanding.

Indeed, his example of the balance between notions of China, *China* and china, or Egyptian, Egyptianising (or Egyptian-like) and material culture illustrates clearly the balance between local reactions to global engagement and globally shared ideas, alongside the development of hybridised practices that may arise. Things we consider 'Roman-like' get their meaning through circulation and the specific context of a specific moment in that system of circulation. Similarly, Laurence and Trifilò's study of regional civilian age commemoration patterns illustrates that it was not geographical connectivity that promoted any pattern convergence but the presence of the global institution of the Roman military that resulted in this particular development in local commemoration customs. Even evidence from Italy, itself, is not indicative of a military model, for Italy had a different commemorative pattern than that used by the Roman military in its global scope. In other words, the Roman military acts as an independent network connecting Rome and the provinces that make up the empire, rather than serving as a simple proxy for Rome itself abroad in terms of practices and customs. Furthermore, regional patterns of monument construction remained consistent in terms of the proportions of walls, temples, honorific arches and the like that were constructed, although the absolute number increases across the empire during the second and third centuries AD. The increase in quantity is more evident in sites on a major road, suggesting that connectivity via direct transport routes played a greater role in the quantity of monument construction. Yet the types of bath-houses constructed in military contexts had more to do with social status and elite display than explicit function, for bath-houses associated with auxiliary forts were more like private bathing facilities, whereas those associated with legionaries served a more public and communal function. As a result of these three related yet distinct examples, Laurence and Trifilò argue that cities are both 100% local and 100% global, or 100% specific and 100% generic – they are both at the same time.

The 200% idea may be outlined in an alternative manner, for initially it appears to imply a binary logic and seems to express a passive balance of local and global. It is not that ceramic styles changed to suit their new context, or that architectural forms can be considered either global or local expressions. Rather, these styles and features were transformed from the ground up explicitly and deliberately by the patrons who commissioned these works, and the architects and artists who designed them, as a means of expressing what we see as the paradox of globalising processes: that global engagement can at the same time produce a resurgence of local expression. But most important is the development of hybrid forms that are able to speak to many parties concurrently. These paradoxes of globalisation are active means of social communication, not passive. My point is that discussion of the global and local in the past must take into account the active nature of changes – the deliberate choices made by individuals and groups in their representations of themselves and their designed environments, be they social, cultural, political economic, geographic or other – in response to global engagement. The 200% is, in fact, a mélange of global, local and everything in between. One might argue that the combinations and permutations are infinite.

This may be illustrated at an individual level by the well-known example of Ilulianus of the Mauritanian Zegrensi tribe during the time of Marcus Aurelius (161–180 CE), who had applied for Roman citizenship.[30] Although his citizenship request was accepted, the letter that we have attesting this makes it clear that he is regarded by Rome as Roman only legally, but not in any other sense.[31] How he regards himself, much less how he is regarded by his tribe as a result of citizenship, we do not know. Indeed, he may have chosen to project certain aspects in particular contexts to achieve his aims, diminishing them at other times for different audiences. In short, one is not either/or, but both and all.[32]

The key to the operations of such diversities of identity is the mechanisms by which the engagements and communications take place: networks and connectivity, features that underpin the traits associated with globalisation. The connectivity afforded by regular communication and social involvement between individuals, communities and other social groups is maintained through networks. Often networks are regarded as the visualisation of structure and structural changes that arise from interactions to characterise the organisation of social associations.[33] The focus is on the underlying relationships among the elements of the social system that shape behaviour patterns.[34] In social network theory terminology, the members of the social system under examination are the nodes, while the ties between them represent the connections that regulate the flows of resources and relationships between the members/nodes, and collectively determine the connectivity of the network. Such a description – for this is descriptive – may help us begin to understand the reasons behind the multiple, diverse identities people maintained and projected in connected contexts.

Horden and Purcell's connectivity network of the ancient Mediterranean, for example, is limited to small step links, focusing on the coherence and coalescence of micro-regions,[35] even though they expand those micro-regions across the entire Mediterranean. But connectivity should not be taken as a synonym for proximity or intimacy. Tomlinson has defined proximity as 'a common conscious appearance of the world as more intimate, more compressed, more part of everyday reckoning' while metaphorically, it imparts 'the increasing immediacy and consequentiality of real distanciated relations ... [and thus] takes us beyond the "empirical" condition of connectivity'.[36] In turn, connectivity may create globalised spaces and connecting corridors to bring about cultural compression.[37] In other words, through connectivity we experience real-world distances differently, which thus underwrites the idea of proximity. From a time–space perspective, for example, distance may be measured in travel time rather than space, and that time element will differ depending upon mode of transportation. From a social network perspective, a shared practice may do more to bind people together than the widespread availability, popularity and (unqualified) consumption of a particular artefact type, since the object itself may be reinterpreted in its various local contexts (or cultural imagination: Pitts and Versluys in the present volume, Chapter 1).

As a result, global processes are ideally considered as locatable networks of practices and connections.[38] The connectivities between groups, and the networks between them that develop, maintain and expand upon that connectivity, are the mechanisms that create the processes of globalisation. The networks themselves, therefore, increase connectivity through the more regular movement of individuals, ideas, practices and material culture. Isayev notes in the present volume (Chapter 6) that distance mattered little in the case of mobility, and with it social exposure, in antiquity. She observes that the ancient Italic states not only allowed a high level of movement but that they depended upon it to sustain the dynamism that contributed their growth and influence. Her insightful contribution illustrates the plurality of mobility with regard to globalisation, for mobility not only creates networks – it takes people, after all, to engage with one another – but is additionally generated by them. Sommer's comparison of elite drinking practices across different cultural groups in the Mediterranean highlights this social role in transmitting shared ideas and mutual understandings. Indeed, his survey begins with Near Eastern practices of the Late Bronze Age, which were transmitted to the Phoenicians of the Iron Age, and shared with Greeks and Etruscans, who, in exposing elements that were recognisably in common, thus incorporated, interpreted and transposed those foreign practices in a manner that accorded with their own ritualised elite drinking performances to create new practices of their own age. This continual merging and mixing over time eventually was transported back to Palmyra during the Roman period, where the terminology the Palmyrians drew upon to express the common shared practices came from the global Mediterranean of that era, articulated through Greek, rather than their own terms of the previous millennium.

This leads directly to the second major aspect to consider: that time–space compression, as conceived in today's world, may not be an essential component of ancient globalisation processes. Time–space compression pertains not to globalisation but to globalism, which, as noted by Witcher here, refers to the explanation of how and why the world is organised as it is.

As a result, it may be one outcome of globalising processes but it is not an essential characteristic of globalisation. One key feature of today's global world is certainly the decrease in communication time,[39] but rapid communication is not necessary to create the sense of one-placeness that widespread connectivity encourages. Isayev's consideration of mobility in Italy illustrates that distance does not matter, but that citizenship means more than a territorial boundary.

Neither are technological advancements essential to facilitate the sense of one-placeness associated with globalisation. Morley observes that the speed of travel and communication did not improve dramatically during the period of the Roman empire (contra Laurance and Trifilò, who argue that the road network and the increased size of draft animals may have helped), but rather that the sense of one-placeness is conveyed by improved security for more people than previously against pirates and bandits, increased information about different regions, routes and prices, and common mechanisms, such as coins, weights and measures. Indeed, he argues that with the geographical expansion of the Roman empire, it took longer to communicate throughout the empire than it had previously. The conclusion to be drawn is that networks of shared practices are more effective at conveying the sense of one-placeness in antiquity than any real or perceived compression of time and place as experienced in the modern world.

A WAY FORWARD

From this overview of the contributions to the present volume, several elements emerge. (1) Fuller understanding of the mechanisms of globalisation will help us break down our traditionally binary perspectives. As Pitts notes, globalisation is not a benign enabler of plurality but is a complex series of processes involving inequalities of varying types and forms, social and material. Applying globalisation frameworks to the past is inherently bound up with issues of identity, and, indeed, identities, and for this we need to keep in mind the paradoxical impact of globalisation of the balance between global engagement and local resurgence. (2) The means of globalisation must also be considered more actively: namely the networks between those social groups engaged with one another. As has been illustrated throughout this volume, a fruitful mechanism is to focus on the networks that create the connectivity we associate with globalisation, which include just as much the trade and communication routes as the networks of shared social practices, whose participants form a network through their common actions. (3) Not all elements of contemporary globalisation are necessary for the same sense of one-placeness to be observed in the past. We need to understand the mechanisms that underpin the features of globalisation in order to consider their role in the past. One key example is the time–space compression. We need to ask ourselves what it is that creates a sense of time–space compression, for neither time nor space have actually been compressed.

Finally, it is important to remember that examinations of today's globalising processes have the advantage of constantly emerging and evolving datasets that can be time stamped very closely. Rarely do we have such luxuries of close chronology in antiquity. To identify closely an absolute date for ancient material evidence is rare; working within a framework of fifty to one hundred years is more common, especially for the Roman period, although obviously evidence that can be tightly dated does exist. However, if we could only draw on modern patterns with a similar scale (e.g. 1950–2000 or 1960–2010, or even 1900–2000), we would probably describe alternative patterns of change within globalising processes and perhaps find similar footprints to what we observe in the ancient world. This is one reason why the analogy of today's patterns and processes of globalisation causes difficulties in wholesale application to the ancient world. Awareness of the mechanisms that underpin the symptoms of globalisation will help to alleviate this.

So where does this leave Roman studies? As Nederveen Pieterse eloquently explains, globalisation decentres Rome: Rome is thus globalising by being globalised, and vice versa. This reflexive perception dissolves the dichotomies associated with our previous approaches to interpreting the impact of Roman interaction with others and the development of a Roman world through expanded Roman power, especially the foreign–native dichotomy that has characterised other theoretical models, including hybridisation. It lifts geographic barriers of study that have fostered provincial archaeologies, and it links identity, connectivity and networks. It creates an understanding that is both broad and local, common and diverse, and which illustrates the networks of connection that foster changes in social, economic and political interactions between individuals and groups across the Roman world. Roman studies reflect the consequences of cultural globalisation. Seen in this light, the Roman world is not just a product of globalisation but also an agent of change, and whose networks of connectivities in a variety of cultural contexts (social, economic, political, etc.) enable us at times to relativise otherwise seemingly disparate phenomena.

Globalisation refers to the processes that generate widespread connectivity, not the conditions of such engagements, and yet the processes operate in socially, temporally and geographically particular contexts, and therefore will vary from one experience of globality to another. With this in mind, we most certainly can discuss the Roman world as globalised and globalising. There is no reason for the Roman era to display the same features and characteristics as other periods and places that exhibit traits of globality, since it is the processes that we are using to interrogate social lives of the past, not the patterns themselves. For this reason, and right now, globalisation is the most encompassing model we have to understand the relationships, real and imagined, that existed in the ancient Roman world.

As ancient authors wrote for their contemporary audiences, so we use modern analogies to try to understand past societies, and their interactions with one another, using concepts applicable to today's social complexities. In directly embracing the difficulties of applying modern concepts to the past, many of the contributions here have suggested that certain elements must be ring-fenced or reconfigured in order to make sense alongside the ancient evidence that we have available to us. This is the necessary paradigm reworking Nederveen Pieterse speaks of in his contribution here. As he argues, using globalisation as a framework for understanding the Roman world offsets Euro- and Western-centrism in contemporary discourse, especially with regard to other periods of widespread interconnections, which recalls Armitage's statement that 'the historian's contribution to the study of globalization should therefore be to remind us that we may be living amid only the latest (but probably not the last) of globalization's diverse and disconnected pre-histories'.[40] If we remember that there is no fixed pattern, temporal scale or geographical scope to globalising processes, or fixed impacts arising from them, then this should not vex us. Through this process, globalisation remains a powerful model for understanding the complexities of multicultural interaction in the past. Indeed, archaeological and ancient historical evidence may help us predict how our current society's globalising processes might develop over time, for assessing the longer-term patterns in the past may serve as a means of anticipating future developments in our own society.

NOTES

1. e.g. Appadurai (1990); Giddens (1990, 2002); Hopkins (2002a); Waters (2001).
2. Tomlinson (1999, 89–97).
3. Appadurai (2001).
4. Ghemawat (2011).
5. Clark (1997); Tomlinson (1999); Hopkins (2002b); Nederveen Pieterse (2004, this volume); McNeill (2008); Jennings (2011).

6. Or even later: O'Rourke & Williamson (2002).
7. e.g. Naerebout (2006/7, 154); Greene (2008, 79–80).
8. e.g. Morley (2007a, 94–6).
9. For a broader recent overview, see also Hodos (2010b).
10. Drawing upon Robertson (1992); more recently, see Waters (1995, 1–25); Tomlinson (1999, 1–31).
11. Hodos (2010b).
12. e.g. Hopkins (2002b, 16–17), although discussed in terms of nation-states, as is more common in contemporary discourse of globalisation.
13. e.g. Robertson (1992); Featherstone (1995).
14. Featherstone (1995).
15. See Hopkins (2006) for discussion.
16. Nederveen Pieterse (2001); van Dommelen (2006b).
17. Connectivity: Horden & Purcell (2000); network theories: *Mediterranean Historical Review* (2007); Knappett (2005; 2011); Malkin (2011).
18. Hopkins (2002b, 17–18).
19. Tomlinson (1999); Friedman (2005); Klein (2007); Ghemawat (2011).
20. Lewellen (2002, 8); Nederveen Pieterse (2004; Chapter 10, this volume); McNeill (2008).
21. LaBianca & Scham (2006).
22. e.g. Hodder (1991b).
23. Waters (2001, 7); Jennings (2011).
24. Hopkins (2002b).
25. Bayly (2002, 52–3).
26. Woolf (1998).
27. Personal comment by a UK buyer for Gap, Inc.
28. Woolf (1998, 187–205).
29. Woolf (1998, 205).
30. The Tabula Banasitana: CIL XIII 7335 = ILS 7096.
31. See also Lendon (1997, 150).
32. See also, for example, Wallace Hadrill (2008).
33. e.g. White & Johansen (2005).
34. Malkin et al. (2007, 4).
35. Horden & Purcell (2000, 123).
36. Tomlinson (1999, 3–4).
37. Tomlinson (1999, 7).
38. Castells (1996, 1997, 1998); Inda & Rosaldo (2008, 38, note 8).
39. Going back to Featherstone (1995, 114).
40. Armitage (2004, 173–4).

WORKS CITED

Abulafia, D. 2011. *The Great Sea. A human history of the Mediterranean.* London: Allen Lane.

Abu-Lughod, J. L. 1989. *Before European Hegemony: the world-system A.D. 1250–1350.* Oxford University Press.

Acquaro, E. 1988. Phoenicians and Etruscans, in S. Moscati (ed.), *The Phoenicians,* 532–7. Bompiani: Milan.

Adams, J. N. 2007. *The Regional Diversification of Latin 200 BC – AD 600.* Cambridge University Press.

Addison, E. 2004. The roads to ruins: accessing Islamic heritage in Jordan, in Y. M. Rowan & U. Baram (eds), *Marketing Heritage: archaeology and the consumption of the past,* 229–48. Walnut Creek, CA: Altamira Press.

Albert, M.-T., M. Richon, M. J. Viñals & A. Witcomb (eds). 2012. *Community development through world heritage.* Paris: UNESCO.

Alcock, S., T. N. D'Altroy, K. Morrison & C. Sinopoli (eds). 2001. *Empires: perspectives from archaeology and history.* Cambridge University Press.

Alexandridis, A. 2010. Neutral bodies? Female portrait statue types from the late Republic to the second century CE, in S. Hales & T. Hodos (eds), *Material culture and social identities in the ancient world,* 252–79. Cambridge University Press.

Algaze, G. 1993. *The Uruk World System. The dynamics of expansion of early Mesopotamian civilization.* University of Chicago Press.

Allason-Jones, L. 1999. Women and the Roman army in Britain, in A. Goldsworthy & I. Haynes (eds), *The Roman army as a community,* 41–51. Portsmouth, RI: Journal of Roman Archaeology, Supplementary Series 34.

Allen, J. 2006. *Hostages and Hostage-taking in the Roman empire.* Cambridge University Press.

Allison, P. M. 2004. *Pompeian Households. An analysis of the material culture.* UCLA Press.

Amiotti G. 1980. I Greci ed il massacro degli Italici nell' 88 a.C. *Aevum* 54, 132–9.

Ando, C. 2010. Imperial identities, in T. Whitmarsh (ed.), *Local knowledge and microidentities in the imperial Greek world,* 1–16. Cambridge University Press.

Andreau, J. 1999. *Banking and business in the Roman world.* Cambridge University Press.

Ang, I. 2005. Multiculturalism, in T. Bennett, L. Grossberg & M. Morris (eds), *New keywords in culture and society,* 226–9. Oxford: Blackwell.

Anheier, H. K. & M. Juergensmeyer. 2012. *Encyclopaedia of global studies.* London: Sage.

Appadurai, A. 1986a. Introduction: commodities and the politics of value, in A. Appadurai (ed.), *The Social Life of Things. Commodities in cultural perspective,* 3–63. Cambridge University Press.

Appadurai, A. (ed.). 1986b. *The Social Life of Things. Commodities in cultural perspective.* Cambridge University Press.

Appadurai, A. 1990. Disjuncture and difference in the global cultural economy. *Theory, Culture and Society* 7, 295–310.

Appadurai, A. 1996. *Modernity at Large. Cultural dimensions of globalization.* University of Minnesota Press.

Appadurai, A. 2001. Grassroots globalization and the research imagination, in A. Appadurai (ed.), *Globalization,* 1–21. Duke University Press.

Appadurai, A. 2006. *Fear of Small Numbers. An essay on the geography of anger.* London: Duke University Press.

Armitage, D. 2004. Is there a pre-history of globalization?, in D. Cohen & M. O'Connor (eds), *Comparison and History: Europe in cross-national perspective,* 165–76. New York: Routledge.

Arora, U. P. 1996. *Greeks on India. Skylax to Aristoteles.* Bareilly: ISGARS Indian Society for Greek and Roman Studies 4.

Assmann, J. 1997. *Das kulturelle Gedächtnis. Schrift, erinnerung und politische identität in frühen hochkulturen.* Munich: Beck.

Atakuman, Ç. 2010. Value of heritage in Turkey: history and politics of Turkey's world heritage nominations. *Journal of Mediterranean Archaeology* 23, 107–31.

Aubet, M. E. 1990. Die Phönizier, Tartessos und das frühe Iberien, in U. Gehrig & H. G. Niemeyer (eds), *Die Phönizier im Zeitalter Homers,* 65–74. Mainz: Verlag Philip von Zabern in Wissenschaftliche Buchgesellschaft.

Aubet, M. E. 2001. *The Phoenicians and the West. Politics, colonies and trade.* Cambridge University Press.

Baker, F. 1993. The Berlin Wall: production, preservation and consumption of a 20th century monument. *Antiquity* 67, 709–33.

Balakrishnan, G. 2003a. Introduction, in G. Balakrishnan (ed.), *Debating empire,* vii–xix. London: Verso.

Balakrishnan, G. (ed.). 2003b. *Debating empire.* London: Verso.

Ball, W. 2000. *Rome in the East. The transformation of an empire.* London: Routledge.

Bang, P. 2008. *The Roman Bazaar. A comparative study of trade and markets in a tributary empire.* Cambridge University Press.

Baram, U. & Y. M. Rowan 2004. Archaeology after nationalism: globalisation and the consumption of the past, in Y. M. Rowan & U. Baram (eds), *Marketing*

Heritage: Archaeology and the consumption of the past, 3–23. Walnut Creek, CA: Altamira Press.

Barkan, L. 1999. *Unearthing the Past: Archaeology and aesthetics in the making of rennaissance culture*. London: Yale.

Baudrillard, J. 2003. *Passwords*. London: Verso.

Bauman, J. 2004. Tourism, the ideology of design, and the nationalised past in Zippori/Sepphoris, an Israeli national park, in Y. Rowan & U. Baram (eds), *Marketing and Heritage. Archaeology and consumption of the past*, 205–28. Walnut Creek, CA: Altamira Press.

Bauman, Z. 1995. *Life in Fragments. Essays in postmodern morality*. Cambridge, MA: Basil Blackwell.

Bauman, Z. 1998. *Globalization: The human consequences*. Cambridge: Polity Press.

Bayly, C. A. 2002. 'Archaic' and 'modern' globalization in the Eurasian and African arena, c.1750–1850, in A. G. Hopkins (ed.), *Globalization in World History*, 47–73. London: Pimlico.

Bayly, C. A. 2004. *The Birth of the Modern World, 1780–1914: global connections and comparisons*. Oxford: Wiley-Blackwell.

Beard, M. & J. Henderson. 1995. *Classics: a very short introduction*. Oxford University Press.

Beaujard, P. 2010. From three possible Iron-Age world systems to a single Afro-Eurasian world-system. *Journal of World History* 21, 1–43.

Beck, U. 2004. Cosmopolitical realism: on the distinction between cosmopolitanism in philosophy and the social sciences. *Global Networks* 4, 131–56.

Belén Deamos, M. 2009. Phoenicians in Tartessos, in M. Dietler & C. López-Ruiz (eds), *Colonial Encounters in Ancient Iberia. Phoenician, Greek and indigenous relations*, 193–228. Chicago, IL: University of Chicago Press.

Bellah, R. N. & H. Joas. 2012. *The Axial Age and its consequences*. Cambridge & London: Harvard University Press.

Ben Younès, H. 1995. Tunisie, in V. Krings (ed.), *La civilisation phénicienne et punique. Manuel de recherche*, 796–827. Leiden: Brill.

Benton, C. & T. Fear. 2003. Introduction: from Rome to Buffalo. *Arethusa* 36, 267–70.

Berger, P. L & Luckmann, T. 1966. *The social construction of reality*. New York.

Bernal, M. 1987. *Black Athena: Afroasiatic roots of classical civilization: the fabrication of ancient Greece 1785–1985*. London: Free Association Press.

Bertelli, L. 2001. Hecataeus. From genealogy to historiography, in N. Luraghi (ed.), *The historian's craft in the age of Herodotus*, 67–94. Oxford University Press.

Bichler, R. 2007. *Historiographie – Ethnographie – Utopie. Gesammelte Schriften*. Wiesbaden: Harrassowitz Verlag.

Bidwell, P. 2009. The earliest occurrences of baths at auxiliary forts, in W. Hanson (ed.), *The army and frontiers*, 55–62. Portsmouth, RI: *Journal of Roman Archaeology*, Supplementary Series 74.

Billig, M. 1995. *Banal nationalism*. London: Sage.

Birley, A. 1971. *Septimius Severus. The African emperor*. London: Routledge.

Birley, A. 2001. *Vindolanda's military bath houses*. Hexham: Roman Army Publications.

Bleicken, J. 1981. *Verfassungs- und Sozialgeschichte des Römischen Kaiserreiches*. Paderborn: Verlag Ferdinand Schöningh.

Block, D. I. 1997. *The book of Ezekiel*. Michigan: Wm. B. Eerdmans Publishing.

Blomqvist, J. 1979. *The date and origin of the Greek version of Hanno's periply*. Lund: Kungliga Humanistika Vetenskapssamfundet.

Boeckh, A. 1817. *Die Staatshaushaltung der Athener*. Berlin: Reimer.

Bondanella, P. 1987. *The Eternal City. Roman images in the modern world*. Chapel Hill: University of North Carolina Press.

Bondì, S. F. 1977. Zu einigen Aspekten der phoinikisch-punischen Durchdringung Siziliens, in W. Huß (ed.), *Karthago*, 109–23. Darmstadt: Wege der Forschung.

Bondì, S. F. 1995. Le commerce, les échanges, l'économie, in V. Krings (ed.), *La civilisation phénicienne et punique. Manuel de recherche*, 268–81. Leiden: Brill.

Bondì, S. F. 2005. Il Mediterraneo di Herakles-Melqart. Conclusioni e prospettive, in P. Bernardini & R. Zucca (eds), *Il Mediterraneo di Herakles. Studi e ricerche*, 259–63. Rome: Carocci.

Bonnet, C. 1988. *Melqart. Cultes et mythes de l'Héraclès tyrien en Méditerranée*. Leuven: Peeters.

Bonnet, C. 2009. L'empire et ses religions: Un regard actuel sur la polémique Cumont-Toutain concernant la diffusion des « religions orientales », in H. Cancik & J. Rüpke (eds), *Die Religion des imperium Romanum. Koine und konfrontationen*, 55–74. Tübingen: Mohr Siebeck

Bonnet-Tzavellas, C. 1983. Le dieu Melqart en Phénicie et dans le bassin méditerranéen. Culte national et officiel, in E. Gubel et al. (eds), *Redt Tyrus – Sauvons Tyr – Histoire phénicienne – Fenicische Geschiedenis*, 195–207. Leuven: Peeters.

Boron, A. A. B. 2005. *Empire and Imperialism: a critical reading of Michael Hardt and Antonio Negri*. London: Zed Books.

Bradley, G. & Wilson, J.-P. (eds). 2006. *Greek and Roman Colonization: origins, ideologies and interactions*. Swansea: Classical Press of Wales.

Braudel, F. 1949. *La Méditerranée et le monde méditerranéen à l'époque de Philippe II*. Paris: Le Livre de Poche.

Bravi, A. 2006. Immagini dell'identità giudaica a Roma in epoca flavia. Il Templum Pacis e la menorah sull'Arco di Tito, *Mediterraneo Antico* 9, 449–61.

Bravi, A. 2010. Angemessene Bilder und praktischer Sinn der Kunst. Griechische Bildwerke im Templum Pacis, in C. Reitz (ed.), *Tradition und erneuerung. Mediale strategien in der zeit der Flavier*, Berlin: De Gruyter.

Breeze, D. J. 2007. Frontiers of the Roman empire world heritage site, in R. White & J. Carman (eds), *World Heritage: global challenges, local solutions*, 17–21. Oxford: Archaeopress.

Breeze, D. J. & Jilek, S. 2008. *Frontiers of the Roman Empire. The European dimension of a world heritage site*. Edinburgh: Historic Scotland.

Breeze, D. J. & Young, C. 2008. Frontiers of the Roman empire world heritage site. Summary nomination statement, in D. J. Breeze & S. Jilek (eds), *Frontiers of the Roman Empire. The European dimension of a world heritage site*, 29–35. Edinburgh: Historic Scotland.

Bricault, L. & M. J. Versluys (eds). 2007. *Nile into Tiber. Egypt in the Roman world*. Leiden: Brill.

Bricault, L. & M. J. Versluys (eds). 2010. *Isis on the Nile. Egyptian gods in Hellenistic and Roman Egypt*. Leiden: Brill.

Bricault, L. & M. J. Versluys (eds). 2014. *Power, Politics and the Cults of Isis*. Leiden: Brill.

Bridgman, T. P. 2005. *Hyperboreans. Myth and history in celtic-hellenic contacts*. New York: Routledge.

Broadhead, W. 2001. Rome's migration policy and the so-called ius migrandi, *Cahiers Glotz* 12, 69–89.

Broadhead W. 2002 *Internal migration and the transformation of republican Italy*, Unpublished PhD Thesis, University College London.

Broadhead, W. 2004. Rome and the mobility of the Latins, in C. Moatti (ed.). *La Mobilité des personnes en Méditerranée de l'antiquité à l'époque moderne*, 315–35. Ecole Française de Rome.

Broadhead, W. 2008. Migration and hegemony: fixity and mobility in second-century Italy, in L. De Ligt & S. J. Northwood (eds), *People, Land, and Politics: demographic developments and the transformation of Roman Italy 300 BC-AD 14*, 451–70. Leiden: Brill.

Brook, T. 2008. *Vermeer's Hat. The seventeenth century and the dawn of the global world*. London: Profile Books.

Brooks, N. 2005. Cultural heritage and conflict. The threatened archaeology of the western Sahara. *Journal of North African Studies* 10, 413–39.

Brunner, J. 1968. *Stand on Zanzibar*. London: Orb Books.

Brunt, P. A. 1971. *Italian Manpower 225 BC – AD 14*. Oxford: Clarendon Press.

Buraselis, K. 2007. *Theia dorea. Das göttlich-kaiserliche Geschenk. Studien zur Politik der Severer und zur constitutio Antoniniana*. Vienna: Verlag der Österreichischen Akademie der Wissenschaften.

Burke, P. 2009. *Cultural hybridity*. Cambridge: Polity Press.

Bussels, S. 2012. *The Animated Image. Roman theory on naturalism, vivedness and divine power*. Leiden University Press.

Butcher, K. 2003. *Roman Syria and the Near East*. London: J. Paul Getty Museum Press & The British Museum Press.

Cain, P. J. & A. G. Hopkins. 2001. *British imperialism, 1688–2000*. Harlow: Longman.

Cantor, M. 1875. *Die römischen agrimensoren und ihre stellung in der Geschichte der Feldmesskunst. Eine historisch-mathematische Untersuchung*. Leipzig: Teubner.

Carr, G. 2003. Creolisation, pidginisation and the interpretation of unique artefacts in early Roman Britain, in G. Carr, E. Swift & J. Weekes (eds), *TRAC 2002*.

Proceedings of the twelfth annual Theoretical Roman Archaeology Conference, Canterbury, 2002, 113–25. Oxford: Oxbow.

Carswell, J. 2000. *Blue and White. Chinese porcelain around the world*. London: British Museum Press.

Castells, M. 1996. *The Rise of Network Society: the Information Age: economy, society and culture 1*. Oxford: Blackwell.

Castells, M. 1997. *The Power of Identity: the Information Age: economy, society and culture 2*. Oxford: Blackwell.

Castells, M. 1998. *The End of the Millennium: the Information Age: economy, society and culture 3*. Oxford: Blackwell.

Castells, M. 2006. Nothing new under the sun?, in Ø. LaBianca & S. A. Scham (eds), *Connectivity in Antiquity. Globalization as long-term historical process*, 158–167. London: Equinox.

Castles, S. & J. M. Miller 1993. *The Age of Migration*. London: Palgrave Macmillan.

Cébeillac-Gervasoni, M. 2002. Note relative aux élites du Latium et de la Campanie et à leurs rapports avec la Méditerranée orientale, in C. Müller & C. Hasenohr (eds), *Les italiens dans le monde grec: IIe siècle av. J.-C.-Ier siècle ap. J.-C.: circulation, activités, intégration: actes de la table ronde, Ecole normale supérieur, Paris, 14–16 mai 1998*, 21–8. Paris: Ecole française d'Athènes.

Celestino Pérez, S. 2009. Precolonization and colonization in the interior of Tartessos, in M. Dietler & C. López-Ruiz (eds), *Colonial Encounters in Ancient Iberia. Phoenician, Greek and indiginous relations*, 229–53. University of Chicago Press.

Chase-Dunn, C. 2005. Social evolution and the future of world society. *Journal of World-Systems Research* 11, 171–94.

Clark, I. 1997. *Globalization and Fragmentation: international relations in the twentieth century*. Oxford University Press.

Clarke, D. B. 2003. *The consumer society and the postmodern city*. London: Routledge.

Clarke, K. 1999. *Between Geography and History: hellenistic constructions of the Roman world*. Oxford University Press.

Cohen, A. P. 1985. *The symbolic construction of community*. London: Routledge.

Cohen, W. I. 2000. *East Asia at the Center: Four thousand years of engagement with the world*. New York: Columbia University Press.

Colvin, S. 2011. The koine: a new language for a new world, in A. Erskine & L. Llewellyn-Jones (eds), *Creating a Hellenistic world*, 31–45. Swansea: Classical Press of Wales.

Cook, I. & P. Crang. 1996. The world on a plate: culinary culture, displacement and geographical knowledges. *Journal of Material Culture* 1, 131–53.

Cool, H. E. M. 2004. Some notes on spoons and mortaria, in B. Croxford, H. Eckardt, J. Meade & J. Weekes (eds), *TRAC 2003. Proceedings of the thirteenth annual Theoretical Roman Archaeology Conference, Leicester, 2003*, 28–35. Oxford: Oxbow.

Cool, H. E. M. 2006. *Eating and drinking in Roman Britain*. Cambridge University Press.

Cooley, A. 2007. The publication of Roman official documents in the east, in K. Lomas, R. Whitehouse & J. Wilkins (eds), *Literacy and the state in the Mediterranean*, 203–18. London: Accordia.

Cooper, N. 1996. Searching for the blank generation: consumer choice in Roman and post-Roman Britain, in J. Webster & N. Cooper (eds), *Roman Imperialism: post-colonial perspectives*, 85–98. Leicester Archaeology Monographs 3.

Copeland, T. 2002. Citizenship, education and heritage. *Internet Archaeology* 12.

Cordier, P. 2005. Varius in omni genere vitae: l'acculturation, les identités, le métissage et les faits culturels romains entre histoire et anthropologie, Mètis. Anthropologie des mondes grecs anciens. *Anthropologie, Philologie, Archéologie* 3, 295–305.

Crawford, M. H. 2008. The text of the Lex Irnitana. *Journal of Roman Studies* 98, 182.

Creighton, J. 2000. *Coins and power in Late Iron Age Britain*. Cambridge University Press.

Crielaard, J.P. 1998. Surfing on the Mediterranean web: Cypriot long-distance communications during the 11th and 10th centuries B.C., in V. Karageorghis & N. Stampolidis (eds), *Eastern Mediterranean: Cyprus-Dodecanese-Crete 16th-6th cent. B.C*, 187–206. University of Crete.

Cunliffe, B. 1988. *Greeks, Romans and Barbarians. Spheres of interaction*. London: Guild Publishing.

Cuozzo, M. 2007. Ancient Campania: cultural interaction, political borders and geographical boundaries, in G. Bradley, E. Isayev & C. Riva (eds), *Ancient Italy: regions without boundaries*, 224–67. University of Exeter Press.

Curran, B. 1996. Review of J.-M. Humbert, M. Pantazzi & C. Ziegler (eds), *Egyptomania: Egypt in western art, 1730–1930* (1994). *The Art Bulletin* 78, 739–45.

Cusick, J. G. 1998. Historiography of acculturation: an evaluation of concepts and their application in archaeology, in J. G. Cusick (ed.), *Studies in Culture Contact: interaction, cultural change and archaeology*, 111–38. Illinois: Center for Archaeological Investigations.

Davies, H. 1974. *A walk along the Wall*. London: Weidenfeld and Nicholson.

de Angelis, F. (ed.). 2013. *Regionalism and Globalism in Antiquity: exploring their limits*. Leuven: Peeters.

de Blois, L., P. Funke & J. Hahn (eds). 2006. *The impact of imperial Rome on religions, ritual and religious life in the Roman empire*. Leiden: Brill.

De Haan, N. 2010. *Römische Privatbäder – Entwicklung, verbreitung, struktur und sozialer status*. Frankfurt: Peter Lang.

de Ligt, L. 1991. Demand, supply, distribution: the Roman peasantry between town and countryside II: supply, distribution and a comparative perspective. *MBAH* 10, 33–77.

de Ligt, L. 2012. *Peasants, Citizens and Soldiers. Studies in the demographic history of Roman Italy 225 BC-AD 100*. Cambridge University Press.

de Ligt, L. & S. J. Northwood (eds). 2008. *People, Land, and Politics: demographic developments and the transformation of Roman Italy 300 BC-AD 14*. Leiden: Brill.

de Souza Briggs, X. 2004. Civilization in Color: the multicultural city in three millennia. *City and Community* 3, 311–42.

Delrieux F. 2001. Les Étrangers dans l'épigraphie Iasienne du IIe siècle a.C., in A. Bresson & R. Descat (eds), *Les cités d'Asie mineure occidentale au IIe siècle a.C.*, 137–55. Bordeaux: De Boccard.

Dench, E. 1995. *From Barbarians to New Men. Greek, Roman and modern perceptions of peoples from the Central Apennines*. Oxford: Clarendon Press.

Dench, E. 2005. *Romulus' Asylum: Roman identities from the age of Alexander to the age of Hadrian*. Oxford University Press.

Denemark, R. A., J. Friedman, B. K. Gills & G. Modelski (eds). 2000. *World System History. The social science of long-term change*. London: Routledge.

Derks, T. & N. Roymans. 2009. Introduction, in T. Derks & N. Roymans (eds), *Ethnic Constructs in Antiquity. The role of power and tradition*, 1–9. University of Amsterdam Press.

Desideri, P. (1991). La romanizzazione dell'Impero, in G. Clemente, F. Coarelli & E. Gabba (eds), *L'impero mediterraneo. 2: I principi e il mondo (Storia di Roma*, vol. 2). Torino: Einaudi.

Di Paola, L. 1999. *Viaggi, trasporti e istituzioni. Studi sul cursus publicus*. Dipartimento di scienze dell'Antichità dell'università degli studi di Messina.

Dietler, M. 2010. *Archaeologies of Colonialism. Consumption, entanglement, and violence in ancient Mediterranean France*. Los Angeles: University of California Press.

Dilke, O. A. W. 1971. *The Roman Land Surveyors. An introduction to the agrimensores*. Newton Abbot: David & Charles.

Dobney, K. & A. Ervynck. 2007. To fish or not to fish? Evidence for the possible avoidance of fish consumption during the Iron Age around the North Sea, in C. Haselgrove & T. Moore (eds), *The later Iron Age in Britain and beyond*, 403–18. Oxbow: Oxford.

Donnelly, M. 1986. Foucault's genealogy of the human sciences, in M. Gane (ed.), *Towards a critique of Foucault*, 15–32. London: Routledge.

Douglas, M. & B. Isherwood. 1996. *The World of Goods: towards an anthropology of consumption*. London: Routledge.

Dubuisson, M. 1985. *Le latin de Polybe. Les implications historiques d'un cas de bilinguisme*. Paris: Klincksieck.

Dueck, D. 2012. *Geography in classical antiquity*. Cambridge University Press.

Duncan-Jones, R. P. 1990. *Structure and scale in the Roman economy*. Cambridge University Press.

Eckardt, H. 2000. Illuminating Roman Britain, in G. Fincham, G. Harrison, R. Holland & L. Revell (eds), *TRAC 99. Proceedings of the ninth annual Theoretical Roman Archaeology Conference, Durham, 1999*, 8–21. Oxford: Oxbow.

Eckardt, H. 2002. *Illuminating Roman Britain*. Montagnac: Editions Monique Mergoil.

Edwards, C. 1993. *The politics of immorality in ancient Rome*. Cambridge University Press.

Edwards, C. & G. Woolf (eds). 2003. *Rome the cosmopolis*. Cambridge University Press.

Egri, M. 2007. The use of amphorae for interpreting patterns of consumption, in B. Croxford, N. Ray, R. E. Roth & N. White (eds), *TRAC 2006. Proceedings of the sixteenth annual Theoretical Roman Archaeology Conference, Cambridge, 2006*, 43–58. Oxford: Oxbow.

Eisenstadt, S. N. 1987. Allgemeine einleitung, in S. N. Eisenstadt (ed.), *Griechenland, Israel, Mesopotamien Kulturen der Achsenzeit. Ihre Ursprünge und ihre Vielfalt*, 10–40. Frankfurt.

Eisenstadt, S. N. (ed.). 1987–1992. *Kulturen der Achsenzeit*. I–V.

Engels, D. W. 1978. *Alexander the Great and the logistics of the Macedonian army*. Berkeley: University of California Press.

Engels, J. 2008. Universal history and cultural geography of the Oikoumene in Herodotus' Historiai and Strabo's Geographika, in J. Pigon (ed.), *The Children of Herodotus. Greek and Roman historiography and related genres*, 144–61. Cambridge Scholars Publishing.

Erdkamp, P. 2008. Mobility and migration in Italy in the second century BC, in L. de Ligt & S. J. Northwood (eds), *People, Land, and Politics: demographic developments and the transformation of Roman Italy 300 BC-AD 14*, 417–50. Leiden: Brill.

Erskine, A. 2009. *Roman imperialism*. Edinburgh University Press.

Evans, J. 2001. Material approaches to the identification of different Romano-British site types, in S. James & M. Millett (eds), *Britons and Romans: advancing an archaeological agenda*, 26–35. York: Council for British Archaeology Research Report 125.

Evans, J. 2005. Pottery in urban Romano-British life, in A. Mac Mahon & J. Price (eds), *Roman working lives and urban living*, 145–66. Oxford: Oxbow.

Fabbricotti, E. 1976. I bagni nelle prime ville romane. *Cronache Pompeiane* 2, 29–111.

Farney, G. D. 2007. *Ethnic identity and aristocratic competition in republican Rome*. Cambridge University Press.

Featherstone, M. 1995. *Undoing Culture: globalization, postmodernism and identity*. London: Sage.

Feldman, M. H. 2006. *Diplomacy by Design. Luxury arts and an 'international style' in the ancient Near East, 1400–1200 BCE*. University of Chicago Press.

Ferris, I. 1995. Shoppers' paradise: consumers in Roman Britain, in P. Rush (ed.), *Theoretical Roman Archaeology: second conference proceedings*. Aldershot: Ashgate.

Fieldhouse, D. K. 1973. *Economics and empire 1830–1914*. London: Weidenfeld and Nicolson.

Fincham, G. 2002. Consumer theory and Roman North Africa: a post-colonial approach to the ancient economy, in M. Carruthers, C. van Driel-Murray,

A. Gardner, J. Lucas, L. Revell & E. Swift (eds), *TRAC 2001. Proceedings of the eleventh annual Theoretical Roman Archaeology Conference, Glasgow, 2001*, 34–44. Oxford: Oxbow.

Finlay, R. 1998. The pilgrim art: the culture of porcelain in world history. *Journal of World History* 9, 141–87.

Finlay, R. 2010. *The Pilgrim Art. Cultures of porcelain in world history*. Los Angeles: University of California Press.

Finley, M. I. 1976. Colonies. An attempt at a typology. *Transactions of the Royal Historical Society* 26, 167–88.

Finley, M. I. 1985. *The ancient economy* (second edition). Los Angeles: University of California Press.

Flaig, E. 1999. Über die grenzen der akkulturation. Wider die verdinglichung des kulturbegriffs, in G. Vogt-Spira & B. Rommel (eds), *Rezeption und identität. Die kulturelle Auseinandersetzung Roms mit Greichenland als europäisches Paradigma*, 81–112. Stuttgart: Franz Steiner Verlag.

Flynn, D. O. & A. Giráldez. 2006. Globalization began in 1571, in B. K. Gills & W. R. Thompson (eds), *Globalization and global history*, 232–47. London: Routledge.

Fogolari, G. 1988. La cultura, in G. Fogolari & A. L. Prosdocimi (eds), *I Veneti antichi. Lingua e cultura*, 17–196. Padua: Editoriale Programma.

Foster, R. J. 2006. Tracking globalization. Commodities and value in motion, in C. Tilley, W. Keane, S. Küchler, M. Rowlands & P. Spyer (eds), *Handbook of material culture*, 285–302. London: Sage.

Foucault, M. 1989. *The archaeology of knowledge*. London: Routledge.

Frank, A. G. 1998. *ReOrient: global economy in the Asian age*. Berkeley: University of California Press.

Frank, A. G. & B. K. Gills (eds). 1993. *The World System: from five hundred years to five thousand*. London: Routledge.

Frank, A. G. & B. K. Gills. 2000. The five thousand year world system in theory and praxis, in R. A. Denemark, J. Friedman, B. K. Gills & G. Modelski (eds), *World System History. The social science of long-term change*, 3–23. London: Routledge.

Frankfurter, D. 1998. *Religion in Roman Egypt. Assimilation and resistance*. Princeton University Press

Frankfurter, D. 2000. The consequences of Hellenism in late antique Egypt: religious worlds and actors. *Archiv für Religionsgeschichte* 2, 162–94.

Frere, S. 1978. *Britannia*. London: Routledge.

Friedman, T. 2005. *The World Is Flat: a brief history of the twenty-first century*. New York: Farrar, Straus and Giroux.

Gaffney, V., R. White & H. Goodchild. 2007. *Wroxeter, the Cornovii, and the Urban Process. Final report on the Wroxeter hinterland project 1994–1997. Volume 1. Researching the hinterland*. Portsmouth, RI: *Journal of Roman Archaeology*, Supplementary Series 68.

Garcea, E. A. A. 2005. Postcolonial criticism in one world archaeology: where is North Africa's place? *Archaeologies* 1, 110–17.

Gardner, A. 2003. Seeking a material turn: the artefactuality of the Roman empire, in G. Carr, E. Swift & J. Weekes (eds), *TRAC 2002. Proceedings of the twelfth annual Theoretical Roman Archaeology Conference*, 1–13. Oxford: Oxbow.

Gardner, A. 2007a. *An Archaeology of Identity. Soldiers and society in late Roman Britain*. California: Left Coast Press.

Gardner, A. 2007b. Review of R. Hingley 'globalizing Roman culture'. *Britannia* 38, 389–90.

Gardner, A. 2013. Thinking about Roman imperialism: postcolonialism, globalisation and beyond? *Britannia* 44, 1–25.

Garnsey, P. 1966. The *Lex Iulia* and appeal under the Empire. *Journal of Roman Studies* 6, 167–89.

Garnsey, P. 1985. Grain for Athens, in P. Cartledge & F. D. Harvey (eds), *Crux. Essays in Greek history presented to G.E.M. de Ste. Croix on his 75th birthday*, 62–75. London: Duckworth Publishers.

Gawantka, W. 1975. *Isopolitie. Ein beitrag zur geschichte der zwischenstaatlichen beziehungen in der griechischen Antike*. München: Beck.

Gawlikowski, M. 1971. Inscriptions de Palmyre. *Syria* 48, 407–26.

Gazda, E. K. (ed.). 2002. *The Ancient Art of Emulation. Studies in artistic originality and tradition from the present to classical antiquity*. University of Michigan Press.

Gehrke, H.-J. 1986. *Jenseits von Athen und Sparta. Das Dritte Griechenland und seine Staatenwelt*. München: Beck.

Gehrke, H.-J. 1998. Die Geburt der Erdkunde aus dem Geiste der Geometrie. Überlegungen zur Entstehung und zur Frühgeschichte der wissenschaftlichen Geographie bei den Griechen, in W. Kullmann et al. (eds), *Gattungen wissenschaftlicher Literatur in der Antike*. Tübingen: Gunter Narr Verlag.

Geiger, J. 2009. Review of A. Wallace-Hadrill, Rome's cultural revolution. *Bryn Mawr Classical Review* 2009. 07. 50.

Gell, A. 1998. *Art and Agency. An anthropological theory*. Oxford: Clarendon Press.

Geraghty, R. M. 2007. The impact of globalization in the Roman empire, 200 BC – AD 100. *Journal of Economic History* 67, 1036–61.

Ghemawat, P. 2011. *World 3.0: global prosperity and how to achieve it*. Boston: Harvard Business Press.

Gibson, M. 2007. *Culture and Power. A history of cultural studies*. Oxford: Berg.

Giddens, A. 1990. *The consequences of modernity*. Stanford University Press.

Giddens, A. 1991. *Modernity and Self-identity: self and society in the late modern age*. Cambridge: Polity Press.

Giddens, A. 2002. *Runaway World: how globalization is reshaping our lives*. London: Routledge.

Gilhus, I. S. 2008. Orbis terrarium Romanorum est: globalization processes in the Roman empire, in A. W. Geertz & M. Warburg (eds), *New Religions and Globalization: empirical, theoretical and methodological perspectives*, 131–44. Aarhus University Press.

Gill, S. 2008. *Power and resistance in the new world order*. Basingstoke: Palgrave Macmillan.

Gills, B. K. & W. R. Thompson. 2006. *Globalization and global history*. London: Routledge.

Gisinger, F. 1933. Zur geographischen Grundlage vn Platons Atlantis. *Klio* 26, 32–8.

Godden, G. A. 1979. *Oriental export market porcelain and its influence on European wares*. London: Granada.

Going, C. J. 1987. *The Mansio and Other Sites in the South-eastern Sector of Caesaromagus: the Roman pottery*. Chelmsford Archaeological Trust and Council for British Archaeology.

Goldhill, S. 2011. *Victorian Culture and Classical Antiquity: art, opera, and the proclamation of modernity*. Princeton: Woodstock.

González, J. 1986. The Lex Irnitana. A new copy of the Flavian municipal law. *Journal of Roman Studies* 76, 147–243.

González-Ruibal, A. 2009. Vernacular cosmopolitanism. An archaeological critique of universalistic reason, in L. Meskell (ed.), *Cosmopolitan archaeologies*, 113–39. Durham, NC: Duke University.

González-Ruibal, A. 2010. Colonialism and European archaeology, in J. Lydon & U. Rizvi (eds), *Handbook of postcolonial archaeology*, 37–47. Walnut Creek, CA: Left Coast Press.

Goody, J. 2010a. *Renaissances: the one or the many?* Cambridge University Press.

Goody, J. 2010b. *The Eurasian miracle*. Cambridge: Polity Press.

Gordon, A. F. 1996. *Egyptian and Egyptianizing Scarabs: a typology of steatite, faience and pate scarabs from Punic and other Mediterranean sites*. Oxford University Press.

Gordon, R & J. Reynolds. 2003. Roman inscriptions 1995–2000. *Journal of Roman Studies* 93, 212–94.

Görgemanns, H. 2000. Wahrheit und Fiktion in Platons Atlantis-Erzählung. *Hermes* 128, 405–20.

Gotter, U. 2001. *Akkulturation* als Methodenproblem der historischen Wissenschaften, in S. Altekamp, M. R. Hofter & M. Krumme (eds), *Posthumanistische klassische archäologie. Historizität und wissenschaftlichkeit von interessen und methoden*, 255–86. Berlin: Hirmer Verlag.

Gouldner, A. W. 1960. The norm of reciprocity. A preliminary statement. *American Sociological Review* 25, 161–78.

Graham, M. W. 2006. *News and frontier consciousness in the later Roman empire*. Ann Arbor: University of Michigan Press.

Graves-Brown, P., S. Jones & C. Gamble (eds). 1996. *Cultural Identity and Archaeology. The construction of European communities*. London and New York: Routledge.

Greenblatt, S. 2009. Cultural mobility: a manifesto, in S. Greenblatt, I. Zupanov, R. Meyer-Kalkus, H. Paul, P. Nyíri & F. Pannewick (eds), *Cultural Mobility: a manifesto*, 1–23. Cambridge University Press.

Greene, K. 1986. *The archaeology of the Roman economy*. Berkeley & Los Angeles: University of California Press.

Greene, K. 2008. Learning to consume: consumption and consumerism in the Roman empire. *Journal of Roman Archaeology* 21, 64–82.

Greenfield, J. C. 2001. The *marzeah* as a social institution, in *Al Kanfei Yonah. Collected studies by Jonas C. Greenfield on Semitic philology*, 907–11. Jerusalem.

Grewal, D. S. 2008. *Network Power: the social dynamics of globalization*. London: Yale University Press.

Gruen, E. S. 1998. *Heritage and Hellenism. The reinvention of Jewish tradition*. Berkeley.

Gruen, E. S. 2002. *Diaspora. Jews amidst Greeks and Romans*. Cambridge, MA: Harvard University Press.

Gruen, E. S. (ed.). 2011. *Cultural identity in the ancient Mediterranean*. Los Angeles: Getty Publications.

Gschnitzer, F. 1971. Ἐπι τοῖσδε ἔδωκαν Πραίσιοι Σταλίταις τὰν χώραν... Zu einem Geschäftstyp des griechischen Völkerrechts, in *Kleine Schriften zum griechischen und römischen Altertum. Bd. II. Historische und epigraphische Studien zur Alten Geschichte seit den Perserkriegen*, 121–44. Stuttgart: Franz Steiner Verlag.

Gschnitzer, F. 1974. Proxenos, *RE Suppl.* 13, 629–730.

Habicht, C. 2002. Die Ehren der Proxenoi. Ein Vergleich. *Museum Helveticum* 59, 13–30.

Habinek, T. N. 1998. *The Politics of Latin Literature: writing, identity and empire in ancient Rome*. Princeton University Press.

Haegemans, K. 2000. Elissa, the first queen of Carthage, through Timaeus' eyes. *Ancient Society* 30, 277–291.

Hales, S. & T. Hodos (eds). 2010. *Material culture and social identities in the ancient world*. New York: Cambridge University Press.

Hamilakis, Y. 2007. *The Nation and Its Ruins: antiquity, archaeology, and national imagination in Greece*. Oxford University Press.

Hamlish, T. 2000. Global culture, modern heritage. Re-membering the Chinese imperial collections, in S. Crane (ed.), *Museums and memory*, 137–60. Stanford University Press.

Hardt, M. & A. Negri. 2000. *Empire*. London: Harvard University Press.

Hardwick, L. 2003. *Reception Studies. Greece & Rome: new surveys in the classics* 33. Oxford University Press.

Harper, T. N. 2002. Empire, diaspora, and the languages of globalism, 1850–1914, in A. G. Hopkins (ed.), *Globalization in world history*, 141–66. London: Pimlico.

Harris, A. (ed.). 2007. *Incipient Globalization? Long distance contacts in the sixth century*. Oxford: British Archaeological Reports.

Harris, W. V. 2005. *Rethinking the Mediterranean*. Oxford University Press.

Harris, W. V. 2011. *Maritime Technology in the Ancient Economy: ship-design and navigation*. Portsmouth, RI: *Journal of Roman Archaeology*, Supplementary Series 84.

Harrison, T. 2007. The place of geography in Herodotus' histories, in C. Adams & J. Roy (eds), *Travel, geography and culture in ancient Greece, Egypt and the Near East*, 44–65. Oxford: Leicester Nottingham Studies in Ancient Society 10.

Harvey, D. 1989. *The condition of postmodernity*. Oxford: Blackwell.

Harvey, D. 1996. *Justice, nature and the geography of difference*. Oxford: Blackwell.

Haussler, R. 2007. At the margin of Italy: Ligurians and Celts in north-west Italy, in G. Bradley, E. Isayev & C. Riva (eds), *Ancient Italy, regions without boundaries*, 45–78. University of Exeter Press.

Haverfield, F. 1912. *The Romanization of Roman Britain* (2nd edition). Oxford: Clarendon Press.

Hawkes, G. 2001. An archaeology of food: a case study from Roman Britain, in G. Davies, A. Gardner & K. Lockyear (eds), *TRAC 2000. Proceedings of the tenth annual Theoretical Roman Archaeology Conference, London*, 94–103. Oxford: Oxbow.

Hawthorne, J. 1998. Pottery and paradigms in the early western empire, in C. Forcey, J. Hawthorne & R. Witcher (eds), *TRAC 97. Proceedings of the seventh annual Theoretical Roman Archaeology Conference, Nottingham, 1997*, 160–72. Oxford: Oxbow.

Hazbun, W. 2004. Globalisation, reterritorialisation and the political economy of tourism development in the Middle East. *Geopolitics* 9, 310–41.

Heather, P. 2010. *Empires and Barbarians: The fall of Rome and the birth of Europe*. Oxford University Press.

Hekster, O. 2008. *Rome and its empire. AD 193–284*. Edinburgh University Press.

Held, D. & McGrew, A. G. (eds). 2008. *Globalization Theory: approaches and controversies*. Cambridge: Polity Press.

Higgins, C. 2009. When Syrians, Algerians and Iraqis patrolled Hadrian's Wall. *The Guardian*, 13 October.

Hill, J. D. 2001. Romanisation, gender and class: recent approaches to identity in Britain and their possible consequences, in S. James & M. Millett (eds), *Britons and Romans: advancing an archaeological agenda*, 12–18. York: Council for British Archaeology Research Report 125.

Hill, J. D. 2002. Just about the potter's wheel? Using, making and depositing middle and later Iron Age pots in East Anglia, in A. Woodward & J.D. Hill (eds), *Prehistoric Britain. The ceramic basis*, 143–60. Oxford: Oxbow.

Hill, J. E. 2011a. *The 'Peoples of the West' according to the Weilüe, by Yu Huan* (English trans. J. E. Hill). Draft annotated translation?

Hill, J. E. 2011b. *Through the Jade Gate to Rome: a study of the silk routes during the later Han dynasty*. Charleston, South Carolina: BookSurge.

Hillier, B. & J. Hanson. 1984. *The social logic of space*. Cambridge University Press.

Hin, S. 2008. Counting Romans, in L. de Ligt & S. J. Northwood (eds), *People, Land, and Politics: demographic developments and the transformation of Roman Italy 300 BC-AD 14*, 187–238. Leiden: Brill.

Hind J.R. 1994. Mithradates. *Cambridge Ancient History* Vol. IX, 129–64. Cambridge University Press.

Hingley, R. 1982. Roman Britain: The structure of Roman imperialism and the consequences of imperialism on the development of a peripheral province, in D. Miles (ed.), *The Romano-British Countryside: studies in rural settlement and economy*, 17–52. Oxford: BAR British Series 103.

Hingley, R. 1996. The 'legacy' of Rome: the rise, decline and fall of the theory of Romanization, in J. Webster & N. Cooper (eds), *Roman Imperialism: postcolonial perspectives*, 35–48. Leicester Archaeological Monographs.

Hingley, R. 1997. Resistance and domination: social change in Roman Britain, in D. J. Mattingly (ed.), *Dialogues in Roman imperialism*, 81–100. Portsmouth, RI: *Journal of Roman Archaeology*, Supplementary Series 23.

Hingley, R. 2000. *Roman officers and English gentlemen*. London: Routledge.

Hingley, R. (ed.). 2001a. *Images of Rome. Perceptions of ancient Rome in Europe and the United States of America in the modern age*. Portsmouth, RI: *Journal of Roman Archaeology*, Supplementary Series 44.

Hingley, R. 2001b. Images of Rome, in R. Hingley (ed.), *Images of Rome: perceptions of ancient Rome in Europe and the United States of America in the modern age*, 7–22. Portsmouth, RI: *Journal of Roman Archaeology*, Supplementary Series 44.

Hingley, R. 2005. *Globalizing Roman Culture. Unity, diversity and empire*. London: Routledge.

Hingley, R. 2008. *The Recovery of Roman Britain 1586–1906: a colony so fertile*. Oxford University Press.

Hingley, R. 2010. Cultural diversity and unity: empire and Rome, in S. Hales & T. Hodos (eds), *Material culture and social identities in the ancient world*, 54–75. Cambridge University Press.

Hingley, R. 2011. Globalization and the Roman empire: the genealogy of 'Empire'. *Semanta, Ciencias Sociais e Humanidades* 23, 99–113.

Hingley, R. 2012. *Hadrian's Wall: a life*. Oxford University Press.

Hingley, R. 2013. Romanization, in *Encyclopedia of Global Archaeology*. New York: Springer.

Hingley, R., R.E. Witcher & C. Nesbitt. 2012. Life of an ancient monument: Hadrian's Wall in history. *Antiquity* 86, 760–71.

Hitchner, R. B. 2008. Globalization avant la lettre: globalization and the history of the Roman empire. *New Global Studies* 2, 1–12.

Hobson, J.M. 2004. *The eastern origins of western civilisation*. Cambridge University Press.

Hobson, J.M. 2012. Orientalization in globalization: a sociology of the promiscuous architecture of globalization, c. 500–2010, in J. Nederveen Pieterse & J. Kim (eds), *Globalization and development in East Asia*. New York: Routledge.

Hodder, I. 1991a. *Archaeological Theory in Europe: the last three decades*. London: Routledge.

Hodder, I. 1991b. *Reading the Past: current approaches to interpretation in archaeology* (second edition). Cambridge University Press.

Hodder, I. 2010. Human-thing entanglement: towards an integrated archaeological perspective. *Journal of the Royal Anthropological Institute* 17, 154–77.

Hodder, I. 2012. *Entangled. An archaeology of the relationships between between humans and things.* Oxford: Wiley-Blackwell.

Hodgson, M. G. S. 1974. *The Venture of Islam: conscience and history in a world civilization*, 3 vols. University of Chicago Press.

Hodos, T. 2006. *Local responses to colonization in the Iron Age Mediterranean.* London: Routledge.

Hodos, T. 2009. Colonial engagements in the global Mediterranean Iron Age. *Cambridge Archaeological Journal* 19, 221–41.

Hodos, T. 2010a. Local and global perspectives in the study of social and cultural identities, in S. Hales & T. Hodos (eds), *Material Culture and Social Identities in the Ancient World*, 3–31. Cambridge University Press.

Hodos, T. 2010b. Globalization and colonization: a view from Iron Age Sicily. *Journal of Mediterranean Archaeology* 23, 81–106.

Hoerder, D. 2002. *Cultures in Contact: world migrations in the second millennium.* Durham, NC: Duke University Press.

Hölbl, G. 1986. *Ägyptisches Kulturgut im phönikischen und punishen Sardinien.* I, II. Leiden: Brill.

Hollifield, J. F. 2008. The politics of international migration: how can we 'bring the state back in'?, in C. B. Brettell & J. F. Hollifield (eds), *Migration Theory: talking across disciplines*, 183–238. New York: Routledge.

Hölscher, T. 1987. *Römische Bildsprache als semantisches System.* Heidelberg: Universitätsverlag Winter.

Hölscher, T. 2004. *The language of images in Roman art.* Cambridge University Press.

Hölscher, T. 2008. The concept of roles and the malaise of 'identity': ancient Rome and the modern world, in S. Bell & I. L. Hansen (eds), *Role models in the ancient world*, 42–56. *MAAR Supplement 7.*

Holtorf, C. 2009. A European perspective on indigenous and immigrant archaeologies. *World Archaeology* 41, 672–81.

Hopkins, A. G. 2002a. Introduction: globalization – an agenda for historians, in A. G Hopkins (ed.), *Globalization in world history*, 1–10. London: Pimlico.

Hopkins, A. G. 2002b. The history of globalization – and the globalization of history. In A. G. Hopkins (ed.), *Globalization in world history.* 11–46. London: Pimlico.

Hopkins, A. G. 2006. Introduction: interactions between the universal and the local, in A. G. Hopkins (ed.), *Global History: interactions between the universal and the local*, 1–38. Basingstoke: Palgrave Macmillan.

Hopkins, A. G. 2010. The historiography of globalization and the globalization of regionalism. *Journal of Economic and Social History of the Orient* 53, 19–36.

Hopkins, K. 1978a. Economic growth and towns in classical antiquity, in P. Abrams & E. A. Wrigley (eds), *Towns in Societies: essays in economic history and historical sociology*, 35–77. Cambridge University Press.

Hopkins, K. 1978b. *Conquerors and slaves*. Cambridge University Press.

Hopkins, K., 1980. Taxes and trade in the Roman empire. *Journal of Roman Studies* 70, 101–25.

Hopkins, K. 1983. Introduction, in P. Garnsey, K. Hopkins & C.R. Whittaker (eds), *Trade in the ancient economy*, ix–xxv. London: Hogarth.

Hopkins, K. 2002. Rome, taxes, rent and trade, in W. Schiedel & S. Von Reden (eds), *The ancient economy*, 190–230. Edinburgh University Press.

Hopkins, K. & M. Beard. 2005. *The Colosseum*. London: Profile.

Horden, P. & N. Purcell. 2000. *The Corrupting Sea. A study of Mediterranean history*. London: Blackwell.

Horsfall, N. 1990. Dido in the light of history, in S.J. Harrison (ed.), *Oxford Readings in Vergil's 'Aeneid'*, 127–44. Oxford: Clarendon Press.

Horton, R.J. 1998. *Globalization and the nation state*. London: Macmillan.

Hübner, W. 2000. Mythische geographie, in W. Hübner (ed.), *Geographie und verwandte Wissenschaften*, 19–32. Stuttgart: Geschichte der Mathematik und der Naturwissenschaften in der Antike 2.

Hutton, W. 1802. *The history of the Roman Wall which crosses the Island of Britain from the German Ocean to the Irish Sea*. London: John Nichols.

Inda, J.X. & R. Rosaldo. 2008. Tracking global flows. In J.X. Inda & R. Rosaldo (eds), *The Anthropology of Globalization: a reader*, 3–46. Oxford: Blackwell.

Inglis, D. & R. Robertson. 2006. Discovering the world: cosmopolitanism and globality in the 'Eurasian' renaissance, in G. Delanty (ed.), *Europe and Asia beyond East and West: towards a new cosmopolitanism*, 92–106. London: Routledge.

Insoll, T. 2007. *Archaeology. The conceptual challenge*. London: Duckworth.

Isaac, B. 2004. *The invention of racism in classical antiquity*. Princeton University Press.

Isayev E. forthcoming. *Pausing Motion: human mobility and place, relational paradigms from ancient Italy*.

Jackson, P. (ed.). 2009. *Changing familes, changing food*. London: Palgrave Macmillan.

Jaspers, K. 1949. *Vom Ursprung und Ziel der Geschichte*. Zürich: Fischer Bücherei.

Jenkins, R. 2004. *Social identity* (2nd edition). London: Routledge.

Jennings, J. 2011. *Globalizations and the ancient world*. Cambridge University Press.

Johne, K.-P. 2006. *Die Römer an der Elbe. Das Stromgebiet der Elbe im geographischen Weltbild und im politischen Bewusstsein der griechisch-römischen Antike*. Berlin: Oldenbourg Akademieverlag.

Johnson, M. 1999. *Archaeological Theory: an introduction*. London: Blackwell.

Johnston, D. 1999. *Roman law in context*. Cambridge University Press.

Jones, S. 1997. *The archaeology of ethnicity*. London: Routledge.

Jones, S. & P. Graves-Brown. 1996. Introduction. Archaeology and cultural identity in Europe, in P. Graves-Brown, S. Jones & C. Gamble (eds), *Cultural Identity and Archaeology. The construction of European communities*, 1–24. London: Routledge.

Jörg, C. J. A. 1982. *Porcelain and the Dutch China trade*. The Hague: Martinus Nijhoff.

Joshel, S. R., M. Malamud & M. Wyke. 2001. Introduction, in S. R. Joshel, M. Malamud & D. T. McGuire (eds), *Imperial Projections: ancient Rome in modern popular culture*, 1–22. Baltimore: Johns Hopkins University Press.

Jouffroy, H. 1986. *La construction publique en Italie et dans l'Afrique Romaine*. Strasbourg: Association pour l'étude de la civilisation romaine.

Kaizer, T. 2002. *The Religious Life of Palmyra. A study of the social patterns of worship in the Roman period*. Stuttgart: Franz Steiner Verlag.

Kane, S. (ed.). 2003. *The politics of archaeology and identity in a global context*. Boston: Archaeological Institute of America.

Keaveney, A. 1987. *Rome and the unification of Italy*. Bristol: Pheonix Press.

Kehoe, D. P. 2007. The early Roman empire: production, in W. Scheidel, I. Morris & R. Saller (eds), *The Cambridge economic history of the Greco-Roman world*, 543–69. Cambridge University Press.

Kelly, D. 2009. *Lineages of Empire: the historical roots of British imperial thought*. Oxford University Press.

Kerr, R. & L. Mengoni. 2011. *Chinese export ceramics*. London: V & A Publishing.

Kiely, R. 2010. *Rethinking imperialism*. Basingstoke: Palgrave Macmillan.

King, A. C. 1999. Diet in the Roman world: a regional inter-site comparison of the mammal bones. *Journal of Roman Archaeology* 12, 168–202.

Kistler, E. 1998. *Die 'Opferrinne-Zeremonie'. Bankettideologie am Grab, Orientalisierung und Formierung einer Adelsgesellschaft in Athen*. Stuttgart: Franz Steiner Verlag.

Kistler, E. 2009. Connected. Cultura simposiale intermediterranea e i gruppi elitari nella Sicilia arcaica, in C. Ampolo (ed.), *Immagine e immagini della Sicilia e di altre isole del Mediterraneo antico. Vol. II. Atti delle seste giornate internazionali di studi sull'area elima e la Sicilia occidentale nel contesto mediterraneo, Erice 12–16 ottobre 2006*, 743–62. Pisa: Scuola Normale Superiore.

Kistler, E. 2010a. Achämenidische Becher und die Logik kommensaler Politik im Reich der Achämeniden, in B. Jacobs & R. Rollinger (eds), *Der Achämenidenhof. The Achaemenid court. Akten des 2. Internationalen Kolloquiums zum Thema 'Vorderasien im Spannungsfeld klassischer und altorientalischer Überlieferungen'. Landgut Castelen bei Basel, 23.-25. Mai 2007*, 411–458. Wiesbaden: Classica et Orientalia 2.

Kistler, E. 2010b. Großkönigliches *symbolon* im Osten – exotisches Luxusgut im Westen. Zur Objektbiographie der achämenidischen Glasschale aus Ihringen, in R. Rollinger et al. (eds), *Interkulturalität in der Alten Welt. Vorderasien, Hellas, Ägypten und die vielfältigen Ebenen des Kontakts*, 63–96. Wiesbaden: Philippika. Marburger altertumswissenschaftliche Abhandlungen 34.

Klein, N. 2007. *The Shock Doctrine: the rise of disaster capitalism*. New York: Picador.

Klein, R. 1983. *Die Romrede des Aelius Aristides*. Darmstadt: Wissenschaftliche Buchgesellschaft.

Klein, R. 1995. Zum Kultur- und Geschichtsverständnis in der Romrede des Aelius Aristides, in B. Kühnert et al. (eds), *Prinzipat und Kultur im 1. und 2. Jahrhundert. Wissenschaftliche Tagung der Friedrich-Schiller-Universität Jena und der Iwane-Dshawachischwili-Universität Tbilissi 27.-30. Oktober 1992 in Jena*, 283–292. Bonn: R. Habelt.

Knappett, C. 2005. *Thinking through material culture*. Philadelphia: Pennsylvania University Press.

Knappett, C. 2011. *An Archaeology of Interaction: network perspectives on material culture and society*. Oxford University Press.

Kohl, K.-H. 2000. *Ethnologie – die Wissenschaft vom kulturell Fremden. Eine Einführung*. München: Beck.

Kohl, P. 1987a. The ancient economy, transferable technologies and the Bronze Age world system: a view from the north eastern frontier of the ancient Near East, in M. Rowlands, M. Larsen & K. Kristiansen (eds), *Centre and periphery in the ancient world*, 13–24. Cambridge University Press.

Kohl, P. 1987b. The use and abuse of world systems theory: the case of the pristine west Asian state, in M. Schiffer (ed.), *Advances in archaeological method and theory* 11, 1–35. New York: Springer.

Kohl, P. L. 2004. Making the past profitable in an age of globalization and national ownership: contradictions and considerations, in Y. Rowan & U. Baram (eds), *Marketing and Heritage. Archaeology and consumption of the past*, 295–301. Walnut Creek, CA: AltaMira Press.

Koolhaas, R., S. Boeri, S. Kwinter, N. Tazi & H. U. Obrist (eds). 2001. *Mutations*. New York: Actar.

Kopytoff, I. 1986. The cultural biography of things: commoditization as process, in A. Appadurai (ed.), *The Social Life of Things. Commodities in cultural perspective*, 64–91. Cambridge University Press.

Kowalski, J. 1929. *De Didone graeca et latina*. Krakow: Polska akademja umiejetnosci Rozprawy Wydziau filologicznego 63.1.

Kowalzig, B. 2005. Mapping out *communitas*. Performances of *Theoria* in their sacred and political context, in J. Elsner & I. Rutherford (eds), *Pilgrimage in Greco-Roman and Early Christian Antiquity. Seeing the gods*, 41–72. Oxford University Press.

Kränzlein, A. 1993. Ius municipium. Zu Art. 93 lex Irnitana, in M. J. Schermeier & Z. Végh (eds), *Ars boni et aequi. Festschrift für Wolfgang Waldstein zum 65, Geburtstag*, 177–86. Stuttgart: Franz Steiner Verlag.

Krebs, C. B. 2010. *A Most Dangerous Book: Tacitus's 'Germania' from the Roman empire to the Third Reich*. New York: Norton.

Krishnaswamy, R. & J. C. Hawley (eds). 2008. *The post-colonial and the global*. Minneapolis: University of Minnesota Press.

Kurlansky, M. 2002. *Salt: a world history*. London: Jonathan Cape.

LaBianca, Ø. & S. A. Scham (eds). 2006. *Connectivity in Antiquity. Globalization as long-term historical process*. London: Equinox.

Lafrenz Samuels, K. 2008. Value and significance in archaeology. *Archaeological Dialogues* 15, 71–97.

Lamberti, F. 1993. *'Tabulae Irnitanae'. Municipalità e 'ius Romanum' (Pubblicazioni del Dipartimento di Diritto Romano e Storia della Scienza Romanistica dell'Università degli Studi di Napoli 'Federico II'*, 6. Napoli: E. Jovene.

Laurence, R. 1994. *Roman Pompeii. Space and society.* London: Routledge.

Laurence, R. 1999. *The Roads of Roman Italy. Mobility and cultural change.* Routledge: London.

Laurence, R. 2001a. Roman narratives. The writing of archaeological discourse – a view from Britain? *Archaeological Dialogues* 8, 90–122.

Laurence, R. 2001b. The creation of geography: an interpretation of Britain, in C. Adams & R. Laurence (eds), *Travel and geography in the Roman empire*, 67–93. Routledge: London.

Laurence, R. 2007. *Roman Pompeii. Space and society* (second edition). London: Routledge.

Laurence, R. & J. Berry (eds). 1998. *Cultural identity in the Roman empire.* London: Routledge.

Laurence, R., S. Esmonde Cleary & G. Sears. 2011. *The city in the Roman West.* Cambridge University Press.

Laurence, R. & F. Trifilò. 2011. Vixit Plus Minus. Commemorating the age of the dead – towards a familial Roman life course? in L. Larsson Lovén & M. Harlow (eds), *The family in the imperial and late antique Roman world*, 23–40. London: Continuum.

Law, R. C. C. 1967. The Garamantes and trans-Saharan enterprise in classical times. *The Journal of African History* 8, 181–200.

Leach, S., H. Eckardt, C. Chenery, G. Müldner & M. Lewis. 2010. A lady of York: migration, ethnicity and identity in Roman Britain. *Antiquity* 84, 131–45.

Lederman, R. 1998. Globalization and the future of culture areas. *Annual Review of Anthropology* 27, 427–49.

Leigh M. 2010. Early Roman epic and the maritime moment. *Classical Philology* 105, 265–80.

Lendon, J. E. 1997. *Empire of Honour: the art of government in the Roman world.* Oxford: Clarendon Press.

Lewellen, T. 2002. *The Anthropology of Globalization. Cultural anthropology enters the 21st century.* Westport: Bergin and Garvey.

Liverani, M. 1991. The trade network of Tyre according to Ezek. 27, in M. Cogan & I. Eph'al (eds), *Ah. Assyria (Festschrift Hayyîm Tadmor)*, 65–79. Jerusalem: Magnes Press, Hebrew University.

Liverani, M. 2000a. The Garamantes. A fresh approach. *Libyan Studies* 31, 17–28.

Liverani, M. 2000b. The Libyan caravan road in Herodotus IV.181–185. *Journal of the Economic and Social History of the Orient* 43, 496–520.

Liverani, M. 2001. I garamanti. Ricerche in corso e nuove prospettive. *Studi Storici* 769–84.

Liverani, M. 2003a. Aghram Nadharif and the southern border of the Garamantian Kingdom, in M. Liverani et al. (eds), *Arid Lands in Roman Times. Papers from the international conference, Rome, 9–10 July 2001)*, 23–36. Firenze: All'Insegna del Giglio.

Liverani, M. 2003b. Alle origini del sistema carovaniero sahariano. *Quaderni dell'Accademia delle Scienze di Torino* 11, 117–34.

Liverani, M. 2003c. *Oltre la bibbia. Storia antica di Israele*. Bari: Laterza.

Lo Cascio, E. & P. Malanima. 2005. Cycles and stability. Italian population before the demographic transition (225 B.C. – A.D. 1900). *Rivista di Storia Economica* 21, 197–232.

Lomas, K. 2007. Community and state in northern Italy. The ancient Veneti, in G. Bradley, E. Isayev & C. Riva (eds), *Ancient Italy, regions without boundaries*, 21–44. University of Exeter Press.

Long, C. & S. Labadi. 2010. Introduction, in S. Labadi & C. Long (eds), *Heritage and globalisation*, 1–16. London: Routledge.

Lorcin, P. M. E. 2002. Rome and France in Africa: recovering colonial Algeria's Latin past. *French Historical Studies* 25, 295–329.

Louwe Kooijmans, L. P. 1998. *Between Geleen and Banpo. The agricultural transformation of prehistoric society* (20^e Kroon voordracht). Stichting Nederlands Museum voor Anthropologie en Praehistorie.

Lucasen, J., L. Lucassen & P. Manning (eds). 2010. *Migration History in World History. Multidisciplinary approaches*. Leiden: Brill.

Lucassen, L. 2007. Van divergentie naar convergentie. Migratie en het proces van globalisering, *Tijdschrift voor sociale en economische geschiedenis* 4, 62–83.

Luhmann, N. 1971. Die Weltgesellschaft, *Archiv für Rechts- und Sozialphilosophie* 57, 1–35.

Luhmann, N. 1997. *Die Gesellschaft der Gesellschaft*. Frankfurt am Main: Verlag für Akademische Texte.

Ma, J. 2003. Peer polity interaction in the Hellenistic Age. *Past & Present* 180, 9–39.

Maffi, I. 2009. The emergence of cultural heritage in Jordan. *Journal of Social Archaeology* 9, 5–34.

Magie D. 1950. *Roman rule in Asia Minor*, Vol. I. Princeton University Press.

Malkin, I. 1998. *The Returns of Odysseus. Colonization and ethnicity*. Berkeley: University of California Press.

Malkin, I. 2002. A colonial middle ground. Greek, Etruscan and local elites in the Bay of Naples, in C. L. Lyons & J. K. Papadopoulos (eds), *The archaeology of colonialism*, 151–81. Los Angeles: Getty Information Institute.

Malkin, I. 2004. Postcolonial concepts and ancient Greek colonization. *Modern Language Quarterly* 65, 341–64.

Malkin, I. 2005a. Introduction, in I. Malkin (ed.), *Mediterranean paradigms and classical antiquity*, 1–8. London: Routledge.

Malkin, I. (ed.). 2005b. *Mediterranean paradigms and classical antiquity*. London: Routledge.

Malkin, I. 2005c. Herakles and Melqart. Greeks and Phoenicians in the middle ground, in E. S. Gruen (ed.), *Cultural borrowings and ethnic appropriations in antiquity*, 238–58. Stuttgart: Franz Steiner Verlag.

Malkin, I. 2011. *A Small Greek World. Networks in the ancient Mediterranean*. New York: Oxford University Press.

Malkin, I., C. Constantakopoulu & K. Panagopoulou. 2007. Preface: networks in the ancient Mediterranean. *Mediterranean Historical Review* 22, 1–9.

Malkin, I, C. Constantakopoulou & K. Panagopoulou (eds). 2009. *Greek and Roman networks in the Mediterranean*. London: Routledge.

Manning, P. 2005. *Migration in world history*. London: Routledge.

Marchand, S. 1996. *Down from Olympus: archaeology and philhellenism in Germany, 1750–1970*. London: Princeton University Press.

Marek, C. 1993. Die expedition des Aelius Gallus nach Arabien im Jahre 25 v. Chr. *Chiron* 23, 121–56.

Marvin, M. 2002. The Ludovisi barbarians: the grand manner, in E. K. Gazda (ed.), *The Ancient Art of Emulation. Studies in artistic originality and tradition from the present to classical antiquity*, 205–23. Ann Arbor: University of Michigan Press.

Marx, K. & F. Engels 1964. *Manifest der kommunistischen Partei* [1848], in *Marx-Engels Werke* Vol. IV. Berlin: Dietz.

Mastrocinque, A. 1994. Gli Italici a Iaso, in M. Sordi (ed.), *Emigrazione e immigrazione nel mondo antico*, 237–52. Milan: Vita e pensiero.

Mattingly, D. J. 1996. From one colonialism to another: imperialism and the Maghreb, in J. Webster & N. Cooper (eds), *Roman Imperialism: post-colonial perspectives*, 49–69. School of Archaeological Studies, Leicester University.

Mattingly, D. J. (ed.). 1997. *Dialogues in Roman Imperialism*. Portsmouth, RI: *Journal of Roman Archaeology*, Supplementary Series 23.

Mattingly, D. J. 2004. Being Roman: expressing identity in a provincial setting. *Journal of Roman Archaeology* 17, 5–25.

Mattingly, D. J. 2006. *An Imperial Possession: Britain in the Roman empire*. London: Penguin.

Mattingly, D. J. 2010. Cultural crossovers: global and local identities in the Roman world, in S. Hales & T. Hodos (eds), *Material culture and social identities in the ancient world*, 283–95. New York: Cambridge University Press.

Mattingly, D. J. 2011. *Imperialism, Power and Identity: experiencing the Roman empire*. Princeton University Press.

Mattingly, D. J. D., L. Stone, D. Stirling & N. Ben Lazreg. 2001. Leptiminus (Tunisia). A 'producer' city?, in D. J. Mattingly & J. Salmon (eds), *Economies beyond agriculture in the classical world*, 66–89. London: Routledge.

Mauss, M. 1923/24. Essai sur le don. Forme et raison de l'échange dans les sociétés archaïques. *Annales Sociologiques n.s.* 1, 30–186.

McKay, A. G. 1980. *Römische Häuser, Villen und Paläste*. Zürich: Atlantis.

McLaughlin, J. L. 2001. *The Marzēah in the Prophetic Literature. References and allusions in light of extra-biblical evidence*. Leiden: Supplements to Vetus Testamentum 86.

McLuhan, M. 1964. *Understanding Media. The extensions of man.* New York.

McNeill, W. H. 1963. *The rise of the West.* University of Chicago Press.

McNeill, W. H. 1982. *The pursuit of power.* University of Chicago Press.

McNeill, W. H. 1979. *A world history* (3rd edition). Oxford University Press.

McNeill, W. H. 2008. Globalization: long term process or new era in human affairs. *New Global Studies* 2.1, 1–9.

Meadows, K. 1995. You are what you eat: diet, identity and Romanisation, in S. Cottam, D. Dungworth, S. Scott & J. Taylor (eds), *TRAC 1994. Proceedings of the fourth annual Theoretical Roman Archaeology Conference, Durham,* 133–40. Oxford: Oxbow.

Meiksins Wood, E. 2003. *Empire of capital.* London: Verso.

Meskell, L. 2009. *Cosmopolitan archaeologies.* Durham, NC: Duke University.

Messineo, G. 1983. Tessera hospitalis? *Xenia* 51, 3–4.

Millar, F. 1977. *The Emperor in the Roman world, 31 BC-AD 337.* Ithaca: Cornell University Press.

Millar, F. 1993. *The Roman Near East. 31 BC – AD 337.* Cambridge, MA: Harvard University Press.

Miller, D. 1995a. Consumption and commodities. *Annual Review of Anthropology* 24, 141–61.

Miller, D. 1995b. Consumption as the vanguard of history, in D. Miller (ed.), *Acknowledging consumption,* 1–57. London: Routledge.

Miller, D. 1998. Coca-Cola: a black sweet drink from Trinidad, in D. Miller (ed.), *Material Cultures. Why some things matter,* 169–87. London: Routledge.

Millett, M. 1990a. *The Romanization of Britain. An essay in archaeological interpretation.* Cambridge University Press.

Millett, M. 1990b. Romanization: historical issues and archaeological interpretation, in T. F. C. Blagg & M. Millett (eds), *The Early Roman Empire in the West,* 35–41. Oxford: Oxbow.

Mitteis, L. 1891. *Reichsrecht und Volksrecht in den östlichen Provinzen des römischen Kaiserreichs. Mit Beiträgen zur Kenntnis des griechischen Rechts und der spätrömischen Rechtsentwicklung.* Leipzig: Georg Olms Verlag.

Moatti, C. 1993. *The search for ancient Rome.* London: Thames and Hudson.

Moatti, C. 2004. Introduction, in C. Moatti (ed.). *La mobilité des personnes en Méditerranée de l'antiquité à l'époque moderne.* Ecole Française de Rome.

Moatti, C. & W. Kaiser (eds). 2007. *Gens de passage en Méditerranée de l'Antiquité à l'époque moderne.* Paris: Maisonneuve & Larose.

Mócsy, A. 1974. *Pannonia and Upper Moesia. A history of the middle Danube provinces of the Roman empire.* London: Routledge.

Modelski, G. 2000. World system evolution, in R. A. Denemark, J. Friedman, B. K. Gills & G. Modelski (eds), *World System History. The social science of long-term change,* 24–53. London: Routledge.

Mol, E. 2012. The perception of Egypt in networks of being and becoming. A thing theory approach to Egyptianising objects in Roman domestic contexts, in A. Bokern et al. (eds), *TRAC 2012. Proceedings of the twenty-second annual*

Theoretical Roman Archaeology Conference, Frankfurt aM, 2012, 117–32. Oxford: Oxbow.

Momigliano, A. 1936. Due Punti di Storia Arcaica. *SDHI* 2, 395–6.

Momigliano, A. 1975. The fault of the Greeks. *Daedalus* 104, 9–19.

Mommsen, T. 1907. *Abriß des römischen Staatsrechts*. Leipzig: Verlag von Duncker & Humblot.

Monteil, G. 2004. Samian and consumer choice in Roman London, in B. Croxford, H. Eckardt, J. Meade & J. Weekes (eds), *TRAC 2003. Proceedings of the thirteenth annual Theoretical Roman Archaeology Conference, Leicester, 2003*, 1–15. Oxford: Oxbow.

Moreau, A. M. 1994. *Le mythe de Jason et Médée. Le va-nu-pied et la sorcière*. Paris: Belles lettres.

Morgan, T. 1998. *Literate education in the Hellenistic and Roman worlds*. Cambridge University Press.

Morley, N. 2004. *Theories, models and concepts in ancient history*. London: Routledge.

Morley, N. 2007a. *Trade in classical antiquity*. Cambridge University Press.

Morley, N. 2007b. The early Roman empire: distribution, in W. Scheidel, I. Morris & R. Saller (eds), *The Cambridge economic history of the Greco-Roman world*, 570–91. Cambridge University Press.

Morley, N. 2009. *Antiquity and modernity*. Oxford: Wiley-Blackwell.

Morley, N. 2010. *The Roman Empire. Roots of imperialism*. New York: Pluto Books.

Morley, N. 2011. Status as performance, in S. Knippschild & M. Garcia Morcillo (eds), *Just for Show? Status as performance in classical antiquity*. Cambridge University Press.

Morris, I. 2003. Mediterraneanization. *Mediterranean Historical Review* 18, 30–55.

Morris, I. 2005. Mediterraneanization, in I. Malkin (ed.), *Mediterranean paradigms and classical antiquity*, 30–55. London: Routledge.

Morris, I. & J. G. Manning 2005. Introduction, in I. Morris & J. G. Manning (eds), *The Ancient Economy: evidence and models*, 1–44. Stanford University Press.

Mount, F. 2010. *Full Circle: how the classical world came back to us*. New York: Simon and Schuster.

Mouritsen, H. 1998. *Italian Unification. A study in ancient and modern historiography*. London: *Bulletin of the Institute of Classical Studies*. Supplement 70.

Moyer, I. 2011. *Egypt and the limits of Hellenism*. Cambridge University Press.

Müller, C. & C. Hasenohr. 2002. Gentilices et circulation des Italiens: quelque réflexions méthodologiques, in C. Müller & C. Hasenohr (eds), *Les italiens dans le monde grec: IIe siècle av. J.-C.-Ier siècle ap. J.-C.: circulation, activités, intégration: actes de la table ronde, Ecole normale supérieur, Paris, 14–16 mai 1998*, 11–20. Paris: Ecole française d'Athènes.

Müller, K. E. 1972. *Geschichte der antiken Ethnographie und ethnologischen Theoriebildung. Von den Anfängen bis auf die byzantinischen Historiographen*. Wiesbaden: Franz Steiner Verlag.

Müller, K. E. 1987. *Das magische Universum der Identität. Elementarformen sozialen Verhaltens: ein ethnologischer Grundriss.* Frankfurt am Main: Campus.

Münkler, H. 2007. *Empires.* Cambridge: Polity.

Munzi, M. 2005. *La decolonizzazione del passato. Archeologia e politica in Libia.* Rome: L'Erma di Bretscheider.

Murphy, C. 2008. *Are We Rome? The fall of an empire and the fate of America.* New York: Mariner Books.

Mutschler, F.-H. & A. Mittag (ed.). 2008. *Conceiving the Empire: China and Rome compared.* Oxford University Press.

Naerebout, F. G. 2006–7. Global Romans? Is globalisation a concept that is going to help us understand the Roman empire? *Talanta* 38–9, 149–70.

Naerebout, F. G. 2007. The temple at Ras el-Soda. Is it an Isis temple? Is it Greek, Roman, Egyptian, or neither? And so what?, in L. Bricault, M. J. Versluys & P. G. P. Meyboom (eds), *Nile into Tiber. Egypt in the Roman world,* 506–54. Leiden: Brill.

Nayyar, D. 2006. Globalisation, history and development: a tale of two centuries. *Cambridge Journal of Economics* 30, 137–59.

Nederveen Pieterse, J. 1989. *Empire and Emancipation: power and liberation on a world scale.* New York: Praeger.

Nederveen Pieterse, J. 2001. *Development Theory: deconstructions/reconstructions.* London: Sage.

Nederveen Pieterse, J. 2004. *Globalization and Culture. Global mélange.* Lanham: Rowman and Littlefield.

Nederveen Pieterse, J. 2005. The long nineteenth century is too short. *Victorian Studies* Autumn, 113–25.

Nederveen Pieterse, J. 2006. Oriental globalization: past and present, in G. Delanty (ed.), *Europe and Asia beyond East and West: towards a new cosmopolitanism,* 61–73. London: Routledge.

Nederveen Pieterse, J. 2007. *Ethnicities and Global Multiculture: pants for an octopus.* Lanham: Rowman & Littlefield.

Nederveen Pieterse, J. 2009. *Globalization and Culture. Global mélange* (second edition). Lanham: Rowman and Littlefield.

Nederveen Pieterse, J. 2011a. Global rebalancing: crisis and the east-south turn. *Development and Change* 42, 22–48.

Nederveen Pieterse, J. 2011b. Many renaissances, many modernities? *Theory Culture and Society* 28, 149–61.

Nesselrath, H.-G. 2002. *Platon und die Erfingung von Atlantis.* Leipzig/München: Teubner.

Nicolet, C. 1988. *L'Inventaire du monde. Géographie et politique aux origins de l'Empire romain.* Paris Fayard (= Nicolet, C. 1991. *Space, geography and politics in the early Roman empire).* Ann Arbor: University of Michigan Press.

Niemeyer, H. G. 1989a. *Das frühe Karthago und die phönizische Expansion im Mittelmeerraum.* Göttingen: Vandenhoeck & Ruprecht Gm.

Niemeyer, H. G. 1989b. *Das frühe Karthago und die phönizische Expansion im Mittelmeerraum. Als öffentlicher Vortrag der Joachim Jungius-Gesellschaft der Wissenschaften gehalten am 31. Mai 1988 in Hamburg.* Göttingen: Vandenhoeck & Ruprecht Gm.

Niemeyer, H. G. 1990a. Die phönizischen Niederlassungen im Mittelmeerraum, in U. Gehrig & H. G. Niemeyer (eds), *Die Phönizier im Zeitalter Homers,* 45–64. Mainz: Verlag Phillip von Zabern in Wissenschaftliche Buchgesellschaft.

Niemeyer, H. G. 1990b. The Phoenicians in the Mediterranean. A non-Greek model for expansion and settlement in antiquity, in J.-P. Descoeudres (ed.), *Greek colonists and native populations. Proceedings of the first Australian Congress of Classical Archaeology held in honour of Emeritus Professor A. D. Trendall, Sydney, 9–14 July 1985,* 469–89. Canberra: Humanities Research Centre; Oxford: Clarendon Press.

Niemeyer, H. G. 1995. Expansion et colonisation, in V. Krings (ed.), *La civilisation phénicienne et punique. Manuel de recherche,* 247–67. Leiden: Brill.

Niemeyer, H. G. 2002. Die Phönizier im Mittelmeer. Neue Forschungen zur frühen Expansion, in E. A. Braun-Holzinger (ed.), *Die nahöstlichen Kulturen und Griechenland an der Wende vom 2. zum 1. Jahrtausend v.Chr. Kontinuität und Wandel von Strukturen und Mechanismen kultureller Interaktion,* 177–95. Möhnesee: Bibliopolis.

Norman, K. 2008. The Hadrian's Wall major study: a test for participatory planning in the management of a world heritage site. *Conservation and Management of Archaeological Sites* 9, 140–73.

Nussbaum, M. C. 2006. *Frontiers of Justice: disability, nationality, species membership.* Cambridge, MA: Belknap Press.

Ohler, N. 1989. *The medieval traveller.* Woodbridge: Boydell.

Oliver, G. J. 2007. *War, food, and politics in early Hellenistic Athens.* New York: Oxford University Press.

Oliver, J. H. 1953. *The Ruling Power. A study of the Roman empire in the second century after Christ through the Roman oration of Aelius Aristides.* Philadelphia: American Philosophical Society.

Olivier, L. 2004. The past in the present. Archaeology, memory and time. *Archaeological Dialogues* 10, 204–13.

O'Rourke, K. H. & J. G. Williamson. 2002. When did globalisation begin? *European Review of Economic History* 6, 23–50.

Osborne, R. 1991. The potential mobility of human populations. *Oxford Journal of Archaeology* 10, 231–52.

Osborne, R. 1998. Early Greek colonization? The nature of Greek settlements in the West, in N. Fisher & H. van Wees (eds), *Archaic Greece. New approaches and new evidence,* 251–70. Swansea: Classical Press of Wales.

Osborne, R. 2007. What travelled with Greek pottery? *Mediterranean Historical review* 22, 85–95.

Osborne, R. 2009. What travelled with Greek pottery?, in I. Malkin et al. (eds), *Greek and Roman Networks in the Mediterranean,* 83–93. London: Routledge.

Osborne, R. & C. Vout 2010. A revolution in Roman history? *Journal of Roman Studies* 100, 233–45

Osterhammel, J. 1997. *Kolonialismus. Geschichte, Formen, Folgen.* Munich: Beck

Osterhammel, J. 2009. *Die Verwandlung der Welt. Eine Geschichte des 19. Jahrhunderts.* Munich: Beck.

Osterhammel, J. & N. P. Petersson. 2005. *Globalization: a short history.* Princeton University Press.

Oudshoorn, J. G. 2007. *The Relationship between Roman and Local Law in the Babatha and Salome Komaise Archives. General analysis and three case studies on law of succession, guardianship and marriage.* Leiden: Brill.

Panaro, A. M. 1951. I precendenti del IV libro dell'Eneide. La formazione della leggenda di Didone. *Giornale Italiano di Filologia* 4, 8–32.

Parchami, A. 2009. *Hegemonic Peace and Empire: The pax Romana, Britannica, and Americana.* London: Routledge.

Parker, G. 2008. *The Making of Roman India. Greek culture in the Roman world.* Cambridge University Press.

Parkin, T. G. 1992. *Demography and Roman society.* Chapel Hill: Johns Hopkins University Press.

Parkins, H. E. (ed.). 1997. *Roman Urbanism: beyond the consumer city.* London: Routledge.

Parsons, T. 2010. *The Rule of Empires: those who built them, those who endured them and why they always fell.* Oxford University Press.

Passavant, P. A. & J. Dean (eds). 2004. *Empire's New Clothes: reading Hardt and Negri.* London: Routledge.

Peacock, D. P. S. & D. F. Williams. 1986. *Amphorae and the Roman economy.* London: Longman.

Pearson, M. & M. Shanks. 2001. *Theatre archaeology.* London: Routledge.

Pels, P. 1998. The spirit of matter: on fetish, rarity, fact and fancy, in P. Spyer (ed.), *Border Fetishisms: material objects in unstable places*, 91–121. London: Routledge.

Peña, J. T. 2007. *Roman pottery in the archaeological record.* Cambridge University Press.

Perring, D. 2002. *Town and Country in England. Frameworks for archaeological research.* York: Council for British Archaeology Research Report 134.

Perring, D. & M. Pitts 2013. *Alien Cities. Consumption and the origins of urbanism in Roman Britain.* London: Spoilheap Monograph 7.

Perry, E. 2005. *The aesthetics of emulation in the visual arts of ancient Rome.* Cambridge University Press.

Petras, J. & H. Veltmeyer. 2001. *Globalization Unmasked: imperialism in the 21st century.* London: Zed.

Picard, G.-C. 1982. Der Periplus des Hanno, in W. Huß (ed.), *Karthago*, 182–92. Darmstadt: Beck.

Pickering, J. 1816. *A vocabulary or collection of words and phrases which have been supposed to be peculiar to the United States of America.* New York: Burt Franklin.

Piepenbrink, K. 2001. *Politische Ordnungskonzeptionen in der attischen Demokratie des vierten Jahrhunderts v. Chr. Eine vergleichende Untersuchung zum philosophischen und rhetorischen Diskurs.* Stuttgart: Franz Steiner Verlag.

Pierson, S. 2007. *Collectors, Collections and Museums. The field of Chinese ceramics in Britain, 1560–1960.* Bern: Peter Lang.

Pitts, M. 2005a. Pots and pits: drinking and deposition in late Iron Age south-east Britain. *Oxford Journal of Archaeology* 24, 143–61.

Pitts, M. 2005b. Regional identities and the social use of ceramics, in J. Bruhn, B. Croxford & D. Grigorpoulos (eds), *TRAC 2004. Proceedings of the fourteenth annual Theoretical Roman Archaeology Conference, Durham, 2004,* 50–64. Oxford: Oxbow.

Pitts, M. 2007. The emperor's new clothes? The unity of identity in Roman archaeology. *American Journal of Archaeology* 111, 693–713.

Pitts, M. 2008. Globalizing the local in Roman Britain: an anthropological approach to social change. *Journal of Anthropological Archaeology* 27, 493–506.

Pitts, M. 2010a. Re-thinking the British oppida: networks, kingdoms and identities. *European Journal of Archaeology* 13, 32–63.

Pitts, M. 2010b. Artefact suites and social practice: an integrated approach to Roman provincial finds assemblages. *Facta. A Journal of Roman Material Culture Studies* 4, 125–152.

Pitts, M. 2013. Pots and comparative history. The case of imported Roman fine wares and Chinese porcelain in NW Europe, in M. G. Fulford & E. Durham (eds), *Seeing Red. New economic and social perspectives on Gallo-Roman terra sigillata,* 381–90. London: Institute of Classical Studies.

Pitts, M, D. Dorling & C. Pattie 2007. Oil for food: the global story of edible lipids. *Journal of World Systems Research* 13, 12–32.

Pitts, M. & R. Griffin. 2012. Exploring health and social well-being in late Roman Britain. An intercemetery approach. *American Journal of Archaeology* 116, 253–76.

Pollock, S. 1996. The Sanskrit cosmopolis, 300–1300 CE: transculturalization, vernacularization, and the question of ideology, in J. E. M. Houben (ed.), *Ideology and Status of Sanskrit,* 197–248. Leiden: Brill.

Pomeranz, K. 2000. *The Great Divergence: China, Europe and the making of the modern world economy.* Princeton University Press.

Porter, S. E. 2003. Hanno's Periplus and the book of Acts, in A. Piltz et al. (eds), *For Particular Reasons. Studies in honour of Jerker Blomqvist,* 259–72. Lund: Nordic Academic Press.

Prag, J. R. W. 2006b. Poenus Plane Est – But who were the 'Punickes'? *PBSR* 74, 1–37.

Prag, J. R. W. 2006a. Review of R. Hingley, Globalizing Roman culture: Unity, diversity and Empire. *Journal of Roman Studies* 96, 214–16.

Prosdocimi, A. L. 1988. La lingua, in G. Fogolari & A. L. Prosdocimi (eds), *I Veneti antichi. Lingua e cultura,* 225–422. Padua: Editoriale Programma.

Purcell, N. 1990. Mobility and the polis, in O. Murray & S. Price (eds), *The Greek City from Homer to Alexander,* 29–58. Oxford: Clarendon Press.

Quack, J. F. 2005. Heiligtümer ägyptischer Gottheiten und ihre Ausstattung in Italien, in H. Beck, P. C. Bol & M. Bückling (eds). *Ägypten-Griechenland-Rom. Abwehr und Berührung*, 398–404.

Ray, N. 2006. Consumption and Roman archaeology: beyond Pompeii, in B. Croxford, H. Goodchild, J. Lucas & N. Ray (eds), *TRAC 2005. Proceedings of the fifteenth annual Theoretical Roman Archaeology Conference, Birmingham, 2005*, 25–41. Oxford: Oxbow.

Redfield, R., R. Linton & M. J. Herskovits. 1935. A memorandum for the study of acculturation. *Man* 35, 145–8.

Redlich, F. 1975. Autobiographies as sources for social history. *Vierteljahresschrift für Sozial- und Wirtschaftsgeschichte* 62, 380–90.

Reece, R. 1988. *My Roman Britain*. Cirencester: Cotswold Studies.

Reger, G. 2007. On the road to India with Apollonios of Tyana and Thomas the Apostle. *Mediterranean Historical Review* 22, 257–71.

Rehbein, B. & H. Schwengel. 2008. *Theorien der Globalisierung*. Stuttgart: UTB.

Reichert, F. 2001. *Erfahrung der Welt. Reisen und Kulturbegegnung im späten Mittelalter*. Stuttgart: Kolhammer.

Revell, L. 2007. Military bath-houses in Britain – a comment. *Britannia* 38, 230–37.

Revell, L. 2009. *Roman Imperialism and Local Identities*. Cambridge University Press.

Rhys-Taylor, A. 2010. *Coming to our Senses: a multi-sensory ethnography of class and multiculture in east London*. London: PhD thesis, Goldsmiths.

Richardson, J. 2008. *The Language of Empire: Rome and the idea of empire from the third century BC to the second century AD*. Cambridge University Press.

Riggs, C. 2005. *The Beautiful Burial in Roman Egypt. Art, identity and funerary religion*. Oxford University Press.

Rilinger, R. 1988. *Humiliores – honestiores. Zu einer sozialen Dichotomie im Strafrecht der römischen Kaiserzeit*. Munich: Oldenbourg Akademieverlag.

Rinaldi, M. 1989. *Kraak Porcelain. A moment in the history of trade*. London: Bamboo Publishing.

Ritzer, G. 2012. *The Wiley-Blackwell encyclopaedia of globalization*. Oxford: Wiley-Blackwell.

Rix, H. 1991. *Etruskische texte. Editio minor*. Tubingen: Gunter Narr Verlag.

Robertson, R. 1992. *Globalization. Social theory and global culture*. London: Sage.

Robertson, R. 2003. *The Three Waves of Globalization. A history of a developing global consciousness*. London: Zed Books.

Robertson, R. & D. Inglis. 2006. The global *animus*. In the tracks of world consciousness, in B. K. Gills & W. R. Thompson (eds), *Globalization and global history*, 33–47. London: Routledge.

Robertson, R. & J. A. Scholte 2007. *Encylcopaedia of globalisation*. Abingdon: Routledge.

Rodriguez, A. R. 1997. The Iron Age Iberian peoples of the upper Guadalquivir valley, in M. Díaz-Andreu & S. J. Keay (eds), *The Archaeology of Iberia. The dynamics of change*, 175–91. London: Routledge.

Romm, J. S. 1992. *The edges of the earth in ancient thought.* Princeton University Press.

Rosenberg, J. 2000. *The Follies of Globalisation Theory: polemical essays.* London: Verso.

Rosenstein, N. 2006. Aristocratic values, in N. Rosenstein & R. Morstein-Marx (eds), *A companion to the Roman republic,* 365–82. Oxford: Wiley-Blackwell.

Rostovtzeff, M. I. 1926. *A history of the ancient world, Volume I.* Oxford University Press.

Roth, R. E. 2007. *Styling Romanisation. Pottery and society in Central Italy.* Cambridge University Press.

Rothschild, E. 1998. *Globalization and democracy in historical perspective.* Cambridge: Centre for History and Economics.

Rowlands, M. 2010. Concluding thoughts, in P. van Dommelen & A. B. Knapp (eds), *Material Connections in the Ancient Mediterranean. Mobility, materiality and Mediterranean identities,* 233–47. London: Routledge.

Rujivacharakul, V. 2011. China and china: an introduction to materiality and a history of collecting, in V. Rujivacharakul (ed.), *Collecting China. The world, China and a history of collecting,* 15–28. Newark: University of Delaware Press.

Rüpke, J. 2011. 'Reichsreligion'? Überlegungen zur Religionsgeschichte des antiken Mittelmeerraums in der römischen Zeit. *Historische Zeitschrift* 292, 297–322.

Rutherford, I. 2007. Network theory and theoric networks. *Mediterranean Historical Review* 22, 23–38.

Sainte Croix, G. E. M. D. 2004. The Athenian citizenship laws, in *Athenian democratic origins and other essays,* 233–53. Oxford University Press.

Salazar, N. B. 2010. The Glocalisation of heritage through tourism. Balancing standardisation and differentiation, in S. Labadi & C. Long (eds), *Heritage and Globalisation,* 130–46. London: Routledge.

Saller, R. 2002. Framing the debate over growth in the ancient economy, in W. Schiedel & S. Von Reden (eds), *The ancient economy,* 251–69. Edinburgh University Press.

Saller, R. P. 2005. Framing the debate over growth in the ancient economy, in I. Morris & J. G. Manning (eds), *The Ancient Economy: evidence and models,* 223–38. Stanford University Press.

Salway, R. 1981. *Roman Britain.* Oxford University Press.

Samuels, K. L. 2008. Value and significance in archaeology. *Archaeological Dialogues* 15, 71–97.

Sanmartí, J. 2009. Colonial relations and social change in Iberia (seventh to third centuries BC), in M. Dietler & C. López-Ruiz (eds), *Colonial Encounters in Ancient Iberia. Phoenician, Greek and indiginous relations,* 49–89. University of Chicago Press.

Scheidel, W. 2001. Progress and problems in Roman demography, in W. Scheidel (ed.), *Debating Roman demography,* 1–82. Leiden: Brill.

Scheidel, W. 2004. Human mobility in Roman Italy, I: the free population. *Journal of Roman Studies* 94, 1–26.

Scheidel, W. 2005. Human mobility in Roman Italy, II: the slave population. *Journal of Roman Studies* 95, 64–79.

Scheidel, W. 2006. The demography of Roman state formation in Italy, in M. Jehne & R. Pfeilschifter (eds), *Herrschaft ohne Integration? Rom und Italien in Republikanischer Zeit*, 207–26. Frankfurt: Antike Verlag.

Scheidel, W. 2008. Roman population size: the logic of the debate, in L. de Ligt & S. J. Northwood (eds), *People, Land, and Politics: demographic developments and the transformation of Roman Italy 300 BC-AD 14*, 17–70. Leiden: Brill.

Scheidel, W. 2009a. In search of Roman economic growth. *Journal of Roman Archaeology* 22, 46–70.

Scheidel, W. (ed.). 2009b. *Rome and China: comparative perspectives on ancient world empires*. Oxford University Press.

Scheidel, W. 2009c. Review of R. Rollinger & C. Ulf (eds), Commerce and monetary systems in the ancient world: means of transmission and cultural interaction, Stuttgart 2004. *Ancient West & East* 8, 414–16.

Scheidel, W., I. Morris & R. Saller (eds). 2007. *The Cambridge economic history of the Greco-Roman world*. Cambridge University Press.

Schmidt-Colinet (ed.). 2005. *Lokale Identitäten in Randgebieten des römischen Reiches. Akten des internationalen Symposiums in Wiener Neustadt, 24.-26. April 2003*. Vienna: Phoibos Verlag.

Schneider, J. 1977. Was there a pre-capitalist world system? *Peasant Studies* 6, 20–9.

Schörner, J. (ed.). 2005. *Romanisierung – Romanisation. Theoretische Modelle und praktische Fallbeispiele*, Oxford: British Archaeological Reports.

Schubart, H. 1995. Péninsule ibérique, in V. Krings (ed.), *La civilisation phénicienne et punique. Manuel de recherche*, 743–61. Leiden: Brill.

Schubert, C. 1994. *Perikles Erträge der Forschung*, 285, Darmstadt: Wissenschaftliche Buchgesellschaft.

Schubert, C. 1996. *Land und Raum in der römischen Republik. Die Kunst des Teilens*. Darmstadt: Wissenschaftliche Buchgesellschaft.

Sear, F. 2006. *Roman Theatres: an architectural study*. Oxford University Press.

Seland, E. H. (ed.). 2007. *The Indian Ocean in the Ancient Period. Definite places, translocal exchange*. Oxford: British Archaeological Reports.

Seland, E. H. 2010. *Ports and Political Power in the Periplus. Complex societies and maritime trade on the Indian Ocean in the first century AD*. Oxford: British Archaeological Reports.

Serrati, J. 2006. Neptune's altars: the treaties between Rome and Carthage (509–226 B.C.). *The Classical Quarterly* (New Series) 56, 113–34.

Shami, S. 2001. Prehistories of globalization: circassian identity in motion, in A. Appadurai (ed.), *Globalization*, 220–50. London: Duke University Press.

Shaw, B. D. 1992. Under Russian eyes. *Journal of Roman Studies* 82, 216–28.

Sherratt, A. 1993. What would a Bronze Age world system look like? Relations between temperate Europe and the Mediterranean in later prehistory. *European Journal of Archaeology* 1, 1–57.

Shumate, N. 2006. *Nation, Empire, Decline: Studies in rhetorical continutity from the Roman to the modern era.* London: Duckworth.

Shumsky, N. L. 2008. Noah Webster and the invention of immigration. *The New England Quarterly*, 81, 126–35.

Sidebotham, S. E. 1986. Aelius Gallus and Arabia. *Latomus* 45, 590–602.

Siegert, B. 2003. Translatio imperii. Der cursus publicus im römischen Kaiserreich, in L. Engell et al. (eds), *Medien der Antike*. Weimar: Universitätsverlag.

Silberman, N. A. 1995. Promised lands and chosen peoples. The politics and poetics of archaeological narrative, in P. L. Kohl & C. Fawcett (eds), *Nationalism, politics and the practice of archaeology*, 249–62. Cambridge University Press.

Simshäuser, W. 1992. Stadtrömisches Verfahrensrecht im Spiegel der lex Irnitana. *Zeitschrift der Savigny-Stiftung für Rechtsgeschichte, Romanistische Abteilung* 109, 163–208.

Sitwell, N. H. H. 1986. *Outside the Empire: The world the Romans knew.* London: Paladin.

Sloterdijk, P. 2004. *Im Weltinnenraums des Kapitals. Für eine philosophische Theorie der Globalisierung.* Frankfurt am Main: Suhrkamp.

Smith, A. 1976. *An Enquiry into the Nature and Causes of the Wealth of Nations* [1776], in R. H. Campbell & A. S. Skinner (eds). Oxford University Press; University of Chicago Press.

Smith, C. & L. M. Yarrow (eds). 2012. *Imperialism, cultural politics, and Polybius.* Oxford University Press.

Smith, D. E. 2003. *From Symposium to Eucharist. The banquet in the early Christian world.* Minneapolis: Fortress Press.

Snodgrass, A. M. 1980. *Archaic Greece. The age of experiment.* London: Dent.

Snowden, F. M. 1970. *Blacks in Antiquity: Ethiopians in the Greco-Roman experience.* New Haven: Harvard University Press.

Soja, E. 1996. *Thirdspace. Journeys to Los Angeles and other real-and-imagined places.* Oxford: Blackwell.

Sombart, W. 1967. *Luxury and capitalism.* Ann Arbor: University of Michigan Press.

Sommer, M. 2004a. Die Peripherie als Zentrum. Die Phöniker und der interkontinentale Fernhandel im Weltsystem der Eisenzeit, in R. Rollinger & C. Ulf (eds), *Commerce and Monetary Systems in the Ancient World. Means of transmission and cultural interaction*, 233–44. Stuttgart: Franz Steiner Verlag.

Sommer, M. 2004b. A map of meaning. Approaching cultural identities at the middle Euphrates (1st to 3rd centuries AD). *Egitto e Vicino Oriente* 27, 153–83.

Sommer, M. 2005a. *Die Phönizier. Handelsherren zwischen Orient und Okzident.* Stuttgart: Kröner.

Sommer, M. 2005b. *Roms orientalische Steppengrenze.* Stuttgart: Franz Steiner Verlag.

Sommer, M. 2006. *Der römische Orient. Zwischen Mittelmeer und Tigris.* Darmstadt: Theiss, Konrad.

Sommer, M. 2007. Networks of commerce and knowledge in the Iron Age: the case of the Phoenicians. *Mediterranean Historical Review* 22, 97–111.

Sommer, M. 2009. Shaping Mediterranean economy and trade. Phoenician cultural identities in the Iron Age, in S. Hales & T. Hodos (eds), *Material culture and social identities in the ancient world*, 114–37. Cambridge University Press.

Sommer, M. 2011a. Empire of glory. Weberian categories and the complexities of authority in imperial Rome. *Max Weber Studies* 155–191.

Sommer, M. 2011b. Trans-Saharan long-distance trade and the Helleno-Punic Mediterranean: new perspectives on old texts, in A. Dowler & E. Gavin (eds.), *Money, trade and trade routes in pre-Islamic North Africa.* London: British Museum Press.

Sommer, M. 2011c. Colonies – colonisation – colonialism. A typological reappraisal, *Ancient West & East* 10, 183–93.

Sommer, M. 2013. Elissas lange Reise. Migration, Interkulturalität und die Gründung Karthagos im Spiegel des Mythos, in A.-B. Renger & I. Toral-Niehoff (eds), *Genealogie und migration. Antike Wanderungsmythen.*

Sonnabend, H. 2007. *Die Grenzen der Welt. Geographische Vorstellungen der Antike.* Darmstadt: Primus Verlag.

Späth, T. forthcoming. Acculturation, inculturation ou valeurs universelles? Le moraliste Plutarque entre hellénisation de Rome et romanisation de la Grèce, in M. Bommas (ed.), *Inkulturation und Akkulturation in der Antike.*

Spek, B. van der 2009. Multi-ethnicity and ethnic segregation in Hellenistic Babylonia, in T. Derks & N. Roymans (eds), *Ethnic Constructs in Antiquity. The role of power and tradition*, 101–16. Amsterdam Archaeological Studies.

Stavrianos, A. 1998. *A Global History: from prehistory to the 21st century* (7th edition). New Jersey: Prentice Hall.

Stearns, P. N. 2006. *Consumerism in World History. The global transformation of desire.* London: Routledge.

Stein, G. J. & R. Özbal. 2007. A tale of two *oikumenai*: variation in the expansionary dynamics of ´Ubaid and Uruk Mesopotamia, in E. C. Stone, *Settlement and Society. Essays dedicated to Robert McCormick Adams*, 329–42. Los Angeles: Cotsen Institute of Archaeology.

Steinbeck, J. 1989. Letter to Marion Sheffield Adams, June 27 1961, in J. Steinbeck, *Steinbeck: A Life in Letters.* New York and London: Penguin.

Steinby, C. 2007. *The Roman republican navy from the sixth century to 167 B.C.* Helsinki: Societas Scientiarum Fennica.

Stemberger, G. 1983. *Die römische Herrschaft im Urteil der Juden.* Darmstadt: Wissenschaftliche Buchgesellschaft.

Stemberger, G. 2009. *Das klassische Judentum. Kultur und Geschichte der rabbinischen Zeit.* Munich: Beck.

Stephan, E. 2002. *Honoratioren, Griechen, Polisbürger. Kollektive Identitäten innerhalb der Oberschicht des kaiserzeitlichen Kleinasien.* Göttingen: Vandenhoeck & Ruprecht.

Stoler, A. L. 2008. Imperial debris: reflections on ruins and ruination. *Cultural Anthropology* 23, 191–219.

Stoler, A. L. 2010. *Along the Archival Grain: epistemic anxieties and colonial common sense.* Princeton University Press.

Strocka, V. M. 2010. Der flavische Stil in de römischen Kunst – Einbildung oder Realität, in N. Kramer & C. Reitz (eds), *Tradition und Erneuerung. Mediale Strategien in der Zeit der Flavier* 285, 95–132. Beiträge zur Altertumskunde.

Svenbro, J. & J. Scheid 1985. Byrsa. La ruse d'Èlissa et la fondation de Carthage. *Annales ESC* 40, 328–42.

Swan, V. G. 2009. *Ethnicity, Conquest and Recruitment: two case studies from the northern military provinces.* Portsmouth, RI: *Journal of Roman Archaeology* Supplement.

Swanson, J. T. 1975. The myth of trans-Saharan trade during the Roman era. *The International Journal of African Historical Studies* 8, 582–600.

Sweetman, R. J. 2007. Roman Knossos: the nature of a globalized city. *American Journal of Archaeology* 111, 61–81.

Swift, E. 2003. Transformations in meaning: amber and glass beads across the Roman frontier, in G. Carr, E. Swift & J. Weekes (eds), *TRAC 2002. Proceedings of the twelfth annual Theoretical Roman Archaeology Conference, Canterbury, 2002*, 48–57. Oxford: Oxbow.

Tanner, J. 2003. Finding the Egyptian in early Greek art, in R. Matthews & C. Roemer (eds), *Ancient perspectives on Egypt*, 115–43. Walnut Creek, CA: Left Coast Press.

Taylor, C. 1989. *Sources of the self.* Cambridge, MA: Harvard University Press.

Tchernia, A. 1986. *Le vin de l'Italie romaine: essai d'histoire économique d'après les amphores.* Ecole Française de Rome.

Teixidor, J. 1981. Le thiase de Belastor et de Beelshamen d'après une inscription récemment découverte à Palmyra, *Comptes Rendus de l'Académie des Inscriptions et Belles-Lettres,* 306–14.

ter Keurs, P. 2006. *Condensed Reality. A study of material culture.* Leiden: Leiden University Press.

Terrenato, N. 2001. Ancestor Cults: the perception of ancient Rome in modern Italian culture, in R. Hingley (ed.), *Images of Rome: perceptions of ancient Rome in Europe and the United States in the modern age*, 71–89. Portsmouth, RI: *Journal of Roman Archaeology* Supplement.

Terrenato, N. 2008. The cultural implications of the Roman conquest, in E. Bispham (ed.), *Roman Europe: Short Oxford history of Europe*, 234–64. Oxford University Press.

Thalmann, W. 2011. *Apollonius of Rhodes and the spaces of Hellenism.* New York: Oxford University Press.

Thiel J. H. 1954. *A history of Roman sea-power before the Second Punic War.* Amsterdam: North Holland Publishing.

Thomas, J. 2004. *Archaeology and modernity*. London: Routledge.

Thomas, N. 1991. *Entangled Objects. Exchange, material culture and colonialism in the Pacific*. Cambridge, MA: Harvard University Press.

Thompson, P. 2003. 'Judicious Neology' The imperative of paternalism in Thomas Jefferson's Linguistic Studies. *Early American Studies: An Interdisciplinary Journal* 1, 187–224.

Tilley, C, W. Keane, S. Küchler, M. Rowlands & P. Spyer (eds). 2006. *Handbook of material culture*, 285–302. London: Sage.

Tolia-Kelly, D. P. 2011. Narrating the postcolonial landscape: archaeologies of race at Hadrian's Wall. *Transactions of the Institute of British Geographers* 36, 71–88.

Tomlinson, J. 1999. *Globalization and culture*. Cambridge: Polity Press.

Tomlinson, J. 2003. Globalization and cultural identity, in D. Held & A. G. McGrew (eds), *The Global Transformations Reader: an introduction to the globalization debate*, 269–77. Cambridge: Polity Press.

Tomlinson, J. 2009. *The Culture of Speed. The coming of immediacy*. London: Sage.

Torallas Tovar, S. 2010. Linguistic identity in Graeco-Roman Egypt, in A. Papaconstantinou (ed.), *The Multilingual Experience in Egypt. From the Ptolemies to the Abbasids*, 17–46. Farnham: Ashgate Publishing.

Torelli, M. 1999. The Romanization of Italy, in *Tota Italia. Essays in the cultural formation of Roman Italy*, 1–13. Oxford University Press.

Trentmann, F. 2012. *The Oxford handbook of the history of consumption*. Oxford University Press.

Trigger, B. 2006. *A history of archaeological thought* (second edition). Cambridge University Press.

Trundle, M. 2004. *Greek Mercenaries. From the late archaic period to Alexander*. London: Routledge.

Tuan, Y.-F. 2002. *Space and Place. The perspective of experience*. Minneapolis: University of Minnesota Press.

Ulf, C. 2009. Rethinking cultural contacts. *Ancient West & East* 8, 81–132.

Usherwood, P. 1996. Hadrian's Wall and the new Romans, in T. Faulkner (ed.), *Northumbrian Panorama*, 151–62. London: Octavian.

van der Pijl-Ketel, C. L. 1982. *The ceramic load of the Witte Leeuw (1613)*. Amsterdam: Rijksmuseum.

van der Veen, M, A. Livarda & A. Hill. 2008. New plant foods in Roman Britain – dispersal and social access. *Environmental Archaeology* 13, 11–36.

van Dommelen, P. 1998. Punic persistence. Colonialism and cultural identities in Roman Sardinia, in R. Laurence & J. Berry (eds), *Cultural identity in the Roman empire*, 25–48. London: Routledge.

van Dommelen, P. 2002. Ambiguous matters. Colonialism and local identities in Punic Sardinia, in C. L. Lyons & J. K. Papadopoulos (eds), *The Archaeology of Colonialism. Issues and debates*, 121–47. Los Angeles: Getty Research Institute.

van Dommelen, P. 2005. Colonial interactions and hybrid practices. Phoenician and Carthaginian settlement in the ancient Mediterranean, in G. Stein (ed.),

The Archaeology of Colonial Encounters. Comparative perspectives, 109–41. Santa Fe: SAR Press.

van Dommelen, P. 2006a. The Orientalizing phenomenon: hybridity and material culture in the western Mediterranean, in C. Riva & N. C. Vella (eds), *Debating Orientalization. Multidisciplinary approaches to change in the ancient Mediterranean*, 135–52. London: Monographs in Mediterranean Archaeology 10.

van Dommelen, P. 2006b. Colonial matters. Material culture and postcolonial theory in colonial situations, in C. Tilley, W. Keane, S. Kuechler, M. Rowlands & P. Spyer (eds), *Handbook of Material Culture*, 267–308. London: Sage.

van Dommelen, P. & A. B. Knapp. 2010a. *Material Connections in the Ancient Mediterranean. Mobility, materiality and Mediterranean identities*. London: Routledge.

van Dommelen, P. & A. B. Knapp (eds), 2010b. Introduction, in P. van Dommelen & A. B Knapp (eds), *Material Connections in the Ancient Mediterranean. Mobility, materiality and Mediterranean identities*. London: Routledge

van Dommelen, P. & Terrenato, N. 2007. *Articulating Local Cultures: power and identity under the expanding Roman republic*. Portsmouth, RI: *Journal of Roman Archaeology, Supplementary Series* 63.

van Nijf, O. 2006. Global Players: athletes and performers in the hellenistic and Roman world, in I. Nielsen (ed.), *Zwischen kult und gesellschaft: Kosmopolitische Zentren des antiken Mittelmeerraumes als Aktionsraum von Kultvereinen und Religionsgemeinschaften*, 225–35. Kissing/Augsburg Camelion Verlag: Hephaiston 24.

Vance, N. 1997. *The victorians and ancient Rome*. Oxford: Blackwell.

Versluys, M. J. 2008. Exploring identities in the Phoenician, Hellenistic and Roman East. *Bibliotheca Orientalis* 65, 342–56.

Versluys, M. J. 2010a. Understanding Egypt in Egypt and beyond, in L. Bricault & M. J. Versluys (eds), *Isis on the Nile. Egyptian gods in hellenistic and Roman Egypt*, 6–37. Leiden: Brill.

Versluys, M. J. 2010b. Review of G. Parker, The making of Roman India. *Bryn Mawr Classical Review* 02.56.

Versluys, M. J. 2013. Material culture and identity in the late Roman Republic (ca. 200 BC – ca. 20 BC), in J. DeRose Evans (ed.), *A companion to the archaeology of the Roman republic*, 647–62. Oxford: Blackwell.

Versluys, M. J. 2014. Understanding objects in motion. An *archaeological* dialogue on Romanization. *Archaeological Dialogues* 21 (1), 1–20.

Versluys, M. J. forthcoming. Egypt as part of the Roman *koine*: mnemohistory and the Iseum Campense in Rome, in J. F. Quack & C. Witschel (eds), *Religious flows in the Roman empire*. Tübingen: Mohr Siebeck.

Veyne, P. 1979. L'Hellénisation de Rome et la problématique des acculturations. *Diogène* 196, 1–29.

Veyne, P. 1999, L'identité grecque devant Rome et l'Empereur, *Revue des Études Grecques* 112, 510–67.

Veyne, P. 2008. *Foucault. Sa pensée, sa personne*. Paris: Editions Albin Michel.

Vlassopoulos, K. 2007. Beyond and below the polis: networks, associations, and the writing of Greek history. *Mediterranean Historical Review* 22, 11–22.

Volker, T. 1954. *Porcelain and the Dutch East India Company.* Leiden: Brill.

von Droste, B. 2012 World heritage and globalization: UNESCO's contribution to the development of global ethics, in M.-T. Albert, M. Richon, M.J. Viñals & A. Witcomb (eds), *Community development through world heritage*, 10–15. Paris: UNESCO.

Wagner, P. 2008. *Modernity as Experience and Interpretation: a new sociology of modernity.* Cambridge: Polity Press.

Walbank, F.W. 1970. *Polybius I. A historical commentary on Polybius.* Oxford University Press.

Wallace, C. 2006. Long-lived samian? *Britannia* 37, 259–72.

Wallace-Hadrill, A. 2007. The creation and expression of identity: the Roman world, in S.E. Alcock & R. Osborne (eds), *Classical archaeology*, 355–80. Oxford: Wiley-Blackwell.

Wallace-Hadrill, A. 2008. *Rome's cultural revolution.* Cambridge University Press.

Wallerstein, I. 1974. *The modern world system, Vol. I.* New York: Academic Press.

Wallerstein, I. 1980. *The Modern World System, Vol. II. Mercantilism and the consolidation of European world economy.* New York: Academic Press.

Wallerstein, I. 1989. *The Modern World System, Vol. III. The second great expansion of the capitalist world economy, 1730–1840.* New York: Academic Press.

Wallerstein, I. 1993. World system versus world-systems. A critique, in A.G. Frank & B.K. Gills (eds), *The World System. Five hundred years or five thousand?*, 292–96. London: Routledge.

Walter, U. 1993. *An der Polis teilhaben. Bürgerstaat und Zugehörigkeit im archaischen Griechenland.* Stuttgart.

Warnaby, G., D. Medway & D. Bennison. 2010. Notions of materiality and linearity: the challenges of marketing the Hadrian's Wall place 'product'. *Environment and Planning A* 42, 1365–82.

Waters, M. 1995. *Globalization.* London: Routledge.

Waters, M. 2001. *Globalization* (2nd edition). London: Routledge.

Weatherill, L. 1993. The meaning of consumer behaviour in late seventeenth- and early eighteenth-century England, in J. Brewer & R. Porter (eds), *Consumption and the world of goods*, 206–27. London: Routledge.

Weatherill, L. 1996. *Consumer behaviour and material culture in Britain 1660–1760* (second edition). London: Routledge.

Weber, M. 2005. *Wirtschaft und Gesellschaft. Grundriß der verstehenden Soziologie.* Frankfurt am Main: Mohr Siebeck.

Webster, J. 1996. Roman imperialism and the 'post-imperial age', in J. Webster & N. Cooper (eds), *Roman Imperialism: post-colonial perspectives*, 1–18. Leicester Archaeological Monographs.

Webster, J. 1997. A negotiated syncretism: readings on the development of Romano-Celtic religion, in D.J. Mattingly (ed.), *Dialogues in Roman imperialism,* 165–84. Portsmouth, RI: *Journal of Roman Archaeology,* Supplementary Series 23.

Webster, J. 2001. Creolizing the Roman provinces. *American Journal of Archaeology* 105, 209–25.

Webster, N. 1828. *An American dictionary of the English language.* New York: S. Converse.

Wells, P. S. 1999. *The Barbarians Speak. How the conquered peoples shaped Roman Europe.* Princeton University Press.

Wells, P. S. 2012. *How Ancient Europeans Saw the World. Vision, patterns, and she shaping of the mind in prehistoric times.* Princeton University Press.

Werner, M. & B. Zimmermann. 2006. Beyond comparison: *histoire croisée* and the challenge of reflexivity. *History & Theory* 45, 30–50.

Wes, M. A. 1990. *Michael Rostovtzeff, historian in exile.* Stuttgart: Franz Steiner Verlag.

Westhead, D. 1991. Norms of citizenship in ancient Greece, in A. Molho et al. (eds), *City States in Classical Antiquity and Medieval Italy. Athens and Rome. Florence and Venice,* 135–54. Stuttgart: Franz Steiner Verlag.

White, D. R. & U. C. Johansen. 2005. *Network Analysis and Ethnographic Problems: process models of a Turkish nomad clan.* Lanham: Lexington Books.

Whitmarsh, T. 2001. *Greek Literature and the Roman Empire: the politics of imitation.* Oxford University Press.

Whitmarsh, T. 2010a. Thinking local, in T. Whitmarsh (ed.), *Local knowledge and microidentities in the imperial Greek world,* 1–16. Oxford University Press.

Whitmarsh, T. (ed.). 2010b. *Local knowledge and microidentities in the imperial Greek world.* Oxford University Press.

Whittaker, C. R. 1994. *Frontiers of the Roman Empire: a social and economic study.* Baltimore: Johns Hopkins University Press.

Whittaker, C. R. 1995. Do theories of the ancient city matter?, in T. J. Cornell & K. Lomas (eds), *Urban society in Roman Italy,* 9–26. London: UCL Press.

Whittaker, C. R. 2009. Ethnic discourse of the frontiers of Roman Africa, in T. Derks & N. Roymans (eds), *Ethnic Constructs in Antiquity. The role of power and tradition,* 189–205. University of Amsterdam Press.

Wilhite, D. E. 2007. *Tertullian the African: an anthropological reading of Tertullian's context and identities.* Berlin: De Gruyter.

Wilkinson, D. 2000. Civilizations, world systems and hegemonies, in R. A. Denemark, J. Friedman, B. K. Gills & G. Modelski (eds), *World System History. The social science of long-term change,* 54–84. London: Routledge.

Wilkinson, R. G. 2005. *The impact of inequality.* London: Routledge.

Wilkinson, R. G. & K. Pickett, 2010. *The Spirit Level. Why equality is better for everyone.* London: Penguin.

Williamson, G. 2005. Aspects of identity, in C. Howego, V. Heuchert & A. Burnett (eds), *Coinage and identity in the Roman Provinces,* 19–27. Oxford University Press.

Willis, I. 2007. The empire never ended, in L. Hardwick & C. Gillespie (eds), *Classics in post-colonial worlds,* 329–48. Oxford University Press.

Willis, S. 1996. The Romanization of pottery assemblages in the east and north-east of England during the first century A.D.: a comparative analysis. *Britannia* 27, 179–221.

Willis, S. 2011. Samian ware and society in Roman Britain and beyond. *Britannia* 42, 167–242.

Wilson, A. 2009. Approaches to quantifying Roman trade, in A. Bowman & A. Wilson (eds), *Quantifying the Roman Economy: methods and problems*, 213–49. Oxford University Press.

Wilson, A. J. N. 1966. *Emigration from Italy in the Republican Age of Rome*. Manchester University Press.

Wimmer, A. & N. Glick Schiller. Methodological nationalism and beyond: nation-state building, migration and the social sciences. *Global Networks* 2, 301–34.

Witcher, R. E. 2000. Globalisation and Roman imperialism, in E. Herring & K. Lomas (eds), *The emergence of state identities in Italy in the first millennium B.C.*, 213–25. London: Accordia Research Institute.

Witcher, R. E. 2010. The fabulous tales of the common people, part 2: encountering Hadrian's Wall. *Public Archaeology* 9, 211–38.

Witcher, R. E., D. P. Tolia-Kelly & R. Hingley 2010. Archaeologies of landscape: excavating the materialities of Hadrian's Wall. *Journal of Material Culture* 15, 105–28.

Wolf, A. 2009. *Homers Reise. Auf den Spuren des Odysseus*. Köln: Böhlau.

Wolf, J. G. 2011. *Die Lex Irnitana. Ein römisches Stadtrecht aus Spanien*. Darmstadt: Wissenschaftliche Buchgesellschaft.

Wolff, H. J. 1979. *Das Problem der Konkurrenz von Rechtsordnungen in der Antike (Sitzungsberichte der Heidelberger Akademie der Wissenschaften. Philosophisch-historische Klasse)*, Abh. 5, Heidelberg: Winter.

Woolf, G. 1990. World-systems analysis and the Roman empire. *Journal of Roman Archaeology* 3, 44–58.

Woolf, G. 1992. The unity and diversity of Romanisation. *Journal of Roman Archaeology* 5, 349–53.

Woolf, G. 1993. European social development and Roman imperialism, in P. Brun, S. van der Leeuw & C. R. Whittaker (eds), *Frontières d'empire. Nature et signification des frontières romaines*, 13–20. Paris: Mémoires du Musée de Préhistoire d'Ile-de-France No. 5.

Woolf, G. 1997. Beyond Romans and Natives. *World Archaeology* 28, 339–50.

Woolf, G. 1998. *Becoming Roman. The origins of provincial civilization in Gaul*. Cambridge University Press.

Woolf, G. 2005. A sea of faith?, in I. Malkin (ed.), *Mediterranean paradigms and classical antiquity*, 126–43. London: Routledge.

Woolf, G. 2009. Cruptorix and his kind. Talking ethnicity on the middle ground, in T. Derks & N. Roymans (eds), *Ethnic Constructs in Antiquity. The role of power and tradition*, 207–17. University of Amsterdam Press.

Woolf, G. 2010. Afterword: the local and the global in the Graeco-Roman east, in T. Whitmarsh (ed.), *Local knowledge and microidentities in the imperial Greek world*, 189–200. Oxford University Press.

Woolf, G. 2011. *Tales of the Barbarians: ethnography and empire in the Roman west*. Oxford: Wiley-Blackwell.

Young, G.K. 2001. *Rome's Eastern Trade: international commerce and imperial policy 31 BC – AD 305*. London: Routledge.

Zahrnt, M. 1995. Identitätsvorstellungen in den östlichen Provinzen am Beispiel der Romrede des Aelius Aristides, in H. van Hesberg (ed.), *Was ist eigentlich Provinz? Zur Beschreibung eines Bewußtseins*. Köln: Archäologisches Institut.

Zanker, P. 2007. *Die römische Kunst*. Munich: Beck.

INDEX

Lightning Source UK Ltd.
Milton Keynes UK
UKHW012257191218
334303UK00009B/104/P